SCHOOL, COURT, PUBLIC ADMINISTRATION

Number 83

SCHOOL, COURT, PUBLIC ADMINISTRATION:
Judaism and its Institutions in Talmudic Babylonia

by
Jacob Neusner

SCHOOL, COURT, PUBLIC ADMINISTRATION
Judaism and its Institutions in Talmudic Babylonia

by
Jacob Neusner

Scholars Press
Atlanta, Georgia

SCHOOL, COURT, PUBLIC ADMINISTRATION
Judaism and its Institutions in Talmudic Babylonia

Library of Congress Cataloging in Publication Data

Neusner, Jacob, 1932-
School, court, public administration.

(Brown Judaic studies ; no. 83)
1. Talmudic academies. 2. Rabinnical courts--Iraq--Babylonia. 3. Rabbis--Iraq--Babylonia--Office. 4. Jews--Iraq--Babylonia--Politics and government. I. Title. II. Series.
BM502.N38 1987 296.6'0935 87-4632
ISBN 1-55540-115-5 (alk. paper)

Printed in the United States of America
on acid-free paper

For

my dear friend
and colleague

CALVIN GOLDSCHEIDER

Judaic Studies and Sociology,
at Brown University

and
his wife

FRANCES KOBRIN GOLDSCHEIDER

Sociology,
at Brown University

on the occasion of
their fourth wedding anniversary

August 18, 1987

In their union
they brought happiness to a whole world beyond themselves,
and, among their many friends and thankful colleagues,
my wife and I celebrate their joy.

CONTENTS

Preface

This book introduces the three principal institutions of the Judaism represented by the Talmud of Babylonia (a.k.a. the Bavli), the school, the court, and the administrative institution of government and public policy of the life of the community of Israel, the Jewish people wherever located. These three categories, of course, derive from our construction of society, not the processes of category-formation of the Talmud, and therefore serve as metaphors, distinguishing three functions that, in the rabbinic-Judaic structure of portrayed in the Bavli, were united in the person and institution of the sage. In the view of the writing produced in his circles, he formed the institutional foundation of Israel, the Jewish people. The on-going and enduring life of the community came to realization in him. He was the school, the court, the administration, all at once and all together. For his person, in his "session" (*metivta, yeshivah*) encompassed the labor of teaching disciples, administering the law entrusted to him to apply, and settling those cases that were assigned to his jurisdiction.

An analogy to the social institutionalization represented by the sage presents itself. If a professor at the Harvard Law School served also as the dean of the Harvard Medical School and the Harvard Divinity School, did the work of the entirety of the Massachusetts Legislature, and – in his person – accomplished the tasks of the various Commonwealth Departments of public administration, but doing all of these things only for the Unitarians, intellectuals, and unbelievers of Cambridge and Somerville, Massachusetts, and if a counterpart professor at New York University served the same functions for the Judaic society of Manhattan and the Bronx, and yet another in Chicago but only for the Polish-American community, another in Berkeley but only for the naturalists, another in Atlanta and Dallas and Phoenix and Miami each with his constituency of obedient believers, we should have a rough analogy to the position and function of the rabbi in the politics and government of Babylonian Jewry in Iranian-Sasanian times, so far as the Talmud of Babylonia portrays matters. Each sector of the larger imperial society governed important aspects of its own affairs, under the loose supervision of the Iranian government. Called the millet-system, the mode of sorting out minority affairs set in place by the Persian Iranians under Cyrus, restored by the Parthian Iranian government of the Arsacids, ca. 200 B.C. to A.D. 226, and renewed by the Sasanian Iranian government from 226 through 640, left in the hands of the diverse religious-social-cultural communities the administration of trivial matters of no concern to the lords of state, made a place for sages' government in just this way. In the case of the

Jews, sages served the purpose – or at least, so their literature, for Israel the only surviving writings of the time and place – claims.

The reason these institutions – school, court, government bureaus of administration – are important to the Talmud of Babylonia, therefore to Judaism, is simple. The Bavli portrays a complete religious system, inclusive not only of world view and way of life but also, and especially, of institutions and on-going instrumentalities of policy and power. The Bavli's authorship understood by religion the encompassing and exhaustive account of all that mattered in social reality on earth and in heaven. Accordingly, in the view of the Judaism that took shape in late antiquity and flourished from then to now, religion – in this case, Judaism, or, in mythic language, the Torah – shapes culture, defines politics, gives coherence to society, and, it must follow, deeply infuses the institutions of politics and culture. Anyone who hopes to understand the formative age of Judaism, in the first seven centuries of the Common Era (A.D.), will therefore investigate not only the beliefs and religious behavior of the Jews who adopted the Judaism at hand, but also – and especially – the institutions that gave full social expression and effected complete realization of these beliefs and patterns of behavior. The Judaism represented by the Bavli derived from sages, who were, as I have made clear, at once lawyers, teachers and masters, judges and administrators, holy men, wonder workers, and, of course, theologians, legislators, and jurisprudents. The institutions they formed in the period at hand, as represented by the Bavli, dictated the future history of Judaism, determining its on-going life and character. Even today, in order to understand the religious life of the Judaism of the State of Israel, we have still to refer to the Bavli and its institutional pattern and program: school or yeshiva, court (governing, in modern times, matters of personal status and various other questions assigned to the rabbinic courts by the State of Israel), and also administration in some specific matters as well.

We in the Protestant sector of the West, with our two-hundred-year-old tradition of the separation of religion from politics, may forget that religion constitutes a powerful political and institutional fact in most societies and cultures. In the Protestant model, we tend to see religion as individual and familial, a matter principally important in the home, while we prefer our politics to take a neutral (or consensus) position on matters of religious interest. To take the place of religion in the corporate model, which the diversity of the West cannot sustain, we moreover frame a civil religion, which a variety of groups may make their own, and with which pretty much everyone can identify equally and comfortably. In these ways we lose sight of the critical role that religion has played, and plays today, in the politics of most of humankind, including the democracies of the West. The relationship between the religious ideas people hold and the political and cultural institutions they build for the sustenance and definition of their culture in my judgment forms one critical subject of inquiry when we study religion. That is because religious systems – world-views, ways of life, addressed to a particular social group – demand not merely assent but obedience, address not only the individual and family, but the large and encompassing questions of society and culture. Religion is public and political, that is its nature. Religion is therefore something people do together, and religion is available for analysis and interpretation among the other important social and political institutions by which humanity sustains an on-going life together.

Such stress on religion as personal and familial renders questions of institutions and the forming of public policy remote. An interest in the topics covered in this book will not strike as urgent scholars of religion and its nature and meaning. The explanation for the stress, in the study of contemporary religion, including Judaism, on matters of belief in preference to issues of behavior in a shared society, lies in the definition of permissible difference in North America and the place of religion in that difference. Specifically, in North American society, defined as it is by Protestant conceptions, it is permissible to be different in religion, and religion is a matter of what is personal and private. Hence Judaism as a religion encompasses what is personal and familial. The Jews as a political entity then put forth a separate system, one that concerns not religion, which is not supposed to intervene in political action, but public policy. Judaism in public policy produces political action in favor of the State of Israel, or Soviet Jewry, or other important matters of the corporate community. Judaism in private affects the individual and the family and is not supposed to play a role in politics at all. That pattern conforms to the Protestant model of religion, and the Jews have accomplished conformity to it by the formation of two Judaisms. A consideration of the Protestant pattern, which separates not the institutions of Church from the activities of the state, but the entire public polity from the inner life, will show us how to make sense of the presence of the two Judaisms of North America.

Here in Protestant North America, so remarkably free and tolerant of diversity, people commonly see religion as something personal and private, prayer, for example, therefore speaks for the individual. Rabbis, for their part, play slight role not only in politics but even in the politics of the Jewish community, with its public policy and its institutions. A larger prejudice that religion and rite speak to the heart of the particular person accounts for the trivialization of the rabbinate, by contrast to the enormous and public role of the rabbis whom we shall study in this book. What can be changed by rite then is first of all personal and private, not social, not an issue of culture, not affective in politics, not part of the public interest. What people do when they respond to religion, therefore, affects an interior world – a world with little bearing on the realities of public discourse: what – in general terms – should we do about nuclear weapons or in terms of Judaism how we should organize and imagine society. The transformations of religion do not involve the world, or even of the self as representative of other selves, but mainly the individual at the most unique and unrepresentative. If God speaks to me in particular, then the message, by definition, is mine – not someone else's. Religion, the totality of these private messages (within the present theory) therefore does not make itself available for communication in public discourse, and that by definition too. Religion plays no public role. It is a matter not of publicactivity but of what people happen to believe or do in private, a matter mainly of the heart.

But in our own day, throughout the history of the West, and certainly in late antique Babylonia, religion has been and now is public, political, social, economic. The Jews form a group not merely because they agree on certain propositions on which outsiders do not concur, but because they exhibit certain public traits that differentiate them from others. Their group moreover forms policy for the whole – public policy – and acts upon that policy. Religion as a powerful force in shaping politics and culture, economic action and social organization, at home and in the encompassing society, finds its counterpart, within Jewry in the power of the community of the Jews to generate a Judaism.

School, court, and bureau of administration – these roles defining the public life of the sage or rabbi therefore present an example of religion as public, corporate, political. The importance in examining the way these roles for religion worked themselves out in the Judaism of the dual Torah represented by the Bavli hardly requires specification. For nothing humanity has made constitutes a less personal, a less private, a less trivial fact of human life than religion. Religion however is understood in Protestant North America as something private and interior, individual and subjective: how I feel all by myself, not what I do with other people. Religion is something you believe, all by yourself, not something you do with other people. The prevailing attitude of mind identifies religion with belief, to the near-exclusion of behavior. Religion is understood as a personal state of mind or an individual's personal and private attitude. When we study religion, the present picture suggests, we ask about not society but self, not about culture and community but about conscience and character. Religion speaks of individuals and not groups: faith and its substance, and, beyond faith, the things that faith represents: faith reified, hence, religion.

William Scott Green further comments in more general terms as follows:

> The basic attitude of mind characteristic of the study of religion holds that religion is certainly in your soul, likely in your heart, perhaps in your mind, but never in your body. That attitude encourages us to construe religion cerebrally and individually, to think in terms of beliefs and the believer, rather than in terms of behavior and community. The lens provided by this prejudice draws our attention to the intense and obsessive belief called "faith," so religion is understood as a state of mind, the object of intellectual or emotional commitment, the result of decisions to believe or to have faith. According to this model, people have religion but they do not do their religion. Thus we tend to devalue behavior and performance, to make it epiphenomenal and of course to emphasize thinking and reflecting, the practice of theology, as a primary

> activity of religious people....The famous slogan that "ritual recapitulates myth" follows this model by assigning priority to the story and to peoples' believing the story, and makes behavior simply an imitation, an aping, a mere acting out.[1]

Now as we reflect on Green's observations, we of course recognize what is at stake. It is the definition of religion, or, rather, what matters in or about religion, emerging from Protestant theology and Protestant religious experience.

For when we lay heavy emphasis on faith to the exclusion of works, on the individual to rather than on society, conscience instead of culture, when we treat behavior and performance by groups as less important and thinking, reflecting, theology and belief as more important, we simply adopt as normative for academic scholarship convictions critical to the Protestant Reformation. The Bavli sees things otherwise. And it is not alone. All of the Judaisms of history, the historical, classical forms of Christianity, Roman Catholic and Orthodox – every known religious system has placed emphasis at least equally on religion as a matter of works and not faith alone, behavior and community as well as belief and conscience. Religion is something that people *do*, and they do it together. Religion is not something people merely *have*, as individuals. Since the entire civilization of the West, from the fourth century onward, carried forward the convictions of Christianity, not about the individual alone but about politics and culture, we may hardly find surprising the Roman Catholic conviction that religion flourishes not alone in heart and mind, but in eternal social forms: the Church, in former times, the state as well. This brings us to the book at hand.

In my *History of the Jews in Babylonia* I took up the sages' sayings and stories concerning the on-going institutions represented by my principal document, the Bavli, and described those institutions within three categories: school, court, administration. I found that the sage or rabbi, as represented in the Bavli, took public definition as master with disciples, so I invoked the analogy of the school; he also judged certain trivial cases, so appeared to be something like the judge of a small claims' court; he furthermore administered certain on-going aspects of public life and carried out public policy, and, consequently, I invoked the metaphor of administration. In this book I survey each of those three institutions, as these emerge in pertinent sayings and stories. I have dealt in other reprises of my results concerning the Jews' political history, their relationships with other religions, their inner politics, and the sages' role in the religio-mythic life of the community, in these books:

Israel and Iran in Talmudic Times. A Political History. Lanham, 1986: University Press of America *Studies in Judaism* Series. Condensation of

[1] Personal letter, January 17, 1985.

materials in *A History of the Jews in Babylonia* II-V, parts of chapter one of each volume.

Judaism, Christianity, and Zoroastrianism in Talmudic Babylonia. Lanham, 1986: University Press of America *Studies in Judaism* Series. Condensation of materials in *A History of the Jews in Babylonia* II-V, parts of chapter one of each volume and of *Aphrahat and Judaism* (Leiden, 1970: E. J. Brill).

Israel's Politics in Sasanian Iran. Jewish Self-Government in Talmudic Times. Lanham, 1986: University Press of America Studies in Judaism Series. Condensation of materials in *A History of the Jews in Babylonia* II-V, parts of chapter two of each volume.

The Wonder-Working Lawyers of Talmudic Babylonia. The Theory and Practice of Judaism in its Formative Age. Lanham, 1987: University Press of America Studies in Judaism. Reprise of materials in *A History of the Jews in Babylonia* II-V.

To portray the character of the institutions of Judaism in the formative age, I present selected chapters of my *History of the Jews in Babylonia* (Leiden, 1966, 1968, 1969: E. J. Brill) III-V. The chapters reproduced here correspond to the original as follows: Chapter One, *The Schools*, comes from Volume Five Chapter Five; Chapter Two, *The Rabbinical Court and Daily Life* , derives from Volume III, Chapter Five; Chapters Three and Four, *Babylonian Jewish Government (I): The Rabbi as Administrator* and *Babylonian Jewish Government (II): The Rabbi as Judge* correspond to Volume IV, Chapters Three and Four, respectively. I express thanks to my publisher, E. J. Brill, for permission to reprint some of the results of the larger work, more than twenty years after the original appearance. My *History of the Jews in Babylonia* II-V remains in print in the original edition, with full bibliographies and notes as well as indices available there; Volume I has been reprinted by Scholars Press in Brown Judaic Studies. In reproducing these chapters I have not removed cross-references and other indications of their original origin. To do so would have vastly increased the cost of producing the books and therefore contradicted my purpose, which is to make available to a new generation results that in my judgment remain firm and sure. Readers will, I hope, grant indulgence for the infelicities involved in simply reproducing the original text. The alternative was to reset the type, and the costs hardly commensurate to the need.

I am proud that this work has lasted for nearly a quater of a century and now gains a new generation of readers, but I shall be still happier when others produce fresher and still better work than I was able to accomplish in the first decade of my scholarly career, beginning with the conclusion of my *Life of Yohanan ben Zakkai* (Leiden, 1962: E. J. Brill), and ending with the completion of the edited books, *The Formation of the Babylonian Talmud. Studies on the Achievements of Late Nineteenth and Twentieth Century Historical and Literary-*

Critical Research (Leiden, 1970: Brill), *The Modern Study of the Mishnah* (Leiden, 1973: Brill). These marked the turning in a new direction altogether. As I move toward the conclusion of the third decade and take up yet another new set of problems, these of a more abstract order than I have ever attempted, I take great pride in my beginnings, even as, in one work after another, I strive to render obsolete each prior study. With God's grace I shall continue to render my entire corpus obsolete by newer, fresher, more abstract and imaginative work than I have ever done before. That, at any rate, is my ambition as I move through the last half of the fifth decade of life: not to run out of ideas, never to take entire satisfaction with what is done.

Since my dear friends and colleagues, Calvin and Francis Kobrin Goldscheider, ornament the field of sociology, it is appropriate that this contribution of data to their larger theoretical inquiry bear a dedication to them on the occasion of our general celebration of an event that has brought so much pleasure to so many people.

JACOB NEUSNER

The Second Day of Hanukkah, 5747
December 28, 1986

Program in Judaic Studies
Brown University
Providence, Rhode Island 02912-1826 U.S.A.

CHAPTER ONE

THE SCHOOLS

I. Introduction

Babylonian Jewry hardly constituted an important social and religious group within Iranian society. As we have seen, while the Jews found themselves persecuted from time to time, they were left alone for most of Sasanian history, being severely troubled only briefly under Yazdagird II and Peroz, and again under Khusro II. Anti-Semitism as a political, religious, or cultural doctrine was unknown. Normal tensions between differing religious groups were not exaggerated. Jews now played no substantial part in international events. They may have fought in the army, but probably not in large numbers, though they normally favored the Iranian cause. The intricate politics of the Sasanian court involved few if any Jews, at any rate none we know about. I doubt that the exilarch himself amounted to much in Ctesiphon. He governed an inconsequential community which demanded little attention.[1] True, it was better to support him than to permit the Jews to evolve some other means of government and administration remote from the state's knowledge or control. But from the perspective of the government, the Jews and their ruler carried little weight. Strikingly, only once in this period did Jewry play a significant part in the selection of an emperor, and then they chose the wrong man.

We have noticed that the Jewish sources provide practically no direct and significant information on Sasanian dynastic and court affairs, Iranian-Byzantine relations, Christian life and problems, Mazdean beliefs and practices, and the like. They are indifferent to outsiders, like the sources produced by every other subordinated communi-

[1] This is merely an impression, based on the small role of the Jews in contemporary politics, both at home and abroad. I do not think the numbers of Jews had diminished. What changed was the political role open to the community. In Parthian and into early Sasanian times, the Jews played a very active part in politics. Later on it seems to me they did not. Perhaps the turning-inward which we shall note later on (below, p. 134) with reference to the life of the schools also characterized the community's interest in participating in politics.

ty. Their sole interest is in the inner life of the Jewish group. As I have already said,[1] the Jewish sources thus impose their own perspective on our studies. They naturally lead us to regard the Jews as more important than they actually were in the context of Babylonian society and politics as a whole. And within Jewry, the Jewish data concentrate on the affairs of those responsible for their editing and preservation, the rabbis.

The Jewish community included some wealthy merchants and tradesmen, but by and large it was, like the Christian one, part of the lowerclass. It was composed mainly of farmers and workers, unimportant people. Their affairs counted for very little.[2] The rabbinical courts had to adjudicate cases about a couple of onions or a piece of cloth or a date-palm, never about thousands of *zuz* of silk or large tracts of real estate. We ought, therefore, to be able to say something about the social and economic history of Babylonia's working class—at least, of the Jewish part of it. One might expect that we could provide a detailed description of the everyday life of artisans at their stalls and farmers in their fields, an account of the economic history of the submerged part of society. The fact is that so far we cannot.[3] Paradoxically, a substantial document deriving from the poorer part of society and pertaining entirely to the private life of a *millet*-community contains very little explicit, detailed information on the everyday life of that community. Just as Talmudic and cognate literature tells us practically nothing about the political and religious context of Babylonian Jewish history, so it leaves us mostly ignorant of the social and economic life of Babylonian Jews.

What we do know about is the life of the great schools of Sura and Pumbedita, where, as I said, the Babylonian Talmud itself was eventually compiled, and, of still greater importance, afterward given final form. The schools may not in *their* day have constituted the most im-

---

[1] Vol. IV, pp. 125-131, 279-283.

[2] Vol. IV, pp. 251-253.

[3] At least, we cannot do so on the basis of Talmudic materials as we now understand them. I know no equivalent to the strikingly original economic studies of R. S. Lopez, *The Birth of Europe* (London, 1966), pp. 258-303, for example, and I think the reason is, in some measure, that the kinds of data available to Lopez are not available to students of Middle Eastern history in Sasanian times. He can, for example, describe the workings of major commercial ventures and movements and give an account of the life of farmers and workers. Perhaps economic history may evolve out of the laws I have supposed were actually applied to, or in some ways shaped the life of, ordinary folk. I am still dubious, however, that the evidence is sufficient for a really wide-ranging and imaginative account such as that of Lopez.

portant or influential force in the shaping of the political or social history of Babylonian Jewry everywhere. But they were the force which later on succeeded in preserving a record of itself and then exercised the predominant influence in the shaping of everyday life and of political and historical events in Jewry, both in Babylonia and elsewhere, for many centuries to come. We therefore focus attention on the life of the schools, not because we are certain that in the period of which we speak the schools merited so much attention, but because, first, they are all we know; second, they later became the most important institution deriving from earlier times. We must never lose sight of these facts. A carpenter of Nazareth who lived and died outside the mainstream of history turns out to have been the most consequential (or, at least, written-about) figure in his day, although that does not mean we have much credible information about him. In the case of the great rabbis and rabbinical schools, the abundance of information and the later importance accorded to it combine to distort our perspective on what really mattered in their own times.

II. Geonic and Medieval Traditions on the Later Masters

Earlier writing of "Talmudic history" consisted of the effort to weave various stories into a unitary account, generally following the conventions as to the order of generations supplied by the Geonic and later traditions. Thus dating a given rabbi early or late, ascription to his sayings of much consequence, organization of information around schools and by generations—these historiographical tasks have depended less upon internal evidence, which is thin and frequently ambiguous, than upon what the post-Talmudic, particularly Geonic, writers said. Therefore for the purposes of Talmudic historiography, it became more interesting to investigate the intentions and insights of, or even the textual traditions pertaining to, Geonim, particularly R. Sherira, than to concentrate narrowly on the Talmudic evidences. This sort of investigation leads directly to the egregious remarks of M. Beer (see above, pp. 48-52), who would write a history of the exilarchate in later Sasanian times out of the mind of R. Sherira. Rather than repeat these inquiries (which have proved their value, such as it is), we had best consider just what the later sources consist of, and then turn directly to the Talmudic evidences. We have not got sufficient manuscript evidence to justify much confidence in choosing between variant chronological readings of the later materials, and we have not got sufficient historical material to determine the accuracy of post-Talmudic writers. R. Sherira provides the following:

> In all the years of Rava there was only one academy [which was] in Pumbedita. After Rava they [the authoritative sages] were divided [into] two schools. R. Naḥman b. Yiẓḥaq was in Pumbedita four years. He died in the year 667 [= 356]. R. Papa was in Nersh, which is near Sura. He ruled there twelve years and died in 687 [= 376].
>
> (*Letter of R. Sherira-Gaon*, ed. B. M. Lewin, p. 89, 1. 7-14.)

> After R. Naḥman b. Yiẓḥaq there ruled in Pumbedita a number of Geonim. R. Ḥama was in Pumbedita and died in the year 688 [= 377]...
>
> (*ibid.* p. 89, 1. 15-17.)

> After him [R. Ḥama] R. Zevid ruled in Pumbedita, and died in the year 696 [= 385]. After him R. Dimi of Nehardea ruled. He died in the year 699 [= 388]. After him Rafram ruled. He died in the year 706 [= 395]. After him R. Aḥa the son of Rava ruled. He died in the year 730 [419]. In all these years after R. Papa, R. Ashi was Gaon in Mata Meḥasia [Lewin, n. 10, adds a comment, "and the academy was moved from Sura to Mata Meḥasia."] and he pulled down the synagogue of the school and [re]built it [as in b.B.B. 3b]. He decreed a number of excellent ordinances and ordained festivals and fasts which pertained only to the exilarch and in Nehardea [the exilarch's residence]. He arranged the festival of the exilarch in his place, because he [R. Ashi] was exceptional,[1] and the greatness and Torah [of R. Ashi] were abundant. Huna b. Nathan, exilarch in these days, and Maremar and Mar Zuṭra who were after him—all were subject to R. Ashi and set [held] their festivals in Mata Meḥasia[2]...
>
> (*ibid.* p. 90, 1.5 through p. 91, 1.10.)

> And what R. Ashi did was not annulled afterward...
>
> (*ibid.* p. 91, 1.17.)

> After R. Ashi there were two academies... Annually, when the exilarch was in Mata Meḥasia (for the festival was ordained in the school house), they [the rabbis of Mata Meḥasia] went before him [the exilarch], and [so did] the rabbis of Pumbedita. So was this matter conducted until the end of a hundred years from this time. The exilarch[s] thus wielded severe authority and great power in the days of the Persians and in the days of the Ishmaelites, for they would purchase the exilarchate with substantial funds and would greatly torment and persecute the rabbis...
>
> (*ibid.* p. 92, 1.6-15.)

---

[1] *WHWH MPLYG*, var. *MYPLYG*. Alternatively: "He was separate."

[2] Here R. Sherira quotes b. Giṭ. 59a, about "Torah and greatness in one place."

R. Ashi held power in his school close to sixty years...
(*ibid.* p. 93, 1.15-16.)

...and he died in the year 738 [= 427].
(*ibid.* p. 94, 1.6-7.)

After him R. Yemar ruled in Mata Meḥasia. He died in the year 743 [= 432]. After him was R. Idi b. Abin. He died in the year 763 [= 452]. After him was R. Naḥman b. R. Huna. He died in the year 766 [= 455]. A persecution occurred, for Yazdagird decreed to prohibit the Sabbath.
(*ibid.* p. 94, 1. 8 through p. 95, 1. 2.)

And R. Ṭavyumi ruled in Meḥasia (and he is [the same as] Mar b. R. Ashi), and died in the year 799 [= 468] at the end of the Day of Atonement. After him was Rabbah Tosfa'ah. He died in the year 781 [= 470]. And on the fourth day of the week [Wednesday] which was the thirteenth of Kislev in the year 811 [= 500] Rabbana 'Abina b. R. Huna, who is Rabina, died, and this was [= marked] the end of instruction.[1]
(*ibid.* p. 95, 1. 5-9.)

In these years there ruled in Pumbedita R. Geviha of Be Ketil, who died in the year 744 [= 422]. After him was Rafram of Pumbedita, who died in the year 754 [= 443]. After him was R. Reḥumi ... who died in the year 760 [= 449] on the eve of the persecution which Yazdagird decreed. After him ruled R. Sama b. Rava, and at his time and at [the time of] Mar b. R. Ashi,—we have heard from the ancients and [moreover] have seen written in the books of their remembrances—they besought mercy so that a snake swallowed Yazdagird [II], the king, in his bedroom, and thus the persecution was annulled. In the days of R. Sama, on the Sabbath of Ṭevet in the year 781 [= 470] Rabbana 'Amemar b. Mar Yenuqa and Huna Mar b. R. Ashi, the exilarch, and Mesharsheya b. Peqod were imprisoned. And on the eighteenth day of Ṭevet Huna b. Mar Zuṭra the Prince [Nasi = exilarch] and Mesharsheya were killed, and in Adar of the same year Rabbana 'Amemar b. Mar Yenuqa was killed. In the year 871 [= 470] all the synagogues of Babylonia were closed, and the children of Jews were seized by the Magi.
(*ibid.* p. 96, 1. 1 through p. 97, 1. 9.)[2]

And in the year 787 [= 476] R. Sama b. Rava died. After him ruled R. Yosi. In his days was [came] the end of instruction, and the Talmud was completed.
(*ibid.* p. 97, 1. 10-13.)

And most of the Saboraic rabbis died in a few years, for so did the Geonim explain in the books of their remembrances in the chronicles: In the year 815 [= 504] died Rabbana Sama b. Rabbana Yehudai in

[1] *SWP HWR'H.*

[2] As above, pp. 60-69.

[the month of] Sivan, and they say that he was a judge. On the first of the week [Sunday] which was the fourth in Adar of the year 817 [= 506] R. Aḥai b. R. Huna died. In Nisan of the same year R. Reḥumi died... In the year 817 [= 506] in [the month of] Kislev died R. Samuel b. Judah of Pumbedita. In Adar died Rabina b. 'Amoẓia. And in the year 819 [= 508] died R. Huna the exilarch. In the year 822 [= 511] on the Day of Atonement there was a storm. R. Aḥai b. Rabbah b. Abbuhah died.

(*ibid.* p. 97, 1. 14 through p. 98, 1. 18.)

And in the year 826 [= 515] R. Taḥna and Mar Zuṭra the sons of R. Ḥinnena died. There remained Rabbah Joseph Gaon in our school [= Pumbedita] for a number of years. Afterwards R. 'Aina' was in Sura and R. Simonia in Pumbedita. And afterwards [came] R. Rabbai of [the town of] Rob. He was of our school, and they say he was a Gaon. There were [now] years of persecution and troubles at the end of the kingdom of the Persians, so that they [the rabbis] were unable to hold sessions and to arrange academies and to ordain Geonic practices until after some years. Then the rabbis came from Pumbedita to the vicinity of Nehardea, to the city of Piruz Shabur. These are the Geonim who were in our city after these things at the end of the kingdom of the Persians: from that year 900 [= 589] ruled Mar Hanan from 'Ashiqiyya. After him ruled Mar R. Mari, our forefather, son of Mar R. Dimi... After him ruled in Sura R. Mar b. R. Huna in the year 902 [= 591]... After him ruled in Nehardea R. Ḥinenai of Be Gihra, and in his days Maḥmad went forth to the world...

(*ibid.* p. 99, 1. 1 to p. 100, 1. 12.)

What is striking in R. Sherira's account, first of all, is his reference to written records possessed by the school of Pumbedita and prepared by his predecessors. Whether these records included the dates of the deaths of great rabbis or not is unclear. He refers specifically to a written report of the miraculous death of Yazdagird. He seems to underline this source, probably because its contents were incredible: "We have *heard* from the ancients... and *seen* written in the books of their remembrances." The other reference to a written source concerns the Saboraic rabbis. R. Sherira is interested in two schools, Pumbedita and Sura, as if no others existed. The appearance of R. Ashi in Mata Meḥasia requires the identification of that academy with the one in Sura, although these were different places.[1] The "break-up" of the

[1] See Gerson D. Cohen, *Book of Tradition*, p. 121, note to 1. 7; W. Bacher, *s.v.* "Matah Meḥasya," JE VIII, 374-5, and M. Beer, "'Iyunim beIggeret R. Sherira Ga'on," *Bar Ilan Yearbook*, IV-V (1956-1965), pp. 187-191.

Beer notes that there is no mention in the Talmud of the move of the exilarch's festival to Sura. R. Sherira regarded it as exceptionally important. He notes that the "subjugation" of Huna bar Nathan is not clearly defined.

"unified school" of R. Ashi apparently accounts for the reestablishment (if that is what happened) of the school of Pumbedita. What seems more likely is that many schools existed. In any event the one at Pumbedita was not suppressed or closed by R. Ashi, but perhaps lost some sort of legal authority or influence on the formation of traditions. In any event upon this basis one can hardly compose a history of the schools. We learn mainly the names of the heads of two important academies, but little more than that.

According to R. Sherira, the exilarch not only utterly subordinated himself to the head of the school of Mata Meḥasia, but actually paid his respects in a public ceremony as a sign of that subordination. According to his view, when other Jews came to pay their homage to the exilarch, they came to the place of R. Ashi, not to that of the exilarch. R. Ashi moreover issued decrees pertaining specifically to Nehardea and the exilarchate. R. Sherira furthermore stresses that what R. Ashi ordained remained valid later on. His assertion is dubious in the light of his later complaint that the exilarch bought his office from the Iranian government and used it to make trouble for the rabbis. I doubt that the leading schoolmen dominated the exilarchate, for if they had, R. Sherira would not have had reason to extend his complaint against exilarchic predominance of Islamic times back into the days of the later Sasanians. It seems on the face of it that R. Ashi's exceptional influence over Huna b. Nathan produced a singular situation which did not quickly repeat itself. But R. Ashi's school remained in Mata Meḥasia and continued as the leading school. As to the Saboraic period, R. Sherira's meaning is that it was brief and ended in the final years of Sasanian rule, not that all the Saboraim individually died young.

Remembering that R. Sherira, a descendant of the Pumbeditan school, represents a tradition hostile to the exilarch, we may somewhat differently reconstruct matters. The exilarch, faced with trouble in the academies, decided to dominate by support and found an agent for his purpose in R. Ashi, the ambitious head of Sura. He persuaded R. Ashi to move to Mata Meḥasia, thus getting rid of the unpleasant associations of Sura, financed his building programs there, and accepted his decisions as *the* authoritative interpretations of the law, thus making his academy *de facto* the primary one and putting Pumbedita in second place (thus R. Sherira's "were subject to" would mean "were forced to accept his legal decisions.") On the other hand the exilarch came every year to the festival of the Mata Meḥasian academy, and the rabbis there ceremonially acknowledged his authority (= passed in front of him) during this annual visit of inspection. And so did those of Pumbedita and all other schools who had to come to Mata Meḥasia for the annual festival and review of the rabbinical corps. R. Ashi was established under the exilarch as a little Mobad Mobadan under the Shah, and the system he set up lasted as a means of exilarchic control of the rabbis for a century.

The traditions in *SOZ* pertain mostly to exilarchs and were cited above.[1] We here review the names and approximate dates of the sages mentioned there:

After 363	R. Ḥananel
Ca. 400	Rava and Rabina
After 484	R. Safra
	R. Aḥa of Difti
Ca. 525	Rabina
	R. Aḥa of Difti b. R. Ḥanilai
	R. Mari and Mar Ḥanina Rava

The sages listed above appear in *SOZ* as having served the exilarchs of their day.[2] To this list we should add the names of Mar R. Ḥanina, R. Sama, and R. Yiẓḥaq, who were Mar Zuṭra's sages according to the legend of Mar Zuṭra's rebellion. Why *SOZ* does not list them in the earlier sequence I cannot say for sure. Probably the reason is that the Mar Zuṭra legend is completely separate from the earlier material. The *SOZ* list strikingly omits practically all the men designated by R. Sherira as heads of schools. R. Ashi's distinction, his supposed superiority to the exilarch, his direction of exilarchic ritual affairs—none of these "facts" so important to R. Sherira even appears. But, as we have already observed, what R. Sherira knows is unknown to the *SOZ*, including even the fifth century persecutions. We do find a Rabina [= Rabbana 'Abina b. R. Huna] mentioned by both as the "end of instruction," but the source of the statement for both R. Sherira and *SOZ* was the famous Talmudic passage:

> R. Ashi and Rabina [were] the end of instruction [*hora'ah*].
>
> (b. B.M. 86a)

The rabbis associated with the exilarch Huna Mar b. R. Ashi were Mesharsheya and Rabbana 'Amemar b. Mar Yenuqa, about whom

[1] Pp. 95-97.

[2] *SOZ* ed. Grossberg, pp. 47-49. There follows the story of the birth of Mar Zuṭra and his revolt, p. 49ff.

SOZ knows nothing, As a matter of fact, not a single name appearing on the *SOZ*'s list of important rabbis who served the exilarchate in the late fourth, fifth, and sixth centuries is even known to R. Sherira as a major rabbinical figure. While R. Sherira provides a history of the two great schools that survived to his own time, and chiefly his own, Pumbedita, *SOZ* concentrates on exilarchic history and presumably exilarchic rabbis. The author may indeed have had access to exilarchic archives just as R. Sherira used academic ones. Neither, however, provides an organized list of all the names of major rabbis in these centuries.

Seder Tannaim veAmoraim contains the following

> And after him [R. Naḥman b. Yiẓḥaq, who died in 667 (= 356)] R. Papa [died] in 686 [= 375], and after him R. Zevid [died] in the year 696 [= 385] and after him R. Dimi of Nehardea [died] in the year 699 [= 388], and after him R. Kahana [died] in the year 702 [= 391], and after him Mar Zuṭra [died] in the year 724 [= 413]. And on that very day there was a great rumbling in the world, and the earth quaked. And after him R. Aḥa b. Rava [died] in the year 730 [= 419]. ...And after him Rabina [died] in the year 733 [= 422], and after him R. Ashi [died] in the year 738 [= 427]. In the year 742 [= 431] R. Yemar was gathered in... In the year 753 [= 442] R. Huna the exilarch was gathered in.[1] In the year 762 [= 451] R. Idi b. Aba was gathered in. In the year 766 [= 455] R. Naḥman b. R. Huna was gathered in, and 'Ardezur the king of the Persians decreed...[2] In the year 779 [= 468] Rabbah b. R. Ashi was gathered in. In the year 782 [= 471] was gathered in R. Ḥama b. Rava, and Huna b. Mar Zuṭra exilarch was killed... In the year 811 [= 500] Rabina was gathered in, [which marked] the end of instruction, and the Talmud was completed.
>
> And the Saboraic rabbis followed, and these are their names: R. Aḥai of Bet Ḥatom; R. Geviha of 'Argizta; R. Aḥa b. Nehilai; Rabbana Sama b. Rabbana Judah; R. Samuel of Pumbedita; Rabina b. 'Umẓia; R. Aḥadbuy b. Qaṭina; and Mar Zuṭra b. R. Ḥama. In their times Maḥumaṭ went forth, in the year 928 [= 617].
>
> (ed. Grosberg, pp. 64-66.)

Seder Tannaim veAmoraim evidently depends upon some of the data of the letter of R. Sherira. The dates are similar or identical for the most part; more important, the focus of interest is the same. Exilarchs appear only rarely, while by contrast, heads of Sura and Pumbedita are never omitted. The discrepancies are minor and unimportant. In fact little if anything appears in the later list which has not been borrowed

[1] As above, p. 136.
[2] As above, p. 61.

from the earlier one. The chief interest is Sura. I do not think the *Seder Tannaim veAmoraim* contains any independent information of value.

The twelfth-century *Book of Tradition* of Abraham Ibn Daud best illustrates the state of the question in medieval and into modern times:

> The fifth generation [of Babylonian Amoraim] was that of R. Naḥman bar Isaac, R. Papa, and R. Huna the son of R. Joshua... R. Papa became head of the academy in Naresh, a city close by Sura, served for nineteen years in that office, and he died in 4132 [= 372]. After R. Naḥman bar Isaac passed away, R. Ḥama of Nehardea became head of the academy of Nehardea. He, too, died in 4132 [= 372], after a term of fifteen years. As for R. Huna the son of R. Joshua, his name is not recorded among the heads of the academies.
>
> The sixth generation was that of R. Ashi and the heads of the academies who lived in his days... During R. Papa's term, in 4127 [= 367], R. Ashi became head of the academy of Sura for sixty years. In the fifth year of his office, R. Papa and R. Ḥama passed away. R. Zevid became head of the academy of Pumbedita for eight years and died in 4140 [= 380]. He was succeeded by R. Dimi [who served] for three years and died in 4143 [= 383]. His successor was Rafram bar Papa who died in the same year. His successor was R. Kahana the second [who served] for twenty-eight years and died in 4171 [= 411]. His successor was R. Aḥa the son of Rava [who served] for two years and died in 4173 [= 413]. Thus, R. Papa as well as these six heads of academies all passed away within the lifetime of R. Ashi. R. Ashi passed away in 4187 [= 427], which is equivalent to 738 of the Seleucid Era. He began to commit the Talmud to writing.
>
> The seventh generation was that of Meremar, Mar bar R. Ashi, and their colleagues. After the death of R. Ashi, his successor as head of the academy of Sura was Meremar [who served] for five years and died in 4192 [= 432]. His successor was R. Idi bar Abin [who served] for twenty years and died in 4212 [= 452]. His successor was R. Naḥman bar Huna [who served] for three years and died in 4215 [= 455]. Following these men, Mar bar R. Ashi succeeded to his father's post for thirteen years. Since those were good years, he was called R. Ṭavyomi.[1] He died in 4228 [= 468], which is equivalent to 779 of the Seleucid Era. His successor was Rabbah Tosefa'ah [who served] for six years and died in 4234 [= 474]. These five men had been disciples of R. Ashi. Although some, like Meremar and R. Idi b. Abin, were [also] his colleagues, the others were disciples.
>
> In the year of Rabbah Tosefa'ah's death [= 474], the Persian Empire decreed frightful persecutions against the Jews...
>
> (ed. and trans. Gerson D. Cohen, pp. 34, 1. 47 through p. 36, 1. 83.)

---

[1] Ibn Daud obviously knows nothing of the persecutions of Yazdagird or dates them later on. In any event, it is a peculiar etymology. On the relationship of Ibn

At the time that these men were heads of the academy in Sura, the following were heads of the academy in Pumbedita: R. Geviha of Be Ketil became head of the academy in the year of R. Ashi's death for six years, and he died in 4193 [= 433]. His successor was Rafram [who served] for ten years and died in 4203 [= 443]. His successor was R. Reḥumi [who served] for thirteen years and died in 4216 [= 456]. He was succeeded by R. Sama the son of Rava, who passed away in 4236 [= 456]. He was succeeded by R. Sama the son of Rava, who passed away in 4236 [= 476].

(ed. and trans. Gerson D. Cohen, p. 42, 1. 165-173.)

The first generation [of the Saboraim] was that of Rabbah Yosi,[1] who marks the beginning of the Saboraic rabbis. He served as head of the academy after Rabina for thirty-eight years,[2] until 4274 [= 514]. In the twenty-fourth year of his presidency, which was the year 4260 [= 500] and 811 of the Seleucid Era and 123 before the Muslim reckoning, the Talmud was sealed ... Rabbah Yosi died in 4274 [= 514]. The second generation of the Saboraic rabbis was that of R. Aḥai bar Huna and his colleagues. R. Aḥai served as head of the academy for one year and died in 4275 [= 515]. He was succeeded by R. Samuel bar Rava, [who served] for three years and died in 4278 [= 518]. He was succeeded by Rabina of 'Umẓa [who served] for one year and died in 4279 [= 519]. His successor was R. Teḥina who served for seven years and died in 4286 [= 526]. He was succeeded by R. Simona and R. 'Aina', the latter in Sura and the former in Pumbedita. R. Simona lived until 4300 [= 540]. All these were of one generation.

The second generation also included the disciples of R. Simona and R. 'Aina'. However their names were not recorded, inasmuch as the academies were closed for about fifty years after R. Simona's death until 4349 [= 589] because of the hostility of the Persian kings and their persecutions.

The third generation was that of R. Ḥanan of Ashiqiyya, who took over from the disciples of R. Simona and R. 'Aina'. He was followed by R. Mari, R. Huna, R. Ḥanina, and R. Ḥinena, respectively. All these were of one generation. R. Ḥanan of Ashiqiyya became head of the academy in 4349 [= 589]. He was followed by these four heads of the academy, whose terms of service, however, are not recorded.

Daud's account to that of R. Sherira, see below, pp. 144 ff. See Cohen, *op. cit.*, p. 123 on 1. 77.

1 Cohen comments (p. 43 n. to 1.3) that since Rabina was supposed to mark the end of the Amoraic period and Rabbah Yosi the beginning of the Saboraic one, Ibn Daud also inferred that Rabbah Yosi succeeded to Rabina's post, although R. Sherira does not say so.

2 Cohen comments (p. 126, n. to 1.4) that Ibn Daud's dates are traceable to R. Sherira's letter.

Sherira		*SOZ*
Sura (= Nersh, Mata Mehasia)	*Pumbedita*	*After 363:*
R. Papa, d. 376	Naḥman b. Yiẓḥaq, d. 356	R. Ḥananel
R. Ashi, d. 427	R. Ḥama, d. 377	Rava and Rabina
	R. Zevid, d. 385	
	R. Dimi, d. 388	
	Rafram, d. 395	
	R. Aḥa b. Raba, d. 419	
R. Yemar, d. 432	R. Geviha, d. 422	
R. Idi b. Abin, d. 452	Rafram of Pumbedita, d. 443	
R. Naḥman b. R. Huna, d. 455	R. Reḥumi, d. 449	
R. Ṭavyumi = Mar b. R. Ashi, d. 468	R. Sama b. Rava, d. 476	
		After 484:
Rabbah Tosfa'ah, d. 470	R. Yosi	R. Safra
Rabina (= R. Abina b. R. Huna), d. 500		R. Aḥa of Difti
Saboraim		Rabina
		Ca. 525:
Rabbana Sama b. R. Judah, d. 504		
R. Aḥai b. R. Huna, d. 506		
R. Reḥumi, d. 506		R. Aḥa of Difti b. R. Hanilai
R. Samuel b. Judah, d. 506		
Rabina b. 'Amoẓia, d. 506		R. Mari and Mar Ḥanina Rava
R. Aḥai b. Rabbah b. Abbuhah, d. 511		
R. Taḥna and Mar Zuṭra sons of R. Ḥinnena, d. 515		
Sura	*Pumbedita*	
R. 'Aina'	Rabbah Joseph Gaon	
	R. Simonia	
	R. Rabbai of Rob	
	R. Ḥanan from 'Ashiqiyya, (ca. 589)	
	R. Mari b. R. Dimi	
R. Mar b. R. Huna, d. 591		
R. Ḥinenai of Be Gihra ca. 640		

> The fourth generation was that of R. Isaac. In his days the Muslim Empire prevailed over the Persian Empire...
>
> (ed. and trans. Gerson D. Cohen, pp. 43, 1. 1 through p. 44, 1. 31.)

Ibn Daud has obviously drawn heavily on the letter of R. Sherira. Yet, as Gerson Cohen points out,[1] while the two lists of the bearers of rabbinical tradition are similar, there are major discrepancies between

[1] Pp. 177-188.

Seder Tannaim veAmoraim	*Sefer Ha Qabbalah*	
	Sura	*Pumbedita*
R. Papa, d. 375	[R. Papa (Nersh), d. 372]	
R. Zevid, d. 385	[R. Ḥama (Nehardea), d. 372]	
R. Dimi, d. 388	R. Ashi (367-427)	Zevid, d. 380
R. Kahana, d. 391		Dimi, d. 383
Mar Zuṭra, d. 413		Rafram b. Papa, d. 383
R. Aḥa b. Rava, d. 419		Kahana II, d. 411
Rabina, d. 422		Aḥa b. Rava, d. 413
R. Ashi, d. 427	Maremar, d. 432	Geviha, d. 433
R. Yemar, d. 431	Idi b. Abin, d. 452	Rafram, d. 443
R. Idi b. Aba, d. 451	Naḥman b. Huna, d. 455	Reḥumi, d. 456
R. Naḥman b. R. Huna, d. 455	Mar b. R. Ashi, d. 468	Sama b. Rava, d. 476
Rabbah b. R. Ashi, d. 468	Rabbah Tosfa'ah, d. 474	
R. Ḥama b. Rava, d. 471		
Rabina, d. 500		
Saboraim	*Saboraim*	
R. Aḥai of Bet Hatom	Rabbah Yosi, d. 514	
R. Geviha of 'Argizta	Aḥai b. Huna, d. 515	
R. Aḥa b. Nehilai	Samuel b. Rava, d. 518	
Rabban Sama b. R. Judah	Rabina of 'Umẓa, d. 519	
R. Samuel of Pumbedita	Teḥina, d. 526 [= Taḥna?]	
Rabina b. 'Umẓia	'Aina' - Simona, d. 540	
R. Aḥadbuy b. Qaṭina	——	
Mar Zuṭra b. R. Ḥama	Academies closed 540-589	
	——	
	Ḥanan of 'Ashiqiyya, 589-?	
	Mari	
	Huna	
	Ḥanina	
	Ḥinena	
	Yiẓḥaq, ca. 640	

them. The one of greatest interest here concerns the dates of Rabina's death and the redaction of the Babylonian Talmud. But the lists of students and leaders of each generation differ markedly. Sherira moreover described the Saboraic age as a brief one, while Ibn Daud found in it five generations, lasting one hundred eighty-seven years; I have cited only part. Sherira dates the beginning of the Geonic period at 589, while Ibn Daud sets it in 689. Cohen points out that while Halevy held Ibn Daud had never even seen Sherira's letter, most scholars disagree. Cohen notes, "The affinities between the two works are much too marked to be dismissed as mere coincidence."[1] The length of the

[1] P. 179.

rabbis' terms of office is pretty much identical in the two lists. Some have held that Ibn Daud used R. Sherira's letter but also another source, Samuel ibn Nagrela's *Introduction to the Talmud.* Cohen persuasively rejects the theory of Abraham Epstein, which was based upon the view that Ibn Daud did indeed draw from Samuel ibn Nagrela. He notes that Ibn Daud's list is more closely related to R. Sherira's letter than to the *Seder Tannaim veAmoraim.*[1] Where he diverges, "This would merely indicate that his basic source was a digest of Sherira, rather than a corrupted text of the *Epistle* itself."

We obviously cannot make facile use of the Geonic and medieval lists. The divergences are striking. We have little knowledge of the sources of data, none at all of the basis for assigning dates to the various rabbis. It is significant that Talmudic evidences standing by themselves and universally available have been able to produce little or no unanimity of opinion on even the most fundamental questions among Geonic and medieval historians. Granted the tendency of *SOZ* to concentrate on exilarchic history, we should nonetheless have expected, on account of that very interest, more extensive reference to R. Ashi than we have uncovered. In fact we do not know much more than the later chroniclers tell us, and what they tell us is too fragmentary to permit a continuous and detailed account of academic history. Yet I think we may take as fact the assignment of various sages to the several schools, even though why one school should be subsumed under another is obscure. I see no reason to doubt that R. Sherira knew who was in Pumbedita and Sura, where records of earlier authorities were preserved. Other schools, such as those in Nehardea, Nersh, Pum Nehara, are generally ignored in Geonic traditions.[2]

III. The Ritual of "Being a Rabbi"

The rabbi functioned in Jewish society as a judge and administrator, for into his hands the exilarch had much earlier committed the court-system of the community. But the sage lived in a society, the school, in some ways quite separate from that of Jewry as a whole. The rabbinical academy was, to be sure, a law-school, and some of its graduates did serve as judges and administrators of the law. We should however err by regarding the school as a center for merely legal study. It was a kind

---

1 P. 186.

2 See Y. S. Ẓuri, *Rav Ashi* (Bilgoraj, 1924), pp. 3-18.

of Jewish monastery, much like the Christian one as the locus for a peculiar kind of religious living. Only one of its functions concerned those parts of the revealed Torah to be applied in everyday life through the Jewish judiciary. The school was a holy community. In it men learned to live a holy life and to become saints. When they left, sages continued to live by the discipline of the schools, and they invested great efforts in teaching that discipline by example and precept to ordinary folk. It was through the academy that Pharisaic-Rabbinical Judaism proposed to conquer the Jewish people and transform it into a true replica of Mosaic revelation as rabbis understood and expounded that revelation.

The school therefore should be seen not merely as a social force,[1] but also and especially as a *religious* phenomenon. It embodied the central myth of Pharisaic-Rabbinical Judaism, the belief that the Mosaic Scriptures constituted divine revelation, but only a part of it. At Sinai God had handed down a dual revelation, the written part known to one and all, but also the oral part preserved by the great Scriptural heroes, passed on by prophets to various ancestors in the obscure past of Pharisaism, finally and most openly handed down to the rabbis of the Palestinian, and now, the Babylonian schools as well.[2] The "whole Torah" thus consisted of both written and oral parts. That "whole Torah" was studied by David, augmented by Ezekiel, legislated by Ezra, and embodied in the schools and by the rabbinical sages of every period in Israelite history from Moses to the present. It was a singular, linear conception of revelation preserved only by the few, but pertaining to the many, and in time capable of bringing salvation to all.

The Pharisaic-Rabbinical myth further regarded Moses as "our rabbi," the first and prototypical figure of the schools. It held that whoever embodied the teachings of Moses "our rabbi" would thereby conform to the will of God—and not to God's will alone, but also to his *way*. The schools believed that in heaven God and the angels studied Torah just as rabbis did on earth. God donned phylacteries like a rabbi. He prayed in the rabbinical mode. He carried out the acts of compassion called for by rabbinical ethics. He guided the affairs of the world according to the rules of Torah, just like the rabbi in his court. One

---

[1] See below, Chapter Seven.

[2] Whether Babylonian schools had existed before R. Judah the Prince to preserve the oral tradition was a moot point in the traditions, as we have seen, Vol. I, pp. 170-172.

exegesis of the Creation-legend taught that God had looked into the Torah and therefrom had created the world. Moreover, heaven above was aware of what the rabbis in particular thought, said, and did below. The myth of Torah was many-sided. It included the striking detail that whatever the most recent rabbi was destined to discover through proper, disciplined exegesis of the tradition was as much a part of the way revealed to Moses as was a sentence of Scripture itself. It was therefore possible to participate in the giving of the law by appropriate, logical inquiry into the law. God, studying and living by Torah, was believed to subject himself to these same rules of logical inquiry, so if an earthly court through logic and tradition overruled the testimony, delivered through natural miracles, of the heavenly one, God would rejoice, crying out, "My sons have conquered me! My sons have conquered me!"

In a word, we are considering a religious-mythical system in which earth and heaven corresponded to one another. The Torah was the nexus and the model for both. The heavenly paradigm was embodied upon earth. Moses "our rabbi" was the pattern for the ordinary sage of the streets of Pumbedita and Sura. And God participated in the system, for it was his image which, in the end, formed that cosmic paradigm. The rabbi and school constituted the projection of heaven onto earth. Honor was due him more than to the scroll of the Torah, for through his learning and logic he might even alter the very content of Mosaic revelation. Intelligence and logical acuteness signified the possession of spiritual grace, so marking the rabbi as a holy man in much the same way as other expressions of supernatural favor, such as the ability to raise the dead, set apart the holy men of other communities. The rabbi *was* "Torah," not merely because he lived by it, but because at his best he constituted as compelling an embodiment of the heavenly model as did a scroll of the Torah itself.

The schools, like other holy communities, imposed their own particular rituals in the first instance intended for the disciples and masters. Later, it was hoped, all Israel would conform to those rituals and so join the circle of master and disciples. The schools' discipline transformed ordinary, natural actions, gestures, and functions into rituals—the rituals of "being a rabbi". Everyone ate. Rabbis did so in a "rabbinical" manner. That is to say, what others may have regarded as matters of mere etiquette, formalities and conventions intended to render eating aesthetically agreeable, rabbis regarded as matters of "Torah," something to be learned as part of the holy way. It was "Torah" to do things one way, and to do them otherwise was "ignorance" (though not heresy, for theology was not at issue). The master of Torah, whether disciple or teacher, would demonstrate his mastery not merely through what he said in the discussion of legal traditions or what he did in court. He would do so by how he sat at the table, by what ritual formulae he recited before eating one or another species of fruit or vegetable, by how he washed his hands. Everyone had to relieve himself, dress himself, conduct normal social relations. The sage would do so according to "Torah". The personality traits of men might vary. Those expected of and inculcated into a sage were of a single sacred fabric.

One must repeatedly stress the fundamental difference between the way of "Torah" and other ways to salvation explored by other holy men and sacred communities. The rabbi at no point would admit that his particular rites were imposed upon him alone, apart from all Israel. He ardently "spread Torah" among the Jews at large. He believed he had to, because "Torah" was revealed to all Israel at Sinai and required of all Israel afterward. Hence if he was right that Moses was "our rabbi" and God kept the commandments, he had to ask of everyone what he demanded of himself, conformity to the way of "Torah." His task was facilitated by the widespread belief that Moses had indeed revealed "the Torah," and that some sort of interpretation quite naturally was required to apply it to everyday affairs. The written part of "Torah" therefore naturally shaped the life of ordinary pious folk. What the rabbi had to accomplish was to persuade the outsider that the written part of the Torah was not exhaustive but partial and incomplete, requiring further elaboration and completion through the oral traditions he alone possessed and embodied.

The final element in the rabbinical Torah-myth concerned salvation. It took many forms. One salvific teaching held that had Israel not sinned—that is, disobeyed divine revelation or Torah—the Scriptures would have closed with the story of the conquest of Palestine. From that eschatological time forward, the sacred community would have lived in eternal peace under the divine law. Keeping the Torah was therefore the guarantee of salvation. The opposite was said in many forms as well. Israel had sinned, therefore God had called Assyrians against Samaria, Babylonians and Romans against Jerusalem. But in his mercy he would be equally faithful to restore the fortunes of the people when they through suffering and repentence had expiated the result and the cause of their sin. So in both negative and positive forms, the Torah-myth told of a necessary connection between the salvation of the people (and of the world) and the state of "Torah" among them. If, for example, all Israel would properly keep a single Sabbath, the Messiah would come. Of special interest here is the saying of R. Papa cited above, that the rule of the pagans depended upon the sin of Israel. If Israel would constitute a full and complete replication of "Torah," that is, of heaven, then pagan rule would come to an end. It would end, as I said earlier,[1] because all Israel then, like some few rabbis even now, would attain to the creative theurgical powers inherent in Torah. Just as God had created the world through "Torah," so saintly rabbis could now create animals and men. Rabbis quite practically asserted their magical power, by holding that they should not pay for the building of walls around their cities, "because rabbis do not require protection." Some rabbis enjoyed the general protection of heaven granted to those who do heaven's will and conform to its revealed word. But a few rabbis could quite independently of heaven exercise the power of Torah, and in doing so, they performed specific magical works such as those just mentioned. They probably would have regarded their power as a foretaste of salvation and as a demonstration of the power inherent in "Torah". Like the wonders of prophecy, the magic of some few rabbis provided a secular authentication for other aspects of their activities. But it was a part of the broader salvific pattern revealed long ago and supposed to come to fruition when Israel had made itself worthy through its embodiment of Torah, that is, as I said, through its perfect replication of heaven.

We shall here review the late fourth and fifth century evidences of the ritual of "being a rabbi" and later on examine other components of that estate. Many rabbinical sayings on proper behavior pertained not only to rabbis but to ordinary folk as well. They therefore cannot be interpreted as singularly characteristic rituals of "being a rabbi," although they obviously reflect the values of the academy. Among such sayings are R. Naḥman b. Isaac's, that one should not keep a wild dog,[2] as well as dicta concerning good health, such as the following:

> Mar b. R. Ashi had to urinate at a bridge. He was told, "Lo, your mother-in-law is coming." He replied, "[Even] in her ear."
>
> (b. Bekh. 44b)

> *For this let every one that is godly pray unto Thee for a time of finding* (Ps. 32:6). Mar Zuṭra [interpreted] 'for a time of finding' to refer to [finding] a privy. (b. Ber. 8a)

---

[1] Vol. IV, pp. 401-402.

[2] b. Shab. 53b.

The latter saying means that one should be grateful to live near a privy. The former stresses that under certain circumstances one should not restrain oneself from performing one's natural functions. Such advice would have been equally salutary for everyone; what characterizes the rabbis is that they took it. They further would have regarded as seriously negligent any rabbis who behaved contrary to good advice universally available from rabbinical lore.[1]

Some teachings concerning eating may have been intended for ordinary folk as well as rabbis. Others clearly were supposed to be carried out only by disciples of sages; by following them, the disciples would give evidence of their status. In the former category are the following:

> Amemar, Mar Zuṭra, and R. Ashi were once seated [at a meal]. Fresh vegetables were brought before them before the fourth hour. Amemar and R. Ashi ate [them] but Mar Zuṭra did not eat them. They said to him, "What is your opinion? Is it [in accord with] R. Isaac who said, 'It is forbidden to converse with anyone who eats fresh vegetables before the fourth hour because [his breath] smells bad?' But we are eating, and lo, you have been conversing with us!" He replied to them, "I follow the other saying of R. Isaac, who said, 'It is forbidden for a man to eat fresh vegetables before the fourth hour.'"
>
> (b. Ber. 44b)

What is striking in the second saying is the absence of a reason for R. Isaac's prohibition. In the former exemplum of R. Isaac's saying the prohibition obviously would apply to anyone; it was quite neutral, naturalistic. In the latter the absence of a reason renders the rule a matter of rabbinical etiquette alone: This is how a sage does things. He who wishes to live by rabbinical rules therefore will follow R. Isaac's rule without question. (In the commentaries, the prohibition against conversing with others constitutes the difference; in the latter case one ought not to eat vegetables early in the day, but if he does, he may continue to talk with other people.) An exchange such as this could not have taken place outside of the schools. There people would not ordinarily have known what R. Isaac had said about bad breath's resulting from eating vegetables too early in the morning. If ordinary people refrained, the reason would not have been attached to a master's

[1] See for example Vol. IV, pp. 300, 388, on having sexual relations in the daytime. The rabbis regarded it as unwise, since demons would be attracted on that account. But urban dwellers ignored the rabbinical view. They were not on that account heretics, but merely behaved foolishly.

name. I doubt there would have been an explicit reason to begin with. The simple matter of when one ate fresh vegetables thus entered into the rite of "being a rabbi."

Similarly, we may be sure that rabbinical sayings on drinking wine applied not only to sages:

> R. Huna b. R. Joshua said, "If a person drinks wine, even though his heart is closed like a virgin, the wine opens it..."
>
> (b. B.B. 12b)

Mar Zuṭra b. R. Naḥman advised parents to teach their children not habitually to drink wine or eat meat.[1] Obviously, counsel not to become accustomed to meat and wine pertained to anyone. Yet more rigorous asceticism would have been expected primarily from disciples of the sages. The question was raised, for example, whether a certain substance was too luxurious for ordinary use.[2] Similarly, Mar b. Rabina would fast the entire year except for three holidays, which were Shavu'ot, Purim, and the eve of Day of Atonement.[3] Repeated fasting and other forms of abstinence characterized holy men, and no one seriously expected that ordinary people would do likewise. Yet holy men such as sages did not regard their rites as suitable only for themselves. Hence the advice not to become accustomed to meat and wine would have extended the fundamentally ascetic value of the sage to the life of a wider circle.

The following story illustrates peculiar legal considerations characteristic of rabbis' meals and not normally found elsewhere:

> R. Papa and R. Huna b. R. Joshua joined their bread together. But by the time R. Huna b. R. Joshua ate one [piece], R. Papa ate four. He [R. Huna] said to him, "Divide with me." "You have accepted [me as a partner]," he [R. Papa] replied. [Thereupon] he raised all these objections ... and he answered him by [the teaching regarding ... and finally, they made the requested division]. He [R. Huna] then went and joined bread with Rabina. By the time R. Huna b. R. Joshua ate one [piece], Rabina ate eight. He said, "A hundred Papa's rather than one Rabina." (b. Pes. 89b)[4]

[1] b. Ḥul. 84a. See also b. Shab. 119a, the sons of R. Papa b. Abba ate meat and drank wine daily.

[2] b. Shab. 50b. Note that the form of the saying is identical with that cited earlier, "Amemar, Mar Zuṭra, and R. Ashi were sitting, and such-and-such was brought before them." This is clearly a conventional form for the transmission of sayings such as this one. Whether the form was reserved for particular sorts of laws or not I cannot say.

[3] b. Pes. 68b.

[4] Trans. H. Freedman (London, 1948), p. 476.

Here the issue concerned the division of food originally contributed by each party to a common meal. Since R. Papa ate faster than R. Huna b. R. Joshua, a legal issue was raised, namely, whether R. Huna could legitimately withdraw. He won the argument and ended the common meal. No one can imagine that lay people sharing a meal would have disputed over the food in a similarly erudite manner. I should suppose that one who wished to depart with his food could do so, and none would expect him to supply weighty legal arguments, replete with learned citations, in justification. This story exemplifies how the sage would conduct himself at an ordinary meal by considerations not applicable to outsiders.

Early Pharisaism had laid great stress upon ritual purity in eating ordinary, that is, not consecrated, food. Now, one who was ritually pure could claim the privilege of saying grace after the meal, as in the following story:

> R. Papa, R. Huna b. R. Joshua, and Rava b. Samuel were eating together. R. Papa said to them, "Let me say grace, because nine *kavs* of water have been thrown on me." Rava b. Samuel said to them, "'...but for others, forty *se'ahs* of water are required.' Let me say grace, since forty *se'ahs* of water have been thrown on me." R. Huna said to them, "Let me say the grace, since I have had neither the one nor the other on me. [That is, I did not require the purification from uncleanness to begin with, not having suffered the emission of semen which would have necessitated it.]"
>
> (b. Ber. 22b)

We see therefore that the rabbinical rules continued to stress a measure of cleanness from ritual impurity, though in no way to the same degree as in the early centuries of the common era; then a *ḥaver* was characterized specifically by his refraining from eating unconsecrated food in a state of ritual impurity.

In the normal course of events sages would have eaten mostly with each other, since they spent most of their time while at the school-sessions in one another's company. These meals began and ended with appropriate blessings and grace.[1] The discussion of what blessings were to be said over particular foods was central to the schools' legal inquiry. Similarly, the saying of grace after meals produced numerous knotty legal problems. Both rites probably were peculiar to rabbis. The very many difficulties met by rabbis in learning the law pertaining to them

[1] On blessings over food, see also Vol. II, pp. 170-6, III, pp. 158-178, and IV, pp. 329-330.

suggest so. Further, not a single instance of an outsider's saying grace or asking the sages about laws pertaining to blessings or grace exists in Babylonian traditions. By contrast, we have many examples of sages' eating together and saying grace with one another, including both legal dicta and stories. I therefore suppose that while ordinary people might have expressed gratitude to the divinity for food they ate, they would not regularly have done so in the forms prescribed by the schools. Hence singular rites signifying whether a man was part of the rabbinical estate must have included those connected with eating. Since sacred meals of various kinds usually marked the existence of a holy community or brotherhood in ancient religions, one can hardly think otherwise. What is remarkable here as elsewhere, on the contrary, is the rabbis' insistance that everyone was supposed to do just as they did. But at this time I doubt that outsiders did so. I know no evidence that the rabbis now made an effort, through curses or promises, to see people did conform.

One important rule about eating was that food should not be thrown:

> Amemar, Mar Zuṭra, and R. Ashi were once eating together. Dates and pomegranates were served to them. Mar Zuṭra took some and threw them in front of R. Ashi as his portion. He [R. Ashi] said to him [Mar Zuṭra], "Does not your honor agree [that edibles should not be thrown]?" He replied, "That was taught with reference to bread..."
>
> (b. Ber. 50b)

The discussion proceeds to analyze Mar Zuṭra's action in the light of such teachings.

Sayings and stories about the proper blessings for various foods include the following:

> Mar Zuṭra made [dough baked in a hole in the ground] the basis of his meal, and blessed it, "...who brings forth bread from the earth," and said three blessings after it [even though others held such a dough did not constitute real bread].
>
> (b. Ber. 38a)

> Mar b. R. Ashi stated, "Over honey of the date-palm we say, 'By whose word all things exist.'"
>
> (b. Ber. 38a)

> R. Ashi said, "When we were at R. Kahana's, he told us that over a broth of beets in which not much flour is stirred the blessing is 'Who creates the fruit of the ground,' but for a broth of turnip in which much flour is stirred, the blessing is, 'Who creates all kinds of foods.' Later

[he retracted and] said that the blessing for both is, 'Who creates the fruit of the ground,' since the flour is put in only to make the mixture coalesce."

(b. Ber. 39a)

[If whole loaves and pieces of bread are set together, some say one may bless the pieces, and this serves for the whole loaves; others, that one should bless the whole loaf.] Mar b. Rabina used to put the broken piece under the whole loaf and then break the bread [and bless it, thus satisfying the opinions of both authorities.] R. Ashi said, "I saw R. Kahana take two and break one [loaf on the Sabbath]." Rabina said to R. Ashi, "Does this not look greedy"? He replied, "He does not do so ordinarily, but only today [on the Sabbath]..."

(b. Ber. 39b)

R. Papa was once at the house of R. Huna b. R. Nathan. After they had eaten the meal, edibles were set before them, and R. Papa took some and began eating. It was said to him, "Does not the master hold that after the meal is finished one may not eat [further]?" He replied, "*Removed* is the proper term. [That is, so long as grace has not been said, one may eat until the table has been cleared.]"

(b. Ber. 42a)

R. Mesharsheya said, "Over garden narcissus, the blessing is, 'Who creates fragrant woods.' Over wild narcissus—'Who creates fragrant herbs.'" Mar Zuṭra said, "One who smells a citron or quince should say, 'Blessed is he who has given a sweet smell to fruits.'"...

R. Papa was once visiting R. Huna b. R. 'Iqa. Oil and myrtle were brought before him, and he took the myrtle, blessed it first, and then blessed the oil. R. Huna said to him, "Does not your honor hold that the law follows..."

(b. Ber. 43b)

R. Papa said, "Water also [requires a blessing after it is drunk.]"

(b. Ber. 44b)

We note, first of all, that many of the teachings about liturgies in connection with foods were handed on at meals, as is quite natural. Yet ordinary folk, not regularly eating their meals with sages, would have had little opportunity to master such laws. The complicated rules about uncommon foods or foods not obviously covered by earlier rulings likewise could have meant little to the common people. It is moreover striking that the rules were taught in connection with actual deeds of major authorities. These paradigmatic stories never included reference to the presence of persons other than rabbis and their disciples. We therefore find little reason to suppose outsiders were present. We have no evidence whatever to suggest that rabbis undertook instruction of ordinary folk about the rules of blessing food.

The same situation pertains to grace after meals, which now as before remained a rite unique to the sages and their circle. Some of the stories pertain to special situations, such as grace at the home of a mourner or at a wedding banquet, as follows:

> R. Assi came to the house of R. Ashi on the occasion of the wedding-feast of Mar his son, and said six benedictions ... R. Ashi came to the house of R. Kahana [on the occasion of a wedding banquet]. The first day he said all the [wedding] benedictions. Afterward, if there were new guests, he repeated them, but if not, he [said only some of them...]
>
> (b. Ket. 8a)

> Mar Zuṭra visited R. Ashi when R. Ashi had suffered a bereavement [lit.: something happened to him]. In the grace after the meal he said a blessing, "Who is good and does good. God of truth, true judge, who judges in righteousness and takes away in justice, who rules over his world to do as he pleases in it, for all his ways are justice. All is his, and we are his people and his servants. For all [things] we are obliged to thank and bless him. He who fences in the breaches of Israel will close up this breach in Israel for life."
>
> (b. Ber. 46b)

The behaviour of R. Ashi thus was cited as evidence of how one is supposed to say the grace at the wedding feast. Rabbinical behavior in this circumstance as in others was regarded as authoritative revelation of the correct law. The blessing of Mar Zuṭra may have been his own composition of scriptural and rabbinical sayings. From that time onward, though, it would have become the conventional form for his disciples, and still later, for disciples of those masters who accepted their liturgy. Further sayings and stories about the grace after meals include the following:

> R. Papa said, "The law is that food which forms an integral part of the meal, when taken in the course of the meal, requires no blessing either before or afterward. Food not integrally part of the meal taken in the course of the meal requires a blessing before but not after [being covered by the grace]. Food taken after the meal requires a blessing both before and after [thus constituting a separate meal]."
>
> (b. Ber. 41b)

> As to breaking off in the middle of grace to join others who have finished eating and wish now to form a quorum of three], did not R. Papa break off for Abba Mar his son, he and another with him?...
>
> (b. Ber. 45b)

> Judah b. Maremar, Mar b. R. Ashi, and R. Aḥa from Difti took a meal together. None was superior to the other [in age or in learning], so as to have the privilege of saying grace. [They thereupon discussed

the Mishnaic law which should guide them, and concluded it is better for the blessing to be said separately.] They said [the grace] individually. When they came before Maremar, he said to them, "You have performed the obligation of grace, but not of saying grace in a quorum [*zimmun*]..."

(b. Ber. 45b)

If one came and found three persons saying grace, what does he say after them? R. Zevid said, "Blessed and to be blessed..." R. Papa said, "He answers, 'Amen.'"

(b. Ber. 45b)

Amemar, Mar Zuṭra, and R. Ashi were sitting at a meal. R. Aḥa b. Rava was waiting on them. Amemar recited a separate blessing for each cup [of wine], Mar Zuṭra recited a blessing over the first and last cup [after grace], while R. Ashi recited over the first cup but no more. Said R. Aḥa b. Rava to them, "According to whose opinion are we to act..."

(b. Pes. 103b)

To summarize: Grace, like blessings for food, was carefully studied in schools. The deeds of the masters were closely observed. No occasion more laden with ritual than eating existed in the lives of the sages. The rite of blessing food and saying grace was particularly central to the ritual of "being a rabbi."

The mode and manner of dressing oneself certainly entered into the ritual of "being a rabbi." Covering one's head was regarded as a sign of piety, therefore required of the sage above all:

R. Huna b. R. Joshua would not walk four cubits bareheaded. He said, "The *Shekhinah* is above my head."

(b. Qid. 31a)

Similarly, R. Ashi pointed out that a *gavra rabbah*, one expert at legal dialectic, required a *sudarium*, or kerchief, for his head.[1] How rabbis donned various articles of clothing on the Sabbath similarly would be observed and carefully recorded.[2]

Since some of the sages were regarded as "living Torahs," their deeds as much as their words constituted a source of law. Thus the recollections not merely of schoolmen, but also of members of the family of a particularly reliable sage would serve as satisfactory precedent:

---

[1] b. Qid. 8a. On *gavra rabbah*, see Vol. III, p. 134. As to peculiar garments for rabbis, see S. Krauss, "Ṭalitam shel Talmidei Ḥakhamim," *Bloch Jubilee Volume* (Budapest, 1905), pp. 83-97. There Krauss argues that such a characteristic cloak or garment was not worn by rabbis.

[2] b. Shab. 61a, how Mar b. Rabina put on shoes on the Sabbath.

> The wife of R. Ashi sifted flour on the topside of a table [on a festival]. R. Ashi said, "This [wife] of ours is the daughter of Rami b. Ḥama, and Rami b. Ḥama was a master of deeds, so if she did not see [this] in the house of parents she would not have done [it]."
>
> (b. Beẓ. 29b)

Reports by a master of what he himself had done were equally satisfactory evidence.[1] Further, deeds were constantly measured against the teaching of earlier masters:

> [Rav Judah had said that if a person saying the Prayer wished to spit, he should do so into his robe or scarf]. Rabina once was standing [in Prayer] behind R. Ashi and wanted to spit. He spat behind himself. R. Ashi said to him, "Do you not accept the teaching of Rav Judah that one should cover it with his scarf?" Rabina replied, "I am squeamish."
>
> (b. Ber. 24b)

In such a circumstance, it was not likely that disciples would ignore the precedents of early masters. Just as in the courts these precedents were binding, so in the schools, homes, synagogues, and elsewhere the words of the ancients echoed with authority in the minds of the disciples. In time a profoundly conservative impact would make itself felt on the personality of the disciple. He would first consciously, then unconsciously, shape himself into the mold of the former generations, and later on would produce the same impact upon his own disciples.

That impact affected not only custom of dress, speech, or eating, but also the formation of the disciple's personality. The schools debated about the traits most desirable in a rabbi. The issues were characteristically academic: Should a master be harsh or merciful? Should a disciple show modesty or pride? The following exemplifies the range of discussion in the later period:

> R. Ashi said, "A disciple of the sages who is not as hard as iron is not disciple of the sages [quoting Jer. 23:29]." Rabina said, "Even so, a man should train himself to be gentle [quoting Qoh. 11:10]."
>
> (b. Ta'anit 4a)

On the other hand, R. Yosi b. Abin explained to R. Ashi that he had abandoned his studies with R. Yosi of Derokert because the latter had showed no mercy to his children. He had cursed his son and daughter, the former for misusing the magical powers in prayer which he had

[1] b. Beẓ. 25b, R. Naḥman b. Isaac said he had carried Mar Samuel from the sun to the shade.

mastered, the latter for being so beautiful as to become a source of distraction for men.[1] R. Ashi taught that arrogance is a blemish.[2] On the other hand, commenting on the saying that a disciple of the sages should posses an eighth [of pride], R. Huna b. R. Joshua said:

> "It crowns him like the awn of the grain."

To this, R. Ashi countered:

> "Every man with pride in him will eventually be degraded..."
>
> (b. Soṭ. 5a)

Naturally rabbis supposed there was a direct causal relationship between personal virtue and worldly events. R. Papa was unable to make rain, for instance, until he showed himself truly humble. Then rain fell in buckets.[3] The belief in an intrinsic relationship between events in the natural world and the moral virtues of sages was also illustrated by R. Papa's belief that he had met an accident because he had failed to help a begger.[4] Reenforced by the expectation that heaven would reward virtuous character as well as right conduct, the schools' effort to reshape the disciple's personality would have achieved considerable success. Yet "being a rabbi" did not consist merely of exhibiting the traits of pride or humility, harshness or gentility, any more than it amounted to sporting peculiar clothing and performing natural functions in a singularly "rabbinical" fashion.

The two central *rituals* of "being a rabbi" were study and discipleship. Study as a merely *natural* action would entail learning of traditions and executing them—in this context, in school or in court. Study became a ritual action when it was endowed with values extrinsic to its ordinary, intellectual character, such as when set into the highly mythic context I have already described. When a disciple memorized his master's traditions and actions, carrying out the former where appropriate and imitating the latter when possible, he participated in that myth, learning what God had taught for just such memorization. His study was thereby endowed with the sanctity which ordinarily pertained to prayer or other cultic matters. Study lost its primary referent in intellectual activity, let alone attainment. The *act* of study itself became holy, so that its original purpose, which was mastery of

---

[1] b. Ta'anit 24a.
[2] b. Meg. 29a.
[3] b. Ta'anit 24b.
[4] b. B.B. 10a.

particular bodies of information, ceased to matter to the exclusion of all other considerations. What now mattered was piety, but this piety was expressed through the rites of studying. Repeating the words of the oral revelation, even without comprehending them, produced reward, just as imitating the master resulted in merit, even if the disciple was not really able to explain the reasons for his actions. The separation of the value or sanctity of the act of study from the this-worldly, cognitive result of learning therefore transformed studying from a natural to a ritual action. That separation was accomplished in part by myth, as I said, and in part by the powerful impact of the academic environment itself.

A striking illustration of the distinction between mere learning and learning as part of ritual life derives from Mar Zuṭra's comment on Is. 14 : 5, *The Lord has broken the staff of the wicked, the scepter of rulers:*

> Mar Zuṭra said, "These are disciples of the sages who teach public laws to uncultivated judges."
>
> (b. Shab. 139a)

The fact that the "uncultivated judge" would know the law did not matter, for he still was what he had been, uncultivated or "ignorant." Thus mere knowledge of the laws did not transform an ordinary person, however powerful, into a sage. This passage is extremely important for political history. It suggests that the exilarch was now getting rabbinical students to teach civil law to non-rabbis in lay law-schools and was using these trainees as judges in its courts to compete with the rabbis. No wonder R. Sherira and *SOZ* have utterly divergent lists. Perhaps the "Lord broke them" refers to some sort of misfortune —plague, persecution—affecting the teachers in these schools.

That learning carried with it a far more than naturalistic valence is further seen in the saying of Amemar:

> "A sage is better than [or, superior to] a prophet, as Scripture says, *And a prophet has a heart of wisdom.* (Ps. 90:12)."
>
> (b. B.B. 12a)

What had characterized the prophet was, Amemar said, sagacity. Since the prophet was supposed to reveal the divine will, it was not inconsequential that his revelation depended not upon gifts of the spirit but upon learning—but learning of a peculiar sort.

One way in which that peculiarity found form was in the schools' stress on "learning and deed." The uncultivated judge could be relied upon to learn and apply part of the law, to be sure, but no one expected that he would also embody all of it. On the other hand, the following saying shows the rabbis' stress on shaping one's way of life in all respects through "Torah":

> R. Papa said, "Scripture said, *That you may learn them and observe to do them* (Deut. 5:1), [meaning] Whoever participates in the [merit for] doing participates in the [merit for] studying, and whoever does not, does not."
>
> (b. Yev. 109b)

R. Papa's saying reflects an earlier viewpoint, that the purpose of "Torah" lay in the creation of a new personality, a new man, and not merely in the acquisition of learning, however sacred its origin. Here we must underline the rabbis' perspective. They studied "Torah" because they believed it was revealed at Sinai, therefore holy. But they expected that their studies would produce a profound transformation of themselves and their little community. Further sayings on studying include the following:

> R. Zevid said, "He [who studies Scripture and Mishnah] is worthy of inheriting two worlds, this one and the one to come..."
>
> (b. Ḥul. 44b)

> R. Mesharsheya said to his sons, "When you wish to come before your teacher to learn, first review your Mishnah and then go to your teacher. When you are sitting before your teacher, look at the mouth of your teacher, as it is written, *But thine eyes shall see they teacher* (Is. 30:20); and when you study any teaching, do so by the side of water, for as the water is drawn out [= MŠKY], so your learning may be prolonged. Be on the dustheaps of Mata Meḥasia rather than in the palaces [ʾPDNY] of Pumbedita. Eat a stinking fish rather than *kutḥa* which breaks rocks."
>
> (b. Ker. 6a)[1]

The rabbis generally shared R. Zevid's certainty of great rewards now and in eternity on account of their study of Torah.[2]

Our earlier remarks ought not to obscure the rabbis' high expectations of actual accomplishment in learning. While, as I said, they stressed the *act* of study without reference to its achievement if any, at the same time they possessed very old traditions on how best to pursue their task. This tradition included much practical advice on how to acquire and preserve learning. R. Mesharsheya's advice to his sons

[1] Trans. I. Porusch (London, 1948), p. 38.

[2] Below, pp. 174-178.

exemplifies this rich source of distilled experience. Part of that experience was perfectly reasonable. Reviewing before classes, concentrating on the teacher, staying near the great schools—these things would make sense in any circumstance. On the other hand the advice to study by a body of water "so that your learning may be prolonged" has little to do with the practical problems of memorizing and reasoning. It rather relates to the rabbis' view of a supernatural correspondence between their own study and those aspects of nature which the rabbis looked upon as symbolic of their activities—and they many times compared Torah to "living waters." Rabina advised that those who make their studies accessible to the public will retain their learning.[1] R. Ashi warned that one who is stubborn in a quarrel or unyielding in a dispute deserves to be smitten with leprosy.[2] While his saying was a general one, it would apply with special force to the argumentative life of the academies.

No role whatever was assigned to women. They did not study in the Babylonian schools. The life of "Torah" was effectively closed to them. On the other hand mothers would encourage their sons to study Torah. Mar b. Rabina's mother would prepare seven garments for seven days of the week to facilitate his learning.[3] Rabina explained how the merit of study of the Torah applied to womenfolk. Women acquire merit when they arrange for their sons' education in Scripture and Mishnah, and when they *wait* for their husbands to return from the schools.[4] Since that return was often postponed by months or even years, it was no small sacrifice. But the schools were entirely male institutions; no equivalent religious communities existed for women. The disciples lived not only an ascetic life, but, in the months at school, a celibate one as well. It was therefore a kind of temporary monastic community, especially for the students from distant places. From the wives also it demanded celibacy.

The central human relationship in the schools was between the disciple and master. Long ago it had been taught that the master took the place of the father. The father brought the son into this world, but the master would lead him into the world to come. Whatever honor was due the father was all the more so owing to the master. But the master did not merely replace the father. He also required the vener-

---

1 b. ʿEruv. 53a.
2 b. Sanh. 110a.
3 b. ʿEruv. 65a.
4 b. Soṭ. 21a.

ation and reverence owing to the Torah. The extreme forms of respect which evolved over the centuries constitute the unique and most striking rituals attached to "being a rabbi." If, as we have seen, study was an act of piety, then the master to some extent was its object. That is not to suggest that the master was regarded as in any sense divine. But the forms of respect reserved for the divinity or for the Torah were not too different, in appropriate circumstances, from those owing to the master. In any event the forms of respect for the master constituted part of the ritual of "being a rabbi," and I think the most important part.

It was the "service of the disciples of the sages" [*shimush talmidei ḥakhamim*] which ultimately separated the true sage from the merely learned man. It had earlier been taught that if one had studied Scripture and Mishnah but did not attend upon disciples of the sages, he was regarded as a Samaritan, a boor, an *ʿam haʾareẓ*. To these epithets, R. Aha b. Jacob added:

> "Behold, such a one is a Magus [MGWŠ]."
>
> (b. Soṭ. 22a)

The discussion continued with a popular saying that the Magus mumbles and does not know what he is saying, just as the Tanna recites and does not know what he is saying. I find it incredible that R. Aḥa could claim to see no difference between a learned Jew and a learned Mazdean except that the former attended and served the sages. Obviously he knew gross differences. That attendance—meaning not merely service but rather imitation, study of the master as much as of the Torah—constituted a vital part of "Torah" because the master exemplified the "whole Torah," including the oral part of it. Mastery of Scripture and Mishnah, written and oral Torah, without observation and imitation of the sage meant little. The whole Torah was not in books nor in words to be memorized, but only to be found in whole and complete form in the master. That is why the forms of respect for the master were so vital to the mythic life of the schools.

Ordinary folk could reasonably be expected to carry out most of the rites characteristic of the rabbinical estate. True, ordinary folk were supposed to honor all rabbis, but that honor was quite different from the constant humility displayed by disciple before his particular master. The real difference was not the depth of submission but the constant attendance and attention. On the rare occasions when a great rabbi appeared in public, the ordinary people could be just as humble as his private entourage, or more so. But the one thing they could not do was keep it up, wait on him constantly, and so learn all his little ways. They just did not have the time—or the interest. Of all human relationships open to rabbis, therefore, it was this one which was most thoroughly ritualized, the most utterly divorced from natural forms of human intercourse. The basis for the rite is best summarized thus: If the master is a living Torah, source of revelation of the oral tradition given at Sinai and embodied now in the master himself, then the disciple had best humbly imitate each and every gesture of that living Torah and so prepare himself as the nexus of the transmission of this same oral tradition to the coming generation.

Submission to the master produced several sorts of tensions. First, the master's knowledge, so much greater than the disciple's, must have intimidated the latter, and as this phenomenon reproduced itself one generation after the other, it led to exaggerating the attainments of the ancients and denigrating one's own:

> Rava said, "We are like a finger in wax as regards reasoning." R. Ashi said, "We are like a finger in the well as regards forgetting."
> (b. ʿEruv. 53a)

That is to say, "just as a finger cannot penetrate wax, so we cannot penetrate reasoning; just as a finger cannot bring up water from a well, so easily do we forget that we have learned." Both similes come at the end of a long line of sayings on the glories of the ancients and the limitations of the moderns. It was an attitude inculcated by the schools, inherent in the belief that perfection had been revealed at Sinai, only to be slowly but inevitably forgotten, stage by stage to suffer attrition through the ages. Master's and disciple's relationships must have been embittered, moreover, by the hardness fostered in the sage, who had to maintain his point with vigor in his quest for truth. Thus the master's arrogance, produced by pride in his very real achievements, would have troubled his relationships with children and disciples alike:

> Why is it not common for disciples of the sages to produce sons who are disciples of the sages?... Mar Zuṭra said, "Because they [high-handedly] overrule the community." R. Ashi said, "Because they call men *asses*."
> (b. Ned. 81a)

R. Ashi and Mar Zuṭra certainly condemned the qualities they cited to account for the sages' failure in raising their own sons in the tradition, but they also must have found it common for sages to behave arrogantly and to call people disrespectful names. A current example of ritualistic behavior between master and disciple is as follows:

> It has been taught [in Tannaitic tradition], "A man should not drink water and hand [the cup] to his disciple unless he first pours some out." It happened once that a man drank some water and without pouring any out gave [the cup] to his disciple. The disciple was squeamish and did not like to drink, and he died of thirst. There and then they laid down a rule that a man should not drink and give [the cup] to his disciple without pouring some out. R. Ashi said, "Consequently if a disciple pours out in front of his teacher, this shows no disrespect." Do not spit anything out in front of your teacher except pumpkin and leek, for they are like a wick of lead.
>
> (b. Tamid 27a)[1]

Many other forms of respect were long ago established, and the strata of sayings of late fourth- and fifth-century masters is not especially rich in new rites; we have no reason whatever to doubt that the ancient patterns varied much.

While the masters encouraged large numbers of disciples to attend the schools,[2] relations between disciple and master proved stormy. For example, R. Papa cursed students who acted disrespectfully:

> R. Huna b. Manoaḥ, R. Samuel b. Idi, and R. Ḥiyya of Vestania had studied with Rava. When he died, they came to R. Papa. Whenever he said to them a saying which did not seem reasonable to them, they would gesture [mockingly] at one another. R. Papa's heart grew faint [but in a dream, he was encouraged to believe they would die]. The next day when they parted from him, he said to them, "May the rabbis go *in* peace [a greeting paid to the deceased]."
>
> (b. Ta'anit 9a-b)

R. Papa similarly prayed for peace from the insolence of one of his students.[3] But usually the sage did not have to rely either on prayers or on divine intervention to keep the students in line. Social pressures in the school, a small and closely-knit society, must have been tremendous. Further, the master could excommunicate the disciple, thus cutting him off from normal intercourse within his community. Banning a disciple would invariably have proved effective so long as the disciple chose to remain within the rabbinical estate. Since he would have been indoctrinated in its values for a long time, he would

[1] Trans. Maurice Simon (London 1948), p. 9.

[2] See Rabina's saying in b. Meg. 10a, for example.

[3] b. Ta'anit 9b.

have been more susceptible than ordinary folk to the power of the ban.[1] We have the following sayings on the subject:

> When a disciple of Mar Zuṭra the pious would incur a ban, he [Mar Zuṭra] would first excommunicate himself and then the disciple. On reaching home, he raised the ban from himself and then from the disciple.
>
> (b. Ned. 7b)[2]

> R. Papa said, "May [such-and-so] befall me if I have ever put a disciple in excommunication."
>
> (b. M.Q. 17a)

Both sayings indicate that the ban was considered an extreme measure, not to be lightly invoked against the disciples.

This survey of late fourth and fifth century data on the singular rituals of "being a rabbi" by no means constitutes a complete or full account of rabbinical in-group rites. Many earlier sayings and stories, not germane to our historical period, would be required to fill out this portrait. I have said nothing, for example, about particular rabbinical modes of speech, though we know the rabbis had their "own" words for some objects, and little enough about rabbinical styles of dress, carrying out natural functions, etiquette at table, behavior with peers and superiors, and the like. What is important is that all of these matters were "Torah," required learning, and, properly done, exhibited sagacity. One recalls the story of Rav's student who hid under the master's bed to observe how Rav and his wife carried on their sex life. When the master discovered the disciple, the latter explained, "Rabbi, it is Torah and I need to learn." Whether or not this ingenious excuse for voyeurism persuaded Rav is unimportant. What is important is that within "Torah" were included numerous aspects of ordinary life which other Jews did not likely consider of religious consequence at all. Because of their belief that the school on earth corresponded to the school in heaven, the rabbis endowed with ritual value their particular ways of doing everyday tasks and of carrying out natural functions and relationships. For the same reason they held, as I have stressed, that following the rabbinical mode constituted both the demonstration of wisdom and the authentication of true sanctity. Yet this was only one such means of authentication, for the rabbis, like the society as a whole, believed in both worldly and supernatural recognition of their worth.

---

[1] See below, pp. 273ff.

[2] See also b. M.Q. 17a.

It would be a grave misjudgment to regard the master-disciple relationship as sterile and stifling, or to assess the inner life of the schools as did Gibbon the men of Byzantium, who

> held in their lifeless hands the riches of their fathers, without inheriting the spirit which had created and improved that sacred patrimony; they read, they praised, they compiled, but their languid souls seemed alike incapable of thought and action... Not a single idea has been added to the speculative systems of antiquity, and a succession of patient disciples became in their turn the dogmatic teachers of the next servile generation...[1]

The master taught the disciple, but did not seek to intimidate him. The disciple revered the master, sought to imitate his virtues, attain his holy way of living, transmit his heritage. But he was not expected to, and did not, surrender his own personality or give up his own critical judgment. If relations proved stormy, the reason was that the disciples preserved the freedom to judge and regarded reason and accurate traditions as holier than the opinion even of a beloved teacher. The master was a "living Torah," but not God. Servility was not confused with respect. Honor did not demand self-abnegation. On the contrary, the creative faculties of the disciples must have been carefully nurtured and enhanced, for the legacy of each generation greatly differs from that of the former ones. After several centuries of scholastic discipline, servile students and dogmatic teachers ought to have created nothing; as Gibbon said of the Byzantine schools:

> Not a single composition of history, philosophy, or literature has been saved from oblivion by the intrinsic beauties of style, or sentiment, or original fancy, or even of successful imitation.

The contrary was the case. What testifies to the vivid and original intellects of the rabbinical schools is the Babylonian Talmud itself, the product not of servility, on the one side, or dogmatism, on the other, but of keen minds, an exceptionally critical imagination, and an utterly independent spirit. We must, therefore, not lose sight of the deeply mythic-religious foundations for the ritual of "being a rabbi." If we ignore the vitality of the Torah-myth that permeated and vivified the schools, we shall not perceive the very source of their creative life and achievement. The schools gave pedantry a cool welcome, for mere learning was insufficient. The masters and disciples took the opinions

[1] Cited by Peter Gay, *The Enlightenment... The Rise of Modern Paganism* (N.Y., 1968), p. 213.

and knowledge of the early generations into their care, respectfully learning them, reverently handing them on. But these they digested and made their own. Their minds were filled with the learning of other, earlier men, but their wisdom was their own.

IV. The Glory of the Sage on Earth

The glory, or honor (KBWD), of the sage on earth presented a curious combination of practical with spiritual advantages. The rabbi felt himself, first of all, to be singularly fortunate because of his mastery of Torah. Among the many sayings in praise of the rabbinical status is the following of Rabina:

> What does Scripture say of the rabbis? Rabina said, "*They that love him shall be as the sun when he goes forth in his might* (Judges 5:31)."
>
> (b. B.B. 8b)

The joy of study, the sense of serving God as he had said he wanted to be served, the confident hope that in doing so, men would find salvation and the Messiah finally be brought nearer—these were the sage's earthly glories, the truest rewards of his situation. He moreover enjoyed the trust that his activity in study and observance produced blessing in this sorry life:

> Mar b. Rabina made a wedding banquet for his son. He saw that the rabbis were making merry too much. He brought a cup worth four hundred *zuz* and broke it before them, and they were saddened.
>
> R. Ashi made a wedding banquet for his son. He saw that the rabbis were making merry too much. He brought a cup of crystal and broke it before them and they were saddened.
>
> The rabbis said to R. Hamnuna Zuṭi [the younger] at the wedding banquet of Mar b. Rabina, "Let the master sing for us." He said [sang] to them, "Woe is us, that we die, woe is us, that we die!" They said to him, "And we—what shall we answer after you?" He said to them, "Oh Torah! Oh commandment!—they shield us!"
>
> (b. Ber. 30b-31a)

The faith that Torah and commandments shield from death was the rabbi's chief glory, producing not pride or self-righteousness, to be sure, but rather the confidence of enjoying divine grace. Every man was destined to die, but the rabbi might enjoy the illusion that Torah would protect him in the world to come.[1] And moreover, the rabbi had

[1] Calculations of rabbinical lifespans curiously seem to indicate a much longer than average life. The average life-expectancy was in the low 30s, while we have

the inner certainty that, come what may, he might go forth to the day's task "like the sun when he goes forth in his might."

The rabbi saw himself, moreover, as the new priest, who now did by study of the Torah what the former priests had done by sacrifices—made atonement for the world. This is not to say he did not pray for the rebuilding of the temple. But he meanwhile substituted for it. Thus Amemar, Mar Zuṭra, and R. Ashi discussed the bringing of a gift of fruit to themselves as rabbis according to the legal regulations for bringing heave-offering to the priesthood of old.[1]

The ordinary people assuredly paid due respect to the holy men of the community. Talmudic discussions (e.g. b. Qid. 33a) make it clear that the rabbis were normally greeted with particular respect. In the earlier generation Abaye and others had to avoid disturbing people, by making detours so as to prevent the necessity of formally rising and greeting of the sage. Rabina regarded it as impudent for a man not to cover his head before a sage:

> Rabina was seated before R. Jeremiah of Difti. A certain man passed before him and did not cover his head. He said, "How full of gall is this man!" He [R. Jeremiah] said to him [Rabina]: "Perhaps he comes from Mata Meḥasia, where rabbis are commonplace." [Rashi: "Rabbis are so numerous that the people's hearts are arrogant toward them, as if they come from them."]
>
> (b. Qid. 33a)

Naturally the needs of rabbis when addressing large public assemblies were carefully attended to. Amemar and Mar Zuṭra were carried on the shoulders of the people when they came to lecture on the Sabbath before Passover, on account of the sages' nervousness.[2]

The honor paid by sage to sage, however, like the homage of the

---

numerous examples of rabbis who lived considerably longer than that. Quite apart from the claim of one hundred twenty years for several earlier worthies (Moses, Yoḥanan ben Zakkai, 'Aqiva), for example, we may suppose that stories about rabbis' dying at forty or sixty may be taken seriously. But the commentaries understand the saying to pertain to the world to come. On the other hand, average lifespans are usually brought down by infant mortality, which in antiquity probably averaged about 50%. So relative length of life for adults must be evaluated by comparison with the relative lengths of life of those who got past the age of two—that is, of only half the population. Within this group one would expect to find the rabbis doing well because their studies necessitated, and also provided, a quiet, protected life, and only the relatively healthy and well-to-do—that is, the well-fed and well-clothed—had the time and ability to pursue them. So the favorable result is arrived at by selection from a favored group.

[1] b. B.M. 12a.

[2] b. Beẓ. 25b.

disciples for the masters, was of another order entirely. First of all, a rabbi could not renounce his honor, according to some authorities,[1] and this meant that sages believed heaven would exact the honor due a sage even if he did not care to do so for himself. Second, among themselves sages were quick to point out lapses in the required respect. When a rabbi did not break off praying to greet another though it was permissible not to do so, it was regarded as a sign of disrespect.[2] The sages would show great respect, to the contrary, by appropriate hospitality. This was frequently recorded, as in the following:

> R. Joshua b. R. Idi visited R. Ashi. A calf a third fully grown was prepared for him...
>
> (b. Shab. 11a)

> R. Papa and R. Huna b. R. Joshua visited the house of R. Idi's son [= R. Joshua], who prepared a calf a third fully grown for them...
>
> (b. Shab. 136a)

It was expected that sages would accompany their guests on their journey. The reward naturally was specified:

> Rabina accompanied Rava b. Isaac four cubits in a city [a minimal distance]. Danger threatened, but he was saved...
>
> (b. Soṭ. 46b)

Similarly, R. Mordecai accompanied R. Ashi for a considerable distance as a sign of respect.[3] Disciples were also expected to accompany their masters. It was central to discipleship to do so.

When travelling from place to place, leading authorities would pay their respects to local masters:

> R. Papa happened to come to Tav'akh. He said, "If there is a rabbinical disciple here, I shall go and greet him." A certain old lady said to him, "There is here a rabbinical disciple, and R. Samuel is his name, and he studies Mishnah. May it be God's will that you may be like him!" He [R. Papa] said, "Since she blesses me by him, I infer that he is a fearer of heaven." He went to him. He [R. Samuel] prepared[4] for him an ox and prepared[5] for him a conflict of Mishnaic teachings...
>
> (b. Nid. 33b)

---

[1] b. Qid. 32a-b. Compare R. Ashi, b. Qid. 32b and in b. Soṭ. 41b.
[2] b. Ber. 14a.
[3] b. Soṭ. 46b.
[4] Lit.: threw.
[5] Lit.: threw.

As it turned out, the ox was better baked than the legal conundrum. Whether or not provincial sages achieved much mastery of the traditions, it is striking that the head of the school did what he could to pay them respect. (It is also remarkable that the old lady could point to only one rabbinical disciple [= ẒWRB' MYRBNN], and not to a single disciple of the sages [TLMYD ḤKhM], in the whole town!)

When sages died, they would be given eulogies, which were not normally provided for lesser folk. The funeral orations for Rabina and R. Ashi are recorded as follows:

> When Rabina died, a certain professional eulogizer opened as follows:
> "Palms, sway your head
> For one who was righteous as a palm
> Let us raise up lament[1] like the oceans[2]
> For one who made nights[1] like days[2] [in study]..."
>
> R. Ashi said to Bar Qipoq, "On that day [on which I shall die], what will you say?" He replied,
>
> "If among the cedars a spark falls,
> What will become of the moss on the wall?
> If Leviathan is caught with a hook
> What will become of the little fish?
> If drought[3] befall a bubbling brook,
> What will become of the pond-water?"
>
> Bar Abin said to him, "God forbid that of hooks and flames we should speak with reference to the righteous!" "And what would you say?" He responded:
>
> "Weep for the mourners
> And not for the mourned,
> For he goes to his rest
> But we to [our] sorrow."
>
> R. Ashi's mind weakened [he was offended] against them, and their knees were turned backward [so that they were both crippled]. On that day [of R. Ashi's death], they did not come to eulogize him, and this [illustrates] the saying of R. Ashi, "Neither Bar Qipoq nor Bar Abin shall bare [his shoulder for me," as is done at the death of the head of a school].[4]
>
> (b. M.Q. 25b)

---

[1] LYLWT.

[2] YMYM.

[3] See trans. H. M. Lazarus (London, 1948), p. 160, n. 6.

[4] On HLYẒ, see also Lazarus, p. 161, n. 2 for an alternative explanation. The circulation of "saying of R. Ashi" seems to me significant, though I do not know what it means.

R. Naḥman b. Isaac moreover taught that after death, the disciples of the sages would feast with the splendor of the *Shekhinah* in the world to come.[1] R. Papa said that one might mourn a sage even away from the, mourning-place and even on the intermediate days of the festival week, Ḥanukkah, or Purim; and

> R. Kahana lamented for R. Zevid of Nehardea at Pum-Nahara...
>
> (b. M.Q. 27b)

Clearly, the glory of the sage in life as in death constituted one of the central motifs of rabbinic Judaism. Like the *ẓaddiq* of later Hasidism, he was the cedar, Leviathan, the running brook, the righteous man, setting the standard for lesser folk, at least so far as his disciples were concerned.

A different sort of earthly glory derived from the rabbis' control of the Jewish court and administrative structure of Babylonia.[2] They there faced the strong temptation to favor their own estate over outsiders, and not a few in former times had boasted that they had been unable or unwilling to overcome that temptation.[3] Some now held it was wrong to show favor to rabbis:

> Mar b. R. Ashi said, "I am unfit to judge the suit of a disciple of the sages, for he is as dear to me as myself, and a man cannot see [something] to his own disadvantage."
>
> (b. Shab. 119a)

Since the Jewish government was responsible for tax collections among the Jews, the rabbis' claim that they were exempted from the headtax[4] conflicted with their judicial-administrative duties. While it is doubtful that they were able to sustain that claim, they clearly were able to use their administrative powers to free themselves from other, local obligations they found abhorrent. Thus as responsible local administrators, they had to provide for the defensive walls of the towns. Rav Judah had held that the rabbis, who do not require protection of earthly walls, are not required to contribute to the building of the

---

[1] b. B.B. 10a.

[2] See below, pp. 259ff., for a discussion of the working of the Jewish government to the sages' own advantage.

[3] Vol. III, pp. 126-130, Vol. IV, p. 135. Note, for instance, the saying of Rava, "May I be rewarded, for when a disciple came to my court, I did not go to sleep before I had sought points in his favor," b. Shab. 119a, which precedes the saying of Mar. b. R. Ashi cited here.

[4] Vol. IV, pp. 85-91.

walls, though even orphans must do so.[1] R. Ashi illustrated the reason for this exemption:

> Rava b. Meḥasia in the name of R. Ḥama b. Guria in the name of Rav said, "Any city whose roofs are higher than [those of the] synagogue will in the end be destroyed ..." Rav Ashi said, "I made it so that Mata Meḥasia would not be destroyed." And lo, it was destroyed? Yes, but not [on account of] that particular sin.
>
> (b. Shab. 11a)

Rabbis knew what accounted for misfortune, what must be done to avert evil. Their knowledge of Torah thus yielded substantial practical consequence. By teaching the right way and leading the communities from error, they could prevent disaster. If they therefore enjoyed some little benefit as a result of their knowledge, it was no more than eventually accrued to one and all.

In any event, I do not think the rabbis' economic advantage was ever an articulated motive in rabbinical legislation or administration, even though it may have been present, and certainly things worked out to their advantage. While it is clear that rabbis did enjoy numerous economic benefits on account of their magical and legal powers, it is equally certain that they never set forth self-consciously to pursue their own gain. R. Papa attributed his wealth to having married a priest's daughter[2] or to his beer-manufacturing activities.[3] While he inquired whether beer might be used in place of wine for ritual purposes, there is no evidence that he so ruled for his own benefit when he got the chance. In general, heads of the schools enjoyed great wealth. Other rabbis profited from the fantasies people attached to their powers. But in general, undistinguished fellows, such as the rabbinical disciple R. Papa met at Tav'akh, could not have profited much.

These evidences of earthly honor contain little that is supernatural, but the basis for much, perhaps most, of the worldly glory of the rabbi lay in the belief in his heavenly power. As I have stressed, the rabbinical academy was far more than a mere law school; it constituted in some measure an equivalent to the monastery, and in still greater measure embodied the holy community of which, rabbis supposed, prophets had prophesied. The rabbi was far more than a politician or judge. In the sage's view, his power derived *not* from worldly sources,

---

[1] b. B.B. 8a.
[2] b. Pes. 49a.
[3] b. Pes. 113a.

such as exilarchic support or Iranian approval,[1] but from heavenly ones. It follows that the rabbis' legal knowledge, while vital, would have counted for nothing without the conviction that knowledge of Torah, including law, produced supernatural as well as political power.

v. The Power of the Sage in Heaven: Introduction

The supernatural environment in which the rabbis lived produced the widespread expectation that some men would enjoy divine favor and even exercise superhuman powers. People generally believed in a supernatural God, who had not only made the world and directed the destinies of men, but who also directly or through angels, demons, and other forces and powers affected the lives of individual men. But that God could be served through appropriate cultic and, in the case of Judaism, Christianity, and Mazdaism, moral actions. For Jews God was conceived essentially according to the model of man,[2] though much greater in dimension to be sure, and he responded pretty much as did men to those who pleased or displeased him. One way of achieving divine favor was through appropriate humility before him, demonstrated through constant, humble obedience, in the Jewish instance to his commandments. Another was to beseech divine blessing in prayer and to hasten to acknowledge divine grace through the same medium.

Those men who were believed, or at least believed themselves, to be especially adept in divine service would thus be assumed to have acquired unusual merits and therefore to enjoy exceptional divine favor. The puissance of some such men could be relied upon in times of crisis or in situations of great need. They were supposed to enjoy powers most men did not have, first of all exercised through prayer. But, as I

[1] See below, pp. 244ff.

[2] The profound anthropomorphisms of both the rabbis and ordinary Jews generally have embarassed philosophical theologians of medieval and modern Judaism. Stories representing God in the form of a man—to take one of many instances at random, the opening passage of b. A.Z. 2a-b, where God takes a scroll of the law to his bosom, or b. Pes. 94a-b, an example of Shiʿur Qomah speculation, in which the dimensions of God are described—are mostly explained away. Yet, as Gershom Scholem has emphasized on the basis of mystical materials, we err by dismissing as mere conceits what the rabbis took very seriously indeed and preserved in their traditions. Obviously, what we refer to as "seeing God as a cosmic man" would have been corrected by the sages, who would have cited the Scriptures in Genesis, Ezekiel, and elsewhere to describe man as in the image of God. But for the purposes of the history of religions, it hardly matters.

have already pointed out,[1] it was possible for a few such men to exercise, quite independently of the will of the divinity, some of the powers of the divinity and of the cultic sancta, in the Jewish case inherent in Torah. For the schools and for the communities accessible to rabbinical influence, the rabbi was such a man. The rabbi was the expert on theology, on the nature of the supernatural world, the names of God. He was the authority on the time and form of prayer. His prayers were more effective than those of others because of his sanctity and merits, derived from his knowledge of Torah and peculiar observances. His prayers both in general and for particular purposes were believed effective. He could bless and curse. Angels visited him. Demons sometimes served him, either willingly or coerced by the power of his Torah. He was an authority on the meaning of dreams and omens, could avert witchcraft and prepare amulets.

We shall now survey sayings and stories pertinent to the rabbi's supernatural situation. We begin with tales illustrating the general expectations of the miraculous, and then examine stories showing rabbi's magical powers, his ability to exercise the black arts of cursing, laying on the evil eye, and commanding the demons. We shall then consider the rabbi's interpretations of heavenly messages. We next turn to the scientific skills attributed to holy men in general, mastery of astrology and of medicine, to see to what degree the rabbi was supposed to have attained knowledge generally believed to be part of the exact sciences of antiquity. We finally review the schools' theological, liturgical, and exegetical traditions, attributed to late fourth and fifth century masters.

The rabbis were not the only men in Jewry who were supposed to be skilled in supernatural arts or believed to possess divine favor. As we shall see,[2] Jews used magical bowls as a domestic prophylactic. Some of those bowls were prepared by Jews who were not representatives of rabbinical schools known to us, probably not rabbis at all. Yet even here, certain important rabbinical figures were cited as especially potent in driving away Lilith, Ghul, and other demons. Moreover, we may safely presume that Jews unrelated to the rabbinical schools practiced magic of various kinds, as was certainly the case in the Roman empire of the day.[3] Jewish magic was highly reputed; in Antioch for

---

[1] Vol. IV, pp. 353-362.

[2] Below, pp. 217ff.

[3] See most recently Stanley Kazan, "Isaac of Antioch's Homily against the Jews," *Oriens Christianus* 49, 1965, p. 59, and esp. n. 34.

example, a cult of the Maccabean martyrs, believed responsible for miraculous cures, was venerated, and eventually taken over by the Christian church, which was unable to extirpate it. Of greater consequence to our study is the Jew, thoroughly at home in the synagogue, who composed, in the *Book of Mysteries* (*Sefer HaRazim*),[1] a compendium of prayers and sacrifices to be offered to pagan and Jewish deities in magical ceremonies, including an invocation to Helios in transliterated Greek, all this in excellent Mishnaic Hebrew.

Such a person, who certainly worshipped Yahweh as the supreme God presiding over the seventh, or highest, heaven, must stand midway on a continuum between the extremes, the Jew who paid no attention to the Scriptures or Judaism or Yahweh, but simply practiced pagan magic without scruple, on the one hand, and the rabbi, on the other. The one who took over pagan magic but made it part of a picture of the cosmos in which Yahweh was supreme above the pagan deities, such as the author of the *Book of Mysteries*, stood in the middle. By contrast, the rabbi supposedly does not practice "magic" at all, but his merits are so effective that he can call down divine blessings or curses or acts of power in his prayers. Thus the opposite of the Jewish magician represented as no different from a pagan magician in the magical papyri and bowls was the rabbi who through study of Torah directly mastered its creative and miraculous powers. Yet the Jewish practitioners of bowl-magic could not have wholly disregarded rabbinical magic, for they explicitly included references to a leading rabbi. It would be unwise, therefore, to postulate that the various sorts of Jewish magicians and clients had little or no contact with one another. What is clear, on the other hand, is that the rabbis wanted nothing to do with other kinds of magicians and disapproved of any acts of theurgy not done by rabbis.

Within rabbinical magic and supernaturalism we must distinguish between contingent rewards for merit and reliably effective magic. Examples of both occur in our sources. Rainmaking, as we shall see, appears as a rabbinical function, but it relied upon the generalized expectation that learning produces merit, which further produces a claim on the deity for performance of the service requested. Mastery of Torah-power was different from miracles produced by divine grace

---

1 Ed. M. Margolioth (Jerusalem, 1967). Professor Baruch A. Levine's appendix demonstrates philological relationships between the language of the magical bowls and that of the *Sefer HaRazim*. This implies a common corpus of Jewish magical expressions and praxis.

elicited through right action. That difference, quite obviously, derives not from the actual events—we can be sure of that—but from the viewpoint and expectations of those who fantasized about those events. If the rabbi's own mastery of Torah led him to believe he possessed power he could exert independent of heaven, for example in his ability to order demons to do his will, then he could rely not upon heavenly reward for merits, but upon the magical power inherent in Torah and available to a master of Torah. On the other hand if he believed that when he prayed for rain, the prayer would be granted because of his merits, the granting of the prayer may be thought a miracle, but no magic was involved. This theoretical distinction willl help to clarify the data we are about to consider (below, sections vi-ix).

Among the central supernatural beliefs of the schools was that their affairs were directly supervised from heaven. It was said, for example, that when Rava died, R. Ashi was born.[1] Likewise Huna b. Nathan could not become exilarch while R. Ashi was still alive, for one "sovereignty" cannot begin before another one has concluded. This view was explicitly attributed to the "angel of death." While the chronology of Rava and R. Ashi is highly dubious,[2] the conviction is significant: Heaven arranged things so that great leadership would neither cease from the schools nor conflict in time. Of greater interest is the following story, which can easily be duplicated many times:

> [Abaye had ridiculed the view that one may cut off palm-branches during the festival week.] R. Ashi had a forest in Shelania'. He went to cut it down during the festival week. R. Shila' of Shelania' said to R. Ashi, "What is your opinion?... [Do you rely on an opinion contrary to Abaye? But Abaye ridiculed that opinion]" ... He said to him, "I have not heard it." [That is to say, it is not reasonable to me.] The hatchet then slipped [from the heft] as if to cut off his leg. He left off his task and returned [after the festival week].
>
> (b. M.Q. 12b)

While stories were told of how earlier sages had rejected the testimony of the natural world,[3] the later schools had no such compunction. They fully expected that the forces of nature would conspire to reveal, then to enforce, the correct view of the law. They felt certain, as I said, of a close correspondence between the fate of man and his moral character,

[1] b. Qid. 72b.

[2] Rava died in 352; according to the same chronology, R. Ashi became head of the school of Mata Meḥasia in 367, holding office for sixty years. I do not believe anyone could ever have headed a school at the age of fifteen or sixteen years.

[3] The most famous concerns R. Eliezer b. Hyrcanus, see b. B.M. 59b-60a.

also between the doings of nature and the deeds of men. R. Naḥman b. Isaac, of the preceding generation, had said for instance that one who rejoices on the Sabbath will be saved from the subjugation of exile, citing Deut. 33 : 29,[1] and that if a man gives his dues to the priest, he will get rich, citing Numbers 5 : 10.[2] Mar Zuṭra or R. Ashi held that saying the *Shema'* would similarly protect in bed the person who said it.[3] Hence saying the *Shema'* acted as a kind of prophylactic incantation, against demons or, presumably liliths, just as in some of the bowls, *mezuzot*, and elsewhere. At the same time, few expected so exact a correspondence between deeds and destiny. Mar Zuṭra explicitly stated that heaven does not behave like a storekeeper, adding up merits and balancing them against sins.[4]

VI. Miracles. Rain Making

The distinction between what was miraculous and what was merely part of the natural order of things remains a highly subjective matter. What we might care to regard as "miraculous", meaning unnatural, would not necessarily have seemed so then. For example, when R. Ashi promised he would insure that Mata Meḥasia would never be destroyed, he was not pledging to work magic or make a miracle. He simply held that if a city's roofs were higher than the synagogue's, in the end it would be destroyed. He therefore made certain that the synagogue of Mata Meḥasia was taller than other buildings.[5] Had the city endured for an impressive period, it might have seemed miraculous to those prone to make such judgments, but to R. Ashi it would have appeared perfectly normal and natural.

On the other hand, the following story tells us what was certainly regarded at that time as miraculous:

> And Mar b. Rabina was going through the valley of 'Aravot and thirsted for water. A miracle [NYS'] was done for him. A well of water was created for him, and he drank [from it].
>
> (b. Ber. 54a)

> Another time he was walking through the Manor of Maḥoza and a wild camel fell on him, but the wall of a house fell, and he went [and escaped] into it. Whenever he would come to 'Aravot he would say the

---

1 b. Shab. 118b.
2 b. Ber. 63a.
3 b. Ber. 5a, as an exegesis of Ps. 149 : 6.
4 b. Qid. 40a.
5 b. Shab. 11a. See above, p. 173.

> blessing, "Blessed is he who did for me a miracle in ʿAravot and with the camel." When he passed the Manor of Maḥoza he would say the blessing, "Blessed is he who did for me a miracle with the camel and in ʿAravot."[1]
>
> (b. Ber. 54a)

Miracles such as these were not done by any gesture or word of the rabbi, but by accident, that is, attributed to divine grace. The sage could not conjure the well of water, nor by a flick of the hand bring down the building, much as he might have wanted to. A miracle therefore had to happen quite independently of the actions of the person for whom it was done. At the same time it was counted as a sign of heavenly favor. The wise man would make certain of showing appropriate gratitude.

One did not have to be a sage to be granted miracles. Even rabbis believed ordinary people received them. On the other hand the sages thought that some of their own number could make rain. Rain came on account of their prayers, merits, or both. Rain-making would have to be included in the category of miracles, but not magic, for from the rabbi's viewpoint nothing he did independently could bring on the rain. He could only beseech heaven's favor to bestow it. The rabbis however expressed considerable confidence in their power to bring rain and even to stop it when they wanted. As to the latter:

> [Regarding rain on the eve of the Sabbath, which was inconvenient and regarded as a curse] Amemar said, "If people did not need [rain, even on that day] we should seek mercy and cancel it [have it cease]."
>
> (b. Taʿanit 8b)

> R. Papa decreed a fast [for rain], but no rain came. His heart grew faint. He sipped a plate of grits and besought mercy, but rain still did not come. R. Naḥman b. ʾUshpazati [or, ʾUshparati] said to him, "If the master will sip another plate of grits, rain will come." He was humiliated. Rain [then] came.
>
> (b. Taʿanit 24b)

> ...Did not R. Papa once when coming to the synagogue at Avi-Gobar ordain a fast, and rain fell before noon...
>
> (b. Taʿanit 26a)

We see that the rabbi regarded his prayers as reliably effective in making rain, but sometimes no more so than the fast of the community as a whole. Moreover, the moral condition of the rabbi entered into the

[1] On saying a prayer of thanksgiving before a rabbi for a miracle, see Mar Zuṭra and R. Ashi, b. Ber. 54b.

matter. If he was not sufficiently humble, hence desperate, it was hopeless. One recalls that the disciples of Rava, Rabbah, and Abaye preserved three stories of how the several masters had recognized and commented upon the disparity of the learning and miraculous power between their generation and the former one. Their generation was more learned but less able to bring rain, they said. Abaye had explained that the ancients gave their lives for the sanctification of God's name, while "we do not do so." Rabbah said that this generation is not good enough to warrant miracles. Rava added that the "Holy One blessed be he requires the heart," and the ancients were more sincere at prayer than were the moderns.[1] In any event, the rabbis were believed to exert greater influence in the heavenly court than did others. They regarded it as part of their duty as community officials to avert trouble and to prolong prosperity:

> R. Ashi said, "I saw R. Kahana, when there was trouble in the world, throw off his cloak, clasp his hands, and pray, saying, 'Like a slave before his master [do I pray].' When there was peace, he would take up his cloak and cover himself, fold himself [in the cloak] and pray, *Prepare to meet your God, O Israel* (Amos 4:12)."
>
> (b. Shab. 10a)

We do not know the result. Evidently the rabbis found it satisfactory; at very least, empirical evidence did not destroy their credibility for either themselves or the community.[2]

VII. MAGIC

Integral to the supernatural environment were both belief in magic and knowledge of the distinction between magic and "true religion." Religion had nothing whatever to do with magic; *magician* was a term of abuse, denoting not quack but subversive. Deeds and prayer approved by society and part of the established cult or religion were in no way seen as magic or incantation. Mastery of enchantment or demons was never regarded as magical if the rabbis did it, but disreputable if others did it. For the rabbis, the difference between religion and magic was simple. *They* did not practice magic, but "Torah" empowered them to do supernatural deeds—which seem to an observer to be exactly the things magicians did. The difference between magic and religion thus

[1] Vol. IV, pp. 357-8, from b. Sanh. 106b, b. Ber. 20a. and b. Ta'anit 24a-b.

[2] Note also the perfectly naturalistic remarks of R. Zevid about meteorological signs, b. B.B. 147a.

drawn in late antiquity is wholly conventional.[1] What is important is that such a belief in the difference actually functioned.

The general background of belief in magic naturally produced a further expectation that the instrumentalities of magic, such as amulets and charms, reliably worked. R. Papa moreover held that plagues were due to witchcraft.[2] It also is clear that witchcraft was believed in, not only by ordinary folk, but also by the sages themselves.

> If someone gives a piece of bread to a child, he must inform the mother. What should he do? He smears it with oil or puts rouge on it. But now that we are afraid of witchcraft, what is to be done? R. Papa said, "He smears the child with some of the substance [he has put on the bread. Butter or jam will not suggest witchcraft.]"
>
> (b. Beẓ. 16a = b. Shab. 10b)

No one seriously doubted that witches existed and practiced witchcraft against children. Amulets had long ago been accepted as bearing medical or other merit. R. Papa explained how one tested the quality of amulets:

> R. Papa said, "It is clear to me that if three amulets [work] for three people three times, the man [who made them] is approved and the amulet is approved. If three amulets [work] for three people once, the man [who made them] is approved but not the amulet. If one amulet [works] for three men, the amulet is approved but not the man [who made it]." [But] R. Papa asked, "If three amulets [work for] one man—what would be the consequence? The amulet certainly is not approved, but is the man [who made them] approved or not? Do we say, 'Lo, he healed [the man who used the amulet]'? Or perhaps [we conclude] that the star [MZL'] of that man is [responsible], for it receives writings."[3] The question stands.
>
> (b. Shab. 61b)
>
> "I saw Qarna's father blow his nose violently, and streamers of silk issued from his nostrils."
>
> (b. Shab. 67b)

R. Papa commented on what a magician can and cannot produce. R. Eleazar had earlier said that a magician cannot make a creature smaller than a barley-corn. R. Papa added that a magician cannot make some-

---

[1] See vol. IV pp. 360-62.

[2] b. Hor. 10a.

[3] "Or perhaps, it is this man's fate to be susceptible to writings", so H. Freedman, trans., *Shabbath* (London, 1948), p. 287. But the word is *star*, not fate! On the practically universal belief in astrology, and the widespread assumption among rabbis that astrology applies to Israel as much as to the nations, see vol. IV, pp. 330-334.

thing even as large as a camel, for "the creatures larger than barley he can collect, and the others he cannot."[1]

The rabbis' normative theory of magic contained two theses. Some supposed that if magic worked, it was a sign of heavenly approval of the man's merits, and hence magic posed no danger to good theology. Others regarded magic as "diminishing the power of the heavenly agents."[2] Magic in the mind of the latter party corresponded to natural science in the modern world. If man could control or coerce nature on his own, he would not need to depend upon heaven.

We have already noted a substantial increase in the number of instances of rabbinical practice of magic in the first half of the fourth century.[3] The late fourth- and early fifth-century schools, by contrast, preserved only a few rabbinical accounts of magical deeds, including the following:

> R. Judah HYNDW'[4] related, "Once we were going in a ship and saw a precious stone surrounded by a snake. A diver went down to bring it up. The snake came and wanted to swallow up the ship. A raven came and bit off its head. The waters turned into blood. A second snake came and took [the head] and hung it [on the decapitated snake] and it lived. Once again it came and wanted to swallow up the ship. Again the bird came and cut off its head. He [or *it*—the diver? the snake? the bird?] took the jewel and threw it into the ship. We had some salted fowl with us. We put [rubbed] it on them. They took [the jewel] and flew away with it."
>
> (b. B.B. 74b)

On using an ant for healing a fever, Abaye had earlier taught that one takes the ant, throws it into a brass tube, and seals it with lead. Then he shakes it, lifts it up, and says, "Your burden on me, and mine on you." Concerning this teaching, R. Aḥa b. R. Huna said to R. Ashi:

---

[1] b. Sanh. 67b. I do not understand the language, "These he assembles/collects," from KNP. Rashi *ad loc.* explains that "it is easy to gather together large creatures and they are collected together to him, but a small creature is not gathered, for it has not got the strength [or power] to come from a distant place." H. Freedman, trans., *Sanhedrin* (London, 1948), p. 460, translates, "...But these [larger than a barley corn] he can [magically] collect [and so produce the illusion that he has magically created them]; the others he cannot." I do not see the basis for his bracketed addition at the end. There is no word about *illusion* here.

[2] b. Sanh. 67b, R. Ḥanina *vs.* R. Yoḥanan.

[3] Vol. IV, pp. 391-402.

[4] The Indian? He was a convert to Judaism, see b. Qid. 22b, Mar Zuṭra visited him when he was dying, and seized his slave, since he was a convert who had produced no Jewish heirs. See Hyman, *Sefer Toledot Tannaim ve Amoraim* (London, 1910) II, p. 575.

"But perhaps someone else had already found the ant and cast *his* illness on it? Rather let him say, 'My burden *and* your burden on you.' But if this is impossible,[1] let him take a new pitcher, go to the river and say to it, 'River, O river, take back the water you gave me, for the journey that chanced to me came in its day and departed in its day."

(b. Shab. 66b)[2]

Neither of the above accounts tells us much about the state of rabbinical magic. The story of R. Judah merely indicates a general readiness to accept as true fabulous stories about magical jewels. In preserving such fables, the rabbis showed only that they believed them, not that they could do much to effect magic. Moreover, the prayer or merit of the rabbi played no part whatever in the fables. The story of R. Judah could have been told by anyone. It reflects no particular rabbinical characteristics whatever. The continuation of, or comment on, Abaye's cure for fever is similarly of slight probative value. I imagine that all that was actually attributed to R. Aḥa was the correction of the formula to be recited to the ant in the tube. If so, all we have is some evidence that the earlier magical beliefs and practices persisted with little change, but also not much augmented. More consequential evidence of the state of rabbinical magic derives from stories about actual rabbinical power over the unseen world through unnatural means.

VIII. Curses, the Evil Eye, and Demons

It was, to begin with, dangerous to offend a rabbi. As we noted earlier,[3] heaven itself would avenge an insult to a sage. R. Papa moreover reported that when a man made derogatory remarks about Mar Samuel, a log rolled off the roof and broke his skull.[4] The rabbi himself could assure unfortunate results for actions or words that displeased him; he did not have to wait for heaven's judgment. For example when R. Aḥa b. Jacob succeeded in writing a perfect Torah-scroll on the exact measurements of calf-skin recommended in the law, "the rabbis set their eyes on him," and he died.[5] Whether the evil eye came on account of jealousy, as in this case, or for more substantial cause, what is important is that the rabbi was a powerful and potentially dangerous man.

[1] This may be a continuation of Abaye's saying, rather than of R. Aḥa's.
[2] Trans. H. Freedman, p. 318, with minor revisions.
[3] p. 170.
[4] b. Ber. 19a.
[5] b. B.B. 14a.

Even in the course of routine greetings, something might go amiss and produce tragedy, as in the following:

> R. Papa and R. Huna b. R. Joshua were going along the way. They met R. Ḥanina b. R. 'Iqa'. They said to him, "Now that we see you, we offer for you two blessings, 'Blessed is he that has shared of his wisdom with those that fear him' as well as 'Blessed is he who has kept us in life, sustained us, and brought us to this time.'" He replied to them, "I too—when I saw you, I counted it for myself [as seeing] sixty myriads of the house of Israel, so I offered for you three blessings, the two [you said] and in addition, 'Blessed is he who discerns mysteries.'" They answered him, "Are you so clever as all that?" They set their eyes against him, and he died.
>
> (b. Ber. 58b)

Why the rabbis were irritated by R. Ḥanina is unclear. Some have supposed they thought his praise excessive, therefore sarcastic. But whatever the reason, the fact is they were believed to have murdered him through unnatural means. The ability to manipulate the evil eye thus was clearly attributed to rabbis.

Everyone, including rabbis, believed in demons. Mar b. R. Ashi stated that he personally had seen the demon of destruction, "and he gores like an ox."[1] Advice on dealing with demons included apotropaic and prophylactic counsel. R. Kahana avoided them altogether, R. Ashi said.[2] Long ago, it had been taught that one should not drink wine "in pairs," that is, two cups at a time, for doing so supposedly attracted demons. R. Ashi reported that he had seen R. Ḥanania b. Bibi go out and gaze upon the street after drinking each cup.[3] On the same matter, R. Papa reported advice received directly from a demon:

> R. Papa said, "Joseph the demon told me,' For two we kill, for four we do not kill, but for four we harm ... And if a man forgot and happened to go out [after drinking in pairs], what is his remedy? Let him take his right-hand thumb in his left-hand and his left-hand thumb in his right hand and say thus, 'You and I, surely that is three.' But if he hears someone saying, 'You and I, surely that is four,' let him reply, 'You and I are surely five.' And if hears one saying, 'You and I are six,' let him retort, 'You and I are seven.' This once happened until a hundred and one, and the demon burst.'"
>
> (b. Pes. 110a)

Mar Zuṭra taught a remedy for the evil eye similar to the one for drinking in pairs:

[1] b. Soṭ. 48a.
[2] b. Pes. 111b.
[3] b. Pes. 110a.

"If a man entering a town fears the evil eye, let him take the thumb of his right hand in his left hand and the thumb of his left hand in his right hand and say, 'I, so-and-so, am of the seed of Joseph over which the evil eye has no power...' If he is afraid of his own evil eye, he should look at the side of his left nostril."

(b. Ber. 55b)

Amemar was told by the chief of sorceresses how to behave if he met a sorceress. He should say the following imprecation:

"Hot dung in perforated baskets for your mouths, O witches! May your heads become bald! May the wind carry away your crumbs! May your species be scattered! May the wind carry off the new saffron you hold! You sorceresses, so long as he [God] showed grace to me and to you, I did not come among [you]. Now that I have come among you, your grace and my grace have cooled."

(b. Pes. 110a-b)

It is striking that the editor of the Babylonian Talmud here remarked, "In the West, they are not particular about pairs." To explain this anomaly, it is said that when a person is "not particular about pairs," the demons are similarly indifferent, but if one is "particular about pairs," the demons make sure to be "particular" too. (It is as if the demons were careful to enforce the individual's superstitions, whatever they might be.) It was thereupon remarked that R. Dimi was particular even about marks on a barrel. That is, he took care not to incise an even number of marks indicating the quantities sold. Once a barrel burst when an even number of marks had been made on it.[1] R. Papa moreover taught that if two men violate the rabbinical teaching against permitting a dog, a palm tree, a snake, a swine, or a woman to pass between two men, they should quote a biblical verse beginning with the word *'el* (God).[2]

Rabbis could do much more than merely counsel. Some of them could force demons into their service or otherwise control them:

Certain stevedores were carrying a keg of wine. They wanted to rest, so they set it under a drain-pipe, and the keg burst [since demons are to be found there]. They came before Mar b. R. Ashi. He took out *shofars* and excommunicated him [the demon]. He [the demon] came before him [Mar b. R. Ashi]. [Mar b. R. Ashi] said to him, "Why did you do this [destruction]?" The demon replied, "What should I do when they set it down right in my ear!" "And as for you," [Mar b. R. Ashi] replied, "What were you doing in a place where people are com-

[1] b. Pes. 110b.
[2] b. Pes. 111a.

> monly found [in large numbers]? You are in the wrong. Go, pay [for the damages]." [The demon] replied, "Now let the Master set a time so that I may pay." They agreed on a time. When the appointed date came, he [the demon] defaulted. When [the demon finally] came, [Mar b. R. Ashi] said to him, "Why did you not come at your appointed time?" He replied, "Whatever is tied up, sealed, measured, or counted—we have no right to take. But if we find something that has been abandoned [we may take it]."[1] (b. Ḥul. 105b)
>
> A demon in the service of R. Papa went to bring water from the river. He tarried. When the demon returned, he was asked, "Why are you so late?" He replied, "I waited until the bad water passed." Meanwhile he saw that they poured off a little water from the mouth of the jug. He said, "Had I known you were used to doing it thus, I should not have tarried."
>
> (b. Ḥul. 105b-106a)

These stories contain no hint as to why demons were believed to obey rabbis. In earlier times, Abaye was told that in heaven it had been proclaimed concerning him, "Take heed of Naḥmani and of his Torah". Certain rabbis could pray so effectively that demons would be handed over into their power by a gracious heaven. So rabbis could cope, perhaps better than other people, with the world of demons. They avoided drinking two cups of wine at a time and practiced other measures either to keep demons away or to control them. No evidence exists that belief in demons was disapproved, or that magic used against them was eschewed by rabbis or used, with distaste, only to please or meet the needs of ordinary folk. It was just as integral to the character of the rabbi to use Torah against demons as to use it for deciding court-cases. Summoning a demon to court for a case of damages caused by him is neatly symbolic of the extent of "Torah." The measures earlier used to control demons included prayer, incantation, repeating Torah-sayings, astrological fortune-telling, and the like, only a few of which measures we have seen illustrated in data from this period. The writing of bowls for the same purpose was, by contrast, never mentioned at all.

IX. Visions, Dreams, and Other Heavenly Revelations

Demons did not regularly serve as a link between heaven and earth, though they occasionally revealed to men secrets of the unseen world. At the same time they were subject to rabbinical authority. When

[1] I assume the meaning is that the demon was unable to collect sufficient funds on time, because of the prohibition he specified.

heaven wished to communicate with the Babylonian Jews, it might have recourse to several established media. People generally believed in the regularity and reliability of revelations through dreams, visions, and other means such as omens, wonders, astrology, signs, random exclamations of maniacs and children, and the like. What is of special interest here is to see whether the rabbis claimed to enjoy special prerogatives in this regard.

While early Pharisaism held that prophecy had come to an end with Malachi, prophecy theoretically could continue, according to some authorities. These authorities would probably have given short shrift to anyone who seriously claimed to be a prophet. Now, R. Ṭavyumi held, omens come from idiots:

> Mar b. R. Ashi was in the manor of Maḥoza, and heard a certain idiot exclaim, "The head of the acedemy who will rule in Mata Meḥasia signs his name Ṭavyumi." He said, "Who among the rabbis signs his Ṭavyumi? I do. I infer that as for me, the hour [Š'T'] is standing [advantageously]..."
>
> (b. B.B. 12b)

As a result of the imbecile's proclamation, Mar b. R. Ashi supposedly took measures to ensure his election, first of all by impeding that of his rival in Mata Meḥasia. There can be no doubt that he seriously believed that he had received a heavenly revelation or that people generally expected such things to happen. We cannot however imagine that such messages were directed exclusively or mainly to rabbis. We have not got the slightest evidence that rabbis believed themselves unique in this regard.

On the other hand rabbis did suppose the angels showed them special favor. Some rabbis regularly received visits from, and held conversations with, angels. R. Bibi b. Abaye, for example, claimed to have had frequent seances with the angel of death.[1] When R. Huna b. R. Joshua was dying, he saw a vision which included hearing the actual words of God. He later reported the vision, and the message he had received from God entered into the theological discourse of the rabbis as an *authoritative* ethical statement. God had told the angels, "Since he does not insist upon his rights, do not be particular with him [but let him go]."[2]

The schools held that rabbis were particularly adept at the interpretation of dreams. They possessed, first of all, an ancient corpus of infor-

[1] b. Ḥag. 5a.
[2] b. R.H. 17a.

mation on the meanings of particular signs and omens revealed in dreams. R. Papa for instance taught that seeing a white horse in a dream is a favorable omen.[1] If one saw unfavorable omens however, fasting could prove effective to counteract them. Rav had long ago taught that fasting is potent against a dream. R. Joseph had added one might fast for that purpose even on the Sabbath. R. Joshua b. R. Idi actually did so, declining to participate in a meal at R. Ashi's house because he was fasting on account of a dream.[2]

One should not for one minute suppose that the messages derived from dreams affected only trivial or theological matters.[3] Supernaturalism, including this aspect of it, played a significant role in the formation of law and the evaluation of legal opinions as well. R. Ashi, for example, received a message through a dream from King Manasseh. The message pertained to a legal question. The next day, R. Ashi said, he would teach it in his school as authoritative law. The story is as follows:

> The school of R. Ashi arose [from study] at the [passage of] "the three kings."[4] He said, "Tomorrow we shall begin with *our colleagues*."[5] [When R. Ashi went to sleep], Manasseh came and appeared to him in his dream. Manasseh said to R. Ashi, "Your *colleague* and the *colleague* of your father do you [now] call us? [If I am merely your colleague, then let me test your knowledge of Torah.] From what portion of the bread is [the piece for reciting] the blessing over bread to be taken?" R. Ashi replied, "I do not know." Manasseh said to him, "You do not [even] know from what part of the bread one takes the piece for blessing! Yet you call me *our colleague*!?" R. Ashi replied, "Teach me, and tomorrow I shall expound it in your name at the school session." Manasseh said to him, "From the part that is baked into a crust." R. Ashi said to Manasseh, "Since you are so wise, what is the reason that you bowed down in worship of the stars?" He replied, "If you were there, you would have seized the skirt of your garment and run after me." The next day, R. Ashi said to the rabbis, "We shall open with the *rabbis*..."
>
> (b. Sanh. 102b)

---

[1] b. Sanh. 93a.

[2] b. Shab. 11a.

[3] Although R. Ashi did say that just as one cannot find grain without straw, so there could be no dream without meaningless details, b. Ned. 8a.

[4] Mishnah Sanhedrin 11 : 1. The three kings who have no portion in the world to come, including Manasseh.

[5] ḤBRYN. The kings of ancient Israel were supposed to have been students of Torah. Hence Manasseh, Ahab, and Jeroboam were all "our colleagues." Yet R. Ashi did not refer to them as "our rabbis," and so he reflected disrespect for the ancient royal masters of Torah who had sinned so as to be excluded from the world to come.

R. Ashi's discourse then stressed that Ahab was the father of idolatry; he now made no mention whatever of Manasseh in that connection.

The rabbis possessed means to cope with problems brought on by dreams. For example, they knew how to overcome not only dreams they could remember, but even dreams they only thought or feared they *may* have dreamt, as in the following:

> Amemar, Mar Zuṭra, and R. Ashi were once sitting together. They agreed that each of them should teach a saying the others had not heard. One opened thus, "If someone saw a dream but does not know [remember] what he saw, let him stand before the priests when they spread out their hands [in the priestly benediction in the synagogue] and say [the following prayer]: 'Lord of the world, I am yours, and my dreams are yours. I have dreamed a dream, but I do not know what it is [portends]. Whether I dreamed concerning myself or whether my friends dreamed concerning me or whether I dreamed concerning others—if [these dreams] are good, strengthen and fortify them like the dreams of Joseph. But if they necessitate healing, then heal them as the waters of Marah [were healed] by the hand of Moses our rabbi, as Miriam [was healed] from her leprosy, as Hezekiah [was healed] from his ailment, and as the waters of Jericho [were healed] by Elisha. Just as you have turned the curse of the Evil Balaam into a blessing, so change all my dreams for me to good.' And he should conclude his prayer right along with the priests, so that the congregation will [unanimously] respond 'Amen'. But if not, then let him say, '[You who are] majestic in the heights and dwell in power, you are peace and your name is peace. May it be pleasing before you to bestow upon us peace.'"
>
> (b. Ber. 55b)

The reason the rabbis among others took dreams so seriously clearly was their belief that dreams not only predicted, but actually shaped events. Hence it was important to seek divine grace to avert the evil consequence a dream might portend. Strikingly, rabbis reported that what they had dreamed about their own academies came true:

> R. Papa and R. Huna b. R. Joshua saw dreams. R. Papa, who [saw in his dream that he] went into a marsh, was made head of a school. R. Huna b. R. Joshua who [saw in his dream that he] went up to a forest became head of the men of the *Kallah*.[1] Some say that both [saw in their dreams that they went into] a marsh. But [the difference was] R. Papa was carrying a drum and therefore was made head of a school. R. Huna b. R. Joshua was not carrying a drum and therefore was made [only] head of the men of the *Kallah*. R. Ashi reported, "I went into a marsh

[1] See vol. IV, p. 384.

> [in my dream] and was carrying a drum and made a loud noise with it."[1]
> (b. Ber. 57a)

Tradition taught that if one saw a goose in a dream, he may hope for wisdom. If he dreamt of having sexual relations with one, he would become head of an academy. R. Ashi reported,

> "[In a dream] I saw one and had sexual relations with her and was raised to a high position."
> (b. Ber. 57a)

We have observed that dreams possessed an intrinsic force to affect events. Heaven might bestow good dreams but could be relied upon to help the worthy man overcome the effects of whatever he had dreamed. We cannot suppose that the rabbis were either the sole dreamers or the only interpreters of dreams. What is important in these traditions is that rabbis, sharing the popular faith, felt that their particular affairs—elections as heads of schools, teaching the law and theology in them—were subject to the influence of dreaming. They moreover composed prayers to cope with not only what had been seen but also what might have been seen by the dreamer, his friends, and anyone else. We may therefore generalize that the rabbis differed from outsiders little if at all in their view of the supernatural world but recorded a claim to be able to cope better than anyone else with the doings of that world.

x. The Science of Astrology

No sage now denied the accuracy of astrology, which was almost universally believed to be an exact science. Earlier debate had centered upon whether "Israel" was under the influence of the stars, but by the fourth century few Babylonian authorities doubted that Jews were subjected to planetary power as much as everyone else.[2] Astrology found a place in rabbinical theology somewhat in this way: God had created the world and could intervene in it in response to merits or in answer to prayer. But the day-to-day running of the heavenly court and its earthly counterpart lay in the hands of ministers, including the angels of the stars (as in Daniel 10) and planets. Their power varied like that of courtiers according to the positions of their stars. The guide to the cosmic administration was the science of astrology.

---

[1] This would account for his exceptional prestige as possessing both Torah [= heading an academy] and worldly greatness.

[2] Vol. IV, pp. 330-334.

In this time too, the rabbis believed not only in astrology but also in its direct pertinence to the destiny of Israel. That belief earlier had been qualified, for merits, prayer, and the like could affect destiny as well. Indeed, the following saying of R. Ashi may represent the remnant of an anti-astrological polemic:

> Did not R. Ashi say, "I and Dimi bar Qaquzeta were [both born] on the first day of the week [Sunday]. I am a king, and he is the chief of the thieves..."
>
> (b. Shab. 156a)

If so, what difference can the stars have made? In context, however it, means nothing of the sort. The passage begins with the citation of R. Joshua b. Levi's saying that a person born on Sunday shall be a man "without one thing in him." That "one thing" becomes the problem. Obviously, it cannot be "one virtue," because of the above saying of R. Ashi. It means rather "completely virtuous" or "completely wicked," just as light and darkness were both created on Sunday. The same passage includes a Palestinian discourse. R. Ḥanina told his disciples, "Go out and tell the son of Levi, 'Not the constellation of the day, but that of the *hour* is the determining influence.'" I think it clear, therefore, that in context R. Ashi's saying constitutes not a rejection of astrology but rather the observation of an astrological anomaly. If so, it is clear he believed as much as did the earlier Palestinian, R. Ḥanina, in the truth of astrological information, whether pertinent to Israel or to the nations. In fact, further sayings of R. Ashi make his position quite obvious:

> [One born under Mars will be a shedder of blood.] R. Ashi said, "A surgeon, a thief, a ritual-slaughterer, or a circumciser."
>
> (b. Shab. 156a)
>
> [The proof, Abaye said, that prophecy has not been taken from the wise is that a great man makes a statement, and the same is then reported in the name of another great authority. Rava countered, "It is not so strange, for perhaps both were born under the same star." Rava added that the proof is this, that a great man makes a statement and then the same is reported in the name of R. ʿAqiva b. Joseph—a far greater man, so that being born under the same star does not matter.] R. Ashi said, "What is so strange in this? Perhaps in this matter he was born under the very same star [Lit.: He is a son of his star]..."

The "immunity from planetary influence" of which the editor of the anti-astrological pericope speaks in b. Shab. 156a-b must mean something other than that Israel is not in the slightest measure subjected to the control of the stars.[1] It probably means that "Israel has no star" in precisely the *way* the nations do, because Israel's fate is shaped not only by the stars but also by ethical merits, divine intervention—which takes the form of altering the astrological patterns—and similar supernatural means. The point must be that Israel is not subjected *only* to natural laws, including astrological ones, but *also* to supernatural forces. Pagans acquire no merit, therefore are *wholly* subjected to planetary government.

Further evidence on the astrological beliefs of the sages includes the following:

> [The serpent injected lust into Eve. Lustfulness departed from Israel at Mt. Sinai. Idolaters did not stand at Mount Sinai, and therefore their lustfulness did not depart.] R. Aḥa b. Rava asked R. Ashi, "What [is the situation] with respect to converts [to Judaism]?" He replied, "Even though they were not [present at Mount Sinai to have their lust removed], their stars were [present at Mount Sinai], as it is written, *Neither with you only do I make this covenant ... but with him that stands here with us this day before the Lord and also with him that is not here with us this day* (Deut. 29:14)."
>
> (b. Shab. 146a)

> Rabina said, "...if a man is frightened but sees nothing, [the reason is] that his star sees. What is the remedy? He should recite the *Shema'*... [But if he cannot say the *Shema'*], he should say this formula, 'The goat at the butcher's is fatter than I am.'"
>
> (b. Meg. 3a)

Both R. Ashi and Rabina adhered to the widespread belief that not only nations but also individuals were assigned to specific stars. More striking still, R. Ashi interpreted Scripture in support of his belief: "He that is not here with us this day" nonetheless is represented by his star.

Since the rabbis generally accepted the accuracy of astrological predictions for Israel as a whole and for individual Jews, it is remarkable that after Samuel, nowhere do we find a claim that a rabbi possessed advanced astrological learning or the skill to cast a horoscope. On the contrary from the end of the third century onward not a single astrological saying is attributed to a major master. That fact is susceptible of several explanations. First of all, one might suppose that astrological sayings were suppressed by the school, or editor, which certainly held "Israel has no star." But the evidences examined here and earlier were not suppressed, and while some of them persisted despite the super-

---

[1] Vol. IV, pp. 333-4.

scription contrary to their content,[1] many of the astrological stories cannot possibly have been either misunderstood or ignored by such a school. So I think it unlikely that pertinent sayings have been suppressed, though obviously one can come only very tentatively to such an opinion. Second, it is possible that after Samuel, who boasted of his knowledge of the stars while (to be sure) leaving only a few neutral sayings to attest to that knowledge, the astrological traditions of Nehardea were lost. This is not implausible, for the school of Nehardea was destroyed by Odenathus in his raid in 363, and while some of the masters, and more important, the memorizers, survived, surely others did not. Third, and I think most likely, the schools probably possessed to begin with a very thin store of astrological information.[2] Whatever the state of popular and rabbinical belief about astrology, astrological sciences were pursued not in Jewish schools but chiefly in Babylonian ones. The rabbis had no special access to astrological traditions. The ancient condemnation of Jeremiah may have made a limited impression upon their assessment of astrology, but it probably inhibited serious study of the subject by rabbinical masters and disciples. It was a science, but a science best left in the hands of the gentile sages; not a black art and not entirely false, but also not really "Torah." This attitude, it seems to me, would best explain the fact that for the whole of the fourth and fifth centuries, we find not a single astrological saying, except for a few commonplaces,[3] despite the considerable number of stories indicating belief in astrology. Astrologers, like doctors of medicine, were necessary for the state and for society. They did not, however, come from rabbinical schools, and, as I said, their knowledge was probably not a part of "Torah."

XI. Medical Traditions

The rabbis were not physicians.[4] While holy men of other communities effected healings through either the power of their prayers or the wisdom of their medicine, the rabbis now did nothing of the sort. No

[1] As I argued earlier, see p. 192, n.1.

[2] For an astronomical comment of R. Ashi, see b. Ber. 58b.

[3] I cannot regard the sayings about being born under Venus, Mars, and so on as revealing any profound knowledge of astrological science or as indicating that the rabbis did preserve accurate or sophisticated information on the subject. On astrology in Mesopotamian Christianity see C. H. Kraeling, *The Christian Building* (Locust Valley, 1967), pp. 125-6.

[4] Vol. IV, pp. 363-370.

miraculous healing is attributed to a sage in the late fourth or fifth century rabbinical traditions. A profession of medicine existed within the Jewish community but by and large did not include rabbis. Rabbis did not receive fees for medical advice and did not regularly practice medicine. On the other hand their traditions included some attention to physiological and therapeutic matters. The sages required medical information in order to study important areas of law, for example, the laws pertaining to circumcision, length of pregnancy, and the like. They were moreover men of wide-ranging interests. It was quite natural for them to acquire[1] and transmit information on matters in which they neither required nor claimed special competence. They furthermore had a lively interest in questions of good health generally. Whatever they could find out about preserving health and avoiding sickness, particularly about matters of the bowels and proper cuisine, was carefully recorded.

We have a number of stories of rabbis' administering medical therapy, including the following:

> R. Aḥa b. Joseph suffered from asthma, so he went to Mar 'Uqba, who advised him to drink three [gold denar] weights of *ḥiltit* on three days. He did so on Thursday and Friday...
>
> (b. Shab. 140a)

> Rabin of Nersh used [for the cure of the bellyache] of the daughter of R. Ashi one hundred fifty of grains [of long pepper], and it cured her.
>
> (b. Giṭ. 69b)

These are perfectly naturalistic remedies, used to heal specific ailments by means of herbs.

Of a more magical character was the recitation of various Scriptures in the healing process:

> [R. Yoḥanan had said, "For an inflammatory fever, let one take an iron knife, go where thorn-hedges are to be found, and tie a white twisted thread to (a hedge). On the first day, he must slightly notch it [the knife? the hedge?] and say, *And the angel of the Lord appeared unto him* (Ex. 3:2). On the following day, he makes a small notch and says, *And Moses said, I will turn aside now and see*. The next day he makes a small notch and says, *And when the Lord saw that he turned aside to see* (Ex. 3:4)."] R. Aḥa b. Raba said to R. Ashi, "Then let him say, *Draw not nigh it*
>
> (b. Shab. 67a)[2]

[1] In the mid-fourth century, many medical sayings came down from Tai tribesmen. Now we find few similar phenomena, probably in part because Shapur II had effectively sealed Babylonia off from the Tai incursions; but see R. Papa, b. A.Z. 29a.

[2] Trans. H. Freedman, *Sabbath* (London, 1948), p. 319.

> A mad dog rubbed itself in the market-place against R. Huna b. R. Joshua. He stripped off his clothes and ran, saying, "I have fulfilled in myself, *Wisdom preserveth the life of him who has it* (Qoh. 7:12)."
>
> (b. Yoma 84a)

We have already noted that R. Aḥa and R. Ashi discussed what a man should say when healing himself from a daily fever through casting his sickness upon an ant.[1] The sages also used ordinary remedies for their own ailments, preserving the record of having done so through discussions of the law, for instance, of whether it was permitted to use such remedies on the Sabbath. Thus Rabina visiting R. Ashi observed that the latter was soaking his foot in vinegar to reduce swelling caused by an ass's having trampled him. He asked whether it is permitted to do so on the Sabbath.[2]

What is striking in these stories is the absence of the attribution to rabbis themselves of supernatural powers of healing. While they knew popular medicine and applied it, they possessed little more knowledge than ordinary midwives or similar folk. They did know how to enlist the power of appropriate Scriptures, which they invoked as incantations. They also knew appropriate magical formulae, such as the one brought to bear upon the ant. But, as in the case of astrology, medical skills and traditions were not assiduously cultivated in the schools and scarcely constituted a vital element of "Torah," though they certainly were regarded as part of "Torah" largely for legal considerations. The advanced medical sciences of the day made little impact upon the schools. When we recall that the later Sasanians, particularly Kavad and Khusro, encouraged the founding of medical schools in their empire, we find the rabbis' commonplace knowledge primitive by contrast.

Measures to prevent injury and disease nonetheless were taken, and the corpus of rabbinical traditions included a few valuable, if not exceptional, pieces of advice. R. Papa, for example, advised that one should wear shoes in a house where a cat is found; the cat may kill a snake, and the bones may stick into the man's foot and endanger his life.[3] He likewise counseled to eat more than normal when one is away from home.[4] He would eat a piece of bread at every *parasang* in order to prevent digestive troubles. He taught that circumcision should not be performed on a south-wind-day. Citing Psalm 116 : 6, *The Lord*

[1] b. Shab. 66b, above, pp. 182-183.
[2] b. Shab. 109a.
[3] b. Pes. 112b.
[4] b. Ta'anit 11a.

preserves the simple, he explained that many people disregard this precaution and yet come to no harm. He also said one should not be bled on such a day.[1] Mar Zuṭra cited I Sam. 1 : 20, concerning the length of pregnancy, to prove that if a woman bears at seven months, she can give birth before the month is completed.[2] R. Papa insisted that the surgeon who performs a circumcision must also suck out the wound.[3] R. Ashi defined the condition of dozing:

> "A sleep which is no sleep; waking which is no waking. The man answers when he is called, but cannot recall an argument; if reminded, he remembers it." (b. Ta'anit 12b)[4]

Advice on the properties of food required only ordinary, routine observation of everyday processes. R. Huna b. R. Joshua noted that wine opens the heart.[5] R. Papa noted that the fourth hour is generally mealtime for most people.[6] R. Papa, who was, as we saw, a brewer of beer, noted the healing qualities of Egyptian beer for the bowels.[7] It serves as a laxative for the constipated, as a binder for him who has diarrhoea. If one is unable to obey a call of nature, R. Aḥa b. Raba said to R. Ashi, he should not think of other things but concentrate on this one necessity[8]. Mar b. R. Ashi taught that one should not restrain his urine, as we noted earlier.[9] Just as Abaye's foster-mother taught him numerous medical traditions which he later handed on in the schools, so R. Papa cited his wife's practice in neutralizing the evil effects of vegetables. She used eighty Persian twigs in cooking them.[10]

xii. The Mind of the Schools (i): Theology

As we have already noticed, the corpus of sayings attributed to the final generations named[11] in the Babylonian Talmud proved insub-

[1] b. Yev. 72a.
[2] b. R.H. 11a.
[3] b. Shab. 133b.
[4] See also b. Meg. 18b.
[5] b. B.B. 12b.
[6] b. Pes. 12b.
[7] b. Shab. 110a.
[8] b. Shab. 82a. This is in precisely the same form as the medical traditions cited earlier in the names of R. Aḥa and R. Ashi. That is, a saying of an earlier generation is examined. R. Aḥa b. Raba then says to R. Ashi that there is a fault in the earlier tradition, which should be corrected thus and so. The fault is not one of transmission but of content or logic.
[9] b. Bekh. 44b. See above, p. 150.
[10] b. Ber. 44b.
[11] The Saboraic masters were generally anonymous, so far as the Babylonian

stantial. Teachings about God and closely related matters similarly are hardly numerous. We do not know whether anyone made an effort to systematize, even to organize, his theological thought. Since sayings germane to theological issues were edited in the conventional form of discrete comments, in the context of dialectical discussions, or as exegeses of Scriptures, we should hardly expect otherwise. Yet while in relationship to legal matters, we have a sufficient number of traditions of the several masters to attempt a formulation of legal philosophies on particular issues, the contrary is the case for metaphysical and theological subjects. All we have are a few bits and pieces.

Earlier it seemed clear that some of the rabbinical sayings were esoteric, others exoteric.[1] The following are obviously for public consumption:

> R. Ashi said, "If a man considered doing a *mizvah* and perforce did not do it, Scripture credits it to him as if he had [actually] done it..." (b. Ber. 6a)

> R. Papa said, "The reward of [attending] the house of mourning [comes on account of] silence." Mar Zutra said, "The reward for keeping a fast [comes on account of] the charity [one distributes in connection with the fast.]" R. Ashi said, "The reward of the house of banqueting [comes on account of] the words [spoken in praise of the bride and groom]." (b. Ber. 6b)

These sayings pertain to the concerns of ordinary folk. Nothing in them refers to secret doctrines of the divine nature. They all are edifying, for they encourage people to carry out the commandments. In the first instance, people are assured that even giving thought to doing a commandment merits reward. In the second are specified the actions which provoke heavenly reward for the doing of various duties.

Part of the rabbis' astral mysticism in the *Merkavah*-tradition concerned the layout and design of the heavens. The heavens were divided into seven parts, and God sits enthroned above the seventh or highest heaven. Concerning this mystery, we have only one saying:

> R. Aḥa b. Jacob said, "There is still another heaven above the heads of the *ḥayyot* [living creatures], as it is written, *And over the heads of the ḥayyot there was a likeness of a firmament, like the color of the terrible ice, stretched forth over their heads above* (Ezek. 1:22)." (b. Ḥag. 13a)

Talmud is concerned. The Geonic traditions are our only source for information about them. At the same time, it is self-evident that the contribution of the Saboraic masters to the formation of the Babylonian Talmud was substantial.

[1] Vol. IV, pp. 315-324.

Sayings such as this one probably were kept secret by the sages.

Teachings on the personality and humanity of God may not have been private at all. We have no indication who would have heard the following:

> R. Papa said, "There is no grief before [on the part of] the Holy One blessed be he, as Scripture says, *Honor and majesty are before him. Strength and beauty are in his sanctuary* (Ps. 96:6)."
>
> (b. Ḥag. 5b)

> R. Papa pointed out the following contradiction: "It is written, *God is angry every day* (Ps. 7:12) and it is also written, *Who could stand before his anger* (Nah. 1:6). But there is no contradiction. No individual can stand before his anger, but he is angry with men collectively [and the merits of some atone for the rest]."
>
> (b. A.Z. 4a)

The exegesis of theological as legal scriptures was a strictly academic enterprise, a central mode of rabbinic thought. Yet the results of these exegeses have nothing to do with secret doctrines. The thought that God, like man, had emotions and that these emotions were approximately the same as those of human beings distressed no one. The rabbis were in no way disturbed by anthropomorphism, although certain anthropomorphic expressions in Scripture may have been found gross. On the contrary, as I said, they envisioned God in the image of rabbinical man. It was perfectly natural to speculate about what was written in the *tefillin* which God placed on his left arm; R. Aḥa b. Rava so speculated with R. Ashi.[1] In this connection, the sensible remarks of Professor R. J. Z. Werblowsky (in his *Prolegomenon* to A. Marmorstein's *Doctrine of Merits in Old Rabbinic Literature* [reprinted in N.Y., 1968], pp. xiv-xv) are particularly germane:

> ...Anthropomorphism i.e., the attribution of human, bodily as well as mental or psychological, qualities to the divine is a well-known phenomenon and problem in the history of religions. Anthropomorphism does not become less anthropomorphic by being reduced to mental or psychological expressions i.e., to anthropopathism (e.g. God loves, is wroth, has pity etc.). God may have no ears, or his ears may be said to be purely metaphorical, yet he is still said to "hear" prayers. Even if these mental and feeling qualities are pruned away by suitable allegorical exegesis, we are still left with a basic irreducible anthropomorphism: the conception of the Deity in "personalistic" terms, i.e. in analogy to the only type of "person" we really know—the human person...

[1] b. Ber. 6a-b.

> Indeed, it appears as if non-pagan, monotheistic religion is caught on the horns of an uncomfortable dilemma: either advocate a "negative theology" in which God easily becomes a bloodless abstraction, First Cause, or cosmic principle, or else risk to speak of God in human, all-too-human terms as Father, Shepherd, King and Lover. The rabbis boldly chose the latter risk, on the assumption that only by means of anthropomorphic imagery could the full, actual, vital relevance of God to our lives be brought out. *The rabbis, it seems, could take this risk with equanimity since actual anthropomorphism was not considered a real danger by them.* They could, therefore, permit themselves considerable latitude of expression. In this respect too the rabbis simply continued the biblical tradition.

It seems to me the rabbis normally meant just what they said, however, and if they used anthropomorphic language, as they did, the reason was not that they were not afraid of the "danger" of anthropomorphism, but rather they were not aware that it was a danger to begin with, but found it quite natural and normal for their theological thought.

These few sayings of late fourth- and fifth-century masters directly pertinent to the nature and doings of God depend upon a long theological tradition. They however exhibit no development of earlier themes. We can best comprehend them as continuations, with little elaboration, of ancient models. Thus the belief that specific actions generate rewards constitutes an element in the classic view that God rewards good deeds and punishes sin. Men were supposed to serve God and submit to his will. The God whom they serve lives in the highest heaven, above all heavenly as well as earthly creatures, who in various forms exist to do his will. He is never grieved but sometimes angry. His anger is briefer than man's and generally is directed at the community, which could bear up under its weight, rather than at the individual, who could not. These random thoughts hardly exhausted the mind of the schools on so central a theological subject. The religious world-view of the rabbis included the workings of the evil creatures and demons whom they might master through Torah, as well as angels and other amiable supernatural creatures who would cooperate with pious sages. That world-view comprehended faith in revelation not only through Scripture and exegesis, but also through omens, dreams, and natural science (astrology). It affirmed that prayers and magical formulae such as incantations might affect the natural world and effect men's wishes. All of these constitute important components of rabbinical theology, which took account of a world populated above and below with beings responsible to carry out the divine will.

XIII. The Mind of the Schools (II): Liturgy

Further insight into the religious ideas of the schools derives from prayers composed by the rabbis and rules promulgated on how to pray. It is clear, first of all, that the few sayings considered earlier cannot exhaust the range of theological ideas or provide a full description of the way in which the rabbis viewed the world and God's role in it. Further, we can hardly distinguish between the liturgical contribution of one generation and that of the next. The profound conservatism of the schools is clearly revealed in the scholastic prayers, often consisting of arrangements of scriptural passages, rarely expressing an idea one can associate with a particular individual or time. We now have only a few compositions:

> When Mar b. Rabina would conclude his Prayer, he would say this [meditation]: "O my God, guard my tongue from evil and my lips from speaking lies. To those that curse me may my soul be dumb. May my soul be like dust to all. Open my heart with your Torah. May my soul pursue your commandments. Save me from an evil encounter, the evil impulse, an evil woman, and from all the evils that threaten to come into the world. Concerning all who think evil against me—quickly annul their intention and spoil their plans. *May the words of my mouth and the reasonings of my heart be pleasing before you, Lord, my rock and redeemer* (Ps. 19:15)."
>
> (b. Ber. 17a)

> When Mar Zuṭra would climb into bed, he would say, "I forgive all who have vexed me..."
>
> (b. Meg. 28a)

Upon the basis of these payers we can hardly characterize the religious situation of the schools. Yet we may discern a religious attitude corresponding to the humble and submissive personality described earlier as inculcated in the school, particularly through submission to the master. We notice, first of all, stress upon the virtue of submission itself, both to man and to God. The disciple is to be "like dust to all" on earth, as an exercise in being "like dust" to heaven as well. The Torah opens man's heart, whereupon the soul pursues the doing of commandments. Consequently one may ask God to save him from various evils, especially—in the charged intellectual atmosphere of the schools this would have been important—from all who devise evil thoughts against him. The need to forgive all who have irritated oneself reflects a day filled with conflict. It nonetheless would be far-fetched to assign these prayers to the situation of schoolhouse alone. They have persisted in various settings long after this period, and the former is included in the prayer said three times daily by pious Jews. Yet in the first place they came from the schools and certainly pertained to the spiritual circumstance of sages.

Coming at the end of a long tradition of liturgical development, the sages now had to choose among several alternative compositions. Prizing each, R. Papa held that all should be preserved:

> [What is the blessing said after reading the *Megillah* of Esther?] "Blessed are you O Lord ... who espoused our quarrel and vindicated our cause and ... Blessed are you O Lord who avenges Israel on all their enemies." Rava says, "[One concludes], 'The God who saves.'" R. Papa said, "Therefore let us say them all, 'Blessed are you O Lord who avenges Israel on all their enemies, the God who saves.'"
>
> (b. Meg. 21b)

> When the agent of the congregation [in repeating the Prayer] reaches the paragraph, 'We give thanks,' what does the congregation say? Rav replied, "We give thanks to you ... because we are able to give you thanks." Samuel said, "God of all flesh, seeing that we give you thanks." The men of Nehardea in the name of R. Simlai said, "Blessings and thanksgiving to your great name because you have kept us alive and preserved us, seeing that we give you thanks..." R. Papa said, "Therefore let us say them all."
>
> (b. Soṭ. 40a)[1]

Willingness to include the preferences of the several authorities and schools doubtless facilitated the promulgation of a single liturgy for Babylonia. If that was R. Papa's intention, one can understand his hesitation to exclude anyone's tradition. We have no evidence, however, that the local synagogues now followed a single pattern in every detail, though the main outline of the prayers had long ago been standardized.

Being lawyers, the sages paid as close attention to the forms and procedures of prayer as to those of litigation in court. They raised to the level of legal inquiry and precision the private devotions of ordinary folk as well as the public prayers of the congregation. They did so because they took seriously the obligation to pray, and because they believed that heaven expected proper prayer as well as true justice from the Jewish community. Thus if someone was freed of his obligation to recite the *Shema'*, this had to be spelled out. R. Papa discussed the circumstances in which one did not have to say the *Shema'*.[2] Rabina

---

[1] See also b. Ta'anit 6b-7a.

[2] b. Ber. 11a, 16a.

taught that saying the *Shema'* mentally was equivalent to reciting it out loud.[1] Abaye and Rava had earlier debated whether one might recite the *Shema'* if manure is being carried by. When the dung is hard like potsherds, Amemar said it was forbidden, and Mar Zuṭra, it was permitted to say the *Shema'* near by.[2] R. Papa held that the snout of a pig is like manure being carried past, even when the pig had just washed in the river.[3] We have already observed that saying the *Shema'* was believed to drive away demons. In these sayings, on the other hand, the apotropaic aspect of the *Shema'* was ignored, its liturgical-rational side emphasized. In legal discussions the rabbis likewise silently passed over the magical value of the *mezuzah*, *tefillin*, and other holy objects, even though in other contexts they were not reticent about it.

The same legal precision pertained to saying the Prayer (Eighteen Benedictions). It had earlier been taught that if a man needs to consult nature he should not say the Prayer. This teaching was qualified, for if he can hold himself in, his prayer will be regarded as valid. R. Zevid taught that he should be able to do so long enough to walk a *parasang*.[4] R. Ashi taught,[5] "Guard your orifices at the time when you are standing in Prayer before me" as an interpretation of Qoh. 4 : 17. The manner in which the leading authorities said the Prayer in special circumstances was carefully recorded.[6]

While blessings of food and grace after meals seemed mostly a private rabbinical rite, Sanctification of wine [*Qiddush*] for the Sabbath and festivals as well as for the conclusion of Sabbaths was entirely public and probably done by most Jews. In this matter the sage would demonstrate the right way by doing so for his disciples and others among whom he lived, or he might be given the honor of saying the Sanctification for the entire synagogue, as in the following stories:

> R. Ashi said, "When we were at the house of R. Papa, he used to say the Sanctification for us [the students], and when the sharecroppers came from the fields, he used to say it again for them."
>
> (b. R.H. 29b)
>
> When R. Ashi visited Maḥoza, [the people] said to him, "Let the master recite the Great Sanctification [*Qiddush*] for us." He [not knowing what they meant] thought it over, "What is the Great Sanctification?

---

1 b. Ber. 20b.
2 b. Ber. 25a, see also R. Papa, b. Yoma 30a.
3 b. Ber. 25b.
4 b. Ber. 23a.
5 *Ibid.*
6 b. Ber. 30a, Maremar, Mar Zuṭra, R. Ashi.

Let us see. For all blessings [of *Qiddush*] we first say, '...who creates the fruit of the vine.'" He said just that. He saw an old man bend [his head] and drink. Thereupon he applied to himself, *The wise man, his eyes are in his head* (Qoh. 2:14).

(b. Pes. 106a)

The younger and elder sons of R. Ḥisda said to R. Ashi, "Amemar once visited our town. We had no wine, so we brought him beer [for *Havdalah*] but he would not recite *Havdalah* [over it], so *he passed the night in fasting* (Dan. 6:19) [because one should not eat without reciting *Havdalah* at the end of the Sabbath or festival]. The next day, we got wine for him ... The following year he visited us again. We offered him beer. He said, 'If so, it is the wine of the country,' and he recited *Havdalah* over it and ate..."

(b. Pes. 107a)[1]

The sage would be given particular respect and the privilege of praying in behalf of others. R. Ashi's visit to Maḥoza underlines the problem of local variations. He simply did not know what was meant in Maḥoza by "the Great *Qiddush*" and obviously would have been embarrassed had he been required to confess his ignorance. The need for rabbis to adjust themselves to local custom is illustrated in the third story. We may therefore distinguish between the provenance of laws about saying Grace and that of the laws on blessing wine in various other ritual circumstances. The blessings and Grace were essentially limited to the academic table, while the public, synagogual Sanctification of wine for other purposes was not. The master would therefore recite such liturgies for the entire community or synagogue, rather than for the school house only.

XIV. THE MIND OF THE SCHOOLS (III): EXEGESIS

As in other matters, so in exegesis, the legacy of these generations was not rich. Whatever the actual state of their contribution, we know very little of what the sages said about Scripture. In general we shall notice the continuation of earlier convictions, particularly the anachronistic assignment to Scriptural times and characters of the traits and values of the contemporary schools. Thus Rava or R. Ashi taught that Abraham "our father" had kept the entire Torah, meaning both the written and the oral parts of it.[2] R. Ashi taught that Manoaḥ did

[1] Further sayings on *Havdalah* are in b. Pes. 8a, R. Papa, R. Zevid, and Rabina; b. Ber. 29, Mar Zuṭra on including *Havdalah* in the abbreviated version of the Prayer.

[2] b. Yoma 28b.

not even attend a school for Scripture (let alone an academy for study of Mishnah and other disciplines of the oral Torah) with reference to Gen. 24 : 61.[1] Wisdom, not age, produced the order of the generations of Shem, R. Zevid of Nehardea taught with reference to Gen. 10 : 21.[2] R. Papa said that Abraham had been exhorted by God not to marry an idolatress or a bondwoman so that his seed should not be ascribed to her.[3]

R. Ashi and R. Papa held that during the years in the wilderness, Moses dwelt in the camp of the Levites.[4] Hence "bringing forth him that cursed" must mean that he was brought forth thence into the camp of the Israelites, where he would be stoned. R. Papa discussed the problem of Ex. 23 : 28, *And I will send the hornet before you*, which he interpreted to mean that the hornet stood on the Jordan river and squirted poison across to blind the Canaanites. He also discussed Amos 2 : 9, *Yet I destroyed the Amorite before them*. He held that there actually were two hornets, one in the time of Moses, which did not cross the Jordan, the other in the time of Joshua, which did.[5] R. Papa interpreted *strong drink* of Num. 28 : 7 as an expression connecting drink, satiation, and plenty,[6] and inferred from there that when a person has his fill of wine, it is because he drank in large gulps, rather than sipping his wine.

On the apparently pointless list of Palestinian towns in Josh. 15 : 22, we have the following exchange:

> R. Huna b. Nathan asked R. Ashi, "What is the point of the verse *Qinah and Dimonah and Adadah?* He replied, "The text is enumerating the towns in the land of Israel." R. Huna replied, "Do I not know [that]? But I want to tell you that R. Gevihah from [Be] Argiza learned a lesson from these names: 'Whoever has cause for indigation [*Qinah*] against his neighbor and yet holds his peace [*Domem*], He that abides for all eternity [*'ade'ad*] shall espouse his cause.'" R. Ashi replied, "If so, the verse *ziklag and Madmanah and Sansanah* (Joshua 15:31) should also convey a lesson." He replied, "If R. Gevihah from [Be] Argiza were here, he would derive a lesson from it... [as follows]: 'If a man has just cause of complaint against his neighbor for taking away his livelihood [*za'akat legima*] and yet holds his peace [*domem*], he that abides in the bush [*shokni sneh*] will espouse his cause.'"
>
> (b. Giṭ. 7a)[7]

---

[1] b. 'Eruv. 18b.
[2] b. Sanh. 69b.
[3] b. Yev. 100b with reference to Gen. 17 : 7.
[4] b. Sanh. 42b-43a. This is part of an exegesis of Lev. 24 : 14 with reference to the death of the blasphemer.
[5] b. Soṭ. 36a.
[6] b. Suk. 49b.
[7] Trans. Maurice Simon, *Giṭṭin* (London, 1948), pp. 22-3, with minor revisions.

It is striking that the stress upon humility, forebearance, and restraint in pressing one's own claims ("To those that curse me, may my soul be like dust") noted in liturgical compositions recurs here. One cannot say that the virtue of submissiveness was now urged to a greater degree than earlier, for I know of no way to prove such a thesis. At the same time it is striking that the earlier passivity[1] of rabbinical politics is now extended to personality-traits and ethical behavior.

R. Papa explained how one may both *go down to Timnah* (Judges 14 : 1) and *go up to Timnah* (Gen. 38 : 13), by comparison to Vardina, Be Bari, and the market of Nersh. Those coming from one direction descend, from another, they go up.[2]

R. Ashi held that King David studied Torah until midnight. Then he spent the rest of the night reciting psalms and praises of God.[3] R. Papa held that Solomon never married, on the basis of I Kings 11 : 2. The liaison with Pharoah's daughter was never regarded as a true marriage.[4]

Mar Zuṭra held that the earlier generations were better at exegesis than the later ones:

> "Between *Azel* and *Azel* (I Chron. 8:38 and 9:44) they were laden with four hundred camel [loads] of [notes containing] interpretations."
> (b. Pes. 62b)

On prophetic literature, exegesis of this time was similarly sparse, as if to illustrate Mar Zuṭra's judgment. R. Ashi commented on the old, native-Babylonian tradition that the word *WYHY* indicates "trouble" saying that sometimes it does, and sometimes it does not, but "it came to pass *in the days of*..." always means troubles, as in Is. 7 : 1 and Jer. 1 : 3.[5] On II Chron. 32 : 1 and Is. 14 : 24, we have the following:

> *After these things and the truth thereof* (II Chron. 32:1). Rabina said, "After the Holy One ... had anticipated [events] by an oath. For he reasoned thus, "If I say to Hezekiah, 'I will bring Sennacherib and deliver him into your hands,' he will reply, 'I require neither [victory] nor the [antecedent] terror.' Therefore the Holy One ... forestalled him by swearing that he would bring him [as in Is. 14:24]."
> (b. Sanh. 94b)[6]

[1] See my "Religious Uses of History," *History and Theory* 5, 1966, pp. 153-171.
[2] b. Soṭ. 10a.
[3] b. Ber. 3b, with reference to Ps. 119 : 62 and Prov. 7 : 9.
[4] b. Yev. 76a.
[5] b. Meg. 10b. Compare Vol. I, 2nd rev. ed., p. 164.
[6] Trans. Jacob Schachter and H. Freedman, *Sanhedrin* (London, 1948), pp. 636-7, with minor changes.

R. Ashi held that drunkards and those with long hair defile the temple service, and their punishment was decreed by Ezekiel 44 : 9. Ezekiel had found a tradition and stated it as a law.[1] R. Papa interpreted Ezek. 14 : 12 to mean that the bread referred to was baked out of human dung.[2] He said that the high priest Joshua was punished because his sons married wives unfit for the priesthood and he did not prohibit them from doing so, with reference to Zech. 3 : 1.[3]

Skills in expositing Scripture were cultivated in some schools, where exegesis of non-legal texts was taken very seriously. Thus we find that R. Papa and R. Huna b. R. Joshua specialized in *aggadot*:

> One of the rabbis asked R. Kahana about the meaning of Mount *Sinai*, and he could not give a satisfactory reply. He then said to the questioner], "Why do you not frequent [the school of] R. Papa and R. Huna b. R. Joshua, who make a study[4] of *Aggadah*..."
>
> (b. Shab. 89a)

> "I can prove by logical argument [that a creeping thing] is clean. If a snake that kills and causes much [corpse] uncleanness is itself ritually clean, how much more should a creeping thing which does not kill [and cause corpse-uncleanness] be ritually clean..."
>
> (b. ʿEruv. 13b)

We have now cursorily examined the exegetical legacy of several successive generations.[5] My purpose was to see whether signs of development or change, examples of modification of traditions by later generations in response to contemporary needs or insights, or similar significations of the working of historical processes could be located. Our inquiry has been a complete failure. I have found practically no marks of historical development whatever. Nothing said now could not have been said two centuries earlier. The contrary also was the case. Individual sages may have produced a singular and original exegetical legacy, as I think is the case with Rav, R. Joseph, and a few others. My method of working by generations of sages however has precluded discovery of just what those individual legacies consisted of. I have not been impressed by the collections of sayings of individual masters produced by Bacher.[6] Bacher does not sufficiently delve into the lives and situations of the several sages to provide persuasive

[1] b. Sanh. 22b.
[2] b. ʿEruv. 81a.
[3] b. Sanh. 93b.
[4] Lit.: "who look into..."
[5] Vol. II, pp. 188-240, III, pp. 179-192, and IV, pp. 370-384.
[6] *Die Agada der babylonischen Amoräer* (Frankfurt a/M, 1913).

explanations of characteristics peculiar to a given time, sage, or school. For historical inquiry, therefore, the task still lies before us. The conventional repertoire of rabbinical exegesis requires more careful and searching study into the literary-historical bases for its very conventionality. Until we have a clearer idea of who selected sayings for inclusion in authoritative collections, and of what was the basis for such selections, we shall be unable to proceed. For now what we can say for certain is simply that the preserved rabbinical exegesis of Scriptures reveals remarkably little sign of the working of the usual historical processes. That negative result presumably is evidence rather of the editorial work that produced the Talmud than of the original teaching behind it. If we supposed otherwise, it would indicate that no one's mind changed much for three hundred years. I cannot think of a more unlikely conclusion.

XV. Summary and Conclusions

It would be a gross error to overestimate the differences separating the ordinary people from the rabbinical estate.[1] I think Jewish Babylonia knew the distinction between lay and rabbinical ways of behavior. But I do not think that distinction was invariably critical. In general, merely conventional social manners or customs were deepened into spiritual conceptions[2] and magnified by deeply mythic ways of thinking. On the streets of the villages however the ordinary folk would have seen the rabbi as still another holy, therefore, exceptional man to be sure, but heart and soul at one in community with other Jews. The rabbinical ideal was anti-dualistic. No one conceived of two ways of living a holy life, two virtues, or two salvations, but of only one Torah to be studied and observed by all.

That conception did not erase the numerous distinctive characteristics of rabbinical dress, speech, behavior, and, especially, social relationships. But it probably did blunt the cutting edge of rabbinical separateness. The deep concern felt by rabbis for the conduct of ordinary folk moreover led them to teach, criticize, and try to control everyday affairs. That effort produced considerable impact upon daily

[1] Compare George P. Fedotov, *The Russian Religious Mind. Kievan Christianity, The Tenth to the Thirteenth Centuries* (N.Y., 1960), pp. 273-274. Fedotov's work is an exemplary study in the relationships between ordinary Christians, on the one hand, and scholars and saints on the other.

[2] See Fedotov, p. 211, for examples of a similar process.

life, as we shall see, and therefore tended to reduce the inevitable gap between holy man and layman. Nor was the only unifying force the rabbis' faith that "all Israel," not merely saints, prophets, and sages, stood at Sinai and bore common responsibilities.[1] When we review the primarily distinctive characteristics of the school, we see they could not have created unscaleable walls of social or religious difference.

The sages spent a good part of their earlier years in the rabbinical schools, and ordinary folk obviously did not. Yet the schools were not monasteries in the sense that their denizens usually remained within them for the rest of their lives. Furthermore, disciples who left the schools and remained under their discipline did not engage in ascetic disciplines of an outlandish sort, calculated utterly to divide the sages' way of living from that of normal men. They married. They ate regularly and chose edible food, not wormwood or locusts or refuse. They lived in villages, not in the wilderness. They did not make their livelihood through holy vagrancy. Their clothes were not supposed to be tattered or in rags. These differences between encratites, anchorites, hermetics, stylites, and other specific kinds of holy men on the one hand and the rabbis on the other are obvious, therefore all the more important. The comparison between the rabbinical academy and the monastery is suggestive not only for the similarities but especially for the differences. The sages sought out the society of ordinary Jews, as I said, living in the villages, not in the countryside ("wilderness"). Not engaged in begging ("holy vagrancy"), they owned property and were glad of it. They occupied important and permanent positions in the administration of communal life, and so they came into constant and intimate contact with the lives of the common people. That contact was routine. Access to the rabbinical schools remained open to all, and the rabbis actively proselytized within the community to gain new candidates for their schools.[2] Advantages of birth were minimal. In no

---

[1] For an explanation of the salvific force of this conviction, see vol. VI, pp. 401-2.

[2] I am still unsure of the extent of rabbinical control of the primary schools. I assume that where the great academies were located, the primary schools which everyone attended would pretty much have reflected rabbinical ideas about education and that the curriculum would have been set according to the outlines of the "Oral Torah." But the situation outside of a few centers of rabbinical schooling remains obscure to me. If we suppose that people came from outside the centers in Sura, Pumbedita, and the like to study in them, then it seems reasonable to imagine they had been prepared to study at the advanced level of the schools. But systematic study of the forms and procedures of education is still at too primitive a state to come to any firm opinion.

way did the rabbis form a caste or a clan; marriage counted for little.

What, furthermore, did the peculiarities of the rabbinical way of living amount to? A rabbi could eat with any other Jew in Babylonia, within obvious limitations. The biblical taboos about food were widely observed. The differences between the rabbis' interpretation of the biblical food taboos and those put forward by others probably diminished, as in time the rabbis' growing domination made their unique exegeses seem more commonplace. If on the other hand, the conduct of the rabbinical meal, apart from its content, took a form probably characteristic of the circles of sages alone, the singular forms consisted of no hocus-pocus, but of intelligible blessings of food, in Hebrew to be sure,[1] and grace afterward. And the rabbis were willing in theory and practice to teach others just what these blessings and prayers meant. Nothing in the rabbinical ritual of eating was to be kept secret. A person showed himself "ignorant" if he violated the rituals. His remedy was to go to a sage to study and learn, and this is explicitly recommended.

As to language, the rabbis did have their own words for various objects,[2] and knowing these words was a sign of membership in the rabbinical estate. Yet the rabbis certainly spoke the language of the people, not only when among them but also in the schools. We have not got the slightest evidence that the language of the schools was Hebrew and not Aramaic, though fixed *forms* in Hebrew were creatively used, not merely transmitted from earlier times. In any event, apart from the usual difficulties of dialect and local custom, any rabbi could communicate with any outsider, and, what is more important, rabbis made no effort to formulate a secret or private language for themselves, only a distinctive language supposed appropriate to their scholastic needs and social status. They clearly regarded their speech as "more cultivated" or as evidence of better education, but this certainly did not render their language alien to the community at large.

[1] I do not know how much Hebrew would have been known to ordinary folk I cannot think of a single popular saying attributed to the "people" by the sages which is formulated in other than Aramaic of the time and place, but that proves very little. Scriptures required commentary, and when that commentary is given in public contexts, it usually is in Aramaic, as in the sayings of R. Joseph. On the other hand, the simple words of blessings, which were formalized and easily learned, and the fixed liturgy of grace, like the synagogue prayers, I think everyone knew, and these could not have posed insuperable obstacles.

[2] Vol. III, pp. 65-7.

It merely signified one was part of the in-group, therefore had to be all the more comprehensible to outsiders. Eating, clothing, speech—these everyday commonplaces revealed both particularities and commonalities, but all together, the differences do not amount to much. Advice about health and various natural pocesses and functions diverges not at all from this pattern. Eating vegetables before the fourth hour might make anyone's breath smell bad. Restraining one's natural processes could lead to severe ill-health for everyone. Wine made anyone talk too much.

We therefore cannot locate in the petty everyday rituals of "being a rabbi" any really substantially differentiating characteristics but two. The rabbis' social life, first of all, followed forms wholly alien to those of outsiders. The disciple revered the master as a living Torah and humbled himself before him as before God. The outsider honored him as a learned man, fantasized about his magical powers, submitted to his judicial authority, and accepted his communal influence. These were simply not the same thing. On the one hand stood a living myth, on the other, the merely superficial effects of that myth. The disciple of the sages furthermore conformed to personality-traits and behavior patterns which would have been quite unnatural for ordinary folk. He forced himself into a posture of abject humility with implications far beyond what outsiders could have comprehended or accepted. His reverence for the master was little lower than his fear of the Lord. His imitation of the master's deeds and his preservation of the memory of those deeds shaped a religious discipline quite alien to the workaday life of common people. The humility shown to God and to the master supposedly extended to behavior with everyone else, as if the "soul like dust" to the curses of the streets would be better able humbly to serve the demands of heaven. The personality-traits appropriate to piety thus had to be extended from heaven to earth. Historical events and moral virtues not only corresponded to one another but came into contact in the formation of the sage's personality. The honor paid by a disciple to his master and close imitation of his actions consequently constituted the most striking distinction between the social life of the rabbi and that of the outsider. The service of the disciple of the sages to the master was required of the disciple but of no one else, and a particular disciple moreover served a particular master, not a whole coterie of authorities. It therefore became a highly exceptional relationship. One who had studied not only Scripture but also Mishnah remained a boor, learned but no different from a Magus, unless he had also "served" a master through imitation of the master's *way*, subjecting himself to his discipline and that of the schools.

Study, second, separated rabbi from common folk. The reasons were not—quite obviously—that ordinary people did not understand the need for information, that they were entirely ignorant of the world and its way, or that they knew nothing of Jewish traditions. The people knew something of the Scriptures. They listened to the reading of the Torah in the synagogues. Prophetic writings and, for a long time, passages of wisdom literature were regularly read to them. The masses observed the Sabbath, the festivals, the holy days, food and sex taboos. All these observances required knowledge, and the constant exposure to Scripture and to the sages produced considerable knowledge. We therefore cannot speak of the "learning" of the rabbis in total contrast to the "ignorance" of the masses. Unless we accept the rabbis' belief that included in the revelation at Sinai was the Oral Torah they alone possessed, we need not regard the people as "ignorant" at all. The main thing common folk ordinarily did not know which the rabbis always did know was the one thing that made a common man into a rabbi: *"Torah" learned through discipleship*. It therefore begs the question to speak of the *ʿam ha'areẓ* as "ignorant of Judaism." One does not have to exaggerate the educational attainments of the community as a whole to recognize that learning in the rabbinical traditions did not by itself separate the rabbi from other people. What was important was the rabbi's attitude toward his *own* study. Extrinsic qualities deriving from the mythic context transformed the natural actions of learning facts or ideas or memorizing sayings, which anyone might have done, into the ritual actions unique to the rabbi.

Once in the schools and subject to the sages' awesome influence, the ordinary Jew therefore became transformed, entering a new being. In time to come, most ordinary folk would participate in that new life, so that the *way* of the schools would become *law* for the community. For the present, however, the separateness of the rabbinical estate persisted. That separateness produced its own worldly effects. The rabbi was endowed both in his own mind and in the practical life of society with a glorious reward. Insight into the joy they felt in their lives can be derived from Rabina's saying that the rabbis, "those who love God," shall be "as the sun when he goes forth in his might." Through Torah they did not overcome natural death, but they did find serenity and strength in the conviction that Torah and commandments shielded them in this world and promised the blessings of the world to come.

They moreover saw themselves as the intermediaries between heaven and earth, the new priests, able to offer sacrifices more pleasing to heaven than burnt-offerings. They believed they would be able through Torah in time to come to bring on the restoration of the ancient temple and the establishment of the Messianic kingdom of God. For such achievements the reward of a measure of worldly honor was little enough. The respect of ordinary folk for the rabbis, and of sages for one another, quite naturally corresponded to the sages' view of cosmic realities. The cedar, the Leviathan, the ever-flowing stream—these were appropriate similes for the great men of the schools. The glory of the world to come would prove commensurate, for the sage would feast in the splendor of the *Shekhinah*. Meanwhile, the political instrumentalities of Jewry, ever more dominated by rabbis, would be turned to the advantage of sages. Torah was its own reward, but among its by-products were various tax-exemptions, both real and merely sought-after, and some advantages in court as well.

Of greater consequence were the supernatural powers, including magical ones, supposed to have been exercised by sages. Heaven listened to the prayers of all men, but in meting out blessings, heaven would pay rabbis special heed because of their merits. Sages both decreed communal fasts for rain and also prayed for it, and if rain did not come, regarded it as a lapse in their own, as much as in the community's collective theurgical capacities. Heaven paid special attention to what was said in the schools. The spirits of the dead of ancient times oversaw scholastic discussions and would make an appearance in order to correct erroneous or dishonorable opinions. Everyone believed in witchcraft, sorcery, and other forms of magic. The rabbis claimed to have special powers in these matters, quite independent of the will of heaven, because of their mastery not only of the Torah but also of the Torah's own power. They could therefore issue a reliably effective curse, lay on the evil eye, and compel demons to their service. Joseph the demon served R. Papa, just as Abaye had compelled 'Igrath, queen of demons, to do his will. So stated the authoritative, normative traditions of the schools, compiled by the editors of the Babylonian Talmud.

In this regard, as I have emphasized, the rabbis differed not at all from other holy men of their time and place. Where they differed was in attributing their claim of reliably effective supernatural and magical power to their knowledge of "Torah": "Take need of Naḥmani and his Torah," 'Igrath had said. In this generation, Mar b. R. Ashi could summon a demon to court, call him to account for his tort, excommunicate him, and demand an explanation for his failure to pay damages. R. Papa could likewise order his demon to go to fetch water for the convenience of his household. Rabbis were no different from others who believed that dreams not only conveyed important information, but also could affect the future. They differed *if* they supposed that sages uniquely held conversations with angels, received visions including divine messages, and talked with heavenly creatures.[1] They certainly supposed that singular to the traditions of "Torah" was accurate information both on the interpretation of signs, omens, and visions in dreams and on necessary measures to be taken on account of such visions. They further held that the affairs of the academies and their politics were predicted in dreams and that such predictions were dependable.

We must take special note of the skills normally common to savants in Babylonia and yet not claimed or exercised by rabbis. As we saw, while the sages generally accepted the scientific character of astrology and believed that astrological realities affected Israel's fate as much as the nations', no sage in this period, indeed none for almost two centuries, presented himself as particularly knowledgeable about the stars. No sage we know of cast a horoscope. None made predictions based upon the stars, though as we have seen, they prognosticated upon other bases. We also observed that rabbis never told stories about their miraculous attainments in healing arts. Unlike Christian monks, they practiced neither medicine nor faith-healing. We have not now got a single account of a rabbi's wonderful cure of a sick man. They did believe that reciting Scriptures might effect a cure or serve as a prophylactic. In earlier times, particularly in the third century, however, important authorities, especially Samuel, had claimed to have therapeutic skills and astrological knowledge.[2]

How can we account for what seems to be a remarkable change in the portrayal of the later rabbis? Samuel and presumably others of his generation were brought up in a community much influenced by Babylonian Hellenistic-Iranian culture, wholly open to its skills and values, deeply affected by its political life. The early Babylonian masters pursued studies characteristic of the Babylonian academic environment of the several Semitic, as well as Iranian and Hellenistic communi-

---

1 But I am not clear on this point, since I have no evidence that the sages thought their supernatural skills in communication were unique.

2 Vol. II, pp. 134-144, 147-150.

ties, including of course both medicine and astrology, foremost fields of Babylonian science. Samuel was reported to have had a number of conversations about astrology with 'Avlat, a Persian sage. The rabbinical schools of Samuel's day were relatively new, probably not a century old. Their final curriculum and forms were not yet established. Now, two centuries later, we see that the schools seem far more closed to the sciences of the milieu than earlier. I think the reason lies in a change in the cultural configuration both of the Jewish community and of the schools themselves. On the one hand, unlike Parthian times, the community was isolated from Sasanian politics and international affairs, and such isolation had continued for several hundred years. On the other hand, the schools were ever more engrossed in the traditional sciences. The Palestinian inheritance, on which these sciences were mostly based, included little attention to medicine and astrology, the latter of which was looked upon with little favor by important Palestinian masters.

I think it striking moreover that not a single story of a substantive friendship between a rabbi and a non-Jewish sage or king is told in the late fourth- and fifth-century strata. Samuel and 'Avlat (not to mention Shapur I[1]), Rav Judah and Abidarna,[2] Rava and Bar Sheshakh as well as the mother of Shapur II,[3] to mention four relationships—these have no substantial counterpart.[4] Since the earlier stories were preserved, we may assume those authorities who told them did not look with disfavor on such exceptional relationships, though ordinary folk were supposed to keep their distance. And the converse is also the case. We noted the keen interest of Aphrahat, among other Babylonian Christians, in confronting the issues and ideas of Judaism.[5] By contrast, the Seleucian consistories' records reveal no equivalent interest, only generalized and conventional references to "the Jews."[6] In all, I find little evidence of sustained and productive interrelationships among different groups such as probably existed in the third century and into

---

[1] Vol. II, pp. 64-72.

[2] Vol. III, p. 30.

[3] Vol. IV, pp. 35-39, 63-64.

[4] Except for the single story about Yazdagird and the exilarch. From this story, we learn that the emperor could supposedly quote Scripture. We do not learn about conversations about mutual interests in politics, as with Shapur I, astrology, as with 'Avlat, piety, theology, and the world-to-come, as with Bar Sheshakh, or other supernatural matters, as with 'Ifra Hormizd.

[5] Vol. IV, pp. 20-27.

[6] Above, p. 121, n. 4.

the fourth. The first Shapur's policy of cultural openness had produced considerable exchange between Iranian and other civilizations in Babylonia. The equivalent policies of Khusro I probably did not, at least so far as Jewry was concerned. Part of the reason, as I said, was doubtless the schools' greater concentration on the inherited traditions, which were in process of redaction, and the consequent monopoly of the interests and themes of those traditions upon the mind of the sages.

Our consideration of the theology, liturgy, and biblical exegeses of the rabbis produced few satisfying results. I think the reason is only in part the paucity of information, for my dissatisfaction derived not only from the limited amount of material, but also from the one-dimensional and inadequate results produced by my study of it. I cannot point out a single idea, expressed through theology, prayer, or Scriptural commentary, which either was unique to this period or in some clear way even related to the particular contemporary interests or events of the schools, not to mention of the Jewish community as a whole. It seems unlikely that the severe conformity imposed by the schools on disciples stifled any sort of original contribution. The contrary is the case in the study of the law, even more so in the actual government of the Jewish community, and it is unreasonable to suppose that creative impulses could not or did not thrive in the ways approved by the rabbinical estate. The very existence of the Babylonian Talmud itself, the product of just this period, testifies to the contrary. I therefore suppose that a serious flaw in my method has impeded the effort to derive historically illuminating information. That flaw probably derives from concentration on the generation as a whole. I had assumed that particular concerns or interests provoked by historical events might be revealed in the concentration of a generation's sayings on one theme rather than another, in the formulation of prayers about a specific concern, or in obsession with a given biblical character and in what was said about him. It is now clear that a better way lies through the study of individual masters and groups of masters in particular schools, rather than through the isolation of sayings by whole generations. The reason in part is that the final editing obliterated whatever marks of change, development, and pertinence to daily events may have been found in the original materials. But if that is so, the other part of the reason may be that in the consideration of theological, liturgical, and exegetical questions the individual sages probably served chiefly as continuators, not at all as innovators. They thus left little possibility for articulated response to contemporary issues or discrete problems. In any event, the question must stand over for further study.

The "Judaism" of the rabbis was now in no degree normative, and speaking descriptively, we of course have no right to call the schools "elite." Whatever their aspirations for the future and pretensions in the present, the rabbis, though powerful and influential, constituted a mere minority, seeking to exercise authority without much political support, to dominate without substantial means of coercion. What they wanted to accomplish however was the formation of the kingdom of priests and holy people demanded at Sinai, and to do so according to the revelation of Sinai as they alone possessed it. So admittedly a description of the rabbinical schools is hardly a portrait of the religious life of Babylonian Jewry. Yet, in my view, the rabbis did more and more set the standard, the golden measure, the royal way.[1]

[1] As I said above (pp. xv-xvi), the literary achievements of this period, including the redaction of the Babylonian Talmud, require study in their own terms. I have here omitted all reference to the formation of the Babylonian Talmud because in the future I plan to devote myself to that problem.

CHAPTER TWO

THE RABBINICAL COURT AND DAILY LIFE

I. Introduction

The rabbi gave his best energies to the study and application of the Mishnah, and held his work as judge and student of the law to be the most consequential *religious* activity. His rhetorical, exegetical and hermeneutical studies of the Mishnah, like his theological inquiry, reflected little of the history of Babylonian Jewry. They centered upon timeless and theoretical academic interests. Mishnah-study had its own rules and requirements, unrelated to the realities of daily life. Whether or not Babylonian conditions greatly affected it I cannot say. The few instances in which theoretical law seemed to bear some relevance to practical life appeared to me ambiguous and equivocal. As we have seen, discussions by the chief authorities of this generation dominated laws dealing with the backsliding priest, and yet a plausible conjecture about underlying political and social realities seemed hardly possible. I remain quite unconvinced that one can easily reduce complex legal discussions to social, economic, or political necessities.[1] Legal theory imposes its own dynamic. Sources come down to us from a later period, and we do not know why a particular discussion is attached to a given law, or what has been omitted. So I have not yet found a way to recover historically useful information from academic discussions about the Mishnah and points of law derived from it. That is not to suggest that when the law was applied in the courts, the Mishnaic code did not determine it, for the contrary was the case, as we shall see. I know of no instance in which the law of the Mishnah was purposely ignored, set aside, or even drastically reinterpreted, in making court decisions.[2] The Mishnah was the rabbinical law code, and there was no other. Wherever the rabbis could judge a case, they did so according to the Mishnah, as faithfully and accurately as they knew how. Judging cases frequently required them to restudy points of theoretical law. There must have been a constant interplay between the courts and the

[1] Above, pp. 202-213.
[2] Except in capital cases.

academies, and doubtless new cases would require the academies to consider heretofore unknown or unexamined points of law. Indeed, the reason we have case-reports is that the academicians studied the law necessary to judge them, or studied the cases to see how authoritative judges had understood the law. The cases before us are invariably cited in Talmudic literature not because they were intrinsically interesting or important, but because they might illuminate an issue of commentary upon the Mishnah or clarify a legal principle. I think it likely that case reports were originally preserved by the several courts. The predominance of R. Naḥman's cases as reported by Rava suggests that the court records of the exilarchic jurisdiction were utilized, because of its, and R. Naḥman's, exceptional power and his jurisprudential distinction. They eventually were preserved in preference to the records of other courts, but in a form much different from what they would have exhibited to begin with.[1]

While the extent of the rabbis' actual control of matters of piety and religious observance, including various taboos, finally appeared unclear to me, I have no doubt whatever that their courts decisively judged all kinds of civil matters. They were powerful, and their power is well-attested. Rabbinical courts decided cases deriving from alterations of personal status through marriage or divorce, and all litigations over property (of which changes in personal status merely constituted a part), such as crimes against property, civil torts and damages, contested titles, claims, and inheritances, commercial transactions of all kinds, the issuance and certification of all manner of documents and deeds, and the like. The whole range of internal litigations which the Sasanians left in Jewish hands devolved upon the rabbinical courts. Blessings and curses, promises of male children, threats of death or suffering in the world to come, and the like—these no longer occur. The rabbis decided, and then flogged, excommunicated, or otherwise effected their decrees. We shall speak no more of rabbinical influence, for here it was authority, and not merely prestige, which they possessed and exerted. We shall therefore briefly survey the various case reports produced by the courts of Rav's and Samuel's students. I shall provide only so much information on general legal principles as is needed to understand the subject-matter of the cases, and in each instance add further references to issues discussed in the academies which, I believe, pertained to the activities of the courts.

[3] Below, pp. 305-312.

My effort is not, as I have emphasized, to offer a history of Jewish law, or of the character of Mishnaic text-studies and commentary, but only to derive from legal data as much information as I can for the understanding of Babylonian Jewish social and religious history.[1]

II. Personal Status: Marriage, Levirate Connection, Divorce

Although the rabbis had no special place in the rite of marriage, their influence on the institution was considerable, because the law specified that betrothal was effected through an exchange of property.[2] Whenever property passed from hand to hand, numerous legal issues arose, involving, for example, an assessment of its value for the purposes of betrothal, an issue the rabbinical courts frequently decided, and the provision of a marriage-contract, which protected the woman in the event of divorce by providing her with a year's maintenance.

The only contemporary case involving a suit on an act of betrothal pertained to a woman who was selling silk skeins. A man grabbed one, and she demanded its return. He said, "If I give it to you, will you become betrothed to me?" She took it and remained silent. The case came to R. Naḥman, who ruled that she can claim, "I took my own property back."[3] R. Naḥman insisted on the absolute irrevocability of the gift for purposes of betrothal. Two other adjudications pertained to the responsibilites of a man to his deceased betrothed, and the claim of a man that his bride was not a virgin:

> R. Naḥman, ʿUlla and Abimi son of R. Papi once sat at their studies, with R. Ḥiyya b. Ammi sitting with them, and a man came before them whose betrothed wife had died [before the marriage]. "Go and bury her," they said to him, "or pay her marriage-contract on her account."
> (b. Ket. 53a)[4]
>
> A man came before R. Hamnuna and claimed, "I found an open door."

[1] The further question of whether the rabbinical courts in this period extended the range of their jurisdiction will be discussed below, p. 334.

[2] Of the three means of betrothal specified in Mishnah Qid. 1.1, that through an exchange of money was enforced in rabbinical courts. We know quite specifically that they disapproved of betrothal through sexual relations, and in the earlier period flogged people who did it that way. The absence of such cases for this period may indicate either that the rabbinical viewpoint was ever more widely accepted among the people or that the people did not consult the rabbis. For cases in the earlier generation, see vol. II pp. 268-274.

[3] b. Qid. 13a. See Boaz Cohen, *Jewish and Roman Law* (N.Y. 1966), I, 279ff.

[4] Compare R. Hamnuna, y. Ket. 8.11.

He said, "Lash him with palm-switches. Harlots of Mabrakta lie open to him." (b. Ket. 10a)

In both cases, the claim involved the payment of money, in the former, for the burial expenses, in the latter, for the expense of the marriage-contract.

There were in addition numerous discussions of the laws of betrothal; Rava in the name of R. Naḥman said that a pledged dowry does not effect betrothal,[1] and cited him concerning testimony to a betrothal;[2] betrothal of a minor without her father's knowledge was discussed by R. Naḥman, Kahana, and Hamnuna;[3] R. Joseph b. Manyumi in the name of R. Naḥman said that where it is customary to return the gifts accompanying a betrothal, one does so with the token of betrothal itself.[4] R. Huna discussed the benediction at the celebration of a marriage.[5] A dispute involving adjudication of the terms of the marriage contract came before R. Naḥman.[6] Rav Judah explained the development of the marriage-contract, dating its clause, that all the husband's property was pledged for payment of the marriage-contract, to the time of R. Simeon b. Shetaḥ.[7]

The rabbis also ruled on whether a marriage remained valid in the case of adultery, and whether a woman might remarry under various circumstances. We have already noted that R. Naḥman ruled on remarriage in the exilarch's family.[8] We have several other cases:

A man once went around saying, "Who of the family of Ḥasa is here? Ḥasa has drowned." R. Naḥman ruled, "The fish must have eaten him," and his wife was permitted to remarry. (b. Yev. 121b)

A man was once drowned at Qarna and hauled up three days later at Be Hedya. R. Dimi of Nehardea permitted his wife to marry. (b. Yev. 121a)

A certain woman used to wash her husband's hands every time they had intercourse. One day she brought him water to wash. He said to her, "Nothing happened today." She replied, "If so, it must have been one of the gentile perfume-salesmen. If not you, it was one of them." R. Naḥman said, "She has set her eyes elsewhere, and her declaration has no substance." (b. Ned. 91a-b)

---

1 b. Qid. 8b, and see also *ibid.* 19a.
2 *ibid.* 43a. See also Rav Judah on the same subject, b. Qid. 65b.
3 *ibid.* 44b-45a.
4 b. B.B. 145a.
5 b. Ket. 7a. See above, p. 161.
6 b. Ket. 54a.
7 b. Ket. 82b. R. Huna made an exegesis of its language, y. Yev. 15.3.
8 *ibid.* 60b, see above p. 63.

A second such case judged by R. Naḥman involved a woman who acted irately toward her husband, with a similar result.[1] R. Naḥman ruled that if a woman claimed that her husband is dead *and* that she should be permitted to marry again, she must be granted permission and given her marriage-contract, but if she merely demanded her marriage-contract, she was to be denied.[2] I see no reason why such rules were not enforced in the courts, since the cases above leave no doubt that rabbis ruled effectively in matters of marriage and remarriage.[3]

We noted[4] that the rabbis had very strong ideas about proper conduct between men and woman. A man must not come into contact with a woman, however young or old, and other restrictions were placed to insure chaste behavior. Such moral dicta shaped the decisions of the courts, and in time came to influence the conduct of the people. If, for example, a man claimed that he had not found his bride a virgin, the rabbis assumed that he knew more than proper conduct would have permitted him to know about female anatomy, and hence punished him for licentious behavior. If he could not succeed in making such a claim, as is clear in this case, then in the future, the conduct of others—or at least, their willingness to go to court—would have been affected. But on the whole, it is difficult to see a very direct relationship between the court-actions and effective laws governing marriage, on the one hand, and the rabbis' repressive attitudes toward sex, on the other.[5] The authority of the courts was not to legislate morality, but to decide cases, and the cases mostly involved litigations over property, such as whether a man has to pay the burial expenses of his betrothed, the enforcement of various provisions of the marriage-contract, what constitutes a proper act of betrothal, and the like. These were narrowly legal issues, and did not leave much leeway for the inclusion or enforcement of dicta about moral questions. It was only in the supposed claim

---

[1] b. Ned. 91b.

[2] b. Yev. 117a.

[3] Note also b. B.B. 51b, Rav Judah on payment of the cost of a wife's purchases; b. Ket. 53a, R. Naḥman on whether a woman who sold her marriage-contract to her husband retains the right to the clause reserving inheritance to male children; b. Ket. 28a, R. Sheshet on the collection of a marriage contract by the divorced wife of a priest; b. Ket. 5a-b, Rav Judah on whether women who have been kidnapped are permitted to return to their husbands; b. B.Q. 8b, R. Huna, a woman can say to her husband, I shall not be maintained by you and I shall not work for you, etc.

[4] Above, pp. 142-145.

[5] And see below, pp. 283-286.

of adultery that R. Naḥman was able to decide a broader matter. The wife apparently claimed she had committed adultery. He interpreted the claim as a mere desire for a new marriage, and refused to prohibit the marriage from continuing as before. So whether or not "the sound of a woman's voice is licentious" and the like, when it came to a practical case, R. Naḥman, who knew and supposedly agreed with Samuel's opinions, followed his own judgment, and declined to interpret the woman's behavior as the rabbinical value-system would lead us to suppose he would.

The Scriptures had specified the requirement for the sister-in-law widowed without children to marry her late husband's brother. The Jews in Babylonia were absolutely meticulous about keeping that rule, and they performed the necessary ceremony of *ḥaliẓah*[1] in rabbinical courts. I think the reason is two-fold, first, because of the explicitness of Scripture itself, and second, because of the stress upon the purity of family genealogy which characterized Babylonian Judaism. The Jews were concerned to produce children who would have impeccable ancestry from the viewpoint of Jewish law. The rabbis were believed to possess accurate records about genealogy. Hence the people's interests and the rabbis' power coincided. We have very numerous cases in this generation testifying to complete rabbinical control over the ceremony of *ḥaliẓah* and over the administration of the laws concerning levirate connections, such as the following (among many cases):

> R. Kahana said, "I was once standing before Rav Judah, when he said to me, 'Come, get on this bundle of reeds so you may be included in a quorum of five [for a *ḥaliẓah* ritual].'" "Why five?" he was asked. "In order to publicize the matter," he replied. R. Samuel b. Judah once stood before Rav Judah, when he said to him, "Come get on this bundle of reeds..." (b. Yev. 101b)

The rabbis also reported seeing Rav Judah's actions in connection with *ḥaliẓah*.[2] Additionally, Rav Judah drew up the document necessary for certifying the proper fulfillment of the ritual:

> Rav Judah ordained [the following language] for a deed of *ḥaliẓah*: "We certify that so-and-so daughter of so-and-so brought before us into court her brother-in-law so-and-so, and we have ascertained him to be the paternal brother of the deceased. We told him, 'If you wish to contract the levirate marriage do so, and if not, incline toward her your right foot.' He inclined toward her his right foot and she removed his

[1] The ceremony replacing the actual marriage with a formal act of rejection.

[2] b. Yev. 102b.

> shoe from off his foot and spat out before him a spittle which has been seen by the court upon the ground." R. Ḥiyya b. 'Ivya in the name of Rav Judah concluded the formula as follows, "And we read before them what is written in the Book of the law of Moses." (b. Yev. 39b)

Rav Judah also quoted the text of the document of refusal [of a girl who comes of age and rejects the betrothal arranged for her before that time]:

> Rav Judah said (others say, it was taught in a beraita), "Originally a certification of refusal was drafted, 'I do not like him and I do not want him and I do not desire to be married to him.' When it was seen that it was too long a formula and it was feared that people would mistake it for a document of divorce, the following was instituted, 'On such-and-such day, so-and-so the daughter of so-and-so made a declaration of refusal in our presence.'" (b. Yev. 107b-108a)

It is clear that Rav Judah set the former formula, but in the latter case, he merely reported the necessary language. Hence one may conclude that before his time, the document to be issued in connection with a *ḥaliẓah*-ritual was not standardized. So the rabbinical courts shaped the ceremony by requiring a court-provided document attesting to its proper forms. If so, one may suppose that earlier, no document was issued, and now, with growing rabbinical power the rabbis were able to control matters.

By contrast to the simple application of the laws, academic discussion produced complicated questions and theoretical decisions, as the rabbis explored all kinds of possibilities unrelated to practical issues before their courts. Rabbinical discussions of this, as other matters involved three kinds of questions: the first and simplest (and normally settled by the end of Tannaitic times) was, What is the Scriptural support for such-and-such a practice? R. Sheshet cited a Tannaitic tradition originating with R. Eleazar b. Azariah that a woman subject to levirate marriage has the right to decline to marry her brother-in-law, but may demand a ceremony of *ḥaliẓah* instead, derived from Deut. 25:4-5.[1] Second, the Mishnah's legal principles and the authoritative basis of its rulings were explicated. Such issues in this generation involved the document of refusal, cited above; the discussion of R. Naḥman's report on R. Adda b. Ahavah's and R. Ḥana's discussions on the

[1] b. Yev. 4a. See also b. Sanh. 49b, Rav Judah on how to perform the commandment of *ḥaliẓah*; b. Yev. 60b, R. Huna on Num. 31:17; b. Yev. 54b, R. Huna on Deut. 25:5; b. Yev. 21a, Rav Judah on Eccles. 12:9, proof of the prohibitions of relations in the second degree.

Mishnah, "If a man was married to a minor and to a deaf woman, cohabitation with one of them does not exempt her rival," which, they said, applies only to a case where the widows became subject to him through a brother of his who was of sound senses,[1] and the like. Similarly, R. Naḥman taught Rava about the requirement for witnesses to a ceremony of *ḥaliẓah* and *mi'un* (refusal), citing Tannaitic opinions in the matter.[2] Third, academic rulings not related directly to Mishnah-commentary and questions raised and discussed mainly by later academicians occupied much attention. Such rulings include Rav Judah's, that one in sleep cannot acquire his sister-in-law;[3] R. Sheshet's on the division of property in a levirate marriage;[4] Rav Judah's, that if a woman awaiting levirate marriage died, the levir cannot marry her mother,[5] and others. Questions posed in the academies, or to them from outsiders, include the following:

> Rav Judah asked R. Sheshet, "What is the law in regard to the rival of a woman whom her former husband remarried after her second married, and died?" (b. Yev. 11b)

> R. Ḥisda asked R. Joseph, "Did you hear from Rav Judah whether a betrothed orphan is entitled to maintenance or not?" R. Sheshet was asked, "Is a minor who has refused [the marriage made before her maturity arranged by her father or brother] entitled to maintenance or not?" (b. Ket. 53b)

> The men of Bairi[6] asked R. Sheshet, "Is a woman who is of the second grade of kinship to her husband but not to her levir entitled to claim her marriage-contract from the levir or not?..." He replied, "You have learned this (in a Tannaitic tradition)..." (b. Yev. 85a)

> R. Sheshet was asked, "What is the law in respect of one witness (who testifies that the husband is dead) in the case of a sister-in-law (whose husband died without issue)?..." He replied, "You have learned (in the Mishnah)..." (b. Yev. 96b)

These cases all obviously involve academicians, except for the question of the 'men of Bairi.' The reply, citing a Tannaitic tradition, like the final one quoting a Mishnah, would suggest that the inquiry came from the local academy, and not from the streets, for the sage reminded the questioners that they had studied the matter in school.

---

[1] b. Yev. 110b. There were many other Mishnaic discussions in this generation.
[2] *ibid.* 101b.
[3] b. Yev. 53b-54a.
[4] b. Ket. 82a.
[5] b. Yev. 17b.
[6] Obermeyer, p. 308.

The rabbis' control of divorce procedures was based upon three facts. Their courts enforced the payment of marriage-contract settlements. They had the right to approve or disqualify documents of divorce. And they decreed who might, and might not remarry. The Scriptural injunction that the husband give a bill of divorce was understood by the rabbis to mean that the document prescribed by the rabbinic law must be handed over. For the academic mind, the various ways in which such 'handing over' could be effected produced numerous and ingenious legal queries. But there can be no doubt whatever that the rabbis' theorizing was based upon a wide range of practical experience in enforcing the law. The cases judged by this generation included the following:

A woman came before R. Naḥman [with the plea that he order a divorce on the ground of her husband's impotence]. When he told her, "The commandment of being fruitful and multiplying does not apply to you," she replied, "Does not a woman like myself require a staff in her hand and a hoe for digging her grave?" [That is, children to maintain her and provide for her burial]. "In such a case," he replied, "we certainly compel [the husband to grant a divorce *and* pay the marriage-contract.]" (b. Yev. 65b)

R. Sheshet once compelled a man to consent to give a bill of divorce... Rav Judah once forced the son-in-law of R. Jeremiah Bira'ah to give his wife a bill of divorce, and he cancelled it, whereupon he forced him again. He cancelled it again, and he forced him to give it, and said to the witnesses, "Stuff pumpkins into your ears and write it..." (b. Git. 34a)

A certain man threw a document to his wife and it fell between jars. Afterwards a *mezuzah* was found there. R. Naḥman said, "It is not common to find a *mezuzah* among jars. [Hence that is what the man threw, and not a bill of divorce.]" (b. Git. 19b)

A certain woman appealed to R. Huna [to force payment of her marriage-contract]. He said to her, "What can I do for you, for Rav would not enforce payment of a marriage-contract to a widow?" She said, "Is not the only reason the suspicion that perhaps I have already received part of it? By the Lord of Hosts I swear that I have not received a penny." R. Huna said, "Rav would admit that where the widow takes the oath of her own free will, we enforce payment." A certain woman appealed to Rabbah b. R. Huna. He said, "What can I do for you, since Rav and my father would not enforce payment to a widow of her marriage-contract?" She said to him, "At least grant me maintenance." He replied, "You are not entitled to it, for Rav Judah said in Samuel's name, 'If a woman claims her marriage-contract in the court, she has no claim to maintenance.'" She said to him, "Turn his seat upside down, he gives me both authorities!" They turned his seat over [fulfilling the curse] and put it straight again, but even so he did not escape an illness. Rav Judah said to R. Jeremiah Bira'ah, "Impose a vow on her in the court, and administer an oath outside of it, and see that the report reaches my ears, since I want to make this a precedent." (b. Git. 35a)

These case reports testify to the fact that the rabbis were able not merely to *inspect* bills of divorce, but also to decree that husbands should issue them in certain circumstances.[1] They were prepared to use the full authority of their courts to enforce such orders. They were also called upon to rule about difficult cases, and were asked to require the payment of marriage settlements.

The following cases indicate that the rabbis were the authoritative judges of the validity of divorce documents, and show the close interplay between practical authority and Mishnah-exegesis:

As Rav said to his scribe, R. Huna said to his, "When you are in Shili, write, 'at Shili' even though you were commissioned in Hini, and when in Hini, write 'in Hini,' even though commissioned in Shili..." A certain bill of divorce was dated by the term of office of the *astandar*[2] of Kashkar.[3] R. Naḥman son of R. Ḥisda sent to Rabbah to ask how to deal with it... (b. Git. 80a-b)

A bill of divorce was once found in the court of R. Huna in which it was written, "In Shavire a place by the canal of Rakis," and R. Huna said, "The fear that there may be two such places is to be taken into account." R. Ḥisda said to Rabbah, "Go and look it up carefully, because tonight R. Huna will ask you about it," and he went and looked up and found that the Mishnah teaches, 'Any document which has passed through a court is to be returned [because if the writer had not meant it to be delivered, he would not have brought it to court for confirmation]...' (b. Git. 27)[4]

Without such a case, one might suppose that the Mishnah-commentary was purely theoretical, or that the rabbis were inventing problems to test the ingenuity of their students. The fact that here an applied law actually produced a case requiring further study of the Mishnah should make the contrary clear. While no cases testify to it, such a saying as the following was probably enforced:

R. Ḥisda required [the appropriate declaration that he had witnessed the preparation of a document of divorce] to be made by bearers from

[1] See also R. Naḥman, b. Ket. 77a, on forcing the issuance of bills of divorce.
[2] Obermeyer, p. 92, *astand-dar*.
[3] Capital of Mesene.
[4] See also b. B.M. 18a-b, 20a-b.

> Ctesiphon to Veh-Ardashir, but not vice versa... The reason is that the people of Veh-Ardashir go to Ctesiphon to market, and the inhabitants of Ctesiphon are familiar with their signatures, but not vice versa, because the people of Veh-Ardashir are busy with their marketing. Rabbah b. Abbuha required [such a declaration if the document was brought] from one side of the street to the other; R. Sheshet from one block to another... (b. Git. 6a)

Similarly, R. Ḥanin told how R. Kahana had brought a document from Sura to Nehardea (or the reverse) and asked Rav whether he was supposed to attest to its preparation or not.[1] The report of such a court procedure obviously is quite as valuable as one of a court action. Rabbis similarly ruled on the validity of divorces under other circumstances:

> A certain man went into the synagogue and found a teacher of children, his son, and a third man sitting there. He said, "I want two of you to write a bill of divorce for my wife." Before the bill of divorce was given the teacher died. The question arose, "Do people make a son their agent in place of his father [and hence was it a valid document] or not?" R. Naḥman ruled... (b. Git. 66a)

Had we no such a case report, we might have assumed that the abstruse legal issue was an invention of the academies, rather than the result of an actual event. The rabbis similarly judged difficult matters in connection with the collection of marriage-contracts after divorce.[2] Hence we may conclude that many points of law stated apodictically, as in the following, in fact relate to practical issues:

> If a man said to two persons, "Tell the scribe to write and do you sign"--R. Ḥisda said, "It would be valid, but should not be done". Rabbah b. Bar Ḥanah said, "It is valid and may be done." R. Naḥman said, "It is valid but should not be done." Rabbah said, "It is valid and may not be done..." Rav Judah made a decree that in a bill of divorce [which the husband had ordered with the words] *all of you*, the agents should insert, "He said to us, 'Write either all of you or any one of you. Sign either all of you or any two of you. Convey all of you or any one of you...'" (b. Git. 67b)

The decree of Rav Judah was doubtless enforced, eliminating complex legal questions and simplifying the administration of divorce law.

Legal dicta relate to the grounds for a compulsory issuance of a bill of divorce;[3] to what is the law if a man writes a bill of divorce on a gold

[1] b. Git. 6a-b.

[2] b. Ket. 80a, Rav Judah, reported by 'the judges of Pumbedita,' meaning R. Papa b. Samuel.

[3] E.g., R. Ḥisda, b. Ket. 75a; R. Huna, b. Ket. 48a, etc.

plate and gives it as both the bill of divorce and payment of the marriage-contract;[1] to various conditions under which a bill of divorce is delivered to the woman;[2] to the interpretation of the language of a bill of divorce;[3] to the acceptability of various claims in court with reference to whether a woman was or was not actually divorced;[4] to whether a bill of divorce may be used more than once;[5] to where the witnesses sign a complex instrument of divorce;[6] and to why three witnesses are there required.[7] Such rulings sometimes emerged mainly from discussions of the Mishnah or questions raised in the academies, but they pertained in the end to the practical affairs of the courts.

III. Conduct of Family Affairs

In assessing the influence of the rabbis over popular life, one has to keep in mind both what judges could do, and also what no court could *ever* accomplish. On the one hand, their power to force a man to divorce his wife under certain specified conditions gave the rabbis considerable power to influence a marriage, and to protect the rights and sensibilities of a woman against excesses. Similarly, should marriages come to an end, they had great authority over the practical legal steps to be taken, the preparation and delivery of documents, the arrangement of marriage-settlements ensuring the future maintenance of the woman, and the like. But these all represent extreme cases, when something has gone so far wrong as to come before them in their capacity as lawyers and judges. They had ideals for the normal marriage which would not come to their courts at any time. They tried to affect everyday life even though the things they wanted were beyond the capacity of judges and lawyers to achieve. It was one thing to deal with miscreants and recalcitrants and the extraordinary situations created by them. It was quite another to influence those who ordinarily kept the law, but whose sins, if they did not, were beyond the law's capacity to punish or repair. It was here that the reputation and influence of the rabbis carried more

---

1 Rava asked R. Naḥman, b. Git. 20b.

2 R. Ḥisda vs. Rav Judah, b. Git. 78b; R. Ḥisda, b. B.M. 7a.

3 R. Huna in b. A.Z. 37a, compare y. Git. 4.3, "Why do we specify the date of a bill of divorce?"

4 R. Hamnuna, b. Ket. 22b, b. Git. 64b, R. Ḥisda vs. R. Huna in b. Git. 64a, with reference to the Mishnah.

5 b. Git. 32b, R. Naḥman vs. R. Sheshet. See also b. Qid. 59b.

6 b. B.B. 160a, R. Huna and R. Ḥisda.

7 Rami b. Ezekiel, re Deut. 19:15, why do three have to sign it, *ibid.*

weight than their legal authority. The power of the court thus extended over the abnormal and irregular, but the influence of the rabbi as a man of piety, learning, and sanctity touched the normal and routine.

We have considerated many sayings on the proper conduct between men and woman above,[1] but a considerable number of these sayings seemed to apply to the proper conduct of the sage alone. Of a more general applicability is the following:

> R. Isaac b. Ḥanina in the name of R. Huna said, "All kinds of work which a wife performs for her husband, a menstruant may perform for hers, except the mixing of the cup (of wine), the making of the bed, and the washing of his face, hands, and feet." (b. Ket. 4b)

There was little the rabbis could do to make certain that the wife did not perform such duties. Similarly their view on the proper frequency and time for sexual intercourse was hardly actionable:

> 'That brings forth its fruit in its season' (Ps. 1:3). Rav Judah, or R. Huna, or R. Naḥman said, "This refers to him who has sexual relations every Friday night." (b. Ket. 62b)

The statement preceding the above was Rav Judah's in Samuel's name, that *disciples* are required to have sexual relations every Friday night. The saying attached to a Scripture was of broader intent, requiring everyone to do the same. R. Huna held that a guest is forbidden to have sexual relations, based upon I Sam. 1:19, "And they rose up in the morning... and came to their house in Ramah, and Elkanah knew Hannah his wife..." On this R. Huna commented, "Only then but not before."[2] He also said, "The Jews are holy and do not have sexual relations in the day-time."[3] Such matters as these were well beyond the jurisdiction of rabbinical courts, but not the influence of the rabbis.

I think it unlikely that the courts could do much to force husbands to maintain their families. Evidence derives from the following case:

> When people came before Rav Judah [with a case of non-support] he would tell them, "A *Yarod* (jackal?) bears children and throws them upon the townspeople." When people came before R. Ḥisda, he would say, "Turn a mortar for him upside down in public and have someone stand and say, 'The raven cares for its young but that man does not care for his children.'" (b. Ket. 496)

It was enacted at Usha, a century and a half earlier, that a man must

---

[1] pp. 142ff
[2] b. Ket. 65a.
[3] *ibid.* 65b, also b. Shab. 86a, Nid. 17a.

maintain his minor sons and daughters. These cases indicate that the rabbi did not force a father to maintain his children, even though in theory he was able to do so. Whether he did not because the court lacked effective power cannot be said for certain. The Talmud specifies that if one is wealthy, he may be so compelled, but brings a case dating only from the fourth century. It may have been that poverty prevented very effective court action, but if that that were the case, the effort publicly to shame the man could have backfired, since his obvious inability to do what the judges thought right would have won for him the sympathy of onlookers, to whose opinion the courts were appealing. Hence I think it likely that the courts did not, in this period, do more than appeal to public opinion, not because of any distinction between rich and poor, but because they did not have the power to do more. I do not know why they should have lacked such power, since they could do so much else. But the claim of support for children may have been beyond their jurisdiction, which seems in these matters to have pertained strictly to documents and property-arrangements. One may recall that the rabbis similarly appealed to public opinion in the matter of marriages between Jews and others whom they thought they should not marry for one reason or another. They warned that such marriages would produce defective children and the like.[1] Their stern admonitions were their only source of law-enforcement, and I should suppose that here too, it was because they could not fine, flog, or excommunicate the irresponsible father that they publicly shamed him.

Some rabbinical discussions pertained to far-fetched matters, and could not have been intended for popular attention in any event. Thus R Ḥisda said that if a minor begot a son, he does not come under the laws of a rebellious child;[2] Rav Judah discussed a case of pederasty of a son and father;[3] similar sayings relating to family life would not have pertained to normal public affairs. The discussions on how long a childless couple may remain together probably did not result in court action unless one of the parties sued for divorce, as above,[4] but R.

[1] But they could certainly prevent the children of such unions from claiming the rights of legitimate offspring, as b. Yev. 45b. Where the courts had effective power, they used it. Note also the discussions of whom priests might and might not marry, e.g., R. Sheshet on whether a priest who has defective testicles may marry a divorcee, b. Yev. 76a; R. Huna said that lesbians are prohibited from marrying priests, b. Yev. 76a.

[2] b. Sanh. 68b.

[3] b. Sanh. 54a.

[4] p. 280.

Naḥman's saying that three years must elapse, corresponding to the "three remembrances" of Sarah, Rachel, and Ḥannah, before a childless couple must separate, was surely a matter of speculation, not law. Marriage with certain women was regarded as dangerous, and R. Huna was quoted as saying that such women transmitted malignant diseases from the womb.[1] Whoever heard the saying would have wanted to avoid such a marriage.[2]

IV. Inheritances and Estates

Samuel had warned Rav Judah to keep away transfers of inheritance even from a bad son to a good one,[3] and the law prevented the rabbis from effecting their moral judgments upon legatees in the administration of probate cases. Their power however was substantial, for Babylonian Jews who wished to litigate a will had to come to them for judgment. One must stress that rabbinical authority pertained to *litigation*. Ordinarily, Rav Judah held, a person could simply give his instructions to three men, who might draw up and witness a will, or execute judgment,[4] that is to say, they might make the desired division without the supervision of a rabbinical court. It was in cases of improper or disputed division of an estate that the courts were consulted. Evidence of court authority is as follows:

> To Mari b. Isak (or Ḥana b. Isak) came a brother from Khuzistan, who said to him: "Give me a share in the property of our father." He replied, "I do not know you." The claimant then came to R. Ḥisda, who said to the claimant, "He replied properly," [etc., as above, p. 88].
> (b. Ket. 27b)[5]
>
> A relative of R. Idi b. Abin died and left a date tree [which was disputed by R. Idi and another]. R. Idi claimed, "I am the nearer relative," while the other made a similar claim. Eventually, however, he admitted that R. Idi was the closer relative, and R. Ḥisda assigned to him the tree. R. Idi then demanded the return of the produce consumed from the time he had seized it... (b. B.B. 33a)
>
> A certain man said, "My estate is for my grandmother, and after her death, to my heirs." He had a married daughter who died during the life-

---

[1] b. Yev. 64b.

[2] On the absolution of a wife's vows by the husband, see b. Ket. 71b, R. Huna v. R. Adda b. Ahavah and, R. Kahana; and b. Ned. 78b-79a, R. Ḥisda and R. Kahana.

[3] b. Ket. 53a.

[4] b. B.B. 113b-114a.

[5] See also b. B.M. 39b.

time of both her husband and her grandmother. After her grandmother died, the husband came to lay claim. R. Huna said, "To my heirs, means, even to the heirs of my heirs," and R. 'Anan judged, "To my heirs means, but *not* to the heirs of my heirs." (b. B.B. 125b)

These three cases provide adequate evidence that the rabbis did rule in cases of disputed inheritances. The first is most striking, for it indicates that in this, as in other kinds of law, the rabbis' rule was disputed not so much by competing groups or authorities, as by 'strong men' who simply declined to recognize their rulings, *but who could be forced to do so*. That is the most important fact: R. Ḥisda was able to issue a decree in the face of the intimidation of witnesses by a powerful defendant, and shaped his decree to conform to the circumstances of the case, rather than to the strict requirements of the law. I can think of no better testimony to the authority of Jewish courts in this period than R. Ḥisda's saying, preserved in a court record one need not regard as fabricated or pseudepigraphic for any reason. Obviously, had such a man not been brought to court in a case the rabbis were able to decide, he would have been exempt from the influence of rabbinical authorities, and one supposes that many such figures existed whom the rabbis could, at best, merely curse or threaten. But when a case in which rabbinical jurisdiction was well established came before the court, it was quite another matter. R. Idi's case and the third one illustrate the normal kind of issues of inheritance, the former depending merely on an inquiry into the facts of the matter, the latter, into the requirements of the law. In both instances, rabbinical authority was accepted by all sides, and met no significant opposition.

If so, one must suppose that the many rabbinical dicta about division of inheritances reflected practical realities, but whether they depended upon cases before the rabbinical courts or upon the theoretical study of the law cannot be determined except in specific instances. The cases cited above, particularly the third, would lead to the supposition that the rabbinical discussions came about for either of two reasons, first, because the Mishnah and external traditions presented theoretical points of law which required study, or second, because an actual case demanded clarification of the law. The Palestinians commented on the disagreement between R. Huna and R. 'Anan,[1] and one may suppose that the case report had reached them and called forth their opinion. But in most instances we do not know whether a rabbinical saying reflected an everyday issue before the court, or a matter of merely

[1] b. B.B. 125b-126a.

theoretical Mishnah study. Such a discussion is illustrated by the question of whether a verbal distribution of property using the language of *gift* rather than *inheritance* required an act of possession or not, which R. Hamnuna, R. Naḥman, and R. Sheshet disputed.[1] R. Sheshet supported his decision from a *beraita*, and all three were concerned with the illumination of a Mishnaic law about which contemporary Palestinians likewise were concerned. Similarly, we note the following combination of a case and a theoretical discussion:

> A certain man said to his wife, "My estate shall be his with whom you are pregnant." R. Huna said, "This is assigning to an embryo through the agency of a third party, and it does not acquire possession." R. Naḥman objected against R. Huna's ruling, citing the Mishnah "If a man said, Should my wife bear a male child he shall receive a *maneh*, and she did bear a male child, then he receives the *maneh*." He replied, "As to our Mishnah, I do not know who is its author..." R. Huna follows his own view, for R. Huna said, "A child does not acquire ownership even if the father said, 'After she will have born him.'" R. Naḥman said, "If a person conveys possession through..." But R. Huna said, "Even where he said, 'After she will have born...'" R. Sheshet said, "Whence do I derive it? From the following? 'If a proselyte died and Israelites plundered his estate, and then heard he had a son or that his wife was pregnant, they must return what they have appropriated...'"
>
> (b. B.B. 141b-142a)

Had we no such case, one might have supposed that legal theory alone was at issue. But here we have evidence that R. Huna decided a case according to his own view, which was disputed by R. Naḥman. There is no reason, therefore, to conclude that most such theoretical discussions do not relate to practical cases before the courts, if as in matters of inheritance we have clear evidence of rabbinical authority over the general kind of law at hand. If a rabbi was asked a question about such a law, it may represent a practical issue recently raised either in school or in court. For example, R. Sheshet was asked, "May a son in the grave be heir to his mother to transmit [her estate] to his paternal brothers," to which he replied by citing a Tannaitic tradition.[2] The reply, "You have learned it" would indicate that the questioners were disciples.

For this period, the largest number of cases of inheritance deals with gifts in contemplation of death, not because such cases were especially common, I think, but rather because R. Naḥman was a great innovator

[1] b. B.B. 129a-b.
[2] b. B.B. 159b.

in the law pertaining to such gifts, and hence his court records preserved numerous cases illustrating his viewpoints and actions. We are singularly fortunate in having R. Yaron's thorough study of Jewish law on gifts in contemplation of death,[1] which proves beyond doubt the important place occupied by R. Naḥman in the development of that law. We shall first review the cases and then summarize Yaron's assessment of R. Naḥman's contribution to the law. Among the relevant case-reports are the following:

> A certain [dying] man said: "A half to a daughter, a half to the other daughter, and a third of the fruit to my wife." R. Naḥman who happened to be at Sura was visited by R. Ḥisda, who asked the law in such a case. He replied, "Thus said Samuel, 'Even if he allotted to her one palm tree for its usufruct, she has forfeited her marriage-contract.'" He asked again, "Is it not possible that he held this view only where he allotted a share in the land itself, but not here where only fruit is involved?" He replied, "Do you speak of movables? I certainly do not hold that the law applies to movables." (b. B.B. 132b)
>
> The [dying] mother of Rami b. Ḥama gave her property in writing to Rami b. Ḥama in the evening, but in the morning she gave it in writing to R. ʿUqba b. Ḥama. Rami b. Ḥama came before R. Sheshet, who confirmed him in possession of the property. R. ʿUqba b. Ḥama came to R. Naḥman who did the same. R. Sheshet came before R. Naḥman and said to him, "Why has the Master confirmed R. ʿUqba b. Ḥama? Is it because she retracted? But she died." He replied, "So said Samuel, 'Wherever a person may retract if he recovered, he may also withdraw his gift...'"
>
> The mother of R. ʿAmram the pious had a bag of notes. While she was dying, she said, "Let it be for my son ʿAmram." His brothers appeared before R. Naḥman and claimed, "Surely he did not pull [= make legal acquisition of] the bag." He replied, "The instructions of a dying person are as if they were written and delivered."
>
> The sister of R. Tobi b. R. Mattena gave her possessions in writing to to R. Tobi b. R. Mattena in the morning. In the evening Aḥadboi son of R. Mattena came and wept before her saying, "Now they will say that one is a scholar and the other is not." She gave them in writing to him. He came before R. Naḥman who said "So said Samuel, 'Wherever

[1] Reuven Yaron, *Gifts in Contemplation of Death in Jewish and Roman Law* (Oxford, 1960). Yaron's stress upon the historical development of the law provides a rare and important example of how such researches ought to be conducted, and how fruitful they are for other kinds of historians when they become available. Our task is immeasurably complicated by the fact that we have few studies such as Yaron's, and are therefore faced with the impossibility of knowing just how legal theory has taken shape over a long period of time. In this one instance we are enabled to speculate with some certainty about the role of a given individual, and hence about the conditions he in particular may have faced in shaping the law.

a person may retract if he recovers, he may also withdraw the gift.' "

The sister of R. Dimi b. Joseph had a piece of an orchard. Whenever she fell ill she transferred the ownership of it to him, but when she recovered she withdrew it. Once she fell ill and sent word, "Come and take possession." He replied, "I have no interest." She sent word, "Come and take possession however you like." He went, left for her (a portion) and acquired from her (by means of symbolic acquisition, so that the gift could not be withdrawn). She recovered, retracted, and came before R. Naḥman. He sent for him. He did not come saying, "Why should I come? Surely some was left for her, and an act of acquisition from her also took place." He sent him, "If you do not come I will chastise you with a thorn that causes no blood to flow" [excommunication]. He asked the witnesses how the incident had occurred, and they told him she exclaimed, "Alas that I am dying." He said to them, "If so, the disposal of her estate was due to expectation of death, and he who gives instructions owing to death may [invariably] retract."

(b. B.B. 151a-b)

Other such cases involving the retraction of a gift of a dying man came before R. Huna[1] and R. Jeremiah b. Abba.[2] R. Naḥman's dicta on the gift of a dying man, reported by Rava, included the following: that the validity of a verbal gift of a dying man is a mere provision of the rabbis; that if a dying man said, "Let so-and-so live in this house or eat the fruit of this date tree," his instructions are to be disregarded [these are abstract rights, and cannot be given away without a legal act of transfer] unless he used the following language: "Give this house to so-and-so that he may live in it" or "Give this date tree to so-and-so that he may eat its fruit;" and that if a dying man said, "Give my loan to so-and-so," his loan is acquired by so-and-so.[3] The cases cited above leave no doubt that these discussions reflected actual circumstances, and that judgments were issued by the rabbinical courts on the disposition of gifts of dying testators, not only among rabbis who knew, or thought they knew, the law, as in the case of R. Dimi b. Joseph, but among ordinary people as well.

Yaron's discussion of the cases involving R. Naḥman[4] stresses that some of the rules were not yet well settled. Samuel is the earliest authority quoted by R. Naḥman. The revocability of the gift of a dying

[1] b. B.B. 153a.

[2] *ibid.*

[3] b. B.B. 147b-148a. Other sayings are cited and discussed by R. Huna and R. Naḥman in b. B.B. 133a, if a dying man assigned his estate in writing, under what law does the beneficiary receive it? R. Huna and R. Naḥman, if a dying man consecrated property, b. B.B. 174b; and see R. Huna, b. Shev. 42b, on the same matter; b. B.B. 111a, R. Naḥman oversees a decision of R. Tavla and R. Huna b. Ḥiyya on the share of a daughter in property inherited from the mother.

[4] pp. 73ff.

person, even before recovery, at the donor's pleasure, is at issue. Yaron says, "The rule must have been on the following lines: 'Everyone who, if he had recovered, would have revoked his *deyathiqi* [legacy] may also revoke during his illness'." Yaron discusses also the case of R. Dimi b. Joseph. Samuel had held that "where one give away all his property, it is presumed that he does so because he has given up all hope of survival; therefore when he recovers, the gift lapses. Though here only part of the property is given away, R. Naḥman admits proof of the special circumstances and accordingly cancels the gift. This is an important development since, at least in certain cases, it did away with the rule, by then long established, that a disposition of *part* of the donor's property is *not* revocable."[1] R. Naḥman's contribution was, Yaron indicates, a substantial step forward in the development of rules concerning gifts in contemplation of death. The rabbi in question, R. Dimi b. Joseph, knew the earlier law, and R. Naḥman's action clearly was based upon the changed view of the law that a disposition of part of the dying donor's property is not revocable, now holding that it could indeed be revoked. It is a measure of the authority wielded by R. Naḥman that he was able to alter the law. A lesser contemporary authority could not have done so, for as we have seen, R. Naḥman was quite able and willing to overrule the decisions of other courts, and to force the judges to retract decisions. Because of his high position in the judiciary, by contrast, he was able to make a substantial innovation. It would be important to know why he chose to do so. One could argue that the inner development of the law, which Yaron makes so easily available, required this "step forward.' He could equally well argue that contemporary social life was such as to require the legal innovation. Yet the evidence is not very substantial to support the latter explanation, for we have only one case, and that one involves a rabbi who knew the former law and thought he was acting in conformity with it, to his best advantage. One cannot very well suppose that social policy required a new law unless some compelling reason for it presents itself. R. Naḥman's particular judicial power enabled him to decree as he liked in matters of law, and the reason for his decree must be found not in the society he administered but rather in the law on the basis of which he made his decisions, and in the lapses of which he found reason to innovate.[2]

---

[1] pp. 93ff.

[2] I shall argue (below, pp. 317-338) that in this generation the authority and social legal influence of the rabbis *may* have greatly expanded, and one might suppose

While cases of division of inheritances came before rabbinical courts only in the event of litigation, rabbinical courts regularly administered the estates of orphans, as did Samuel's father and Samuel in Nehardea.[1] Administration of estates did not entail litigation, for orphans' and incompetents' property required court protection. So one can say that here the 'values' of the rabbis must have played a significant part in daily life. Yet such values seem to me of no great consequence for ordinary people, for they were not moral or ethical notions, but narrowly technical and legal ones, which only remotely could have shaped, or even pertained to, the attitudes of the people. I think it useful to distinguish, therefore, between rabbinic 'values' and rabbinic 'laws' or 'procedures,' *even* in matters of legal substance. The 'values' concerning marriage, effected through technical and legal decisions, were of broad popular consequence. Those concerning property and inheritance could not have meant much in an everyday context, and though the very strong powers of the rabbinical courts over all kinds of property litigations were unchallenged by other, competing systems of law, and though the rabbis could do pretty much as they chose in enforcing such laws, the consequences for the formation of popular culture could not have been very profound.

Administration of estates involved two kinds of actions, first, protection of orphans' rights and property, and second, division of estates which had already come under probate. The following cases testify to rabbinical control of both matters:

> Certain orphans who boarded with an old woman had a cow, which she took and sold. Their relatives appealed to R. Naḥman and claimed, "What right had she to sell it?..."
>
> The wine of Rabbana ʿUqba the orphan was pulled [formally acquired] by the purchasers who bought it at four zuz. The price subsequently rose, so that it was worth six. The case came before R. Naḥman, who ruled...
>
> ʿAmram the dyer was guardian of orphans. The relatives came to R.

that the innovations of R. Naḥman reflected that a wider variety of cases was coming to court than heretofore. However even if this was true, it does not have any bearing upon the laws in which clear-cut innovation can be discerned, for in this instance the cases pertaining to early periods leave no doubt that the courts before R. Naḥman's time did have authority and jurisdiction over inheritance law, and the matter of gifts in contemplation of death was earlier discussed and adjudicated. Hence there is here no relationship between social realities and legal theory. Earlier courts had decided such cases, but R. Naḥman, for reasons of law, and *not of social administration*, chose to deal with them in a new way.

[1] Vol. II, pp. 137-138.

> Naḥman and complained that he was clothing himself from the property of the orphans. He said, "He does so to command more respect." "He eats and drinks out of their money, as he is not a man of means," they claimed. "I suggest that he had a valuable find." "But he is spoiling their property..." He said, "Bring evidence and I will remove him..." (b. Git. 52a-b)

These cases indicate that R. Naḥman supervised the administration of orphans' estates, and had the power to protect their property either by the supervision of its disposition or by the replacement of incompetent or dishonest guardians. What is significant is that the relatives could do nothing on their own, but had to come to the court to seek an action. When they did, the court was prepared to interpret the law as favorably as possible for the guardian. Further such cases are as follows:

> A creditor once seized an ox from the herdsman of (his debtor's) orphans. The creditor claimed, "I seized it during the lifetime (of the debtor)," and the herdsman claimed, "It was after his death." They appeared before R. Naḥman who asked the herdsman, "Have you witnesses that he has seized it." "No," he replied. R. Naḥman thereupon ruled, "Since he could have said, 'It came into my possession through purchase,' he can also claim, 'I seized it during the lifetime of the debtor.'" (b. Ket. 84b)

> A certain woman with whom a bag of bonds was deposited claimed to the heirs that she had seized them during the depositor's lifetime in payment of a debt. R. Naḥman said to her, "Have you witnesses that it was claimed from you during his lifetime and that you refused to return it?" "No," she replied. "If so, your seizure took place after death, and is invalid." (b. Ket. 85a)

> A certain man once deposited a silver cup with Ḥasa, who died intestate.[1] The heirs came to R. Naḥman, who said, "I know that Ḥasa was not a wealthy man, and does the depositor not indicate the mark [that it was a silver cup]?" (b. Ket. 85b)

> A certain person built a house on ruins that had belonged to orphans. R. Naḥman confiscated the house from him. May it therefore not be inferred that R. Naḥman holds that he who occupies his neighbor's premises without an agreement must still pay rent? The case is different, for the site had originally been occupied by some men from Kerman, who used to pay a small rent. When the defendant had been told by R. Naḥman to go and make a peaceful settlement with the orphans, he paid no heed. R. Naḥman therefore confiscated the house. (b. B.Q. 21a)

In these cases, the court of R. Naḥman ruled on the rights of orphans' estates and on the disposition of the property of estates in general.

---

[1] b. Yev. 121b, he drowned.

A further category of cases concerns the maintenance of widows and daughters from estates controlled by sons and brothers, as the following:

> Such a case [in which daughters claimed maintenance from the movable property of their deceased father's estate] occurred at Nehardea, and the Nehardean judges issued an order (favoring the daughters). At Pumbedita also R. Ḥana b. Bizna allowed collection. R. Naḥman said to them, "Withdraw, or otherwise I shall order seizure of your (own) houses." (b. Ket. 50b)

> R. ʿAnan sent to R. Huna, "To our colleague Huna, Peace. When this woman presents herself before you, authorize her to collect a tenth of her father's estate." R. Sheshet was sitting before (R. Huna). "Go," R. Huna said to him, "And say to R. ʿAnan—ʿand he who does not deliver the message to him shall be banned—ʿAnan, ʿAnan, from landed or from movable property? And who presides at the meal in a house of mourning.'" R. Sheshet went to R. ʿAnan and said to him, "The Master (R. ʿAnan) is a teacher, and R. Huna is a teacher of the teacher, and he pronounced the ban against anyone who would not convey to you, and had he not said so I should not have said, 'ʿAnan, ʿAnan, from landed or movable property...'" (b. Ket. 69a-b)

(R. ʿAnan complained to Mar ʿUqba about the disrepectful language of R. Huna.) For our interest, it is important to note that the rabbinical courts did dispose of estates, and direct inheritances to be given to various claimants.

The power of the rabbinical court to administer orphans' estates was so considerable, R. Naḥman held, that even after they reach maturity they cannot protest the preceding actions of the court, for otherwise, "what validity is there in the authority of a court?"[1] R. Naḥman held that a minor might sell an estate validly at age eighteen or twenty.[2] Before that time, the court's power to supervise their actions was substantial, and there was little that they could do about it. Laws considering the administration and distribution of estates, not associated with specific cases, are given by R. Naḥman;[3] R. Naḥman in the name of Rabbah b. Abbuha;[4] R. Huna,[5] and R. Ḥisda.[6]

---

[1] b. Yev. 67b, Qid. 42a.

[2] b. B.B. 155a.

[3] b. Git. 50a, Mar Zutra b. R. Naḥman in the name of R. Naḥman, on a claim from orphans sold a widow's house, it is not a valid sale; b. ʿArakh 22a, R. Naḥman on distraint of orphan's property; b. Ket. 100b, R. Naḥman on assessing such property for sale.

[4] b. Ket. 92a, 110a, R. Naḥman in the name of Rabbah b. Abbuha, If orphans collect land for their father's debt.

[5] b. B.M. 39a, R. Huna, on whether a minor may enter the estates of captives.

[6] b. B.B. 52b, R. Ḥisda, on the division of property by brothers.

v. Farm and Marketplace

Except for jurisdiction over land disputes of all kinds,[1] only limited rabbinical influence over agricultural life and procedures can be discerned. Two kinds of law interested the rabbis at study, first, disputes about produce and farm property, and second, enforcement of the agricultural taboos prescribed in Scripture. As to the former, when the cases came to rabbinical courts, the rabbis ruled on them. Examples of such cases are as follows:

> Some market-gardeners once squared accounts, and found that one had five *istiras* too much. The others said to him in the presence of the landowner, "Give him the extra funds," and in the presence of the owner of the land he acquired it from him. Afterwards he reckoned by himself and found that he had nothing left over. He went to consult R. Naḥman, who said, "What can I do for you, for there is the rule laid down by R. Huna in Rav's name [that a transfer of claims in the presence of a third party takes effect immediately]. And for another, they duly acquired from you." Rava said to him, "Does he claim, I am unwilling to pay? He pleads that he does not *owe* the money." R. Naḥman said, "If so, the possession was transferred in error, and in such a case the money must always be returned." (b. Git. 14a)

> A certain sharecropper said to his employers, "Should I cause loss I will quit." He did cause a loss. Rav Judah said, "He must quit without receiving the value of the improvements (he made in the property)." R. Kahana said, "He must quit, but receives them..." (b. B.M. 109a)

> A certain man leased a vineyard for ten barrels of wine, but (the wine produced in the vineyard) turned sour. R. Naḥman ruled...
> (b. B.M. 106b)[2]

These are perfectly routine cases, which reveal little specific rabbinical influence on agricultural life, but were rather normal property disputes. Rabbis' narrowly agricultural rulings mainly related to their own farms. Thus R. Ḥisda told his own workers to remove palms which were growing among the vines, including their roots, since wine is more valuable than the products of the palm.[3] Rav Judah permitted a certain family to retrench the vineyards on the intervening days of a festival.[4] We do not know how widespread to begin with was obedi-

---

[1] See below, pp. 305-312.

[2] The discussion includes a conversation with R. Ashi, which is chronologically impossible. It may be that R. Ashi later commented on the court record, in which case the words "R. Ashi said *to him*" should read, "R. Ashi said."

[3] b. B.Q. 92a.

[4] b. M.Q. 4b.

ence to rabbinic rulings on work, including farm work, which might or might not be carried out on such days. The rabbis' knowledge of agriculture doubtless won the attention of the Jewish farmers, for they were, as we have seen, believed to possess especially sound information about the omens and signs of the natural world. Rav Judah said, for instance, that if fine rain comes down before heavy rain, then rain will continue for some time, but if it follows a heavy downpour, then the rain will cease.[1] Raḥva told how to make a fig tree which does not produce fruit.[2] R. Naḥman explained the difference between drought and famine. When the grain has to be transported by river, that is a sign of drought; but if it must be brought from one province to another, that signifies a famine.[3] These observations reflect nothing about whether the rabbis dicta affected agricultural life. R. Ḥisda said that whoever burns his neighbor's produce will not leave a son to succeed him.[4] This saying was in an exegetical context. Had the matter pertained to the enforcement of law, R. Ḥisda would not have had to make such a curse. The neighbor would simply have sued for damages at court. On the other hand, the decrees of the rabbis concerning property rights, though unattested by cases, were probably carried out. Thus R. Naḥman discussed whether a sharecropper had presumptive right of possession.[5] R. Huna declared barley left in public land to be ownerless, and R. Adda b. Ahavah declared the refuse of boiled dates to be ownerless.[6] Since suit against someone who had misappropriated such property would have to be brought to the rabbinical courts, and in such a case the rabbis would have refused to act upon the claim, these sayings represent cases in which the law was easily enforceable.

The Mishnah had explicitly taught as follows: "Every precept which is dependent on the land [= Palestine] is practised only there, and that which is not dependent on the land is practised both there and abroad, except *'Orlah* and *Kilayim*."[7] Rav Judah interpreted the Mishnah to mean, "Every precept which is a personal obligation—but not related to the soil or its produce—is practiced both in Palestine and abroad, but what is an obligation of the soil, for instance, tithes, applies only in Palestine." But the Pumbeditans ruled that even *'orlah* does not apply

[1] b. Ta'anit 9b.
[2] b. Tamid 30b.
[3] b. Ta'anit 13b.
[4] b. Sotah 11a, with reference to II Sam. 30.
[5] b. B.B. 46b.
[6] b. B.Q. 30b-31a.
[7] b. Qid. 36b-37a.

in the Diaspora, a ruling Rav Judah reported to R. Yoḥanan.[1] While as we have seen[2] in the earlier generation, such laws were in fact observed and enforced in Babylonia, in this time we have the following case:

> R. Ḥanan and R. ʿAnan were walking along a path, when they saw a man sowing diverse seeds together. One said to the other, "Come, master, let us ban him." "You are not clear," he replied. Again they saw another sowing wheat and barley among vines, and one said to the other, "Come let us ban him." "You are not thoroughly informed," he replied... (b. Qid. 39b)

It stands to reason that had the rabbis banned the man, their action would have been confirmed by the courts, and the rabbis therefore were eager to enforce the laws on diverse seeds in the diaspora. But we do not have any evidence pertaining to this period to attest that the people kept these laws. It was the Palestinian view that Babylonia was a land "empty of commandments" for heave-offerings, tithes, and seventh-year laws did not apply there.[3] The same source reports that R. Huna in the name of R. Mattena said that the world was created for three things, *Ḥallah*, tithes, and first-fruits, the second and third of which do not apply in Babylonia.[4] We have already noted that R. Ḥisda continued to receive priestly offerings and tried to force butchers to give them, and have no reason to doubt that when the priests could get their hands on them, they accepted them gladly. M. Beer states,[5] "The law was that the parts of the sacrifices reserved for priestly use were supposed to be given to the priests both in Palestine and abroad, and were called (as in the case of R. Ḥisda above), *gifts*. All butchers were supposed to separate from every ox they slaughtered the three parts for the priests and to give them to appropriate parties." Beer supposes that this was actually done, on the basis of cases involving R. Ḥisda, R. Kahana,[6] and others of the subsequent generation as well. Beer stresses[7] that while the Palestinians did not believe that the Babylonians separated the necessary offerings and tithes, and otherwise obeyed the agricultural taboos except where specified in the Mishnah, in fact these laws *were* kept in Babylonia, omitting the time of the temporary suspension in the days of Odenathus. We have a number of sayings rele-

[1] *ibid.* 39a.
[2] Vol. II p. 260-262.
[3] Gen. R. 37:4.
[4] Gen. R. 1:4.
[5] *Op. cit.*, 107-111.
[6] b. ʿEruv. 8b, and see Beer, *op. cit.*, p. 109, n. 352.
[7] Beer, *op. cit.*, p. 111, n. 366.

vant to these laws,[1] but only the case cited above. On that basis, one can hardly come to a firm opinion on whether the rabbis enforced these laws or not in this period, but on the basis of clear evidence from the earlier and later times,[2] I should suppose that they did when and where they could.

Supervision of farms proved difficult, because of the practical difficulties posed by overseeing a wide territory. The market place was quite another matter. It produced far more litigation than the farm. Indeed, the kinds of laws the rabbis wanted to enforce on the farms were by their nature not susceptible to commonplace litigation, which is probably why we have so few cases to begin with. On the other hand, market transactions involved two or more parties, and anyone who felt wronged and thought he could win in the rabbinical courts would very naturally repair to them for judgment, and the other party had to conform to the courts' decisions willy-nilly. Furthermore, the rabbinical courts were in the towns, and while walking by the wayside one or another rabbi might discover a violation of agricultural taboos, it was far more common for the rabbis to find their way through the markets, not only en route to the academy or to court for instance, than out through the fields. The rabbis had a clearcut responsibility to the exilarch, established by his forceful action in the early generation, to oversee the pricing of goods. This issue had been fought out and settled. So the rabbis' responsibilities required their presence in the marketplace. The combination of law, circumstance, and responsibility subjected the marketplace to close rabbinical supervision, and that supervision was singularly effective.

---

[1] E.g., Rav Judah, in animals of the same species, one may assist intercourse, and it is not forbidden on account of obscenity, b. B.M. 91a-b; Rav Judah on sowing five kinds of seeds in one seedbed, b. Shab. 84b; and see also y. Maʿaserot 4.4, Rav Huna; b. Beẓ. 39b, R. ʿAnan and R. Naḥman; R. Sheshet on why one should not muzzle an ox in its ploughing, b. B.M. 90a; y. Yev. 15.3, R. Sheshet; R. Adda b. Ahavah on mixed seeds in a vineyard, b. Pes. 25a; Raḥvah on driving a goat and a mule together, b. B.Q. 55a. On the firstlings of the flock, b. Bekh. 53b, Rav Judah, b. Tem. 24b, b. Bekh. 3b, 35a, Rav Judah said that it is all right to make a blemish in a firstling before it is born, so that it does not become liable to the priests; b. Bekh. 36b, Rav Judah held that the firstling of an Israelite cannot be examined for blemishes unless a priest is present; b. B.Q. 12b, R. Naḥman in the name of Rabbah b. Abbuha on firstlings in "this time" [when the Temple lies in ruins]; on who may eat heave-offerings, R. Huna, b. Yev. 72a; on other aspects of tithes and heave-offerings, R. Ḥisda, b. Yev. 89a, R. Naḥman in the name of Rabbah b. Abbuha, b. Yev. 74a, R. Sheshet, b. Yev. 73a, etc. On seventh-year, see also Y. Ẓunẓ, *Ha Derashot Be Ysra'el* (Jerusalem 1954), ed. Ḥ. Albeck, p. 295 n. 142.

[2] Vol. II, pp. 260-1, and 260 n. 6.

We shall, as before, examine first relevant cases and then other sayings that could easily have come to practical decision and enforcement. The most important cases of this generation are as follows:

R. Huna said, "The singing of sailors and ploughmen is permitted, but that of weavers is prohibited [being frivolous]." R. Huna abolished singing, and a hundred geese were priced at a *zuz*, and a hundred *se'ahs* of wheat at a *zuz*, but there was no demand for them. R. Ḥisda came and disregarded the order, and a goose was required at a *zuz* but was not to be found. (b. Sot. 48a)

Rav Judah permitted a gloss to be put on fine cloths. (b. B.M. 60b)

Rami b. Ḥama's host sold some wine and erred. Finding him saddened, he asked him why. "I sold wine and erred," he replied. "Then go and retract..." "But I have waited longer than is necessary to show it to a dealer or relative." He sent him to R. Naḥman, who told him, "This rule applies only to the buyer, but the seller can always retract..."[1]

A man had jewelry for sale. He asked sixty, while it was worth fifty, yet had he been offered fifty-five he would have accepted. A man came and reckoned, "If I give him fifty-five it will constitute renunciation. I will give him sixty and then sue him." When he came before R. Ḥisda, the rabbi said to him, "This was taught only of one who buys from a merchant, but when one buys from a private individual, he has no claim of fraud..." (b. B.M. 51a)

Rav Judah said to R. Adda the surveyor, "Do not treat surveying lightly, because every bit of ground is fit for garden saffron." He also told him, "The four cubits on the canal banks you may treat lightly, but those on the river banks do not measure at all..." (b. B.M. 107b)

Certain wool-sellers brought wool to Pum Nahara. The townspeople tried to stop them from selling it. They appealed to Rav Kahana, who said, "They have the right to stop you." They said, "We have money owing to us here." "So," he replied, "you can go and sell enough to sustain you until you collect your debts, but then you must go." (b. B.B. 22a)

R. Huna said to certain tradesmen, "When you buy palm branches from pagans, do not cut it yourselves, but let them cut it and give it to you..." (b. Suk. 30a)[2]

R. Huna (or, Rav Judah) permitted sellers of pot herbs to go and sell during the intervening days of a festival in the marketplace in the ordinary way. R. Kahana objected... (b. M.Q. 13b)

---

[1] On a case involving retraction before R. Naḥman, see b. Ned. 31b, b. B.M. 87a, below.

[2] See Boaz Cohen, *op. cit.*, II, 520.

> There was once a famine in Nehardea and all the people sold their houses. But when wheat came, R. Naḥman told them, "The law is that houses must be returned to their original owners..." (b. Ket. 97a)

These cases testify to extensive authority over the marketplace. The rabbis obviously were able to issue decrees which the market tradesmen and craftsmen obeyed. Whether the results of their decrees were quite so spectacular as the first case would suggest we do not know; numerous stories, however, from earlier times[1] as well as those cited here suggest that what the rabbis said they could enforce. They did not have to *await* the arrival of litigations in their courts in order to do so. Similarly, the rabbis prevented fraud, overcharging, and excess profits, and would use their court powers to force the restitution of funds wrongfully gained. They could in all instances enforce the law just exactly as they saw fit. The rulings of R. Naḥman and R. Ḥisda about retracting a sale indicate that there was no obstacle to the requirement that sales made contrary to rabbinic rules be annulled. Rav Judah's instructions to the surveyor provide an insight into still another aspect of rabbinic control. They apparently hired, and supervised the activities of, public servants not directly connected with litigation in the courts, and these would have provided additional means for amplifying rabbinic power. The adjudication of R. Kahana, the instructions of R. Huna, the forced resale by R. Naḥman, preventing massive impoverishment on account of famine—all these cases similarly indicate the broad extent of rabbinic control of commercial life. It was here, moreover, that the rabbis encountered normal, everyday life, and not merely the exceptional cases arising from criminal or abnormal behavior. While what they did about a peculiarly written, or poorly delivered divorce may have mattered very little, their decrees against excessive profits, concern to prevent violation of the commandment against stealing, their ability to permit or prohibit market-dealings on festivals, their power to prevent gouging and other kinds of reprehensible behavior—these provided means by which their ethical ideas reached large masses of people, shaping the behavior of men who would never make an appearance in any court.

Numerous legal dicta doubtless were applied to everyday commerce, therefore, even though no cases attest to it. Rav Judah, for example, said that a partner can insist that his partner name a price for his share,

---

[1] Vol. II p. 262-268. On the supervision of prices, not merely weights and measures, see II, 111-114.

or allow him to do so, against the view of R. Naḥman.[1] R. Naḥman provided a general principle of usury: all "payment for waiting" is prohibited.[2] R. Huna told R. Naḥman that Prov. 28:8 indicates that usury from heathens leads to loss of wealth.[3] He and R. 'Anan debated whether orphans' money may be lent at interest or not.[4] He forbade an increased price for credit.[5] As to futures, R. Huna and R. Ḥisda debated on whether one may withdraw, R. Huna holding that one may withdraw before the crop actually comes into existence, but not afterward.[6] R. Sheshet cited by R. Huna prohibited borrowing upon the market price.[7] R. Ḥisda dealt with the sale in which the price changed before delivery.[8] R. Huna held that a buyer was permitted to sift the grain in order to test its quality.[9] Observations on coinage included R. Naḥman's, that an "exact" coin is worth more than a normal one.[10] R. Ḥisda discussed with Rava the case of a coin's appreciating in value;[11] and he, R. Huna, and Rav Judah spoke about obsolete coins.[12] Rav Judah ruled on what is a permissible profit.[13] It was a general rule that competition was to be restricted.[14] The rabbis oversaw the payment and proper treatment of laborers. R. Ḥisda said that one must not treat leniently anyone except a hired worker, and R. Huna held that one imposes an oath in case of a court claim, except on a hired worker.[15] R. Ḥisda's saying, that a safe investment would be purchase of a Scroll of the Torah[16] does not necessarily represent a fiction of the rabbinical imagination, for such an object, of constant and possibly increasing value, would indeed constitute a good purchase, and with the prestige of the rabbinate and piety of the people supporting its value, one could make a worse investment. These are examples of the numerous sayings relating to the conduct of commercial life, some of them of legal force, others

---

1 b. B.B. 13a.
2 b. B.M. 63b.
3 b. B.M. 70b, and so should be discouraged.
4 *ibid.* 70a.
5 *ibid.* 65a.
6 b. Yev. 93a; R. Huna v. R. Naḥman, b. B.M. 66b.
7 b. B.M. 72b.
8 b. B.B. 83b-84a.
9 b. B.B. 94a.
10 b. Ḥul. 54b.
11 b. B.Q. 97b.
12 *ibid.* 97a.
13 b. B.M. 40a-b.
14 b. B.B. 21b, as in the case of the wool-merchants in Pum-Nehara.
15 b. Shev. 49a, compare 45b, R. Sheshet in b. B.M. 112a, b. B.Q. 99a.
16 b. B.Q. 88a.

merely observations about the conduct of economic life, but all of them *potentially* enforceable, when necessary, in rabbinical courts.[1]

vi. Suits for Civil Damages and Personal Injury. Crimes against Property

The cases cited above, showing the authority of rabbinical courts and officials over the market place, centered upon normal, everyday matters such as the regulation of prices, market conditions, and the like. But a great number of cases came to trial concerning abnormal matters. While neither the rabbis nor the exilarchate exercised capital jurisdiction over such major crimes as Geniva's sedition,[2] they certainly did judge cases of personal damages, torts, and the like. Their authority was unlimited, supported by the exilarchate, and, through him, by the imperial government. All kinds of disputes over property were theirs to adjudicate, and they did so with great effectiveness. Cases concerning theft of property, injury to property, and personal injury, include the following:

> A certain person cut down a date-tree belonging to his neighbor. When he appeared before the exilarch, the latter said, "I myself saw the place. Three date trees stood in one place. Go and pay thirty-three and a third zuz." [etc. as above, p. 68]. (b. B.Q. 58b)

> A certain man stole the yoke of oxen of his neighbor, and went and ploughed and sowed some seeds, and at last returned them to the owner. When the case came before R. Naḥman he said, "Go and appraise the increment..." [Rava criticized his judgment, and he replied] "Did I not say to you that when I am judging you should not make any suggestions to me, for Huna our colleague said of me that I and 'King Shapur' [= Samuel] are brothers in respect of civil law? That person is a notorious robber and I want to penalize him." (b. B.Q. 96b)

> A person once brought pumpkins to Pum-Nahara, and a crowd assembled and everyone took a pumpkin. He [fearing they would not pay] called out, "Behold they are dedicated to God." The buyers came before R. Kahana, who said to them, "No one may dedicate something which is not his own..." (b. B.B. 88a)

[1] Yet note Rav Judah's exegesis of Ps. 116:9, comparing the marketplace to a cemetery.

[2] R. Mattena said that one who enters a city in which courts are established to inflict the death penalty is freed of the obligation to say a certain prayer, b. Ber. 60a. But the Jewish courts had no such powers. On a rare murder case, see above, p. 221.

A certain old woman came before R. Naḥman and said to him, "The exilarch and all his rabbis are sitting in a stolen Sukkah..." [as above, p. 63]. (b. Suk. 31a)

A certain person showed a heap of wheat belonging to the exilarch and was brought before R. Naḥman, who ordered him to pay... (b. B.Q. 116b)

R. ʿAnan's field was flooded by a dam-burst. He went and restored the fence on land belonging to his neighbor. The latter sued before R. Naḥman. He said to him, "You must restore the land." "But I have become owner by right of occupation," he replied. R. Naḥman [told him that the law does not follow those who hold that if occupation takes place in the presence of the owner without protest, it constitutes a title]. R. ʿAnan said, "This man has tacitly waived his rights because he came and helped me to build the fence." R. Naḥman replied, "This was a waiver given in error. You yourself would not have built the fence had you known that the land was his. Just as you did not know, so he did not know." (b. B.B. 41a)

In a case in which an ass consumed bread and chewed the basket, Rav Judah ordered full payment for the bread but only half-damages for the basket... (b. B.Q. 19b)

Ḥanan the wicked stole a garment and sold it, and was brought to R. Huna. He said to the plaintiff, "Go and redeem your pledge [buy the garment from the purchaser]..." (b. B.Q. 115a)

Ḥanan the wicked boxed someone's ear. He came before R. Huna, who told him to pay a half-zuz in damages... (b. B.Q. 37a)[1]

These cases indicate that cases of theft and damages to property were under the jurisdiction of the rabbinical courts, and the rabbis' law, which did not always conform to what 'common sense' would dictate (as in the case of the date-tree), was brought to bear. The plea of the people who bought, or wanted to buy, pumpkins indicates the readiness of the rabbinical court to judge civil suits of all kinds. The cases against, and in behalf of, the exilarch, the claim against R. ʿAnan for appropriating part of his neighbor's land, and the torts and personal injury cases judged by R. Huna and R. Judah—all testify to a broad range of judgment. One notes also that the courts enjoyed the services of bailiffs or sheriffs to bring malefactors to trial.

Concommitantly, the rabbis applied the rules of evidence and assessment of damages which they studied in their academies. Each of the above cases indicates that jurisdiction over a relatively simple matter

---

[1] Also b. Bekh. 50b.

required complex knowledge, and that knowledge was acquired in the law schools. Rules of procedure, discussed in this generation, included the following: whether a man who occupies premises without the owner's knowledge has to pay rent or not;[1] whether someone who enters ruins and rebuilds them without the permission of the owner, has to return the actual timber and stones to the owner;[2] how damages are to be paid out;[3] how to assess liability for accidental injury and death;[4] how to collect damages when a thief sells stolen goods before the owners have given up hope of recovering them;[5] whether a man is liable to make restitution of priestly dues which he has destroyed;[6] whether a man may take the law into his own hands to protect his interest;[7] and the determination of legal liability in the case of minors.[8] The academic interpretation of II Sam. 23:15-16 is revealing:

> 'And David longed, and said, Oh that one would give me water to drink of the well of Bethlehem which is by the gate. And the three mighty men broke through the host of the Philistines and drew water out of the well of Bethlehem which was by the gate.' What was his difficulty? Rava in the name of R. Naḥman said, "His difficulty was regarding concealed articles damaged by fire..." R. Huna however said, "There were there stacks of barley which belonged to Israelites, but in which Philistines had hidden themselves, and he wondered whether it was permitted to rescue oneself through the destruction of another's property." The answer they sent him was, "It is forbidden to rescue oneself through the destruction of another's property. You however are king, and a king may break through to make a way and nobody is entitled to prevent him..." (b. B.Q. 60b)

So David was told of the right of eminent domain. The preoccupation of the rabbis with matters of civil law in general, and torts in particular, thus resulted from the vast powers they possessed in dealing with just such matters.

---

[1] b. B.M. 65a, R. Naḥman, and R. Ḥisda reporting the academic discussion of the matter in b. B.Q. 20a.

[2] b. B.M. 101a, R. Naḥman and R. Sheshet.

[3] b. B.Q. 9a, R. Huna v. R. Naḥman, and also y. B.Q. 2.2, R. Huna.

[4] b. B.Q. 42a, 49a, R. Adda b. Ahavah.

[5] b. B.Q. 68a, R. Naḥman and R. Sheshet, also b. B.Q. 111b, R. Ḥisda, b. Ḥul. 134a, R. Ḥisda. See b. B.M. 16a, y. B.Q. 1.1.

[6] b. Ḥul. 130b.

[7] b. B.Q. 27b. See Boaz Cohen, *op. cit.*, I, 637f.

[8] R. Naḥman b. Jacob, y. ʿEruv. 7.6, y. M.S. 4.3.

VII. TRANSFERS OF PROPERTY

Yaron provides a helpful, brief summary of the modes of acquisition of property in Talmudic law. He states:

> Tannaitic law fixes certain modes of acquisition—common to both sale and gift but differing according to the nature of the thing to be acquired. Land and slaves are to be acquired by payment of the purchase price, or by deed, or by *ḥazaqa* (seizure), movables by lifting or drawing... Movables can be acquired together with land, by modes of acquisition proper for land. Both land and movables can be acquired by barter, that is to say, on exchange of one object for another; when one party acquires one object (by one of the modes of acquisition mentioned), the other party at the same moment becomes owner of the other object... At some stage a new mode of acquisition—*qinyan sudar*, 'acquisition by kerchief'—made its way into the law, soon to become the mode of acquisition *par excellence*. Indeed, in Talmudic writings *qinyan*—'acquisition' without further qualification refers to this mode. *Qinyan sudar* developed out of barter: the handing over of any object (except money and fruits), even if practically valueless, came to be regarded as valid barter. Thereby... any object, land as well as movables, could be instantly acquired. *Qinyan sudar* was very convenient in a variety of circumstances. It might be used to transfer propery which happened to be at a place other than where the bargain was struck. Formerly in such a case movables could be transferred only by way of barter, but not by sale or gift. It might be used to avoid the cumbersome necessity of lifting each of a number of movables sold. Formerly in a sale of, for example, a thousand jars of wine, acquisition necessitated the lifting of each jar. It might also be used for the purpose of shifting the risk of destruction from the vendor to the purchaser. In a sale of movables, payment of the price did not effect a transfer of ownership... *Qinyan sudar* was frequently employed in cases of gift... *Qinyan sudar* is not referred to in either the Mishnah or the Tosephta. Since it is first discussed by Amoraim of the first generation, it is usually considered an early Amoraic device, but it may conceivably belong to the later Tannaitic era.[1]

From Yaron's discussion, it is clear that some of the modes of acquisition, particularly the *qinyan sudar*, would not yet have been widely known among the people, and we have already cited a case[2] in which the ignorance of a woman of the proper mode of establishing her seizure of a proselyte's land led to grief. So the cases to be considered here largely devolve upon squatter's rights and other disputes over

[1] *op. cit.*, 35-6. On the mode of acquisition by seizure, see Boaz Cohen, *op. cit.*, II, 465ff.

[2] Vol. II, pp. 264-5.

whether the proper mode of acquisition had been correctly effected, and over other complex matters raised by the rabbinic rules. The people in time had to come to understand and abide by the *only* forms of acquisition which would be enforced in rabbinical courts.

Concerning the transfer of immovable property and land, we have the following cases:

> A certain woman once put up a fence on top of another fence on the estate of a proselyte (intending to acquire it) and a man came and hoed a little. The latter than appeared before R. Naḥman, who confirmed it in his possession. The woman came to him and cried. He said to her, "What can I do for you, for you did not take possession properly."
> (b. ʿEruv. 25a)

A proselyte's property was regarded as ownerless. Rav Judah had ruled that if a man threw vegetable seeds into a crevice in the proselyte's land, and another hoed a bit, the latter acquires possession, because the former had made no improvement of the ground.[1] In this case, the woman thought she had made a proper act of acquisition, but she was uninformed of rabbinical law, and hence lost the land.

Further land-tenure disputes include the following:

> [A man once said to his neighbor, "If I sell this land, I shall sell it to you." He went and sold it to another.] A similar case came before R. Ḥisda, who referred it to R. Huna [who decided that since no price had been agreed on, the man cannot claim the field, never having acquired it.]
> (b. A.Z. 72a)

> R. Joseph said, "I know of a case that arose in Dura diReʿuta in which a Jew bought land from a heathen and another came and dug up a little of it, and when the case came before Rav Judah, he assigned the land to the latter... R. Huna bought a field from a heathen, and a Jew came and dug up some of it. He came before R. Naḥman, who confirmed his title to it...
> (b. B.B. 54b-55a)

> A certain man said to another, "What are you doing in this house?" The other replied, "I bought it from you, and have had the use of it for a period of seizure [*ḥazaqa*, that is, for three years, even though no deed was available]." The other replied, "But I have been living in an inner room (and therefore made no protest)." The case came before R. Naḥman, who said to the defendant, "You must prove that you have had constant use of the house..."
>
> A certain man said to another, "I will sell you all the property of Bar Sisin."[2] There was a piece of land called Bar Sisin's, but the seller said, "This is not really the property of Bar Sisin, though it is called Bar

---

[1] b. ʿEruv. 25a.

[2] See also b. B.B. 159b.

Sisin's." The case was brought to R. Naḥman who decided for the purchaser...

A man claimed, "This belonged to my father," and the other, "to my father." One brought witnesses to prove it had belonged to his father and that he had had use of it for the period of seizure, and the other's witnesses only proved he had had use of it for sufficient years to confer title. R. Naḥman said, "The evidence that one has had the use of it cancels that of the other, so the land is assigned to the one who brings evidence that it belonged to his father." He then brought witnesses to prove that the land had belonged to his father. R. Naḥman ruled, "As we put him out, so we can put him in, and we disregard any disrepute that this may bring on the court..." (b. B.B. 29b-31b)

One claimed, "The land belonged to my father," and the other, "to mine," but while one brought witnesses that it had belonged to his father (to the time of his death) the other's witnesses testified that he had had use of it for the period of seizure. R. Ḥisda ruled, "What motive has he (who occupied it) to lie? If he wants, he can claim, 'I bought it from you and have had the use of it for the period of seizure...'" A certain man said, "What are you doing on this land?" He replied, "I bought it from you and have had use of it for the period of seizure."[1] He went and brought witnesses to prove he had had the use of it for two years. R. Naḥman decided that he should restore both the land and the produce... (b. B.B. 33b)

R. Huna said, "If a man consents to sell something through fear of physical violence, the sale is valid..." [Rav Judah and R. Hamnuna questioned this rule]... A certain Taba tied a certain Papi to a tree until he sold his field. Rabbah b. bar Ḥana signed as witness both to a notification [that the sale was made under duress] and to a deed of sale. R. Huna said, "He who signed the notification acted properly, and so did he who signed the deed..." (b. B.B. 48a-b)

There was a case in Dura diRe'uta [where three trees planted at distances of less than eight cubits between them were sold] and when it came before Rav Judah, he said to the buyer, "Go, give him [his share of the ground]..." (b. B.B. 82b-83a)

These cases involve varying principles of law, for instance, whether acquisition is achieved if a price has not been specified, how land is acquired in a purchase from a non-Jew, how conflicting claims involving seizure were to be adjudicated, how various forms of competing testimony were assessed, the validity of a sale under duress, and the definition of what was sold in connection with the sale of trees. They illustrate general principles of law. For instance, the cases found in b. B.B. 29b-33b illustrate the teaching of Rav Judah, that if a man

[1] Rav Judah ruled similarly, b. B.B. 53b-54a.

takes a knife and a rope and announces, "I am going to gather the fruit of so-and so's date tree which I have bought," his statement is accepted, because a man does not ordinarily presume to gather the fruit of trees he does not own,[1] and similar legal definitions pertaining to the rights of seizure. They are important for our purposes because they indicate beyond any doubt that the rabbis' theoretical sayings, their explanations for points of Mishnaic law, and the like were connected with court cases, procedures, and adjudications.

In this generation, academic discussions concerned the following issues: Can produce effect a barter?[2] Can money effect title?[3] Does spreading mattresses on the floor of a proselyte's house effect acquisition?[4] How to make acquisition of trees?[5] If the buyer's vessel stands on the premises of the seller, does the buyer acquire by means of it or not?[6] Other discussions focused on the right of the public to establish domain through usage of a right of way;[7] on the right of the owner of the shore of a stream to use the bed;[8] on establishing a right, through customary usage, to close a window;[9] on the right of a resident of an alley to fence in the space facing his door;[10] on other matters of seizure and establishing a right or title through customary usage;[11] on how to establish a protest to prevent seizure through usage;[12] and the like.[13]

The cases and questions seemed mostly to concern the acquisition of

---

[1] b. B.B. 36a. Several similar statements of Rav Judah are here cited.

[2] R. Naḥman v. R. Sheshet, b. Qid. 28b; see also R. Naḥman, b. Qid. 8a.

[3] R. Naḥman, By biblical law it does, b. B.M. 48a; R. Huna also, b. B.M. 46b-47a.

[4] R. Sheshet, b. B.B. 53b.

[5] R. Huna, b. B.B. 72b.

[6] b. B.B. 85b, R. Sheshet asked R. Huna.

[7] b. B.B. 26b, Rav Judah; see also his saying in b. B.B. 12a, 60b, 100a; b. B.Q. 28a.

[8] R. Naḥman, quoted by Rava, b. B.B. 67b.

[9] b. B.B. 60a.

[10] R. Huna, b. B.B. 11b.

[11] E.g. R. Naḥman on why ploughing confers title through seizure, b. B.B. 36b; on confirming title to land, b. B.B. 47b; on accepting conflicting testimony to establish title through seizure, Rav Judah, b. B.B. 56b; R. Naḥman, b. B.B. 6a, etc.

[12] R. Naḥman, b. B.B. 39a, it need not be in the presence of the holder of the property; R. Naḥman, on drawing up a deed of protest, b. B.B. 39b-40a.

[13] b. Ket. 17b, R. Huna says that one does not acquire ownership of the property of a minor by undisturbed possession even if the minor comes of age; on adjoining courtyards at different levels, R. Huna, b. B.B. 6b; and other matters, R. Naḥman, b. B.B. 12a; R. Sheshet, b. Qid. 20b; R. Ḥisda and R. Qattina on how we know that if one sells a field for sixty years, it does not return to the original owners in the Jubilee, b. B.M. 79a; also b. B.B. 51a, R. Naḥman to R. Huna; Rav Judah sent to Palestine to ask about how a large animal is to be acquired, y. Qid. 1.4.

property theoretically without an owner, that is, squatter's rights, such as to land belonging to a proselyte. Since the proselyte's actions before his conversion—indeed, even his familial relationships—were afterward regarded as being of no account, his property could be seized and held by other Jews.[1] Another apparently ownerless property would have been held by absentee or disinterested owners, for to establish a right of possession through seizure, the claimant had to make use of the land for a considerable period without the complaint of the owner. A third involved land purchased from pagans. These claims, to what was regarded as substantially free land, seem to have dominated litigation in the rabbinical courts. One may therefore infer that normal transfers of property did not regularly produce litigations, and hence the ordinary people must have transacted their business according to law. So everyday exchanges proceeded without much rabbinical interference.

It is striking that most of the cases pertaining to adjudication of land disputes involved contested seizure, rather than such matters as improper acquisition through non-payment of the purchase price, incorrect deeds, or the like. Yaron notes the importance of the innovation, made one assumes no earlier than in the preceding century, of acquisition by means of a kerchief, symbolically representing the object to be bartered, and legalizing sale or gift of objects as a means of formal transferral of possession. *No* cases involving movable property devolved upon improper knowledge of that rule. Cases involving movables are as follows:

> A man once sold an ass to his neighbor. The buyer said, "I will take it to that place, and if it is sold, well and good, but if not, I will return it to you." He took it, but it was not sold, and on his way back it was accidentally injured. R. Naḥman held him liable... (b. B.M. 81a)[2]
>
> There was a certain river boat about which two men were disputing. One said, "It is mine," and so did the other claim. One of them went to court and appealed, "Attach the boat until I bring witnesses to prove it is mine." Would we attach it or not? R. Huna said we should, and Rav Judah said we should not. The man went to look for his witnesses, but did not find them, whereupon he requested the court to release the boat, leaving it to the stronger to possess it. Rav Judah said that we should

---

[1] I should suppose that potential proselytes would have been put off by such a rule, had they known it, for in effect conversion to Judaism would strip them of their wealth. It is perfectly clear that the law was not merely theoretical, for people did grab whatever they could from converts.

[2] Compare b. Ned. 31b.

not release it, and R. Papa said we should. The ruling is that we should not attach it in the first place, but if so, we should *not* release it.

(b. B.B. 34b)

The first case involved a sale on condition, and R. Naḥman held the man liable for damages, on the ground that the return journey differed not at all from the outward one, in that the man would have gladly sold the ass under any circumstances.[1] The second case involved conflicting procedures in adjudicating a difficult claim. We have no cases involving simple conflict over whether or not an object had been properly acquired, and a comparison to the earlier situation suggests[2] that the commonplace procedures now were mostly well known and widely observed. The people therefore had acquired the necessary knowledge of the procedures and policies of the rabbinical courts to prevent unnecessary litigation over matters of improper procedure in normal relationships. The two relevant cases are by no means equivalent. One depends upon what must have been a fairly normal circumstance, a sale on condition that the object be resold. But the other involved not a normal sale, but unusual and actually unacceptable court procedures, which the rabbis most certainly wanted to discourage.

Legal sayings on possession of movables include the following: R. Ḥelbo in the name of R. Huna said, "One can acquire an animal by taking the reins from the seller, but not if it is of a proselyte;"[3] a discussion of R. Naḥman and R. Sheshet on acquisition by means of a utensil;[4] if one was told to acquire ownership like an ass, what is the law? discussed by R. Naḥman, R. Hamnuna, and R. Sheshet.[5]

Adjudication of cases involving gifts and their proper disposition naturally was within the jurisdiction of the courts, and as in the case of inheritances, the rabbis applied the law without opposition or difficulty. One such case dates from this period:

The mother of Rami b. Ḥama gave her property in writing to Rami b. Ḥama in the morning, but in the evening she gave it in writing to Mar ʿUqba b. Ḥama. Rami b. Ḥama came before R. Sheshet who confirmed him in possession. Mar ʿUqba came before R. Naḥman who took similar action. R. Sheshet came to R. Naḥman and said, "Why did you so decide?" "And why," R. Naḥman replied, "did you so act?" "Because," he replied, "(Rami's deed was written) first." "Are we then

[1] See above, p. 302.
[2] Vol. II p. 262ff.
[3] b. B.M. 8b.
[4] *ibid.* 47a.
[5] b. B.B. 143a.

> living in Jerusalem where the hours are inserted?" "Then why did you so act?" "I treated it as a matter at the discretion of the judges." "I too," R. Sheshet said, "treated it as a matter at the discretion of the judges." R. Naḥman replied, "In the first place I am a judge and you are not,[1] and second, you did not first come with this argument."
>
> (b. Ket. 94b)[2]

The similarity of this case to the one involving Rami's mother's will suggests that the laws on apportioning gifts would have been enforced as easily as those on inheritances. R. Sheshet also said that once a gift has come into the possession of the recipient, it cannot be cancelled by the recipient if he merely says "This gift is to be cancelled" or "I do not want it," but if he said, "It is cancelled" or "It is not a gift," his words take effect.[3] R. Naḥman held that a gift given on condition that the recipient return it, which the recipient has then consecrated, is both consecrated and to be returned.[4] Rav Judah said that if a deed of gift is drawn up in secret, it is not enforceable.[5] The legal issues of these sayings thus involved when and whether proper acquisition had taken place.

Cases of acquisition of lost or ownerless property before the courts at this time required decision on two principles, first, whether the owners had truly given up hope of finding the property, in which instance the property had become ownerless and might be kept by the finder (or, in the instance of theft, by the thief or the fence). Second, in the case of conflicting claims of precedence, to which finder did an object belong? We have one case involving the discovery of lost property and efforts to find its owners:

> A certain man once found four *zuz* which had been tied up in a cloth and thrown into the Biran river. When he appeared before Rav Judah, the latter said to him, "Go and announce it..." (b. B.M. 24b)

The ruling meant that the owner had not yet given up hope of finding the object, and therefore it was the finder's task to look for him. R. Naḥman instructed Rava on the same matter:

> Rava once followed R. Naḥman into the street of the leather-dealers... and asked him, "What if one found a purse here?" He replied, "It would belong to the finder." "What if a Jew came and indicated an identification mark?" "It would still belong to the finder." "But if he keeps

[1] See above, pp. 84-87.
[2] Compare b. B.B. 151a, cited above, p. 289.
[3] b. Git. 32a, b. Ker. 24a.
[4] b. B.B. 137b.
[5] b. B.B. 40b.

> protesting?" "It is," R. Naḥman replied, "as if one protested against his house collapsing or against his ship sinking in the sea."
>
> (b. B.M. 24b)

That is to say, the situation was so hopeless that no reasonable person could hope to retrieve his property, and hence from the time it was lost, it should be regarded as having been given up for good by its owners.

R. Naḥman also ruled that if a man sees a coin fall from one of two people, he must return it, as there is no possibility of the rightful owner's giving up hope of finding it.[1] R. Naḥman and R. Sheshet discussed distinguishing marks. R. Sheshet was asked whether *number* was a distinguishing mark, and he cited the Tannaitic tradition to indicate that it was.[2] R. Naḥman was asked whether knowing the place where an article was found is a sign of identification or not, and cited a Tannaitic tradition to indicate that it was not.[3] R. Naḥman and R. Ḥisda both said that if a man lifts up an object found by his neighbor, the neighbor does not thereby acquire the object, but if a laborer finds something, the object belongs to his employer.[4] Such sayings as these do not represent legal innovations, but rather, clarifications or extensions of existing and well-known laws, learned from Tannaitic traditions or from sayings of the preceding generation.

VIII. Collection of Debts and Mortgages. Commercial Documents.

The common course of commercial life, as of marriages and market place transactions noted above, did not lead through the rabbinical courts. People normally made purchases and paid for them, were not cheated or defrauded, faced no disputes about ownership, and therefore did not have to come to rabbinical courts. But the fact that the courts were present to prevent infractions of the regular rules of commercial life, and had the power to do so, affected ordinary people as much as malefactors, for the certainty and security that the law would be enforced led to its predominance over everyday relationships. So if most debts were paid and most mortgages properly collected, then the few cases in hand adumbrate many instances in which

---

[1] b. B.M. 26b.
[2] b. B.M. 23b.
[3] *ibid.*
[4] b. B.M. 10a.

life proceeded in the proper and peaceful way. The courts did have the power to enforce the collection of debts and to oversee the writing and honoring of mortgages, as in the following cases:

> A certain mortgage-note stated an unspecified number of years. The creditor claimed it meant, three, the debtor, two. The creditor anticipated [the court action] and enjoyed the usufruct. Whom do we believe? Rav Judah said, "The land stands in the presumptive possession of the owner [since there is a dispute about the third year, it belongs to the debtor, for he is now owner, and the creditor must repay]." Rav Kahana ruled, "The usufruct is in the presumptive possession of him who enjoyed it..." (b. B.M. 110a)

> A certain man said to his neighbor, "When you repay me, do so before two who have studied the laws." He went and repaid privately. The money was lost (after the lender received it). The lender claimed before R. Naḥman that he had received the money only as a deposit, and that he had said, "Let it remain with me as a deposit until we obtain the two witnesses who have studied the laws, so that the condition may be fulfilled." R. Naḥman said, "Since you admit that you received the money from him, it is a proper repayment. If you desire the condition to be fulfilled, go and bring the money (here), for here am I and R. Sheshet who have studied the laws, *Sifra*, *Sifré*, *Tosefta*, and the whole *Gemara*..." (b. Shev. 41b)

> A certain man claimed of his neighbor, "Give me the hundred *zuz* that I claim from you and here is the document (proving the claim)." He replied, "I have paid you." The other said, "Those were for a different claim." R. Naḥman said, "The document is impaired [there being no document for the other claim, we assume the former to have been paid since the claimant admits receiving the money]."
> (b. Shev. 42a)

> A certain man said to his neighbor, "A hundred *zuz* I counted out to you by the side of this pillar." He replied, "I never passed by the side of this pillar." Witnesses came and testified that he had urinated by the side of that pillar. R. Naḥman ruled, "He is proven a liar..."
> (b. Shev. 34b)

> R. Naḥman gave a practical decision at the exilarch's court [in a case in which the Mishnah applied, "If a man lent money on a field and the lender said to the borrower, 'If you do not repay me in three years, it is mine'—it becomes his."] R. Huna said, "If he so stipulated when lending the money, it becomes completely his. If after, he acquires only in proportion to the money still owed." R. Naḥman said, "Even if after lending the money, the stipulation was made, it becomes completely his." Rav Judah tore up the document [issued by R. Naḥman, as a title]. (b. B.M. 66a)[1]

[1] See above, p. 63.

A minor was once summoned for a [civil] suit before R. Naḥman, who found the boy had neither witnesses nor proof. R. Naḥman ruled him liable.

A certain woman (trustee appointed by the creditor and debtor of a bill of indebtedness) produced a note of debt, but said to the creditor, "I know that this bill was discharged." R. Naḥman accepted her testimony... (b. Sanh. 31a)

R. Sheshet had some money owed to him in Maḥoza for some cloaks. He sent to R. Joseph b. Ḥama, "When you come back from there, bring the money with you." R. Joseph went to them and they gave him the money, and requested that he establish possession (so that they would bear no further liability). At first he agreed, but then he excused himself. When he returned, R. Sheshet said to him, "You acted quite rightly..." (b. Git. 14a)[1]

The final case is striking, because in Parthian times, a similar incident resulted in a different action. Then the Jewish debtors forced the rabbinical agent to issue the bill they requested, by thrashing him until he agreed to do so. In this time, approximately a century and a quarter later, the rabbi was able to arrange things in accordance with the law as he understood it, which indicates that he had more power than his predecessors. These cases show that the rabbinical courts had the right to interpret the language of mortgages, to adjudicate claims involving payments of debts, to rule on the validity of documents in connection with debts, and to assess the credibility of testimony from litigants and witnesses alike. Discussions involved the following issues: If a pledge is lost, is the debt thereby cancelled?[2] Are judicial oaths imposed in the case where the claim for payment of a debt is denied?[3] Is a lost document of loan returned to the owner if the debtor admits that he has not paid the debt?[4] What are the laws pertaining to bonds of indebtedness?[5] For example, what if two men produced bonds of indebtedness against one another?[6] May a creditor recover a debt at any time he chooses?[7] If orphans seize land for a debt owed to their father, can a creditor of his then seize it from them?[8] and other matters.[9]

---

[1] See vol. I, pp. 94-97 for a similar case.
[2] b. Shev. 43b, Samuel v. R. Naḥman.
[3] b. B.M. 5a, R. Naḥman.
[4] b. B.M. 17a, R. Kahana.
[5] R. Huna, R. Ḥisda, b. B.B. 172b; R. Hamnuna, b. B.B. 171b.
[6] b. Ket. 110a, R. Naḥman v. R. Sheshet.
[7] b. Ket. 104a, R. Sheshet.
[8] b. Pes. 31a.
[9] E.g., b. B.B. 157b, R. Naḥman refers a question to Palestine about land which

We have already noted a number of cases in which the proper drawing up and disposition of a document was ruled upon by rabbinical courts.[1] Their powers in this area were of two kinds. First, they could evaluate a document written outside of court, in a normal private commercial transaction, and assess its acceptability. Second, their own courts issued decrees and documents of many kinds, which of course would be easily enforced unless (as in the instance of Rav Judah's action against R. Naḥman's document, cited above)[2] another judge determined that it was of no value. Instances of court-supervision and control of legal and commercial documents include the following:

> A document came to court which was dated six years ahead. The rabbis before Rava thought that it was a post-dated document which is to be deferred and not executed until the date which it bears. R. Naḥman ruled, "This document must have been written by a scribe who was very particular and took into account the six years of Greek rule in Elam which we do not reckon..." R. Aḥa b. Jacob asked, "How do we know that our Era is connected with the Greek rule at all? Why not say it is reckoned from the Exodus from Egypt, omitting the first thousand years? In that case, it is post-dated." R. Naḥman replied, "In the diaspora, the Greek Era alone is used." (b. A.Z. 10a)

> A certain woman wished to deprive her (intended) husband of her estate, and so assigned it in writing to her daughter. After the subsequent marriage and divorce, she came before R. Naḥman (to claim the return of her estate). R. Naḥman tore up the deed. R. ʿAnan went to Mar ʿUqba and said, "See, sir, how Naḥman the boor tears up people's deeds." "Tell me what happened." "It happened in such and such a manner." "Do you speak," he replied, "of a deed a woman intended as a means of evasion? So did R. Ḥanilai b. Idi in the name of Samuel say, 'I am an officially recognized judge and should a deed intended as a means of evasion come into my hand I would tear it up...'"
> (b. Ket. 78b-79a)[3]

> R. Naḥman said, "Never was a bill for inspection [a legal document issued by a court inviting the public to inspect a property put up by an order of the court for sale] drawn up in Nehardea... (b. Ket. 100b)

R. Naḥman ruled that if two deeds were issued in sequence, the later cancels the earlier.[4] R. Huna spoke of various kinds of deeds which

has been mortgaged to several creditors; b. B.M. 16b-17a, R. Naḥman on conflicting claims; b. Ket, 88a, R. Naḥman on the privileges of a creditor, etc.

[1] Above, p. 313.

[2] Above, pp. 63 and 313.

[3] Above, p. 70.

[4] b. Ket. 44a.

effect possession.[1] R. Adda b. Ahavah said that sometimes a deed of acknowledgment of a debt may be drawn before witnesses and without an act of acquisition, and sometimes it may not. If the debtor actually called the witnesses for that purpose, it is to be drawn up.[2] Rav Judah gave instructions on how to draw up a deed of sale of a field, saying that he should specify in it, "Acquire the date trees, other large trees, small trees, and small date-trees."[3] R. Naḥman issued several decrees concerning documents.[4] The cases here cited indicate that the courts ruled on the validity of documents, and disagreements among officials, rather than widespread disinterest or disrespect for such documents, posed a greater obstacle than any other to court action.

IX. Agency and Trust

Cases concerning the power and culpability of agents, and disputes concerning the liability of trustees, came before the rabbinical courts, so the rabbis were able to effect Mishnaic and other Tannaitic laws on these subjects. Rabbinical adjudication of cases of agency in this time included the following:

> A certain woman once gave a man money to buy land. He went and bought it for her without providing for the security of its tenure. [He failed to arrange for the seller to pledge his landed property for the field]. She came before R. Naḥman, who said to the agent, "She can declare, 'I sent you to improve, not to make my position worse.' Go buy it from him without security and then sell it with due security of tenure." (b. B.B. 169b)

The courts were willing to oversee relationships of agency, and to order just practices in such matters. The rabbis similarly discussed the possibility of an agent's disobeying orders,[5] and debated whether or not an agent is presumed to carry out his task.[6] Cases concerning the liability of bailiffs came to court:

> A man once deposited sesame with another, and when he asked him

[1] b. B.B. 77a-b.
[2] b. Sanh. 29b.
[3] b. B.B. 69b.
[4] Weiss, *Dor*, III, 158. On solar vs. lunar calendars, see R. Naḥman, re Is. 60:1 in Gen. R. 6:3.
[5] b. Ket. 99b, R. Naḥman was asked by R. Ḥisda and Rabbah b. R. Huna about a hypothetical case in which an agent disobeyed orders.
[6] R. Naḥman said that he is, b. ʿEruv. 31b-32a.

to return it, the other replied, "You have already taken it." "But surely," he replied, "it was such-and such quantity, and is still lying intact in your jar." "Yours you have taken back, and this is different." R. Ḥisda ruled... (b. Yev. 115b)

A man once deposited jewels with his neighbor. When he asked for them back, he replied, "I do not know where I put them." He came before R. Naḥman who said, "A plea of 'I do not know' is negligence, so go and pay." Yet he did not pay, so R. Naḥman had his house seized. Subsequently the jewels were found, and had appreciated in value. R. Naḥman said, "Let the jewels be returned to their owner, the house to its owner..." (b. B.M. 35a)

Aibu entrusted flax to Ronia. Then (a thief) Shabu came and stole it. But subsequently the identity of the thief became known. The trustee came before R. Naḥman, who held him liable... (b. B.M. 93b)

These rulings of R. Naḥman indicate that the laws of bailment, involving the responsibility of trustees, were enforced without difficulty in rabbinical courts. The rabbis additionally discussed whether he who enters a false plea in case of theft of a deposit is required to take an oath[1] and other oaths in connection with trusteeship;[2] whether he who denies a deposit falsely is considered as if he had misappropriated it,[3] and other matters.[4]

x. Summary and Conclusions

Our survey of cases[5] and of concommitant academic discussions, can leave no doubt whatever of the nature of rabbinic jurisdiction. However ambiguous the role of the rabbis in deciding points of religious observance, when a litigation involving exchanges of property, torts and damages, court-enforced documents, and the like came up, it was the rabbis, and they alone, who decided it for Babylonian Jewry. They may have had difficulty with powerful or recalcitrant individuals,

[1] b. B.Q. 107b, R. Sheshet.

[2] b. B.M. 34b, R. Huna.

[3] b. B.Q. 105b, R. Sheshet.

[4] R. Huna and Rav Judah v. R. Naḥman and R. Yoḥanan, b. B.Q. 118a, and compare b. Ket. 12b, b. B.M. 97b, and 116b, on the conflicting claim, "You have a coin of mine" vs. "I am not certain of it."

[5] It could well be argued that some of the "cases" cited above were in fact theoretical case-formulations of a legal issue. It seems to me that the language of a very few cases is ambivalent, e.g. "Aibu centrusted flax to Ronia," cited above. In most instances, however, my judgment is that actual court-cases obviously are under discussion

but on the whole, their law was *the* law of the Jewish community. The reason was, as we have seen, that they were hired to decide just these cases, and the exilarch himself was expected by the Sasanian government to preside over an orderly and stable Jewish administration. Furthermore, the uncommon character of most litigations, devolving upon relatively abnormal situations, leads me to conclude that most of the people in their normal transactions abided by the law, and hence produced very few, if any, significant cases. Routine law enforcement led to just as routine obedience and conformity to rabbinic regulations and the use of acceptable documents of all kinds.

The tables which follow are intended to provide a summary of the third-century exemplifications of practical, workaday enforcement of the law reported in the Babylonian Talmud. The data are divided into approximate periods, ca. 220 to 265, and 265-310. The dividing line is somewhat arbitrary, for some cases in which R. Naḥman or Rav Judah or others of their generation figure could have taken place in the lifetimes of Rav and Samuel. Similarly, I have excluded cases involving R. Naḥman b. Isaac, Rabbah, Rava, and Abaye, although some of these might have taken place in the period before 310, and some of R. Naḥman's might have happened later on, since he supposedly died in 320. It does seem useful, however, to attempt a rough chronological division of the data. A further difficulty was, How does one determine whether questions derive from outside of the academy or not? I could not be certain, so I have included a reference *only* where it is very clear that the questioner was not a sage. I feel fairly sure that questions on the explanation of a Mishnaic law, or on the contradictions between one and another law, or on the further complexities of a legal issue—all were posed by learned academicians, and not by ordinary people. I have, finally, restricted the tables to Babylonian Talmudic evidence. The reason is that the Palestinian Talmud contains remarkably little data and very few cases at all relating to the students of Rav and Samuel. The intense hatred of Babylonians characteristic of the Palestinian academies deprived the latter of any substantial interest in what the former were actually doing in their courts. Hence I have limited this survey to more reliable data.

I. *b. Berakhot*

	Ca. 220-265	Ca. 265-310
Court Cases	1. 58a, R. Shila flogged for intercourse with gentile woman.	
Questions from Outside the Academy		1. 11b, Question to R. Abba & Yosi.
Stories about Law Enforcement outside of the Academy	1. 40b, Benjamin the Shepherd.	1. 20a, R. Mattena & Matun.

II. *b. Shabbat*

	Ca. 220-265	Ca. 265-310
Court Cases		
Questions from Outside the Academy	1. 139a, Levi from men of Bashkar (?)	
Stories about Law Enforcement outside of the Academy	1. 59b, Levi *re* coronet in Nehardea.	1. 59b, Rabbah b. Abbuha—*re* coronet in Maḥoza. 2. 121b, R. Huna criticizes man for killing hornet.

III. *b. ʿEruvin*

	Ca. 220-265	Ca. 265-310
Court Cases		[1. 25a, R. Naḥman—*re* land acquisition].
Questions from Outside the Academy		1. 80a, to R. Judah b. Oshaiah, Mattena, Rav Judah.
Stories about Law Enforcement outside of the Academy	1. 6a, R. Huna reports Rav's action at Damḥaria.	1. 6b, R. Naḥman at Nehardea. 2. 8a, Rav Judah at Dura diReʿuta.

(*continued*)

	Ca. 220-265	Ca. 265-310
	2. 6b, R. Mattena (supervised by Samuel). 3. 6b, Samuel did not object to practice in Nehardea. 4. 6b, Rav and Samuel in Nehardea (see also 8b). 5. 44b, Samuel flogged Sabbath violators. 6. 74b, Samuel. 7. 100b, Rav at Afsatia.	3. 8a, R. Ḥisda at Sura. 4. 11b, R. Naḥman at exilarchate. 5. 12a, Rav Judah at Dura diRe'uta. 6. 26a, Rabbah b. Abbuha at Maḥoza.

IV. *b. Pesaḥim*

	Ca. 220-265	Ca. 265-310
Court Cases		
Questions from Outside the Academy		
Stories about Law Enforcement outside of the Academy	1. 30a, Samuel to potsellers.	1. 42a, R. Mattena at Papunia. 2. 105a, R. Huna [*re* drinking before Havdalah].

V. *b. Yoma, Sukkah, Beẓah* [= Y., S., B.]

	Ca. 220-265	Ca. 265-310
Court Cases	1. B. 7a, R. Ammi. 2. B. 16b, R. Taḥlifa b. Avdimi.	[1. S. 31a, woman complains to R. Naḥman about theft].
Questions from Outside the Academy		1. B. 4a, Host asks R. Adda b. Ahavah. 2. B. 21a, to R. Huna.
Stories about Law Enforcement outside of the Academy	1. S. 11b, R. Mattena —brought case to Samuel.	1. Y. 81b, R. Giddal b. Menasseh of Bari. 2. S. 30a, R. Huna instructs traders.

VI. *b. Rosh Hashanah, Ta'anit* [= R.H., T.]		
	Ca. 220-265	Ca. 265-310
Court Cases		
Questions from Outside the Academy	1. T. 11b, Mar 'Uqba at Ginzaca	
Stories about Law Enforcement outside of the Academy	1. T. 21b, Samuel proclaimed a fast. 2. T. 24a, Rav proclaimed a fast. [3. T. 28b, Rav did not interfere in synagogue service.]	1. T. 20b, R. Huna's authority over markets, etc. 2. T. 21b, Rav Judah proclaimed a fast. (2) 3. T. 21b, R. Naḥman proclaimed a fast. 4. T. 24a, R. Naḥman proclaimed a fast.

VII. *b. Megillah, Mo'ed Qatan, Ḥagigah* [= M., M.Q., Ḥ.]		
	Ca. 220-265	Ca. 265-310
Court Cases		
Questions from Outside the Academy		
Stories about Law Enforcement outside of the Academy	1. M. 5b, Rav cursed men for planting flax on Purim. [2. M. 22b, Rav did not prostrate himself on synagogue mosaic].	1. M. 24b, R. Huna did not prohibit unfit priest from blessing congregation. 2. M. 27a, R. Huna proclaimed fast. 3. M.Q. 4b, Rav Judah permitted family of Bar Zittai to make *banki* in their vineyards. 4. M.Q. 10a, R. Huna cursed desecrator of festival week. 5. M.Q. 11a, Rav Judah permitted oven-making. 6. M.Q. 13b, R. Huna permitted sellers of

(*continued*)

	Ca. 220-265	Ca. 265-310
		herbs to go about their business in festival week. 7. M.Q. 16b, Woman banned for not giving way to student of R. Naḥman. 8. M.Q. 27b, R. Hamnuna banned people of Daru-Mata for not honoring dead. 9. M.Q. 27b, R. Huna cursed woman for excessive mourning.

VIII. *b. Yevamot*

	Ca. 220-265	Ca. 265-310
Court Cases	[1. 39b, Formula of Ḥaliẓah—ceremony before Rav]. 2. 45a, to Rav. 3. 104a, Rabbah b. Ḥiyya of Ctesiphon. 4. 116a, Rav instructs court scribes on deeds. 5. 121a, R. Shila permits woman to remarry.	[1. 39b, Deed of Ḥaliẓah composed by Rav Judah]. 2. 52a, R. Sheshet flogged for passing by door of father-in-law's house. 3. 65b, Woman pleads before R. Naḥman for divorce because of husband's sterility. 4. 95a, Rav Judah flogged for incest. [5. 115b, Disputed trust—to R. Ḥisda]. [6. 115b, Notes of indebtedness adjudicated by Rabbah b. Abbuha]. 7. 116a, R. Huna instructs court scribes on deeds. 8. 116b, Woman comes to Rav Judah's court *re* presumed death of husband.

(*continued*)

	Ca. 220-265	Ca. 265-310
Questions from Outside the Academy	1. 45a, to Rav.	
Stories about Law Enforcement outside of the Academy	1. 102a, Rav says people normally perform *ḥaliẓah* with a sandal.	1. 102b, Rav Judah 2. 121b, Woman re-married after R. Naḥman exclaimed her husband must be dead.

IX. *b. Ketuvot*

	Ca. 220-265	Ca. 265-310
Court Cases	1,2. 2b [= 3a], Samuel on conditional divorce. 3. 21a, Samuel confirms deed. 4. 60a, Samuel forces woman to suckle child. 5. 80a, R. Ammi—re divorce settlement. [6. 105a, Qarna paid by litigants].	1. 10a, R. Naḥman flogged man who claimed bride was not a virgin. 2. 27b, R. Ḥisda *re* inheritance. 3. 49b, Rav Judah *re* non-support. 4. 50b, Pumbeditan and Nehardean judges *re* support of daughters by father's estate. 5. 54a, R. Naḥman *re* marriage contracts. 6. 69a, R. ʿAnan *re* support of daughter from father's estate. 7. 78b-79a, R. Naḥman *re* deed of evasion. 8. 80a, Rav Judah *re* divorce settlement. 9. 84b, R. Naḥman *re* orphan's property. 10. 85a, R. Naḥman *re* trust. 11. 85b, R. Naḥman *re* trust. 12. 85b, R. Naḥman *re* marriage contract. 13. 91a, R. Naḥman *re* estate.

(*continued*)

	Ca. 220-265	Ca. 265-310
		14. 94b, R. Sheshet *re* conflicting deeds of gift. 15. 97a, R. Naḥman *re* retraction of sale [16. 105a, R. Huna paid by litigants] 17. 106a, R. Naḥman—case referred by R. ʿAnan.
Questions from Outside the Academy		
Stories about Law Enforcement outside of the Academy	1. 23a, Samuel's father guards captives brought to Nehardea for ransom.	

X. *b. Nedarim*, *Nazir*, *Sotah* [= Ned., Naz., S.]

	Ca. 220-265	Ca. 265-310
Court Cases		1. Ned. 7b, R. Ḥisda annuls a vow. 2. Ned. 7b, R. Huna bans for blasphemy. 3. Ned. 21b, R. Huna annuls a vow. 4. Ned. 22b, R. Naḥman annuls a vow. 5. Ned. 27a, R. Huna rules on a vow. 6. Ned. 31b, R. Naḥman rules on the liability of an agent. 7. Ned. 48b, R. Naḥman annuls the force of a vow. [8. Ned. 50b, Rav Judah judges suit.] 9-10. Ned. 91a-b, R. Naḥman refuses to

(*continued*)

	Ca. 220-265	Ca. 265-310
		forbid woman from her husband. (2 cases) 11. S. 48a, R. Huna forbade singing in marketplace.
Questions from Outside the Academy		
Stories about Law Enforcement outside of the Academy		

XI. *b. Gittin*

	Ca. 220-265	Ca. 265-310
Court Cases	1. 6a, R. Kahana asked Rav whether declaration was required. 2. 30a, Samuel *re* divorce. 3. 34a, Samuel *re* divorce.	1. 6a, R. Ḥisda and R. Sheshet required declaration. 2. 14a, R. Naḥman *re* transfer of possession in error. 3. 19b, R. Naḥman had document read to him by court scribes. 4. 19b, R. Naḥman *re* divorce. 5. 27a, R. Huna *re* divorce. 6. 34a, R. Sheshet *re* divorce. 7. 34a, Rav Judah *re* divorce. 8. 35a, R. Huna *re* payment of marriage contract. 9. 39b, R. Naḥman *re* emancipation of slaves. 10. 52a, R. Naḥman *re* orphan's property. 11. 52a, R. Naḥman *re* orphan's property.

(continued)

	Ca. 220–265	Ca. 265–310
		12. 52b, R. Naḥman *re* orphan's property. 13. 63b, R. Naḥman *re* divorce. 14. 66a, R. Naḥman *re* divorce. 15. 80a-b, R. Huna *re* dating divorce documents.
Questions from Outside the Academy		
Stories about Law Enforcement outside of the Academy		1. 14a, R. Sheshet's agent gives quittance in Maḥoza. 2. 46b, R. Huna refuses to redeem slaves.

XII. *b. Qiddushin*

	Ca. 220-265	Ca. 265-310
Court Cases	1. 12b, Rav punished for illegal forms of betrothal. 2. 79b, R. Joseph b. R. Menasia *re* betrothal.	1. 12a, R. Ḥisda on betrothal. [2. 12b, R. Sheshet chastised man for passing etc.] 3. 13a, R. Naḥman *re* betrothal.
Questions from Outside the Academy		
Stories about Law Enforcement outside of the Academy		[1. 39a, R. Ḥanan and ʿAnan *re* enforcing agricultural law]. [2. 70a, *re* excommunication for disrepect to Rav Judah].

XIII. *b. Bava Qama*

	Ca. 220-265	Ca. 265-310
Court Cases	1. 11a, Rav *re* negligent trust. 2. 27b, Samuel *re* damages. 3. 99b, Rav *re* *Kashrut* of food. 4. 117a, Rav *re* theft by confiscation.	1. 12a, R. Naḥman *re* distraint. 2. 19b, Rav Judah *re* damages. 3. 21a, R. Naḥman *re* orphans property. 4. 37a, R. Huna *re* personal injury. [5. 50b, R. Naḥman *re* ritual slaughter]. 6. 58b, R. Naḥman *re* damages. 7. 88b, Rav Judah *re* inheritance. 8. 96b, R. Naḥman *re* increment through theft. 9. 113a, R. Naḥman *re* summons to suit. 10. 115a, R. Huna *re* theft. 11. 116b R. Naḥman *re* theft by confiscation.
Questions from Outside the Academy		
Stories about Law Enforcement outside of the Academy		

XIV. *b. Bava Meẓi'a'*

	Ca. 220-265	Ca. 265-310
Court Cases	1. 14a, Samuel *re* property suit. 2. 16b, Samuel's scribes *re* deeds of transfer. 3. 23b, Rav *re* find. 4. 36a, Rav *re* trust. 5. 49a, Rav *re* futures.	1. 7a, R. Ḥisda—R. Huna *re* coerced temple dedication. 2. 18a-b, R. Huna *re* divorce [= 20a-b]. 3. 24b, Rav Judah *re* find. 4. 35a, R. Naḥman *re* trust.

	6. 70a, Samuel *re* orphan's property. 7. 73a, Rav *re* liability. 8. 96b, Rav *re* liability. 9. 101a, Rav *re* misappropriation of property. 10. 110b, Samuel *re* misappropriation of property.	5. 38b, R. Sheshet *re* estate. 6. 39b, R. Ḥisda *re* estate. 7. 49b, R. Ḥisda *re* futures. 8. 51a, R. Naḥman *re* futures. 9. 66a, R. Naḥman *re* usury. 10. 81a, R. Naḥman *re* trust. 11. 93b, R. Naḥman *re* trust. 12. 109a, R. Naḥman (or Rav Judah) *re* liability for loss. 13. 110a, Rav Judah *re* dispute over debt.
Questions from Outside the Academy		
Stories about Law Enforcement outside of the Academy		

XV. *b. Bava Batra*

	Ca. 220-265	Ca. 265-310
Court Cases	1. 36a, Father of Samuel *re* seizure. 2. 54a, Levi *re* seizure. 3. 111a, R. Nittai *re* inheritance. 4. 143a, Samuel *re* estate. 5. 153a, Rav and Samuel *re* deed of gift.	1. 22a, R. Kahana *re* market supervision. 2. 29b, R. Naḥman *re* seizure. 3. 30a, R. Naḥman *re* seizure. 4. 31a, R. Naḥman *re* seizure. 5. 33a, R. Ḥisda *re* seizure. 6. 33b, R. Ḥisda *re* seizure. 7. 33b, R. Naḥman *re* seizure. 8. 41a, R. Naḥman *re* seizure.

(*continued*)

	Ca. 220-265	Ca. 265-310
		9. 41b, Rav Judah *re* seizure. 10. 48b, R. Huna *re* forced sale. 11. 54b, Rav Judah *re* seizure. 12. 54b, R. Naḥman *re* seizure. 13. 82b-83a, Rav Judah *re* sale. 14. 88a, R. Kahana *re* market supervision. 15. 111a, R. Tavla *re* inheritance. 16. 111a, R. Huna b. Ḥiyya *re* inheritance. 17. 132b, R. Ḥisda *re* inheritance. 18. 141b, R. Huna *re* acquisition. 19. 151a, R. Naḥman and R. Sheshet *re* acquisition of property from dying person. 20. 151a, R. Naḥman *re* acquisition of property from dying person. 21. 151a, R. Naḥman *re* acquisition of property from dying person. 22. 151b, R. Naḥman *re* acquisition of property from dying person. 23. 153a, R. Huna *re* acquisition. 24. 159b, R. Naḥman *re* suit over sale. 25. 159b, R. Naḥman *re* seizure. 26. 169b, R. Naḥman *re* agency.

(*continued*)

	Ca. 220-265	Ca. 265-310
Questions from Outside the Academy	[1. 127a, Men of Akra di. Agma to Samuel *re* inheritances].	
Stories about Law Enforcement outside of the Academy		

XVI. *b. Sanhedrin*

	Ca. 220-265	Ca. 265-310
Court Cases	1. 7b, Rav *re* lawsuit. 2. 29a, Mar 'Uqba *re* lawsuit.	1. 25a, R. Naḥman punished slaughterer [2. 27a-b, Aha b. Jacob *re* murder].[1] 3. 29b, R. Naḥman *re* collection of debt. 4. 31a, R. Naḥman *re* civil suit. 5. 31a, R. Naḥman *re* collection of debt.
Questions from Outside the Academy		
Stories about Law Enforcement outside of the Academy	1. 47b, Samuel did not object to veneration of Rav's grave.	

XVII. *b. 'Avodah Zarah*

	Ca. 220-265	Ca. 265-310
Court Cases	1. 56b, Samuel *re* fitness of wine. 2. 57a, Rav *re* fitness of wine. 3. 68b, Rav *re* mouse in beer.	1. 33b, Rav Judah *re* fitness of wine. 2. 62b, R. Ḥisda *re* fitness of wine.
Questions from Outside the Academy		

[1] Probably ca. 350 A. D.

(*continued*)

	Ca. 220-265	Ca. 265-310
Stories about Law Enforcement outside ot the Academy		1. 72a, R. Ḥisda tells Jewish wine sellers how to pour for gentiles.

XVIII. *b. Horayot, Shevu'ot, Makkot* [= H., Sh., M.]

	Ca. 220-265	Ca. 265-310
Court Cases		1. Sh. 30b, R. Naḥman *re* suit. 2. Sh. 34b, R. Naḥman *re* payment of debt. 3. Sh. 41b, R. Naḥman *re* payment of debt. 4. Sh. 41b, R. Sheshet *re* payment of debt. 5. Sh. 42a, R. Naḥman *re* payment of debt. 6. M. 16b, Rav Judah flogged a man who ate a worm.
Questions from Outside the Academy		
Stories about Law Enforcement outside of the Academy		

XIX. *b. Zevaḥim, Menaḥot, Ḥullin*

	Ca. 220-265	Ca. 265-310
Court Cases		
Questions from Outside the Academy		
Stories about Law Enforcement outside of the Academy	1. Men. 32, Rev on how the people practice *ḥaliẓah.* 2. Ḥul. 44a, Rav *re* supervision of slaughter. 3. Ḥul. 53a, Rav *re*	1 Ḥul. 17b, R. Sheshet examined slaughterers' knives. 2. Ḥul. 48b, R. Naḥman supervised market. 3. Ḥul. 56a, R. Mat-

(*continued*)

	Ca. 220-265	Ca. 265-310
	supervision of slaughter. 4. Ḥul. 59a, Rav *re* supervision of slaughter. 5. Ḥul. 95a-b, Rav *re* supervision of *kashrut*. 6. Ḥul. 96a, Samuel *re* supervision of of porging. 7. Ḥul. 110a, Rav taught prohibition of milk and meat. [8. Ḥul. 131a, Rav told of Levite who snatched priestly dues]	tena *re* supervision of slaughter. 4. Ḥul. 95b, R. Naḥman, R. Huna, R. Ḥisda, consulted about *Kashrut* of meat. 5. Ḥul. 110a-b, R. Ḥisda tries man for eating udders. 6. Ḥul. 132b, R. Naḥman declared man liable for priestly dues. 7. Ḥul. 132b, R. Ḥisda banned butchers of Huẓal for not giving priestly dues for twenty-two years. 8. Ḥul. 141b, Rav Judah flogged man for clipping wings of dam, releasing, retaking it.

XX. *b. Bekhorot*, *ʿArakhin*, *Temurah*, *Keritot*, *Meʿilah*, *Tamid*

	Ca. 220-265	Ca. 265-310
Court Cases		1. Bekh. 50b, R. Huna *re* personal injury.
Questions from Outside the Academy		1. Bekh. 27a-b, Woman asks R. Naḥman *et al.* *re* purity rules applying to heave-offering.
Stories About Law Enforcement outside of the Academy		1. ʿArakh. 29a ,Rav Judah *re* temple dedication in Pumbedita.

XXI. *b. Niddah*

	Ca. 220-265	Ca. 265-310
Court Cases		1. 13b, R. Huna ordered hand cut off for masturbation.
Questions from Outside the Academy		
Stories About Law Enforcement outside of the Academy	1. 25a, Samuel *re* sac of abortion. 2. 25b, Samuel *re* sac of abortion. 3. 66a, Samuel *re* meaning of blood-excretion.	1. 20b, ʿUlla *re* menstrual blood. 2. 20b, Rav Judah *re* menstrual blood (refuses to examine first drop). 3. 20b, Rabbah b. bar Ḥana *re* menstrual blood. 4. 67b, Rav Judah decreed *re* time of immersion in Pumbedita.

XXII. *Summary*

	Ca. 220-265	Ca. 265-310	Total	Approximate Percentage of Total
Civil Law	23	85	108	44.0%
Personal Status	16	24	40	16.3%
Food and Sex Taboos (including slaughter)	15	21	36[1]	14.6%
Fasts, Holidays, Sabbath	10	19	29	17.5%
[Sabbath Limits	7	7	14]	
Synagogue Liturgy	3	2	5	2.0%

[1] Among the many ambiguities of this table, I think this item is the most difficult to evaluate. Most of the "cases" or "exemplifications of law enforcement" cited in the preceding tables, and here counted as one unit, in fact would have far wider applications. The items here listed would easily lead to the supposition that many times, and not merely once or twice, the rabbis gave instructions about ritual slaughter and menstrual blood. Indeed I can hardly regard the items represented by this figure as really to be equated to the specific cases represented elsewhere on the table.

(continued)	Ca. 220-265	Ca. 265-310	Total	
Punishment of Common People for Disrespect to Scholars	—	2	2	.8%
Vows and Dedications	—	7	7	2.8%
Agricultural Rules and Tithing	1	3	4	1.6%
	68	163	231	99.6%
	29.2%	70.8%		

The last table requires little amplification. We see that close to one-half of all cases, questions, and stories which suggest that laws were actually enforced pertained to matters of civil law. Since most actionable matters of personal status involved property transactions and were also brought to court, an additional 16.3% should be added, for a total of 60.3%. Most of those cases deriving from food taboos (8 out of the 15 in b. Ḥullin) were based upon the rabbis' supervision of the market place. So I think it is abundantly clear that where laws were enforced, the main reason was that the rabbis' position as chief judicial officials of the Jewish government made it possible. Their public authority produced, likewise, almost half of the exemplifications of law enforcement pertaining to the sacred calendar (fasts, holidays, and the like), that is, the approximately 14 out of 29 instances concerning the Sabbath boundary. The evidences on other matters are inconsequential. In summary: *the rabbis actually enforced those civil and property laws that their courts were empowered to administer, and very little else.*[1]

One is struck also by the considerably greater number of cases (etc.) deriving from the later period. I had originally regarded it as of no probative value. One must keep in mind, first of all, the vast number of cases contributed by R. Naḥman, whose special circumstances we

[1] And this was *just* what the Persians and Samuel had agreed to. Samuel had said that the law of the government is law, and his saying specifically applied to taxes, property transactions, court bills and documents, and the like. We now see that these were the particular matters over which rabbinical courts exercised effective jurisdiction. So in fact the rabbis were quite properly serving as part of the Persian regime, as they were supposed to, and whatever else they said or did bore no relationship to their official, state-sanctioned functions. Given the meticulous way in which the rabbis clearly carried out their part of the agreement, one can hardly be surprised that the Jews were on the whole not badly treated even in the repressive times of Kartir.

have discussed. We have noted, moreover, the arbitrary assignment of some cases to the period of 265 to 310, which might just as well have happened earlier; but we have omitted cases of Rava and Rabbah which might have taken place before ca. 310. I have, thirdly, excluded the data of the Palestinian Talmud, which I regarded as a distortion, because of the suppression of stories pertaining to the students of Rav, Samuel, and their contemporaries. And yet, the *Yerushalmi* cases concerning Rav and Samuel are not numerous, and do not appreciably alter the proportions we have noted. In Vol. II are cited 4 additional cases (p. 260, y. 'Orlah 3.7, re agricultural law; p. 273, y. Git. 3.8, on requiring a divorce; p. 278, y. Nid. 2.5, 2.7, on menstrual purity; and see also y. 'Eruv. 1.4, Rav oversees a Sabbath-boundary, y. Git. 6.1, Rav on the validity of a divorce, in two cases, and y. Qid. 3.8, Samuel on the validity of a divorce granted under duress). So one may *very* tentatively suppose that the practical authority of the rabbis over Jews outside of the academies did in fact expand during the last half of the third century and afterward. However, until we have considered in volume IV the similar statistics for the first two thirds of the fourth century, we cannot regard the matter as settled. *If* a similar substantial growth in the exemplifications of the enforcement of the law becomes apparent, then we may well conclude that with the passage of time, the rabbis did acquire more and more practical power over the lives of the people.

We have learned, therefore, that while the Mishnah and Amoraic discussions on it constituted a single body of law, these comprehended various *types* of law, not enforced to the same degree or in the same way. Laws pertaining to possession and stable exchange of property, the recognition of changes in personal status, and the like—these were enforced by courts, and the court officials could use coercion. One may assume that for every transaction yielding court action, many more proceeded normally without resort to litigation. The second major *type* of law studied in the academies pertained to religious life, including the application of moral and cultural ideals and the proper observances of religious taboos. A representative of such laws is the following:

> R. Ḥisda said, "It is forbidden to have sexual relations in the daytime." (b. Nid. 17a)

Faithful students would have refrained, therefore, if they knew of R. Ḥisda's teaching. But outside of the academies, there was actually no way whatever for the rabbis to supervise the sex life of the ordinary people. Similarly, the laws about festivals, holidays, fasts, and Sabbath, the prayers of the synagogue, all manner of liturgies—these could not have shaped the practices of the common folk unless the people actually turned to the rabbis for advice. As we have seen, a very substantial minority of the exemplifications of enforcement of practical law pertained to these very matters, 39.3% of those we have considered. Many of these actions involved, however, public supervision by the rabbis of matters easily within their control because of their judicial and political position, especially supervision of the marketplaces, and hence of ritual slaughter, on the one hand, and erection of the Sabbath limits, on the other. There remain, however, some instances in which ordinary people did consult the rabbis about various religious practices and taboos, most of them specifically pertaining to biblical laws which the people believed were revealed at Sinai. Since they planned to keep them, it was natural to consult the rabbis about how to do so. Yet the instructions of the rabbis were here misunderstood as often as not, and so I should suspect that the configuration of popular piety and mores cannot be accurately discerned from a survey of the rabbinical rules on the subject. On the other hand, as I have stressed, the rabbis' personal influence must have exceeded their practical authority. Given their reputation as holy men, physicians, and masters of magic, one can hardly suppose that ordinary people would lightly have ignored rabbinical practice, or openly defied it.

To summarize: The Sasanian government certainly reserved for its own courts jurisdiction over serious criminal cases, particularly those involving state policy. The rabbis, for their part, had unlimited authority in their own schools. They exercised substantial power over the Jewish marketplace and over property transactions, as agents of the exilarchate and hence of the Persian regime. They possessed in addition considerable influence over ordinary affairs of normal people. So the Mishnaic tractates which rabbinical *courts* actually enforced, for various reasons and in various ways, were likely to have been ʿEruvin, possibly parts of Taʿanit, Moʿed Qatan, Nedarim, Shevuʿot, and Niddah, and *most* certainly, Yevamot, Ketuvot, Gittin, Qiddushin, Bava Qama, Bava Meẓiʿa', Bava Batra, and Ḥullin.

The following account gives a helpful portrait of the workaday functions of R. Huna, head of the Sura academy:

> Rava said to Rafram b. Papa, "Tell me some of the excellent things which R. Ḥuna used to do." He said to him, "Of his youth I recall

> nothing, but about his old age, I remember. Every cloudy day they would carry him out in a golden palanquin, and he would survey the whole town. Every wall which looked unsafe he would order torn down. If the owner could rebuild it, he did so, but if not, he [R. Huna] would rebuild it of his own funds. On the eve of every Sabbath, he would send a messenger to the market, and all the vegetables that remained to the market-gardeners, he would buy and throw into the river." (But he should have given it to the poor? Sometimes they would depend on it and would not go and buy. But he should have given it to cattle? He thought that food fit for humans must not be given to cattle. But he should not have bought it at all? This would mislead the gardeners in the future [by not providing sufficient supplies].) "Whenever he discovered a medicine, he would fill a jug with it, and suspend it above the doorstep and announce, 'Whoever wants to, let him come and take.' (Some say, he knew from tradition a medicine for [a certain disease caused by eating with unwashed hands], and he would suspend a jug of water and proclaim, 'Whoever needs it, let him come so that he may save his life from danger.') When he ate bread, he would open his door wide and declare, 'Whoever is in need, let him come and eat.'" Rava said, "All these I can carry out, except the last, for in Maḥoza are many soldiers." (b. Ta'anit 20b-21a)

One is struck by the variety of public responsibilities carried out by the rabbi. He had to see to it that the buildings did not collapse after a rain-storm, as happened on account of their mud-construction. He had to insure that a constant market was maintained, by encouraging the truck-gardeners to provide a steady supply of fresh vegetables. He had to give out medical information, to preserve public health, and to make certain that poor people could benefit from the latest remedies. And he had to provide for the poor, so that no one would starve in his town. Only some of these duties depended upon his political role, namely, the first and second. As judge he could order the destruction of dangerous property; as administrator he had to supervise the marketplace, and use his funds to control supply and prices. But these roles had nothing to do with medical and eleemosynary activities, the former of which depended rather upon his reputation as a man of learning, who had mastered the occult sciences, including medicine. The latter was based upon the fact that he possessed great wealth, accruing from his other positions in politics, administration, and academic life. So we conclude that the rabbi effected the various Mishnaic laws and Oral Traditions in several different ways. We have here emphasized his coercive power, based upon the courts, but extending mostly to litigations over property and market-transactions. Strictly speaking, however he sought to carry out the laws and ensure the people's conformity to them, it was only civil laws, torts, proper court procedures, and some economic dicta—not all of them derived from the rabbinic tradition—which were actually *enforced* by the rabbi. The rabbi could, secondly, *influence* ordinary people because of his reputation as a holy and learned man, his knowledge of medicine and magic, and his supposedly unusual "merit." It would be natural for ordinary people to accept his leadership, even when it was not based upon political or coercive agencies. He could, thirdly, set a public example which others might be encouraged to emulate through promises of heavenly reward or punishment. And in his academy, he could *decree* for his disciples precisely what he wanted.

In the end, therefore, from the rabbi's perspective the most satisfactory situation lay in the academy, and the chief hope for the reformation of Babylonian Jewish life to conform to the Mishnah and rabbinic traditions depended upon the extension of academic mores to as wide a circle of Jews as possible. The first step would have to be the achievement of genuine autonomy, so that the academies served none but their own interests, and no longer depended upon the exilarchate for accreditation as judges, and hence for judicial powers. A stable situation of equality and autonomy was hardly to be hoped for. Either the exilarch would use the academies, or the academies would subvert the exilarch. No middle ground existed, for each laid down a claim to exclusive, uncontingent authority. So the uneasy partnership of nearly a half-century, between the death of Shapur I and the passing of Rav, Samuel, and their adult contemporaries, on the one hand, and the coming of age of Rabbah, Rava, Abaye, R. Joseph, and others of the time of Shapur II, on the other, would inevitably have to be dissolved. Rav and Samuel had humbly and faithfully served the exilarch, and many of their disciples held high places in his administration. But Rav and Samuel had built academies, and their disciples had greatly enhanced the prestige and achievements of these academies. In the next generation, the heads of the schools openly defied the suzerainty of the exilarch, competing with him no longer merely for public recognition, which was now theirs, nor only for a measure of day-to-day power, which he had gladly granted them long ago, but for the crown and sceptre of Babylonian Jewry. Who should rule until the Messiah will come? Indeed whose rule now signifies, according to the common understanding of Genesis 49:10, that the Messiah eventually *will* come, and whose rule will bring him nearer? These were the issues of the coming age.

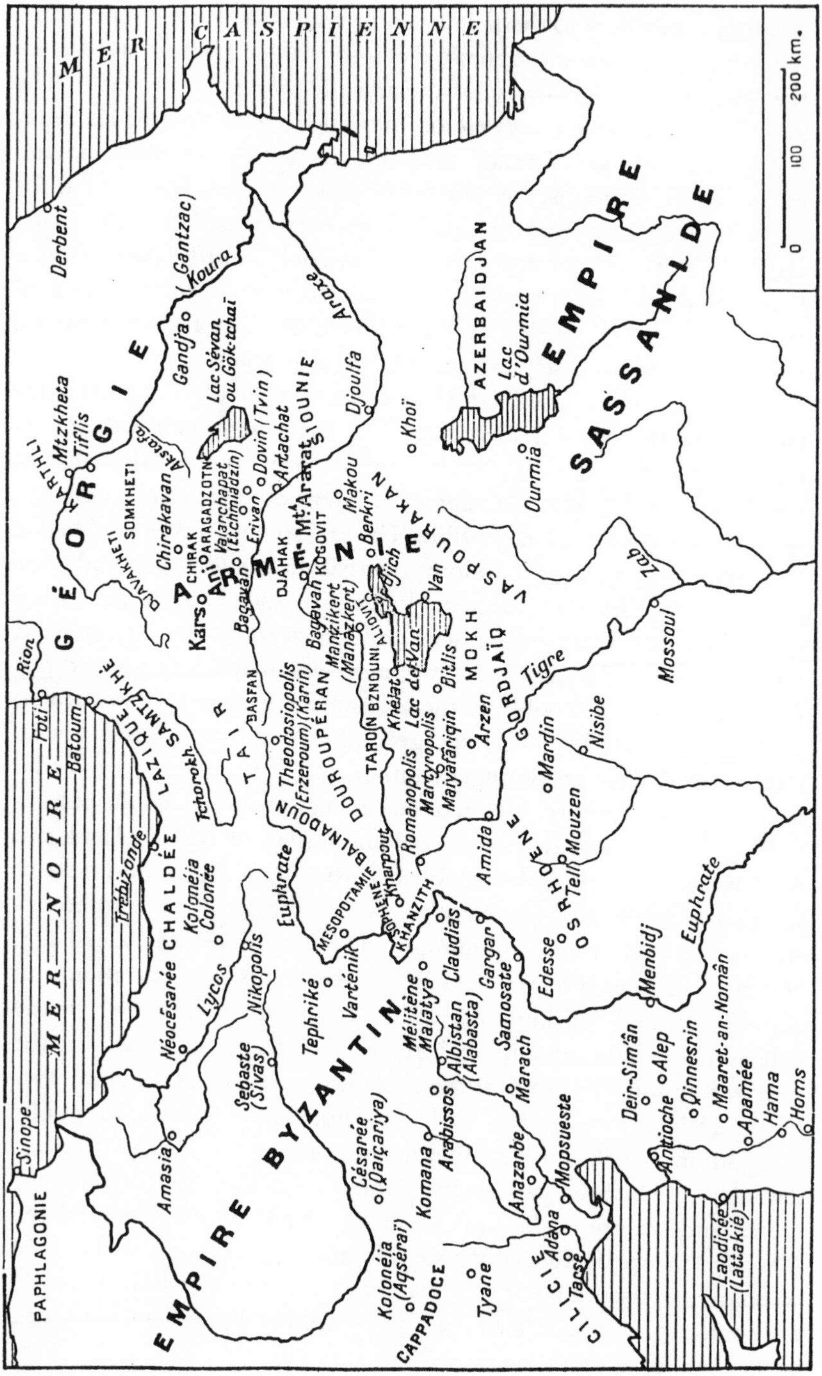

I. Northern Mesopotamia, Armenia, Georgia, and Eastern Anatolia

CHAPTER THREE

BABYLONIAN JEWISH GOVERNMENT (I): THE RABBI AS ADMINISTRATOR

I. Introduction

We cannot too often remind ourselves that all we know about Babylonian Jewry consists of what the rabbis chose to transmit in their schools.[1] Nowhere does that fact become more striking than in the study of the life and culture of ordinary Jews. We have limited archaeological data, the magical incantation bowls and the paintings in the synagogue at Dura-Europos. Rabbinic literature provides little persuasive evidence about what the latter may have meant, or what the former were used for.[2] Our consideration of the external structure of the Jewish government of Babylonia quickly came down to study of germane rabbinic sayings and stories. It was the limited usefulness of these data that became in the end the most obvious and convincing result of our inquiry. All we can say with absolute certainty is that there *was* an exilarchate, and that some rabbis disliked the holder of that of-

[1] I have not repeated the extended discussions found in vol. II, pp. 251-260, 281f, and vol. III, pp. 202-213, about the use of Talmudic sources for social history, or the relationship between the rabbis' legal sayings and the actual behavior of the people, nor have I restated the comparisons between the functions in Jewish society of the rabbis and their schools and those in Mazdean, Christian and Manichaean society of Magi, ascetic monks, and elect, respectively, found in vol. II, pp. 147-151, and vol. III, pp. 195-202 and 266-271. I presuppose knowledge of earlier passages, have absolutely nothing to add to what I have already said on these subjects. I can report no significant modifications in my basic theses. My purpose here is to examine the data on fourth-century rabbis by the procedures and criteria offered and employed in the earlier volumes. What is important is the testing of those theses against the data of a later generation and the consideration of evidence, below (pp. 256ff), possibly pointing to broadening and deepening rabbinical influence. It is striking that the rabbis were now willing to say, "Go and see what the people are doing in the streets," and similar expressions. I have not found many such expressions used earlier in Babylonia. Standing by themselves they prove nothing. But as we shall see, some evidence suggests that the rabbis now could control popular behavior more effectively than in earlier times.

[2] I hope in later research to study the meaning for the history of Babylonian Judaism of the incantation bowls and of the synagogue at Dura Europos. See the brief and preliminary comments in vol. II, pp. 57-64, and also my "Judaism at Dura Europos," *History of Religions* 4, 1, 1966, 81-102.

fice. Were we to accept the opinion of rabbis as fact, we should have to suppose the shadowy exilarch to have been a mere figure-head, a marginal Jew whose religious laxity, luxurious manner of living, and indifference to the sentiments of ordinary folk rendered him irrelevant to the "true life" of Israel. Only by extrapolating from the likely choices and facts of Sasanian politics were we able to suggest that the exilarch was more significant and central in Jewish affairs than some rabbis said. References to the exilarch's servants would lead us to suppose that he built a considerable administration, of which the rabbis and their disciples constituted only a part, though perhaps a most important, influential one. But practically all we know about exilarchic government is what the schools reported.

On the other hand, the rabbis' own aspirations render their literature of historical interest. In fact, they make possible the recovery of aspects of Babylonian Jewish history, if not so much as we might have liked. What was most striking about the rabbis as a group was both their intimate involvement in the everyday life of ordinary Jews and their desire to control, direct, and where necessary, reform it. The reason was that they took most seriously the prophetic conviction about the destiny of Israel. The sacred quality of Israel's group life, the morality and ethics of everyday affairs, and the loyalty of the people to the covenant at Sinai and its revealed legislation—these, and not the power of pagan kingdoms or the sword of Israel itself, would finally decide Israel's destiny. Israel would be saved through *Torah*.[1] Regarding themselves as the best exemplars of the divine will for Israel, the rabbis very much wanted all other Jews to become rabbis. Unlike the Manichaeans, who hardly expected that the hearers would eventually be numbered among the elect, and unlike the Christian nuns and monks, who did not suppose ordinary people bore every single obligation which the ascetics carried out, the rabbis demanded that all Jews conform to rabbinical ideals, that is, to the Torah. It was this ethic which brought the rabbis into contact—and conflict—with ordinary people. They could hardly ignore any means of influence or power over the common life.

It was thus that the rabbinical estate hoped to effect a great reformation of the lives of common folk. Israel should conform to the laws of the whole Torah, meaning in particular those of the Mishnah redacted by R. Judah the Prince, studied in the rabbinical schools, and enforced wherever possible in the Babylonian Jewish courts controlled by the

---

[1] See my "Religious Uses of History," *History and Theory* 5, 2, 153-171.

rabbis. The study and application of that law, both the Written and the Oral Revelation supposedly given to Moses and handed on by him to their own day, constituted the rabbis' conception of the holy life. That life was lived in their schools, and only partially outside of the rabbinical group. The rabbis and disciples conformed to the "Torah" in every detail, or regarded their lapses as sin. The masters could thus effect in the schools the fulfillment of the whole Torah. Outside of the schools, they could not, of course, look for equivalent success. The inertia of more than eight centuries of local customs and traditions, which must have taken shape from the first Jewish settlement in Babylonia, at the start of the sixth century B.C., and continued uninterruptedly to develop from that time to the advent of the rabbinical movement in the second century A.D., was not easily diverted. The rabbis nonetheless tried to reshape the accepted patterns of Jewish living and to reform the ideals and values which underlay them. That salvific aspiration brought them, to begin with, to cooperate with the exilarch, by staffing his courts and administrative agencies. It further preserved their patient willingness to cope with a less than satisfactory situation.

The rabbis did not live in monasteries, though their schools have much in common with monasteries and served many of the same functions.[1] They did not regard themselves as divorced from, or not responsible for, the ordinary folk. Therefore their literature contains considerable data upon the relationships between the laws and doctrines of the rabbis, on the one hand, and the life of the people on the other. Both case-reports and some sayings do testify to the condition of that life.[2] The central issue is, What was the relationship between rabbinical law and the sociology and culture of ordinary Jews? I have as yet found no way to illuminate the life of the streets except from that of the academies.[3] The only aspects of religious sociology open to study therefore are those revealed in the interstices between theoretical rabbinical sayings and actual, practical applications of some laws. So far, I have been able to contribute only the beginnings of an account of how the law was applied.

Some have argued that everyday life is of no interest to the historian, including the historian of religion, who should stress the creative achievements of the saints or elite alone. George Foot Moore wrote, for example, as follows:

---

[1] See vol. III, pp. 195-202.
[2] Vol. II, pp. 249-287, vol. III, pp. 202-213.
[3] See below, pp. 256ff.

> It is primarily the religion of intelligent and religious men that is [here] described ... Such men are always the minority, but they are the true representatives of their religion in any age, teachers and examples to their fellows. No religion has ever succeeded in bringing all of its adherents to its standards of right living ... and in the highest religions the gulf between the intellectual and moral leaders and the superstitious and depraved sediment of society is widest. But it is not from ignorance and superstition that anything can be learned about a religion; at that end, they are all alike.[1]

The supposition that it is the work of only the intelligent and religious men which warrants study seems to me faulty. Morton Smith comments on Moore's assumption that the true picture of a religion must be drawn chiefly from those documents which it accepts as authentic. He says:

> This supposes, obviously, that the religion has not changed substantially in the course of its history. If what was once a minority party has subsequently won control, and if the works of a former majority have been lost by neglect or by suppression, then the documents now accepted as authentic—the propaganda of the former minority—will give a seriously false picture of earlier times. Indeed, even if the triumphant party was one of the major parties aforetime, but was then matched by equally important competitors, there is a danger that it will now represent itself as the one true form of the earlier religion, and dismiss the other ancient forms, which, in their day, had equal claims to legitimacy, as heretical sects.[2]

Nowhere does it seem more dangerous to ignore the issues of everyday life than in the study of Babylonian Talmudic literature, which speaks in one and the same language, using quite historical, descriptive terms, about how things both *were* and *ought* to be. That literature, edited from the perspective and on the basis of the traditions of the schools of Sura and Pumbedita, not only contains almost no evidence about traditions and teachings of other than rabbinical authorities, but suppresses the whole record of pre-rabbinic Babylonian Judaism as if it simply had not existed. If we were seeking a true picture of that earlier period, we simply could not find it in rabbinical literature. But can we suppose that the period from 200 to 500, about which Talmudic traditions allegedly testify, is any more authentically portrayed? I have already argued that our records, while useful, are seriously deficient,

[1] Cited by Morton Smith, "The Work of George Foot Moore," *Harvard Library Bulletin* 15, 2, 1967, p. 175.

[2] *Op. cit.*, pp. 177-178.

first of all, in their *interest* in other-than-rabbinical opinions, second, in their willingness to portray at all, or fairly and objectively, other than rabbinical figures, or events pertaining to other-than-rabbinical circles. To assent to Moore's judgment would require, moreover, a theological judgment, including antecedent theological argument, about what is "true religion," and who may be called its "true representatives." It furthermore begs the question to argue that the "leaders" *actually* led, unless we can find evidence to testify to the wide extent of influence and power over the common life.

To assess rabbinic leadership one needs to study those who were led. Obviously we shall have to suppose there were variations between Jews, even among whole communities. Theologically to evaluate these variations requires the kind of judgments that cannot, in the first instance, be offered by historians of religion. The difficulties we faced[1] in finding in the phenomena themselves a valid distinction between "true religion" and "magic" or "superstition," or between "depraved sediments of society" and "moral leaders," and the like—those dificulties are not inconsequential. They must suggest that we had better describe as carefully and critically as we can, rather than evaluate data upon the basis of unexamined principles of theological judgment. I see no better way to obstruct our understanding of the data at hand than to begin by asking about its orthodoxy, heresy, nobility, immorality, or depravity. In studying the life of Babylonian Jewry, we have, therefore, to attempt a description of the way the Jewish government worked. The rabbis described only their own part in political and social life. So we turn immediately to what we are *able* to consider, namely the activities of the rabbinical courts and the work of the rabbis as administrators and judges.

What were the bases of rabbinical power and influence—leadership, in Moore's term—over the ordinary people? We need, first of all, to distinguish between political *power* and religious *influence*. If a rabbi could resort to court punishments, such as the ban, or the lash, or forcibly require a defendant to accept the court judgment in a case of property litigation, or impose fines, then one may say that he had concrete, coercive, political *power* to carry out the law. Another sort of power was that wielded by the rabbi over people who believed he could curse or bless with actual, measurable results, or who thought he was a holy man, able to bring down the favor or wrath of an ever-interested divinity and his legions of angels and demons, or who accepted his

[1] See vol. III, pp. 110-126.

claim to know just what God wanted of Israel in this particular place and time. That power was no less "coercive" in its way than police power in its several forms. I have chosen to refer to it, however, as "religious influence," to distinguish between what the rabbis could do as agents of the Jewish government and what they could do as holy men. As agents of the Jewish government, the rabbi decided according to rabbinical law cases involving personal status and transfers of property. A few other kinds of cases could be adjudicated by their courts as well, but these were the chief categories of law which rabbinical courts enforced with Iranian and exilarchic support.[1] As holy men, they exerted "religious influence" in a most concrete sense. People either were so frightened of the evil the rabbis could bring down upon them, or so eager for blessings they could promise in this world and in the next, or so impressed by their mastery of supposedly ancient teachings which God had revealed at Mount Sinai, that they submitted to the rabbis. Whether it was against their own will or otherwise hardly matters. They therefore were subjected, or subjected themselves, to the "spiritual power" of the rabbis. That spiritual power was not divorced from material matters. On the contrary, it is quite clear that a curse was believed to be practically effective over crops or commerce, a blessing would generate male children or open the gates of heaven.

The only useful distinction between "power" and "influence" must therefore be located in the basis of coercion. When the rabbi could rely on the exilarch to see to it that a court order was obeyed, he exerted political power. When he had to resort to the curse or ban, he used "religious influence." I do not suppose it was charismatic, in the sense that the appeal of individual rabbis' personalities affected or moved ordinary people. Some of the rabbis exhibited striking personalities, but that had little to do with the response of ordinary people to their orders. It was religion or magic and not personal charisma which influenced the workaday world.

Rabbinical *power*, deriving from the authority and ultimate support of Iranian government through the exilarchate, thus effected the widespread enforcement of civil laws,[2] including property exchanges of all kinds. Supernatural *influence* persuaded ordinary folk to pay close at-

[1] See vol. III, pp. 317-338. That is to say, precisely the terms of the original agreement between Samuel and Shapur.

[2] The chief handicap was the difficulty of administering widely scattered communities. Poor communications, local strong-men, and other centrifugal forces would have limited the enforcement of law even with great support from the exilarchate and the Sasanian bureaus of administration at Ctesiphon.

tention to rabbinical rules about religious and ritual laws, proper behavior in everyday life, matters of morality and ethics not accessible to court action, and the like.[1] It would be a mistake, however, to suppose that these forms of coercion ever were completely distinguished from one another. The judge in court, able to order lashes or excommunication, could also curse the guilty party or cast an evil eye. The administrator of community affairs, dealing with matters which, by their nature, could hardly be brought to court, and in general able to achieve his will through influence rather than political coercion normally was also the court-judge who might try a civil case involving the same recalcitrant. The sinner was a criminal, and vice versa. And the rabbinical judge-administrator was always the holy man, who knew the Torah, whose clothing, speech, and conduct set him apart from other Jews. It seems most useful, however, separately to consider these two aspects of the leadership of the rabbinate and to isolate the kinds of law effected by each. In general we shall see that rabbinical *influence* pertained to ordinary life, to the conduct of normal people in everyday circumstances, as well as to matters of faith, cult, rite, and taboo beyond court jurisdiction. Rabbinical *power* applied to extraordinary matters, such as contested divorces or marriage-contracts, broken contracts, disputed property and real estate, torts, and similar unusual occurrences. The rabbi as an extraordinary, holy man achieved his greatest affect in commonplace and ongoing daily life. The rabbi as lawyer, judge, and administrator, who carried out fundamentally routine, political tasks, related to exceptional events yielding court cases. We consider first the influence of the rabbi in the context of his administration of public affairs; second, in Chapter Four, his power as judge of specific sorts of cases; and finally in Chapter Five, his appearance as a holy man who exemplified the requirements of revelation.[2]

II. The Court

The focal point of rabbinical power and influence over the life of ordinary people was the court, in which both narrowly judicial and more broadly administrative functions were combined.[3] To the rabbis, the academy, not the court, constituted the most important focus of

[1] See vol. III, pp. 234-272.

[2] In general, I shall first cite or summarize case-reports, then, where appropriate, present evidence of rabbinical fulfillment of law, and finally, briefly refer to rabbinical opinions on the law.

[3] See vol. III, pp. 102-110, 130-149.

activities, but it was in court that rabbis normally came together with the common folk.[1] There they were prepared to use all the powers at hand, both political and religious, to enforce the "whole Torah." Nonetheless, matters that came before them as judges and administrators did not, to begin with, encompass the whole of the law. If most people did not keep ritual and moral laws, the rabbis could do little more than issue curses and ominous warnings *and* raise up a generation of disciples to obey it. If most people kept a rite or taboo, they could easily force the deviant person into line. In ligitations of property, on the other hand, their judgment was not disputed.[2]

The rabbis' view of their judicial responsibilities was expressed by Rava:

> When Rava would go to court, he said this: "Of his [my] own free will he [I] goes forth to death, and he [I] does [do] not meet the wishes of his household. He goes [I go] homeward empty-handed, and would that his [my] coming in should be like his [my] going out."
> (b. Yoma 86b-87a)[3]

The dangers of misconstruing a case led to Rava's hope that he might be as free of guilt upon his leaving court as upon entering it.

Given their stress of the merits of forefathers, one cannot be surprised that the rabbis insisted upon genealogical "purity," as much as upon ethical righteousness. Rava held that one proselyte may judge the case of another,[4] but not of a native Jew. R. Joseph earlier had taught that the court must be both pure in righteousness and free of all blemish,[5] including all physical defects.[6] Rava explained the prohibition against judges' taking gifts: as soon as a man receives a gift from another, he becomes so favorably disposed toward him that the latter seems like his own person, and the judge can see in him no wrong.[7]

[1] I do not mean to suggest that the school and court were invariably conducted in different places. We know that cases were decided in the exilarch's palace, so I should assume that in Maḥoza, the school was not the primary site of court functions. Elsewhere, however, cases may well have been tried where classes met. The distinction is meant as a merely functional one.

[2] Vol. III, pp. 317-338.

[3] The passage that follows in b. Yoma 87a was said by Rav, see b. Sanh. 7b, cited in vol. II, p. 115.

[4] b. Yev. 101b, as an exegesis of Deut. 17:15. Proselytes supposedly could not however judge the cases of home-born Jews.

[5] b. Qid. 76b. In context, his saying applied to the Sanhedrin, not to an ordinary court. But the language is simply "bet din."

[6] b. Yev. 101b. This saying is an exegesis of Song 4:7, and both this saying and that cited above seem originally to have formed a single pericope, which referred to "purity" of righteousness, genealogy, and physical appearance.

[7] b. Ket. 105b.

Sayings attributed to these two generations[1] concerning court procedures included Rava's, on whether a man's or a woman's suit is heard first,[2] on administering court oaths,[3] and on issuing subpoenas.[4] Rules of evidence included Rava's, that a man cannot testify against himself, "A man is his own relative, and therefore cannot declare himself wicked."[5] Abaye held, on the other hand, that the silence of the accused is equivalent to assent. If, for example, a witness testifies that a man ate forbidden food and the accused stands mute, the hostile witness is believed.[6] Other traditions reported the same rule of evidence in cases about the defilement of pure food and bestiality committed against an ox. The administration of court-oaths in Rava's court is illustrated by the following stories:

> A woman was once ordered to take an oath at the court of Rava, but when R. Ḥisda's daughter [his wife] said to him, "I know that she is suspected of [taking false] oaths," Rava transferred the oath to her opponent.
>
> (b. Ket. 85a)[7]

> A man with a monetary claim upon his neighbor once came before Rava, demanding of the debtor, "Come and pay me." "I have repaid you," the latter pleaded. "If so," Rava said to him, "Go and swear to him, that you have repaid." He thereupon went and brought a [hollow] cane, placed the money therein, and came before the Court, walking and leaning on it. He said to the plaintiff, "Hold the cane in your hand." He [the defendant] then took a scroll of the Torah and swore that he had repaid him [the plaintiff] all that he had received [the payment] in his hand. The enraged creditor thereupon broke the cane, and the money poured out on the ground. It was thus seen that he [the borrower] had [deceitfully] sworn to the truth.
>
> (b. Ned. 25a)[8]

Rabbah held that an oath generally will be viable because a man will not normally have the effrontery to deny a whole debt, though he may lie about part of it, a principle he derived from Scripture.[9] R. Joseph

---

[1] See vol. III, pp. 220-234, for the sayings of the earlier generation.

[2] b. Yev. 100a.

[3] b. Shev. 38b.

[4] b. Sanh. 8a, B.Q. 113a. See also b. M.Q. 16a, on the biblical origin of the regulation requiring the sending of a court messenger for a subpoena.

[5] b. Yev. 25b, b. Sanh. 9b. Rava did not, of course, invent the principle.

[6] b. Qid. 65b-66a.

[7] Trans. W. Slotki (London, 1948), p. 537. A second oath-story follows.

[8] Trans. H. Freedman (London, 1948), p. 71. See B. Lewin, *Oẓar HaGeonim, Nedarim*, Ap. p. 25.

[9] b. B.M. 3a.

and Rava discussed the penalties to be paid by witnesses whose testimony was convincingly refuted.[1] Rava and Abaye debated about the testimony of such a witness. Abaye said that the perjurer's testimony was retrospectively disqualified, while Rava held the disqualification was only in future cases.[2] Confirmed liars, Abaye held, could not testify even under oath.[3] Rava said that one who lent on interest was also ineligible to testify in a Jewish court, and the following case report indicates his opinion was put into effect:

> Two witness testified against Bar Bithinus. One said, "He lent money on interest in my presence." The other said, "He lent me money on interest." Rava disqualified Bar Bithinus...
>
> (b. Sanh. 25a)[4]

These and other sayings on court procedures and rules were part of a long development. We have no reason to suppose much, if anything, in them was new. What is important is that these sayings most certainly reflect the actual laws of procedure in rabbinical courts. No obstacle prevented the rabbis from conducting the courts according to rules of procedure and evidence which had been worked out in Tannaitic and earlier Amoraic times.

Punishments available in civil cases included flogging, excommunication, and fines, as well as adjudication of a case in favor of an injured plaintiff.[5] Somewhat irregular punishments involved putting out eyes, cutting off hands,[6] and public defamation of an evil-doer. Rava held that one may call the transgressor of the orders of rabbis "sinner", and no libel suit on that account would be entertained in court.[7] He said that flogging now was a substitute for capital punishment.[8] R. Joseph cited an earlier tradition, that while the four modes of capital punishment were no longer in effect, their equivalents were still commonplace. In place of stoning, one may be accidentally trampled to death by a beast, or may fall from a roof; in place of burning comes accidental injury through fire or snake-bite; in place of decapitation, the government or brigands kill by the sword;[9] in place of strangulation, one suffers

---

[1] b. Sanh. 9b.
[2] b. Sanh. 27a. See also Rava in b. Mak. 5a, b. B.Q. 73b.
[3] b. Sanh. 29b.
[4] Trans. Jacob Schachter (London, 1948), pp. 144-145.
[5] Vol. III, pp. 220-229.
[6] Vol. III, p. 221.
[7] b. Sanh. 40a.
[8] b. Sanh. 10a.
[9] As happened to Christian martyrs, see above, p. 25.

drowning or suffocation.[1] The effectiveness of excommunication depended upon widespread ostracism of the excommunicant. When whole groups, such as the butchers of Huẓal, or towns, were excommunicated, it could not have made much difference.[2] On the other hand, Abaye and R. Joseph discussed whether an excommunicant might have sex relations with his wife.[3] If the wife were a faithful Jewess, she could well effectuate the conclusion of their discussion.

A striking story about judicial punishment—in error—is as follows:

> Yemar b. Ḥashu had a money claim against a certain person who died and left a boat. "Go," he said to his agent, "and seize it." He went and seized it, but R. Papa and R. Huna b. R. Joshua met him and told him, "You are seizing on behalf of a creditor and thereby you are causing loss to others, and R. Yoḥanan ruled, 'He who seizes on behalf of a creditor and thereby causes loss to others does not legally acquire it.'" Thereupon they [the rabbis] themselves [who were also creditors of the deceased] seized it. R. Papa rowed the boat while R. Huna b. R. Joshua pulled it by the rope. One then declared, "I have acquired all the ship," and the other so claimed as well. They were met by R. Phineḥas b. 'Ammi who said to them ... When they appeared before Rava, he said to them, "You white geese [rabbis wore a white cloak] that strip the people of their cloaks [giving a decision in their own favor and robbing the other creditors]! Thus ruled R. Naḥman, 'The seizure is valid only if it took place during the lifetime [of the original owner/debtor].'"
>
> (b. Ket. 84b-85a)[4]

What is interesting for our purpose is the willingness of Yemar b. Ḥashu's agent to give up his claim upon the boat to the two rabbis, whose citation of a learned master convinced him that he could not go to court and retain possession of the boat for his master. Since the courts could and did adjudicate all sorts of property claims, ordinary people were not prepared to oppose their judgments, even when these were in the rabbis' own interest.[5]

The combination of punishments available to court officials was probably quite sufficient for their ordinary needs. They could not have had great difficulty in effecting more weighty decisions. As I said, whether people paid attention to excommunication probably depended mostly upon the circumstances. If nearby, they would have been sub-

[1] b. Sanh. 37b. On capital jurisdiction, see below, pp. 186-190.

[2] Vol. I, p. 148; vol. III, p. 227.

[3] b. M.Q. 15b.

[4] Trans W. Slotki, p. 536. On special distinguishing garments worn by rabbis, see below, p. 295ff.

[5] On rabbinical favoritism of rabbis in court, see below, pp. 309ff.

jected to local court influence. If from distant places, they may have been able to ignore or avoid a summons to court and to escape the most bothersome results of the consequent ban. On the other hand, the court could easily determine the division or possession of disputed property, and had no difficulty in putting the decision into effect. Decisions in land disputes, no less than in litigations over movables, would have produced judicial confirmation of rights of ownership. Documents such as deeds of ownership or possession were drawn up by court scribes. In such circumstances, the bailiff of Bar Ḥashu may well have supposed it futile to contend with the learned rabbis for possession of the boat.[1]

Court errors by an official appointed by the exilarchate would not lead to the judge's having to make restitution. On the other hand, R. Joseph held that while an "unauthorized" judge might have to make restitution in the case of error, his decision was still quite valid:

> Mar Zutra b. R. Naḥman judged a case alone and erred. R. Joseph told him, "If both parties accepted you as judge, you do not have to make restitution. Otherwise, go and pay an indemnity."
>
> (b. Sanh. 5a)[2]

There is no doubt, however, that the decision was a valid one. The reference to an unauthorized judge calls to mind the fact that the exilarch could not supervise what people did everywhere and probably did not try to establish a monopoly on courts. If a learned rabbi was consulted by ordinary people to settle their disputes, the decision he made would not be overturned by other, "recognized" courts. (This is very important for the question of setting up and financing independent schools. It would suggest that a group of rich men could keep their own school of rabbis and might find it worth their while.) I should suppose the reason would have been that he ruled according to the same principles of law followed in the authorized courts, namely the rabbinic traditions. Indeed, Abaye and Rava seem in the following source to suppose the possibility of existence of two competing courts in the same town:

> "You shall not form separate sects" (Deut. 14:1). Abaye said, "The warning against separate sects is applicable in a case where there are two courts in the same town, one ruling according to Bet Shammai, the other according to Bet Hillel." ... Rava said, "The prohibition applies to a court in one town which is divided between Shammaites and Hillelites..."
>
> (b. Yev. 14a)

---

[1] On the Jewish court's unlimited jurisdiction over Jewish property, see Salo W. Baron, *Social and Religious History of the Jews*, II, p. 417, n. 39.

[2] See H. Z. Taubes, *Oẓar HaGeonim, Sanhedrin*, p. 28/15A.

The discussion contains no reference to such a situation in Babylonia, so I very much doubt that two courts actually competed with one another in any significant town, certainly not in any village. So the ruling by Mar Zutra b. R. Naḥman may have been given in a town in which a formally established, exilarchic court, staffed by rabbis, was not to be found; or alternately, if such a court existed, the contending parties preferred for some reason to ask for the decision of Mar Zutra.

In addition to the usual judical functions, the courts oversaw the general welfare of the towns.[1] Among court responsibilities were the suppression of rumors and the annulment of vows. Two cases involving rumors were reported:

> A certain woman was allegedly engaged by the well of Be Shifi [with the gift of] the flesh sticking to date stones. R. 'Idi b. 'Abin asked Abaye what was the rule in such a case. Abaye replied, "Even those authorities who say that as a rule we do not suppress rumors would here suppress them, because people will then say that the rabbis examined the gift of betrothal and found it did not contain the value of a perutah." [Since she was never actually engaged, no harm can result in suppressing the rumor.]
>
> (b. Git. 89a)

> A woman was reported to have been betrothed by one of the sons of a certain person. Rava ruled, "Even those authorities who hold that we should not as a rule suppress a rumor would rule that here we should do so...."
>
> (b. Git. 89a-b)

One recalls that Rava held it was permitted to libel a man who broke rabbinical enactments, so libel in general was actionable, and the courts would probably have suppressed and punished libel. Here we again see that the courts would make the effort to suppress rumors in specified circumstances.[2] How they would have done so we can only surmise. They may have issued a public order that such-and-such a rumor was not true and should not be repeated. Anyone violating their order would have been banned as a transgressor of rabbinical rulings. The effectiveness of such a procedure, however, is unattested by any sources. The rabbis clearly *thought* they could suppress rumors, though it may be that in actuality they could only attempt to do so, going through the routine court procedures, without any certain result.

On the other hand, the courts had no difficulty whatever in annuling

[1] We shall consider various other activities of public administration in sections iii-vii, below.

[2] See also b. Yev. 25a = b. M.Q. 18b, Abaye on suppressing rumors.

vows. A faithful Jew who made a vow and later on regretted it could turn to a rabbinical court and seek absolution. The normal ground was that the man had not vowed with such-and-such a situation in mind, and hence the vow was, of itself, invalid. Cases of absolution included the following:

> A man once came before Rabbah b. R. Huna. The rabbi asked, "If ten men had been present to appease you just then, would you have vowed?" The man replied, "No." He thereupon absolved him.
> (b. Ned. 21b)

> Abaye's wife had a daughter. He insisted she marry one of his family, and she wanted her to marry one of her relations. He vowed, "Benefit from me is forbidden to you if you disregard my wishes..." She went, ignored his wish, and married the girl off to one of her relations. Abaye came before R. Joseph for absolution. R. Joseph asked, "Had you known she would disregard your wish, would you have vowed?" Abaye said, "No." R. Joseph absolved him.
> (b. Ned. 23a)[1]

Rabbah held that in the case of a betrothed maiden, either her father or her fiancé may annul her vows.[2] They may also repeat a prescribed formula of confirmation of a vow.[3] R. Joseph held that absolution on the Sabbath may be granted by a single scholar, but not by three ordinary people, for the latter case would resemble a law-suit, which cannot be tried on the Sabbath.[4] The rabbis discussed the possible interpretations of the language of vows. For instance, Rava said that if a man vowed not to eat but ate dust, he had not transgressed his vow.[5]

Rava's court, like R. Naḥman's earlier, seems to have enjoyed appellate status. We have already noted his ruling against two rabbis who had seized property in their own advantage.[6] R. Ḥiyya 'Arika appealed to Rava when dissatisfied with the ruling of another rabbi. Rava thereupon supported the judgment of the lower court of Rabbah b. Shila.[7] Many of the extant case reports derive from Rava's court, more than from any other court of his time, just as the earlier ones were disproportionately from R. Naḥman's. It may be that his close ties with the

---

[1] Note also the case of R. Kahana before R. Joseph, b. Ned. 22b.
[2] b. Ned. 67a.
[3] b. Ned. 69a-b, 70a.
[4] b. Ned. 77a, with Abaye's contrary view.
[5] b. Shev. 22b. On the language of the vows of a Nazir, see Abaye's discussion, b. Nazir 13a, Rava, *ibid.* 17a, etc.
[6] Above, p. 135.
[7] b. Ket. 104b.

exilarch, like those of R. Naḥman, resulted in the preservation of his decisions as binding precedents.[1]

The academies by this time produced few, if any innovations in either the functions or the responsibilities of the court. Long ago, in both Palestine and Babylonia, arrangements for public welfare had been entrusted to the rabbinical judges. The fourth-century rabbis did little more than carry on the tasks first laid down by others, following time-tested rules of procedure, evidence, and punishment. What is important in this time is the steady growth of the effectiveness of the courts, but that did not alter the way they carried on their business.[2]

III. The Court's Eleemosynary Responsibilities

Chief among the court's responsibilities in maintaining the public welfare were the collection and distribution of funds for the poor. The courts could levy sums to be paid for philanthropic purposes. Rabbah, for example, collected a charity contribution from orphans.[3] The court also kept control of such funds until they were disbursed. In Pumbedita, R. Joseph deposited charity funds with a person who was so negligent that the money was stolen. R. Joseph thereupon required the bailiff to pay an indemnity.[4] He explained that since the poor of Pumbedita receive a fixed allowance, the charity funds were stolen from definite plaintiffs, and hence restitution was legally possible. The chief responsibility involved determining who was eligible for charity and how much he would receive, as in the following miracle-story:

> A certain man came before Rava [asking for charity from public funds]. He said to him, "On what do you usually dine?" The man replied, "On fat chicken and old wine." Rava said, "Do you not take into account the burden of the community?" [That is, can you not live more cheaply?] The pauper rejoined, "Do I eat of theirs? I eat of the substance of the All-Merciful, [as it is taught. 'The eyes of all wait for you, and you give them their food in due season' (Ps. 145:15)." 'In their time' is not said, but 'in his time,' teaching that the Holy One blessed be he provides for everyone in his time.'] Meanwhile Rava's sister, whom he had not seen for thirteen years, came and brought him

---

[1] See vol. III, pp. 61-75, with reference to R. Naḥman. I think it clear that the heads of academies produced a vastly disproportionate number of legal sayings, as well as case reports.

[2] On the growth of rabbinical power, see below, pp. 256ff.

[3] b. B.B. 8a. For his distribution of charity funds, see b. B.B. 8b, Abaye's report.

[4] b. B.Q. 93a.

> a fat chicken and old wine. He [the applicant] said, "Just what I was talking about!"[1] Rava replied, "I apologize to you. Come and eat."
> (b. Ket. 67b)[2]

Rava was prepared to compel a man to contribute to charity funds against his will, and did so to R. Nathan b. ʾAmmi.[3] In dealing with cases of non-support, he would try to force the father to take his children off the charity rolls.[4] Following Beer, I should suppose that the rabbis encouraged the needy to turn at first to private people, and only afterward to the communal funds.[5] Beer says that the poor depended upon the rabbi as such, "because of his uprightness and devotion."[6] Forcible collection and division of funds for charity, however, would have involved more than mere respect for the rabbi as a noble-hearted man. The rabbi possessed the power to collect the funds by government, or exilarchic, fiat, as Beer recognizes.[7] The court in fact was the agent of the government, able to act in its behalf and *legally* to acquire property or funds for philanthropic purposes.[8] So the administration of funds for charity, like the collection of taxes, was among the administrative functions of the court. It was as the *judges* of these courts that the rabbis exerted such legal authority, and not merely as reliable philanthropists. Rava held, as we have noted, that orderly provision for the poor was absolutely necessary for good relations with the Iranian government.[9] Doubtless had large numbers of impoverished Jews been neglected within their own community, the government would have had to step in and establish some sort of responsible party to keep order. Rava urged the townspeople of Maḥoza to help one another, so they might retain the right of self-government. Rava pointed out, moreover, that small as well as large contributions would in the end mount up to meaningful sums.[10] Nonetheless, beggars did go from door to door, and it was difficult for folk to know who really needed

[1] Alt.: Rava said, "What a remarkable incident."
[2] For another rule of Rava on distributing charity, see b. R.H. 6a.
[3] b. Ket. 49b.
[4] *ibid.* 49b. See vol. III, p. 284 for a less effective action by Rav Judah.
[5] b. Ned. 65b, see Beer, *Maʿamadam*, p. 139, n. 77.
[6] *op. cit.*, 139-40.
[7] *ibid.* p. 142.
[8] Beer, *op. cit.*, p. 140.
[9] b. B.B. 9a, see above, pp. 54-55. The government may have provided some funds for that purpose, as represented by ʾIfra Hormiz's gifts, see above, pp. 35-39. Note also the references to Shapur I as a philanthropist, vol. II, p. 71, *if* Rav's saying was meant as praise, contrary to my earlier interpretation of b. B.M. 70b.
[10] *ibid.* 9a, in the name of R. Sheshet.

help and who did not. So R. Naḥman b. Isaac (in commenting upon Is. 58:7) said that if a man was really anxious to give to charity, God would make sure that he found fitting recipients for his money, so that he might gain the merit of having assisted them.[1]

Merit could also be acquired by visiting the sick, Rava, R. Joseph, and Abaye all agreed, and Rava said one must visit even a hundred times a day.[2] Nonetheless, we have no evidence whatever that the courts took responsibility to insure that the sick were visited.

iv. The Court and the Marketplace

The courts' power to control litigation of cases arising from market transactions resulted in indirect influence over the marketplace.[3] The courts, however, took a quite direct part in economic life. While the Palestinian rabbis had held that market-supervisors must not fix prices, the exilarch, and, one assumes, the antecedent non-rabbinical Babylonian Jewish courts as well, insisted that prices were to be controlled by court officials. Rav was forced to submit to the Babylonian practice,[4] and from that time onward, the rabbis as court-officers followed the exilarchic requirements. In general, the courts were supposed to maintain an orderly market, to prevent great fluctuation in prices, to insure the constant provision of produce and so prevent famine, and to see to it that the ritual requirements of Judaism were met by the merchants and artisans.[5] Ritual law figured in the following rulings:

> A load of turnips came to Maḥoza [on a festival]. Rava saw that they were withered, and permitted the people to buy them, since they had been picked yesterday....
>
> (b. 'Eruv. 40a)

> A boat-load of *ẓaḥanta* [a fish] came to Sikara. R. Huna b. Ḥinnena went out to inspect it, and since he saw scales [on the boat] he permitted [the fish to be sold]. Rava said to him, "How is it possible to give permission in a place where [scales are] commonly found." He issued an announcement prohibiting the fish, and R. Huna b. Ḥinnena issued one permitting them.
>
> (b. A.Z. 40a)

---

[1] b. B.B. 9b.

[2] b. Ned. 39b.

[3] See vol. III, pp. 295-302, and below, chap. IV sect. IX, pp. 231-233, "Other Commercial Transactions."

[4] Vol. II, p. 112.

[5] On court-supervision of the abbatoir and butcher-shops, see below, pp. 151-156.

In the following inquiry, the concern was for good hygiene:

> The pottery dealer Minyomin once left a pot of honey uncovered. He came to Rava [to ask about it]. Rava said, "What have we to fear [for the law that liquids are prohibited which have been left uncovered applies to water, wine, and milk]?"
>
> (b. Ḥul. 49b)

Rabbah, or Rava, similarly reported a ruling on how clothes-merchants may sell their wares when only gentiles may purchase them.[1] The numerous cases involving sale of or profit from wine touched by a gentile all produced rabbinical rulings about the ritual fitness of marketable wares.[2] There can be no doubt, therefore, that the courts' market-supervision extended, or was extended by the rabbis, to matters of merely ritual concern.

The courts' rulings involved narrowly economic questions as well, so one cannot conclude that the rabbis' were consulted only because of their superior knowledge of the rites and restrictions of Judaism. As court-officers, they had authority over weights, measures, and prices. In general, they used their authority to limit competition and so to protect the rights of the home-born merchants over outside competition. R. Huna b. R. Joshua, for example, said that residents can keep outsiders from setting up in competition, though itinerants cannot prevent other itinerants from coming to town.[3] On this account those who claimed to be rabbis had to prove their rabbinical status, so that they might be exempted from such restrictions and permitted to sell their wares either in direct competition with home-folk or even before the natives were allowed to show their produce.[4] Court supervision of markets assuredly came under the authority of the exilarchate, which had originally required it of the rabbis. Cases illustrating that supervision include the ritual ones cited earlier[5] and above,[6] the special privileges accorded to rabbis, as in the case of R. Dimi,[7] and the litigations involving butchers arising from market-dealings. None of these cases involved supervision of weights, measures, or prices. I see

---

[1] b. Shab. 29b, 46b.

[2] See above, pp. 59-61; for one example, b. A.Z. 57b, a ruling of Rava.

[3] b. B.B. 21b-22a.

[4] See b. B.B. 22a, cited below, and M. Beer, *Ẓiyyon*, 28, 1963, p. 21. Since rabbinical disciples left their native villages to study in the schools, it was important to insure that right.

[5] pp. 59-61.

[6] p. 141.

[7] Below, pp. 151-156.

no reason, however, to think that such supervision had ceased; it was clearly carried on in earlier times.[1] Moreover, one can hardly suppose that officials who could say what wine, fish, and vegetables were suitable for public sale, could not also decide about weights, measures, and prices. As I said earlier[2] when it came to market supervision, the rabbis did not have to wait for litigation to arrive in the courts. They frequented the markets, and were prepared to issue spot-judgments when necessary. The normal, everyday kinds of issues they confronted in the markets allowed them to impose their ethical and moral ideals upon ordinary people. This personal prestige, combined with the power to decide litigations as they chose when in court, would have encouraged most people to conform to their advice and rulings even outside court or the presence of court-officers.

v. The Court and the Farm

Litigations of land disputes produced some court influence over agricultural life, as did the interest of the rabbis[3] in the rights and welfare of laborers and slaves.[4] Agricultural cases, except for property claims, mainly concerned the enforcement of the laws and taboos prescribed by Scripture. The earlier tradition[5] made it explicit that agricultural precepts dependent on "the land," meaning Palestine, were to be practiced only there, while those not dependent on the land, except *'Orlah* and *Kila'im*, apply abroad as well. The Palestinians wrongly thought that Babylonia was "empty of commandments" because of the absence of heave-offerings, tithes, and the like. Rav Judah taught that tithes and other such obligations apply *only* in Palestine and the Pumbeditans held that even *'Orlah*-taboos did not apply abroad. So the rabbinical rulings seem quite unequivocal. Nonetheless, there is considerable evidence that some agricultural taboos certainly *were* observed in Babylonia, both earlier and in this period.[6] The biblical understanding of the ordinary people must have been part of the reason. Finding agricultural laws in Scripture, apparently accustomed from

[1] Vol. II, pp. 111-119, and vol. III, pp. 295-302.

[2] Vol. III, p. 298.

[3] But I know of no cases before the courts, except in the matter of claims for unpaid wages, see below, pp. 244-247.

[4] On workers and slaves, below, pp. 228ff.

[5] Vol. III, pp. 295-298 for a summary of Mishnaic rulings and the opinions of the preceding generation. See also vol. II, pp. 51-52, n. 3, and pp. 260-262.

[6] Note b. A.Z. 22a, evidence that *'orlah*-taboos were really observed. See above, p. 65.

times past to give to the priests their several gifts and to keep such other laws as the Bible seemed to them to demand, the ordinary Jews must have continued to observe the laws. But some Babylonian rabbis for their part said they must do so, and the rabbis yielded to popular opinion (and private interest) and accepted these payments. R. Ḥisda in the preceding generation received priestly gifts. Others now took them.

I can think of no more striking example of the way in which rabbinical authority operated in Babylonia. It was easy for the rabbis to require what the Bible itself clearly demanded, and not much more difficult to convince the people that rabbis knew *how* such laws should be carried out. When, on the other hand, biblical bases for rabbinical teachings and rulings were not obvious or clear, it was difficult for the rabbis to secure widespread conformity to the law as they interpreted it. R. Naḥman b. Isaac taught that the first fruits of the shearing had to be given to the priests in Palestine, but not abroad.[1] We have, however, a number of stories about how leading rabbis of priestly origin actually took priestly parts of slaughtered animals, [MTNT' = gift] including the following:

> Rava once penalized [lit.: fined] a man [for refusing to give priestly dues] by taking away a side of meat, and R. Naḥman b. Isaac did so by taking away his cloak.
>
> (b. Ḥul. 132b)
>
> Abaye said, "At first I would snatch the priestly dues, thinking, 'I am showing zeal for the commandment,' but when I heard the teaching, 'They shall give (Deut. 18:3)—but he shall not take it himself,' I did not snatch it any more, but would say to all, 'Give them to me.' When I heard [a further teaching, that it was wrong to ask for the gifts] I decided not to accept them at all, except on the day before the Day of Atonement, so as to confirm myself as a priest..."
>
> (b. Ḥul. 133a)[2]
>
> R. Joseph said, "A priest in whose neighborhood lives a needy rabbinical disciple may [alt.: should] assign his priestly dues to him..."
>
> (b. Ḥul. 133a)
>
> Rava and R. Safra' once visited the house of Mar Yuḥna' son of R. Ḥana' b. Adda' ... and he prepared for them a third-born calf [or, a calf in its third year]. Rava said to the attendant [a priest who usually received the priestly dues], "Assign to me the [priestly] dues, for I wish to eat the tongue with mustard..."
>
> (b. Ḥul. 133a)

[1] b. Ḥul. 136b.

[2] Trans. Eli Cashdan (London, 1948), p. 753, with minor alterations.

The account reports that R. Safra would not eat the meat thinking Rava ought not to take it from the servant. In a dream he heard the Scripture (Prov. 25:20), "As one that taketh off a garment in cold weather, and as vinegar upon nitre, so is he that sings songs to a heavy heart." R. Safra consulted R. Joseph, who approved his conduct and told him not to worry. The Scripture had come to him, and not to Rava, who had disheartened the attendant, the story closes, because Rava was in bad grace with the divinity, either for his conduct here or for some other reason. Gifts of firstlings were further referred to in the following:

> The daughter of R. Ḥisda [Rava's wife] said to him [Rava] "My father once permitted a firstling..."
>
> (b. Ḥul. 44b)

> Rafram of Pumbedita had a firstling which he gave to a priest while it had no blemish...
>
> (b. Bekh. 36b)

> A certain man brought a firstling before Rava on the eve of a festival towards evening...
>
> (b. Beẓ. 27b)

> A woman proselyte was given by 'Aḥa an animal to fatten. She came to Rava [to ask whether the law of firstlings applies to an animal held in partnership with a heathen].
>
> (b. Bekh. 3b)

Rava was asked whether cattle liable to *'arnona*, the tax on crops and cattle paid in kind, were subject to the law of firstlings or not.[1]

The stories cited above, like those pertaining to the preceding generation, leave no doubt whatever that some priestly dues and firstlings were collected by rabbis who were also priests. Both Abaye and Rava clearly so indicated. Furthermore courts assisted priests to collect those gifts. We may suppose, of course, that where people could avoid, or did not believe themselves liable to give, priestly taxes, they would not do so. Nonetheless, it is beyond doubt that the rabbis in court did support the claims of the priests to receive their ancient dues. These gifts were originally intended to compensate the priests for their activities in the Temple, government, and schools. Despite the advent of other forms of government, the priests continued to demand their due. The people were thus subjected to the exactions of several groups: the Iranian government, the exilarchate, rabbis seeking support for

---

[1] b. Pes. 6a.

their schools, the poor, priests, and so on. The priestly demand, even when turned to the advantage of a rabbinical disciple in need—and I do not suppose it often went to so worthy a recipient—must have weighed heavily on the folk, who slaughtered animals only seldom, and then mainly for festival meals. The additional exaction of the firstlings of the herd, which was surely carried out according to the above evidence, was of equally sound biblical foundation, and many people had no doubts about paying it. Since the priests' claim represented a significant property right, it is important to note that Rava and R. Naḥman b. Isaac proved willing to support the priests in court. Otherwise it would have been difficult indeed for priests to collect their dues, except when voluntarily handed over. With court backing, on the other hand, the priests enjoyed a substantial economic benefit.

In addition to firstlings and the priestly gifts of slaughtered cattle, heave-offering also seems to have been given to the priests of Babylonia in this time. The following account implicitly suggests that Rabbah and R. Huna b. R. Joshua accepted heave-offering:

> Rava said, "Heave-offering produced abroad [outside of Palestine] is not subject to [a certain ruling]." Rabbah neutralized it in a larger quantity [of produce] and used to eat it in the days of his [levitical] impurity. When R. Huna b. R. Joshua happened to have heave-offering of wine, he used to mix two [measures] of *ḥullin* [unconsecrated wine] with one of heave-offering...
>
> (b. Bekh. 27a)[1]

Abaye ruled that camel-riders were forbidden to eat heave-offering.[2] His saying presupposed that it was necessary to eat heave-offering in a state of levitical purity, but whether he intended it as a practical instruction we cannot say. The laws of heave-offering were studied in Rabbah's school by Abaye b. Abin and R. Ḥananiah b. Abin,[3] by Rava[4] and by R. Naḥman b. Isaac,[5] among others. Nothing in the report of their studies indicates that they intended to apply the laws. Whether or not ordinary people gave tithes we do not know. Rava held that the majority of the people of the land do not give tithes.[6] The language

[1] Note also the discussion of R. Naḥman, R. 'Amram, and Rami b. Ḥama, who were asked whether one had to eat heave-offering produced abroad in a state of levitical purity, b. Bekh. 27b.

[2] b. Nid. 14a.

[3] b. Pes. 34a.

[4] b. Shab. 17b.

[5] b. Ber. 39b.

[6] b. Shab. 13a. Compare b. Shab. 23a, Rava said that the majority of ordinary people do tithe.

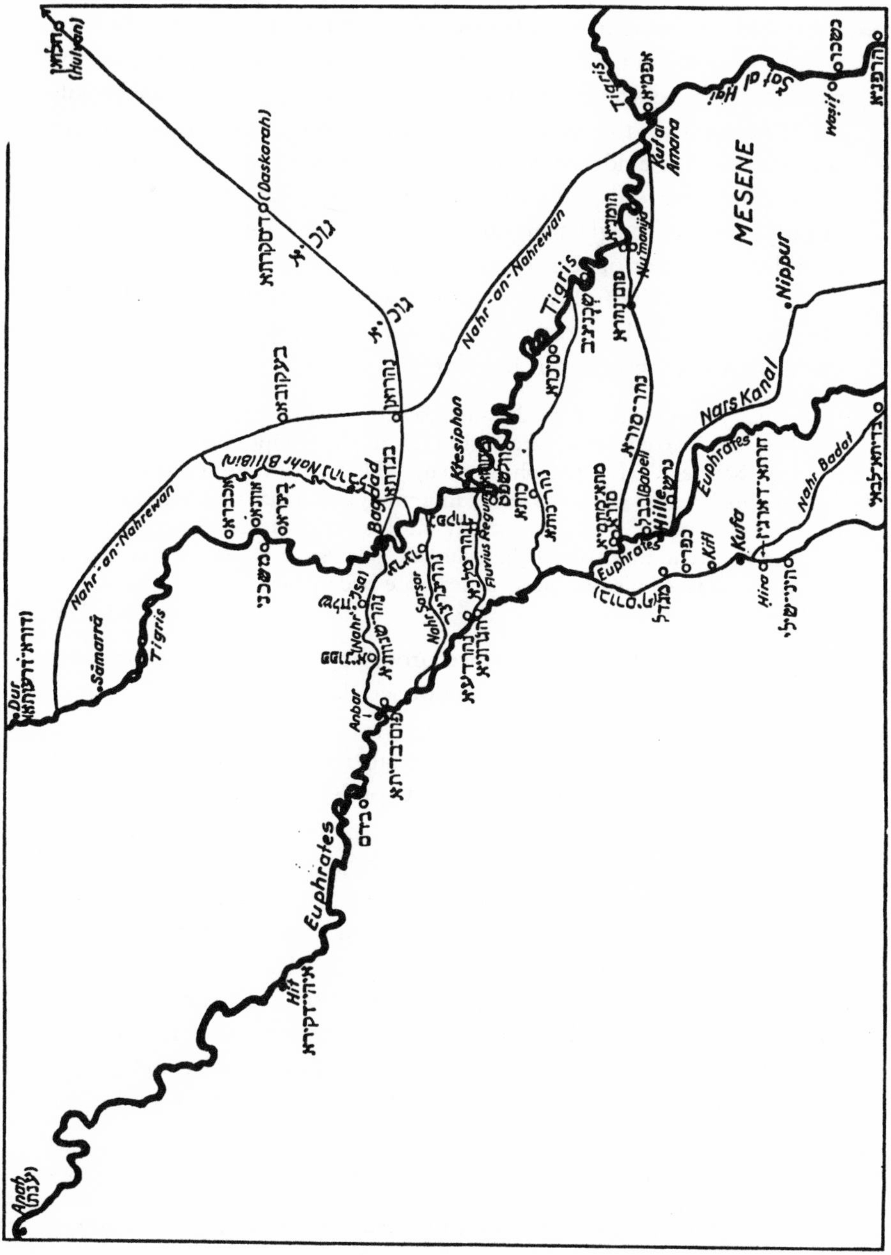

IV. Jacob Obermeyer's Map of Babylonian Jewish Settlements

attributed to him is in the present tense. Abaye held that most of the people of the land *do* separate tithes.[1] Both sayings appear in the context of legal discussions, and do not necessarily indicate that people did tithe, or that the rabbis were even talking about contemporary conditions.[2] The evidence would suggest that the people may not have given tithes, but did present to the priests the heave-offering and the priestly parts of newly-slaughtered animals, the former a negligible item, but the latter of considerable value.

According to the following story it seems possible that R. Joseph, like Samuel before him, did not believe the taboo against sewing mixed seeds had to be observed in Babylonia:

> R. Joseph mixed seeds and sowed. Abaye protested, "But we learned, 'Mixed seeds [are forbidden in the diaspora by a decree] of the Scribes.'" R. Joseph replied, "That poses no difficulty. The Mishnah refers to mixed seeds in a vineyard. This is mixed seeds [not in a vineyard]...." Subsequently R. Joseph corrected himself, citing the fact that Rav sowed the scholars' garden [a vegetable garden for the benefit of his disciples] in separate beds [for different species].
>
> (b. Qid. 39a)

Abaye did not accept the evidence brought when R. Joseph corrected himself, for he thought Rav's action could be explained for other reasons.

Concerning a forbidden mixture of fabrics, R. Papa and Rava left sayings about whether the prohibition applies to slippers and money-bags, respectively.[3]

It was reported to R. Joseph that the people of Khuzistan separated *ḥallah* from bread made with rice, which was not legally necessary. He sent word that a lay Israelite should eat it in their presence, to signify that it was not consecrated as priestly food.[4] The incident suggests that people may have kept laws which the rabbis did not impose or expect them to keep. The context of Abaye's criticism of R. Joseph's orders leads to the inference that it was an ancestral practice and should not be disturbed. It is significant, therefore, that R. Joseph wished to

---

[1] b. Ket. 24a, b. Git. 61a.

[2] Nor does Rabbah's comment on how one weighs tithe, b. Shab. 22b. Note also b. Ber. 47a-b, Abaye and R. Papa on the laws of tithing, b. B.Q. 28a, Rava on the laws of leaving the corner of the field and other matters, in the context of a legal discussion. Note also the discussion of Abaye and Rabbah, b. R.H. 13b, on heave-offering, b. R.H. 15a, on tithing fruit of trees which blossom in the sixth year and ripen in the seventh.

[3] b. Beẓ. 15a.

[4] b. Pes. 50b.

demonstrate publicly the fact that what the rabbis did not regard as holy was *not* to be treated as such. Considerable variation must have characterized local observance.[1]

To summarize: The courts used their power to adjudicate claims against property in order to enforce the donation to the priests of parts of newly-slaughtered animals, and some forms of other priestly dues. The rabbinical judges would penalize those who did not comply. Whether or not the Palestinians thought that the Babylonian Jewish farmers should give tithes and heave-offerings, the Babylonian Jews probably did give heave-offerings, but not tithes, to the priests. The rabbis would have liked to divert that income to their own needy disciples, who, they held, were engaged in work of a sanctity equivalent to making sacrifices in the Temple of old and therefore were entitled to them. The courts did not likely force the priests to make over their dues to rabbinical courts. It also seems that ordinary people did keep agricultural taboos which some rabbis did not believe were required in the diaspora.

VI. The Court and the Synagogue

The court had no control over synagogue affairs, nor did the rabbi occupy a higher place than other Jews in the liturgical life of the community. The priestly caste continued to pronounce its blessings, but otherwise, in the synagogue all Jews were equal. The rabbis' arrangements of prayers[2] were certainly followed in the *schools*, and disciples followed in all details the masters' manner of praying.[3] Earlier masters, as well as those of this generation, clearly regarded study of Torah as intrinsically more sacred than prayer.[4] Abaye said that he prayed only where he studied, rather than going to the synagogue for

---

[1] Stories about how rabbis themselves farmed their lands were preserved, e.g. b. Men. 87a, R. Joseph was able to produce a very desirable kind of wine. Since the rabbis were believed to know many kinds of secrets about the natural world, it would have been normal for people to imitate their ways, and so their reputation as holy men would certainly have enhanced their influence over agricultural practices.

[2] See below, pp. 324-330.

[3] On the role of the rabbis earlier, see vol. II, pp. 274-282, and vol. III, pp. 234-238, and my "Rabbis and Community in Third Century Babylonia," in J. Neusner, ed., *Religions in Antiquity: Essays in Memory of Erwin Ramsdell Goodenough* (Leiden, 1968), pp. 438-459.

[4] See below, pp. 290-295.

that purpose. His saying was quite consistent with earlier ones on the same subject.[1] This attitude probably reflects the above-mentioned fact, that the rabbis played no central role in synagogue life, and what they did not control could not have seemed very important.

The only instance of court exercise of rabbinical authority involving synagogues is as follows:

> There was a synagogue of Jews from Rumakan [near Maḥoza] which opened out into a room where a corpse was deposited [before being buried].[2] The priests wanted to go to pray there, and they came to Rava [and asked him what to do]. He replied, "Take the ark and put it down there [to interpose between the room and the synagogue proper]. Since it is a wooden vessel which is meant to be stationary ... it will form a partition to prevent the passage of defilement." The disciples said to Rava, "But sometimes it is moved while a scroll of the Torah is resting on it, and thus becomes a vessel which is moved both when filled and when empty?" "If so," he answered, "there is no remedy."
>
> (b. Meg. 26b)

The priests' problem had nothing to do with the proper conduct of synagogue prayer, but rather with a matter of ritual defilement. Rava did not order that the ark be left in its place, only that the priests see whether they could so arrange things as to prevent corpse-uncleanness. Rava held that a synagogue-building may be sold or exchanged [for secular purposes], but not rented or pledged.[3] He ruled also that one may make a decrepit ark into a smaller one, but not into a reading-stand,[4] and said that one may turn a synagogue into a school-house of the rabbis, but not the reverse.[5] I should imagine that the disposition of synagogue property might well have been adjudicated in local courts. Other rabbinical laws affecting synagogue life, such as specifications of the lections for various occasions, prayers, and proper conduct in the synagogue, would probably have been outside of effective court jurisdiction. As a holy man, the rabbi could, of course, guide and advise the people, but he could certainly do little contrary to public opinion.

[1] b. Ber. 8a, see vol. III, p. 235 for other such sayings by earlier masters. And contrast b. Meg. 29a, Abaye studied in the synagogue.

[2] Compare the view of R. Assi, b. Meg. 28b.

[3] b. Meg. 26b.

[4] *ibid.* 26b.

[5] *ibid.* 26b-27a. This was consistent with the view that the school was holier than the synagogue. Note also b. Git. 60a, Rabbah and R. Joseph on the Sabbath lections; b. Meg. 24b, 'Ullah b. Rav asked Abaye whether a child dressed in rags is allowed to read the Torah; b. Ber. 62b, Rava held it was not permitted to spit in the synagogue.

The people would have found in the memory of their forefathers' conduct of synagogue prayers a far more compelling source of guidance than the rabbis' teachings, although buttressed by citations of earlier rabbis or by references to Scripture.

As to art in the synagogue, Abaye held that the Torah absolutely forbade making copies of the four faces of Ezekiel's vision (Ez. 1:10). He exposited Ex. 20:20, "You shall not make *with me*" to mean "*Me* you shall not make," and since man is in God's image, the human face cannot be reproduced.[1] The actual practice in synagogues could not have conformed to the rabbinical rules about art, whether strict or lenient, according to Geonic tradition. R. Ḥiyya b. R. Huna said that he observed Abaye and Rava bending to one side and not completely prostrating themselves at prayer.[2] The Geonic tradition of R. Sherira on this passage explained that they, like his forebears, refrained from falling face-down on the floor of the synagogue "but would keep their faces up, and would not touch their faces to the ground, for *perhaps under the dirt there is a floor of stones and mosaic*...."[3] There can be little doubt therefore that in Geonic times, it was believed that synagogue floors had earlier been decorated by mosaics, now covered up by dirt. It was further believed that Abaye and Rava had refrained from prostrating themselves on the floor precisely because doing so would make it seem that they were bowing down to the mosaic on the floor. Abaye and Rava nonetheless prayed in the synagogue of Shaf veYativ in Nehardea, in which a statue of a man was set up.[4] They believed that the *Shekhinah* lived there and in the synagogue in Huẓal, alternatively.[5] They held that the Scripture (Ps. 90:1), "Lord, you have been our dwelling place" referred to both the synagogue and the school house.

VII. The Court and the Abbatoir. Food Taboos

Supervision of the slaughter of cattle was entirely within the courts' powers.[6] The rabbis, first of all, inspected the butcher shops and abat-

[1] b. R.H. 24a, b. A.Z. 43a.

[2] b. Ber. 34b.

[3] *Ozar HaGeonim* ed. B. M. Lewin I, 83, and note 5.

[4] Note also the Geonic tradition (*Ozar HaGeonim* V, c, p. 43) that the *andarta* mentioned in b. R.H. 24b, which stood in the synagogue of Shaf veYativ in Nehardea and so disturbed the rabbis who prayed there was a statue of the king. "The king decreed to set up against the Jews' wishes a statue such as the Persians themselves worshipped."

[5] b. Meg. 29a.

[6] See vol. II, pp. 274-282, III, pp. 259-266.

toirs, to oversee the butchers in the act of slaughter, and to make certain of the sharpness of their knives. They could moreover prohibit both the participation of a sinning butcher and the sale of improper meat in the Jewish marketplace. It was therefore to the advantage of the Jewish butchers to obey the rabbis' rules to begin with. Quite naturally the butchers consulted the rabbis about doubtful matters, as in the following stories:

> Rava examined an arrow for R. Jonah b. Taḥalifa, who slaughtered with it a bird in flight...
>
> (b. Ḥul. 30b)[1]
>
> Certain Tai [Arabs] once came to Ẓikonia [near Pumbedita] and gave the Jewish butchers some rams [to slaughter], saying, "The blood and fat will be for us, and the hide and flesh for you." R. Tobi b. R. Mattena sent the case to R. Joseph and asked what was the law....
>
> (b. Ḥul. 39b)[2]
>
> The case [of a bird] once came to Rabbah, in which the doubt arose as to whether it was clawed or not, and he was about to examine the gullet from the outside when Abaye said to him....
>
> (b. Ḥul. 43b)
>
> An ox belonging to the family of R. ʿUqba was slaughtered. The slaughtering started at the pharynx and was completed at the gullet proper. Rava said, "I will impose the restriction..." Meanwhile the case circulated until it came before R. Abba. He said to his disciples, "The ox should have been permitted ... Go tell [Rava] the son of Joseph b. Ḥama to pay the owner the value of the ox."[3]
>
> (b. Ḥul. 43b)
>
> Rava once declared an animal, which was thought to be a doubtful case of *trefah*,[4] to be permitted and then bought some of the meat.

[1] But the discussion further presupposes that R. Jonah prepared dust in the whole valley where the bird was flying in order to receive its blood as the law required. I therefore suppose that the examination was for theoretical purposes, *or* that the condition of preparing the dust for receiving the blood was not actually met.

[2] It is supposed that the Tai intended to use their share of the animals for their cult.

[3] I do not understand why Rava should have had to repay the ox's owner, unless his decision was not made as a court officer of the exilarchate, for as we have seen above, p. 136, errors made in judgment did not require indemnity unless the judge was "unauthorized." Rava was certainly an authorized judge. It is possible that the incident occurred early in his life ("Go tell the son of R. Joseph b. Ḥama..."), or that R. Abba did not know that Rava was an authorized judge. I should suppose the former to have been the case, since later on Rava's decisions would not have been subjected to the examination of less powerful men than himself. See vol. III, p. 74.

[4] Lit. "torn." Unfit for Jewish use.

[His wife] the daughter of R. Ḥisda said to him, "My father once permitted a firstling but would not buy of its meat."

(b. Ḥul. 44b)

A case of a perforation stopped up by unclean fat came to Rava. He said...

(b. Ḥul. 49b)

A basketful of birds, each with its legs broken, was brought before Rava. He examined each...

(b. Ḥul. 57a)

[The case of a fracture covered with flesh and] tender sinews came before Rava. Rava said, "On what account do we suspect [it to be prohibited]...

(b. Ḥul. 77a)

A case came to Abaye where the bone was broken in a compound fracture, and a fragment had broken off. He held the case over for three festivals. R. Adda b. Mattena said [to the owner], "Go and ask Rava b. R. Joseph b. Ḥama, whose knife is sharp." He took it to him, and Rava said, "Let us see..."

(b. Ḥul. 77a)

There was a certain butcher who was suspected of selling kidney fat for the fat of ileum. [The former is forbidden]. Rava punished [lit.: fined] him [by forbidding him] to sell *even* nuts...

(b. Bekh. 29b-30a)

A certain butcher was insolent to R. Tobi b. Mattenah. Abaye and Rava were appointed to investigate the case, and they banned him. He went and appeased [R. Tobi]...

(b. M.Q. 16a)

Two butchers made an agreement that if either killed on the other's day [for slaughtering and selling meat] the skin of his beast should be torn up. One did violate the other's day, and the other went and tore up the skin. Rava summoned and ordered him to make restitution...

(b. B.B. 9a)

The case-reports cited above provide unequivocal testimony about the nature of the rabbis' authority over the abattoir and butcher-shop. In the instances of R. Jonah's arrow, the clawed bird, the perforation, the birds, and the compound fractures, rabbinic authority was consulted because people or butchers wanted to know whether the meat was fit for Jewish use. The cases of the Tais' rams, the butcher suspected of selling kidney fat, the insolent butcher, and the agreement that was broken, all involved actual rabbinical supervision of the butcher shops themselves. The rabbis' power to enforce both ritual and commercial law was unopposed. The insolent butcher could be banned. One suspected of selling unkosher parts of the animal actually could be driven out of business, so far as the Jewish market was concerned. When a case of contract-violation involving butchers came up, Rava summoned the miscreant to demand restitution. In both ritual and civil cases, therefore, the rabbis were quite able to declare the law and to enforce it.

The rabbis moreover inspected the butchers' implements. Rava stated several rules with regard to the butchers-knife examination, and R. Papa ruled:

> "It must be examined with the flesh of the finger and with the finger-nail, and the examination must be of three edges."
>
> (b. Ḥul. 17b)

Several reports of earlier and later generations concerned how various rabbis actually did examine butchers' knives, in either the abattoir, school, or court. On the whole, therefore, rabbinical authority in these matters extended far beyond the walls of the schoolhouse.[1] The rabbis' power over the markets combined with their reputation as masters of the law to render them effective supervisors.

Food-Taboos: It was probably much more difficult to enforce the food taboos among the ordinary people. The kitchens of Jewish Babylonia could hardly be inspected by the rabbis so thoroughly—if at all—as the abattoirs. Nonetheless, we have some evidence that the rabbis did enforce the food laws whenever they could. The following stories are of interest:

> A young pigeon [prepared for cooking] once fell into a jar of milk sauce. R. Ḥinena b. Rava of Pashrunia permitted it. Rava remarked, "Who except R. Ḥinena ... is so wise as to permit it?"...
>
> (b. Ḥul. 112a)

> The ritually slaughtered meat of R. Mari b. Raḥel was salted together with *trefah* meat. He came before Rava who said to him....
>
> (b. Ḥul. 112b)

> Once a vulture seized a piece of meat in the market and dropped it among the palm-trees belonging to Bar Marion. When the latter ap-

[1] Nonetheless, the inquiry of R. Jonah, cited above, and the decision concerning Rava's duck, which was found with the neck smeared with blood, b. Ḥul. 28a, were probably of narrowly academic venue and do not by themselves prove that the rabbis' authority extended beyond the schoolhouse. The other cases cited above indicate, however, that it most certainly did.

peared before Abaye, Abaye said to him, "Go and take it for yourself..."
(b. B.M. 24b)

A man once came to Rava and asked, "What is the law [about releasing the bird when taking the young] with regard to the *Temah* [a clean bird]?" Rava said [to himself], "Does not this man know that one has to let a clean bird go?" He said to [the inquirer], "Perhaps there was but one young bird or one egg?" He replied, "That is so." Then said Rava, "This surely should not give rise to doubt...." The other sent it away. Rava then set snares for it and caught it...
(b. Ḥul. 141b)[1]

Abaye, moreover, issued rulings about the permissibility of certain kinds of fish[2] and discussed the punishment for eating an eel,[3] which birds are permitted and which prohibited,[4] and the decision concerning an animal or bird which has been clawed by a dog.[5] These few cases of inquiries to the rabbis are suggestive, though not probative. The inquiry about a pigeon in milk sauce would presuppose the specifically rabbinical interpretation of the commandment not to stew a kid in its mother's milk, for this was long ago extended to prohibit contact between meat and dairy products. The case of the meat dropped by a vulture would suggest that an ordinary Jew observed the rules on proper slaughter of meat. The inquiry to Rava indicates a similar interest in keeping the biblical commandment not to take both the mother and the young. That the rabbi was not so scrupulous as the inquirer leads to the supposition that ordinary people kept that particular law more stringently than the rabbis thought they had to. Since it was a biblical ordinance, promising long life as the reward for obedience, people would have been quite strict about it, and assumed that the rabbis would know precisely how required to keep it.

To summarize: We have considered two different settings for the enforcement of ritual laws relating to food. In the cases of slaughtering and selling meat, we have seen that the rabbis' administrative powers as court officers and market supervisers gave them considerable power over butchers. The slaughterers were, therefore, quite likely to consult with, or to receive inspection visits from, rabbis. The rabbis' authority to enforce the laws would, to begin with, have encouraged widespread

---

1 On the tendency of rabbis to favor rabbinical interests in making court decisions, see below, pp. 309ff.

2 b. Suk. 18a.

3 b. Mak. 17b.

4 b. Ḥul. 63a.

5 b. Ḥul. 53a.

compliance. About other food taboos, we have no such certainty. In a few instances, non-academicians asked about the law; of these, one involved a biblical ordinance, one an honest doubt about the rule on ritually-slaughtered meat mixed with non-kosher meat, and the third, an uncooked pigeon in milk. The practices of the people in their homes can hardly be assessed upon the basis of these three cases, nor can we speculate about the extent of rabbinical influence in the domestic enforcement of the food taboos.

VIII. Court and Rite (I): Mourning

We turn to consider other areas of law, mostly ritual in nature, where religious influence, and not political or judicial authority, was the chief means of effectuating the law. The evidence is limited.

We have one case of a rabbi's giving public instruction on mourning rites, as follows:

> Rava told the people of Maḥoza, "You who do not follow the bier [to the burial ground] should begin counting [the days of mourning] as soon as you turn your faces from the city gates."
>
> (b. M.Q. 22a)[1]

We do not know whether the Maḥozans followed Rava's rule. The rabbis had numerous principles about proper mourning rites. The funeral cortege, for example, was supposed to halt and sit seven times, to comfort the mourners or express lamentations en route home from the burial place. When, therefore, R. ʿIvya arranged a "halting and sitting" for his wife, the sister of Rami b. Papa, when she died, R. Joseph said he erred in a number of details, and Abaye and Rava noted other errors committed in that connection. Rava referred to the fact that such "haltings and sittings" may be arranged only where they are local practice.[2]

In general the rabbis had to defer to accepted customs, and could do little to force people to change them. Rava, for example, said that a mourner was permitted to bathe in cold water all seven days of his bereavement and may eat meat and drink wine.[3] Another tradition held that he said the mourner may *not* do so. No stories accompany the

---

[1] Trans. H. M. Lazarus (London, 1948), p. 138. On this passage, see B. M. Lewin, ed., *Oẓar HaGeonim*, *Mashqin*, IV, C, p. 34.

[2] b. B.B. 100b.

[3] b. Taʿanit 13a.

discussion, and if Rava's opinion on the law was in doubt, it can hardly be concluded that ordinary people had received, and were following, his instructions. Rava held, further, that on the Sabbath a mourner may walk about in his cloak, although it has been torn as a sign of mourning. On the Sabbath, Abaye found R. Joseph with his head covered with a handkerchief and asked him why he did so, considering that mourning is not conducted on that day.[1] The various sages clearly had different ideas of proper conduct during a period of mourning. Some were based upon the teaching of R. Judah the Prince, others upon Tannaitic tradition. For one thing, R. Judah the Prince urged the people to follow his practice, when he died, of being buried in a cheap shroud. R. Papa said that the people now commonly buried the dead in a shroud worth a few cents.[2] Whether this practice represented a response to rabbinic instruction, or the continuation of earlier Babylonian practices, or mere poverty, we do not know for sure. If, however, Babylonian custom was similar in this respect to the Palestinian, then R. Judah the Prince's instruction would have been quite necessary there. The influence of the rabbis during close to two centuries, we may infer, would have resulted in the modification of former practices.

The court seems, however, to have had little control over how people buried and mourned for their dead. We have no cases to suggest otherwise. I find it hard to suppose that in funerary matters the people turned to the rabbis as court-officials. On the other hand, the rabbis' own practices, exemplified in the schools and in the behavior of the disciples, would have represented an alternative to earlier, established customs, and, given the rabbis' prestige and supposed supernatural powers,[3] the common people would have regarded their instructions with a mixture of respect and awe. Men who were able to communicate with the dead and the divinity would also know how to pay last respects to deceased relatives. So sensitive a matter as burial of the dead must have proved amenable to rabbinical influence, therefore, even though the courts as such seem to have had little to say about it.[4]

---

[1] b. M.Q. 24a.

[2] b. Ket. 8b. But compare below, p. 196.

[3] See below, pp. 353-362 on the rabbis as "holy men."

[4] If so, however, we have remarkably little evidence to suggest how much influence, if any, rabbis actually had over burial rites and customs.

IX. COURT AND RITE (II): PURITY LAWS

The rabbis were believed by 'Ifra Hormizd to be experts in distinguishing various kinds of blood-excretions from one another.[1] Whether or not that story actually reports a historical incident, it is clear that the rabbis themselves told about the expertness of various masters. The biblical injunctions on levitical purity, concerning, specifically, the commandment to refrain from sexual relations during a woman's menstrual period, were generally obeyed by the people, so far as we can tell. The reason was that the Mosaic law prescribed menstrual taboos. The rabbis praised the Jews for their loyalty to the taboos:

> Rava exposited the Scripture, "And at our doors are all manner of precious fruits" (Song 7:14) as an allusion to the daughters of Israel who tell their husbands about their doors.
>
> (b. 'Eruv. 21b)

In earlier periods, numerous cases were reported of ordinary people, mostly women, who brought samples of blood for rabbinical inspection.[2] For this period, apart from the story about 'Ifra Hormiz(d), no similar accounts were recorded.

On the other hand, we have the following sayings which concern purity laws:

> R. Joseph said, "It once happened in Pumbedita that the infant was made to undergo ritual immersion [to protect heave-offering which may come in contact with her] before her mother...
>
> (b. Nid. 32a)[3]

> Rabbah acted similarly [permitted immersion on the eighth day, instead of the night preceding] at Maḥoza on account of the guards at the city gates [who could not be trusted to refrain from molesting the women at night]....
>
> (b. Nid. 67b)

R. Joseph's report suggests that people were careful to avoid rendering heave-offering unclean. Rabbah's ruling in Maḥoza indicates two facts. First, the women did take a ritual bath when they were supposed to, and second, some people in Maḥoza asked for, and probably accepted, his ruling about the matter. (It cannot be taken for granted that his ruling was considered valid by everybody in the town.) Rava explained that a menstrual woman may perform the normal household

---

[1] Above, p. 35.
[2] Vol. II, pp. 276-277, vol. III, pp. 240-243.
[3] Trans. W. Slotki (London, 1948), p. 222.

tasks for her husband, except making his bed in his presence.[1] Following R. Huna's dictum, that she also may not fill his cup, the wives of the several rabbis did so in a manner different from ordinary days.[2] Other forms of levitical uncleanness were discussed by the rabbis, whether or not practical cases arose, or were likely to arise, for decision.[3] Rava ruled that the lizards of Maḥoza are unclean if their shapes are retained.[4] I do not know the practical implications, if any, of this ruling, or under what circumstances, and for what purpose, it was issued. In fact, the laws of ritual cleanness had been suspended for Babylonian Jewry, and few, if any practical applications of such rulings existed.[5]

To summarize: If, as I suppose, the people continued to observe the taboos concerning menstrual separation, then it seems that the rabbis were consulted on how to do so. Whether the consultation came to them as court officers or as learned and holy men, I cannot say, though I imagine it was, at least in the case of 'Ifra Hormizd, on the latter account.

---

[1] b. Ket. 61a.

[2] Specifically, Abaye's, Rava's and R. Papa's, b. Ket. 61a.

[3] E.g., b. Shab. 28a, Rava on the uncleanness of the skin of an unclean animal; b. B.Q. 25b, Rava on the length of time which the uncleanness arising from a corpse may last; b. 'Eruv. 4b, Rabbah b. R. Huna on whether or not knotted hair constitutes an interposition in a ritual bath; b. Shab. 95b, Rava on five principles in the uncleanness of an earthen vessel; b. Shab. 84b, Rava on the same subject; b. Shab. 58b, Rava vs. Abaye on the uncleanness of a bell and its clapper; b. Ber. 19b, Rava on interposition before uncleanness, etc.; b. Shab. 14a, Rava and Abaye on waters of purification.

[4] b. Nid. 56a.

[5] Clearly, some priests ate their sacred food in a state of ritual purity. Perhaps some who adhered to the old way of the *ḥavurah* did likewise, but I find little grounds to suppose that rabbis ordinarily ate secular food (*ḥullin*) in a state of ritual purity. See my *Fellowship in Judaism* (London, 1963), pp. 22-30.

In fact, the purity laws were originally intended, as later understood by the Sadducees and Temple priesthood, for observance in the Temple alone. It was the Pharisees who made keeping the ritual purity laws (apart from those concerning menstrual purity, to be kept by everyone) a mark of membership in the Pharisaic party, and hence the Pharisees held that one must keep those laws even outside of the Temple, in particular at meal-time. There was no earlier basis in Babylonian Jewry for keeping ritual purity laws, and I suppose most of them would have died away of disuse long before the first rabbis made their way to Babylonia. Hence whether or not the Pharisees and later rabbis thought that one ought to keep ritual purity taboos when eating even ordinary meals, to the ordinary folk such taboos could have seemed wholly unreal, and such a teaching far beyond their expectations of Sinaitic revelation. It is especially noteworthy that priests did eat their consecrated offerings in a state of ritual purity, according to the little evidence we have considered.

x. Court and Rite (iii): Holy Objects

Numerous sayings pertain to *tefillin*, *mezuzot*, and other holy objects, but we have no evidence either that the courts were able to enforce the laws about their sanctity, or that the rabbis greatly affected the conduct of ordinary people in their regard.[1] The following account is suggestive:

> Our [Tannaitic] Rabbis taught, "A linen garment—Bet Shammai say it is exempt from [the requirement of] fringes, and Bet Hillel declare it liable. The law follows Bet Hillel." R. Eliezar b. R. Ẓadoq said, "Is it not a fact that anyone in Jerusalem who attaches blue threads [to linen] causes amazement?" Rabbi said, "If that is so, why did they forbid it? Because people are not well versed in the law."
>
> Rava son of R. Ḥanan said to Rava, "Then let ten people insert [fringes into linen garments] and let them go about in the market place, and so the law will be made known to all." "People will wonder at it all the more." "Then let it be announced at the public lecture." "It is to be feared that people will use imitation blue." "But it is no worse than if it were white?" ... "But it can be announced on public notices?" "And are we to rely upon public notices?" Rava then said, "If in respect of leaven on the Passover or in respect of the Day of Atonement ... we rely on public notices, how much more so may we rely upon them here where only the transgression of a positive precept can be involved..."
>
> (b. Men. 40a)[2]
>
> Rabbah b. R. Huna once visited the house of Rava b. R. Naḥman and saw that the latter was wearing a garment that was folded over, with the fringes inserted in the folded corners. [It became clear that these were improperly inserted, and Rava b. R. Naḥman took off the garment. Rabbah b. R. Huna then said to him,] "Do you think [fringes] are an obligation upon the person? They pertain to the garment. Go and insert the fringes properly."
>
> (b. Men. 41a)

What is interesting in the second account is the fact that the son of the greatest authority of the preceding generation not only did *not* carry out the law properly but did not even know it. The possibility that ordinary people would have known and followed rabbinic injunctions seems all the more remote, especially in the light of the first story. Rava seemed reluctant to announce the law in public, apparently because of the good chance of popular misunderstanding.[3] Whatever

---

[1] Compare vol. III, pp. 238-240.

[2] Trans. Eli Cashdan (London, 1948), p. 246.

[3] See vol. III, pp. 252-259, for astonishing instances of such misunderstanding of rabbinical instruction on ritual matters.

reliance Rava was prepared to place in public notices, in the end, the story does *not* say that such notices were posted or issued.

While a number of sayings pertain to the *mezuzah* and its proper placement, the only stories concern how rabbis placed the *mezuzah* in their own houses.[1]

Abaye explained circumstances affecting the rule prohibiting sexual intercourse in a place where a scroll of the Torah was located.[2] Rava taught some rules for scribes of sacred books.[3] The latter rules could have been enforced if the rabbis had declared that improperly written scrolls could not be used for public lection. We have no evidence that such cases arose, certainly nothing equivalent to the cases indicating rabbinical rule over the abattoir. The former rule also produced no practical results so far as we can tell.

One recalls that an Arab woman brought *tefillin* to Abaye for ransom.[4] The reason was that she thought he would pay well for them, and one may infer that rabbis had the reputation of being especially concerned for the sanctity of *tefillin*. Even if that was the case, it does not prove that they also had any authority, through the courts or otherwise, over how the people handled, used, or manufactured them. On the other hand, as holy men, they would have been believed to know how to make powerful charms, and so their instructions would not usually—when known—have been ignored. Abaye explained how to make *tefillin*, and said that the parchment had to be flawless.[5] We have the following story as well:

> Abaye was once sitting before R. Joseph when the strap of his *tefillin* snapped. He asked R. Joseph, "May one tie it together?..." R. Aḥa b. R. Joseph asked R. Ashi, "May one sew it together, turning the seam on the inside?" He answered, "Go and see what the people do."[6]
>
> (b. Men. 35b)

The latter saying, from the fifth century, indicates that the rabbi did not know the answer but was willing to depend upon popular custom.

[1] Sayings: b. Men. 33b, Rava, the *mezuzah* should be affixed in the handbreadth nearest the street. R. Ḥanina of Sura said the reason was that it should thus protect the entire house. Note also Rava's saying in the same place that faulty doors are exempt from the requirement of a *mezuzah*. Stories: b. Men. 33b, Abaye about the *mezuzot* in Rabbah's house; b. Men. 34a, R. Papa about the *mezuzot* in Mar Samuel's house.

[2] b. Ber. 25b-26a.

[3] b. Men. 29b.

[4] b. Git. 45b, cited above.

[5] b. Men. 35a.

[6] Hebrew: DBR.

In the former case, a disciple inquired of his master, who supplied an answer. Either R. Ashi later on did not know what R. Joseph had said, or the ordinary people eventually learned the proper rabbinic practice so it was necessary only to refer to what they were actually doing. But the latter supposition is unlikely, since it is easier and safer to give a direct answer than to refer to popular custom, chance observation of which is always in danger of yielding an erroneous result. Explaining R. Yannai's opinion, that *tefillin* demand a pure body, Abaye said that he meant one should not pass wind while wearing them, and Rava that one should not sleep in them.[1] Mar. b. Rabina asked R. Naḥman b. Isaac whether *tefillin* may be written on the skin of a clean fish. R. Naḥman b. Isaac replied that Elijah will some day come and answer his question.[2] R. Naḥman thus did not know the answer to the question. Now let us suppose that ordinary people were engaged in the manufacture of *tefillin*, and thought to make use of the skin of a clean fish. Had they asked a rabbi, he would not have known. Had they not done so, but gone ahead and made the *tefillin* in such a fashion, then later on, it would hardly have been easy to instruct them that they were wrong. It would have become rooted in their traditions, and in time to come, the best a rabbi could do when faced with the same question in the school would have been to say, "Go, see what the people are doing." Saying so would not necessarily have meant approval, but rather implied a confession that no tradition existed on the subject, so it would be just as well to do what ordinary folk now did. Not all instances in which the custom of the people was found normative or acceptable are of the same weight, to be sure. Many recent scholars have thought, however, that such a saying would invariably indicate widespread conformity to the law. In some instances it may rather have meant simply that the rabbis had no traditions on a question, or were unwilling to run contrary to folk practice in some minor matter, or were unable to overcome customs of many years' standing.

The evidence that the rabbis as court officers supervised the preparation and use of holy objects is very slight. I see no reason to suppose that their instructions were sought out by ordinary people, or that they made much effort to impose their laws outside of the schools. We simply do not know what ordinary people were doing. We know that *tefillin* were thought to be worn characteristically by disciples of the

---

[1] b. Shab. 49a, 130a.

[2] b. Shab. 108a.

rabbis,[1] and therefore probably not by non-academicians. Laws about *mezuzot* have yielded no probative evidence one way or the other. In Nippur, the equivalents to *mezuzot* were magical bowls. The Jews clearly used them. If so, perhaps common people were following the practices of their non-Jewish neighbors in preparing a prophylactic against demons for their homes, rather than using the rabbinical amulet intended for the same purpose. (But it is also possible that Jews used these bowls first, and that the usage spread to Mandaean and Christian neighbors. Neither Montgomery nor Yamauchi is clear on this point.) It is most striking that the instructions about preparing a Torah-scroll are unaccompanied by evidence as to how they were carried out. Since the Torah-scroll was prepared mostly for synagogues, it may be that the rabbis' lack of control of synagogue life[2] extended even to the preparation of sacred objects used there.

xi. Court and Rite (iv): Holy Days

The rabbinical courts exerted only limited influence over the celebration of the holy days. Whether or not the rabbis preached in the synagogues, outside of them they could direct festival behavior only in a few, highly visible details. Their discussions ranged over all legal technicalities, to be sure, but I seriously doubt outsiders listened to them.[3]

The Days of Awe: Rava said that one who sounds the *shofar* for the sake of making musical noises has fulfilled his obligation in that regard.[4] He also instructed a disciple about the obligation to hear the *shofar* during prayers.[5] Rabbah explained that the requirement to recite kingship, remembrance, and *shofar*, or revelation, Scriptures, was so "that the remembrance of you may come before me for good, through the *shofar*."[6] The obligation to fast on the Day of Atonement, which the Scriptures had imposed, was probably enforced so far as possible by the rabbis. The following story indicates that the rabbis had *some* public authority:

> Rava permitted [ŠR'] the people of Southside [Maḥozan suburb] on the Day of Atonement to walk [pass] through water for the purpose of

[1] See vol. III, p. 130-149.
[2] See above, p. 149.
[3] See vol. II, pp. 279-280, vol. III, pp. 252-259.
[4] b. R.H. 33b.
[5] b. R.H. 34b.
[6] b. R.H. 34b.

> guarding the crop [even though it appeared to be forbidden as act of washing]... R. Joseph permitted the people of Be Tarbu to walk through the water to go hear the lecture [on the Day of Atonement] but did not allow them to return...
>
> (b. Yoma 77b)

Both instances pertained to villagers outside of the towns. In order to encourage their attendance at the rabbis' Atonement lecture, crossing water was permitted. It stands to reason that they had actually asked about the law in at least the latter case, for the subsequent discussion indicates that had permission not been granted, the people would not have come, certainly not in future years, and the rabbis were eager to encourage just such attendance.

Other stories about practices concern the rabbis' own behavior on the Day of Atonement. Rabbah fasted for two days, because of doubt about the right date.[1] Rava would cool off through sitting on fresh twigs, Rabbah through a silver cup.[2] Rabbah's household scraped pumpkins on the Day of Atonement.[3] Sayings on what constituted a culpable act of eating, such as Rava's that chewing pepper or ginger is not punishable, could not have meant much outside of the schools.[4]

Tabernacles: The laws on proper construction of the *sukkah*, on the festival prayers and rites, on preparation of the *lulav* and the like produced numerous legal discussions.[5] Only two stories about actual practice are extant, and both involve rabbis and disciples. Abaye asked R. Joseph why he was sleeping on a certain kind of bed in the *Sukkah*; Rava permitted a disciple, R. Aḥa b. Adda, to sleep outside of the *Sukkah* because of an odor.[6] That people kept the festival is beyond question. But we do not know how they did so.

---

[1] b. R.H. 21a.

[2] b. Yoma 78a.

[3] b. Shab. 115a.

[4] b. Yoma 81b.

[5] E.g. b. ʿEruv. 3a, = b. Suk. 2a, Rabbah on Lev. 23:43 to prove that the *Sukkah* must be less than 20 handbreadths high; b. Suk. 4a, Abaye vs. Rava on the laws pertaining to roof of the *Sukkah*; b. Suk. 7a, Abaye vs. Rava on the walls; b. Suk. 12b, Abaye on whether one may use licorice wood for the roofing; b. Suk. 29a, Rava on what can be kept in the *Sukkah*; b. Suk. 32b, Abaye and Rava on using myrtle for the roofing; b. Suk. 36b, Rava on how to make a *lulav*; b. Suk. 37a-b, Rabbah and Rava on the four species and the *lulav*; b. Suk. 41b, Rava on lending an *etrog*; b. Suk. 44a, Abaye asked Rava about the *lulav* ceremony; b. Suk. 55a, Abaye and Rava on the lections; see also b. Qid. 34a-b, Abaye and Rava; b. A.Z. 3b, Rava, One who is bothered by heat is not obligated to remain in the *Sukkah*.

[6] Abaye, b. Suk. 19b, Rava, b. Suk. 26a.

Passover: The rabbis gave public lectures[1] about proper observance of Passover, in particular on how to observe the strict taboos against using, or even possessing, leaven during the festival. Rava's public lecture is reported as follows:

> Rava lectured, "A woman may not knead in the sun nor with water heated by the sun, nor with water collected from the caldron, and she must not remove her hand from the oven until she has finished all the bread [she must continue working it until baked], and she requires two vessels, one with which she moistens, the other in which she cools her hands."
>
> (b. Pes. 42a)[2]

The lecture was on preparing unleavened bread. Women normally must have had traditions based upon what they had seen their mothers do. Presumably Rava's lecture was intended to teach the ordinary people to conform to the standards of the rabbis. R. Mattena, who had earlier given a public lecture, found that the people simply did not comprehend his instructions, and we do not know what people understood of Rava's, or how they responded. A likely guess is that the women went on doing as their mothers had taught them. On the other hand, because of his supervision of the marketplace, Rava was able to control the sale of wheat:

> A ship of grain foundered in Ḥishta [before Passover]. Rava permitted selling [the wet grain, which had become leaven] to gentiles... and subsequently allowed it to be sold to Jews in small quantities, so that it might be consumed before the festival.
>
> (b. Pes. 40b)

As market-commissioners, rabbis had no difficulty in supervising the sale of products in connection with Passover. No similar circumstance provided them with a basis for controlling home-celebrations. We do not know the origin of such a question as the following:

> R. Naḥman b. Isaac was asked, "If one rents a house to his neighbor from the fourteenth [of Nisan], who is obligated to search out [the leaven]?..." He said to them, "We have learned [in Tannaitic tradition]...."
>
> (b. Pes. 4a)

The question was a technical one, and had nothing to do with such simple, annual tasks as the baking of unleavened bread. The reply, phrased in legal terms, presupposed knowledge and comprehension of

[1] See vol. III, p. 255.

[2] = b. Yoma 28b. Note also Rava's comment on the kneading basins used in Maḥoza, b. Pes. 30b.

the Tannaitic traditions (= "we have learned"). The obligation for searching leaven was probably not assigned to purchasers by the courts.

We see, therefore, three kinds of Passover law. The first involved the sale of produce in the marketplace, the second, the preparation of unleavened bread and other home duties, and the third, other, non-ritual legal issues arising from the technicalities of Passover observance. The rabbis could easily enforce the law in the market. They could encourage observance at home. If consulted on a legal technicality, they could offer an opinion. The first type of law was easily effected through control of the markets. The second and third kinds of law were not litigable and produced no cases for court action. While they were not enforced, observance could be encouraged through rabbinical influence.

The Passover *seder* produced no cases or questions arising from the circumstances of the common life. While numerous stories told what the rabbis said and did in their schools or homes, none at all pertained to people outside of rabbinical circles. The following illustrate the nature of the stories:

> Rava used to drink wine the whole of the day preceding the first evening of Passover, in order to whet his appetite to eat more unleavened bread in the evening...
>
> (b. Pes. 107b)

> Abaye said, "When we were at the Master's [Rabbah's] house, we used to recline on each other's knees. When we came to R. Joseph's house, he remarked to us..."
>
> (b. Pes. 108a)

> Rava counted the beams, while Abaye's mother, when he had drunk one cup, would offer him two cups with her hands. The attendant of R. Naḥman b. Isaac, when he (the rabbi) had drunk two cups, would offer him one cup...
>
> (b. Pes. 110a) [1]

> Meremar asked, "Who recites the *Haggadah* at R. Joseph's?" They told me, "R. Joseph."
>
> (b. Pes. 116b)

> Abaye was sitting [at the Passover meal] before Rabbah. Seeing him dozing, he said to him, "You are dozing, Sir!"....
>
> (b. Pes. 120b)

Stories about how the rabbis conducted themselves at the *seder* were important for the study of the law and were therefore carefully pre-

[1] Preventive magic, see below, p. 335-336.

served in the schools. They do not indicate what ordinary people did in their homes, nor were they intended to. One recalls that the laws of Grace and other blessings for foods and material pleasures produced many accounts of what rabbis said and did, but practically none about life outside of the schools. What happened within rabbinical circles could not have influenced outsiders unless the rabbis made the effort to shape the lives of the common folk *and* had the power to do so. Conduct at meals, including the Passover *Seder*, was far beyond their direct powers of persuasion or influence.

Academic discussions about Passover focussed upon the laws of searching out and removing the leaven.[1] These discussions were technical and frequently involved far-fetched examples, such as Rava's, "If a mouse enters the house with a loaf, is a new search for leaven required?" which evoked a long discussion on the mouse and the loaf.[2] Other issues involved the Scriptural basis for contemporary practice[3] and the interpretation of Scriptures relevant to Passover.[4]

The Intermediate Days of Festivals: It is a paradox that while the rabbis had little power over the actual celebration of festivals, they had a great deal of authority to enforce their beliefs about proper conduct on the intervening, semi-festival days. The reason was that these beliefs pertained mostly to what work on those days was prohibited and what was permitted. Activities which were publicly performed could easily come under their surveillance, and their supervision of the markets placed within their control the artisans and small merchants as well as the farmers who sought to sell their produce. In consequence, while the laws about building the *Sukkah* or searching out leaven or celebrating the Passover meal seem to have affected rabbinical or academic circles alone, with ordinary people hearing lectures about the most basic questions of preparing unleavened bread and similar matters, the laws

---

[1] Rava provided the liturgy of a blessing for the act of searching out the leaven, b. Pes. 7a; on the laws of the search and removal of leaven, see also b. Pes. 4b, Abaye; b. Pes. 6a, Rava, if one turns the house into a granary before thirty days before Passover, he is not obligated to remove the leaven; b. Pes. 8a, Rava said the courtyard does not require a search; b. Pes. 8a, Rabbah b. R. Huna said salt sheds and wax sheds must be searched, etc.

[2] b. Pes. 10b-11a.

[3] b. Pes. 40a, on Ex. 12:17; b. Pes. 39a, R. Reḥumi to Abaye, how do you know that *maror* in Ex. 12:8 refers to a kind of herb? b. Pes. 5a, Rava deduced the prohibition of leaven from noon of the day preceding the Passover seder from Ex. 34:25, see also b. Pes. 120a, Rava on the Scriptural and rabbinical origins of the commandments to consume unleavened bread and bitter herbs.

[4] e.g. R. Naḥman b. Isaac, b. Pes. 6b.

about observing the intermediate days of Tabernacles and Passover produced a number of enforcement-sayings, including the following:

> Rava enacted [’YTQYN] at Maḥoza, “Whatever one carries with great effort must on a festival be carried on a carrying pole. Whatever is normally carried on such a pole must be carried by a yoke...”
>
> (b. Beẓ. 30a)

Rava’s principle was that one should deviate from his normal way of carrying a load, so as to recognize the obligation not to work on the intervening days. We do not know what the people did in response to Rava’s enactment. The following is suggestive:

> Rava b. R. Ḥanin said to Abaye, “We have learned... yet we see that people do this and we do not take them to task!” He replied, “...but let Israel [go their way]. *It is better that they should err in ignorance than presumptuously...*”
>
> (b. Beẓ. 30a)[1]

This is a striking reply, for Abaye apparently thought it hopeless to seek to impose conformity to rabbinical rulings. It was better not to raise some issues to begin with. That does not mean that the rabbis refrained from issuing rulings about the observance of the intermediate festival days, but it does suggest that widespread obedience to the law could *not* be taken for granted. Among other rulings are the following:

> Abaye allowed [ŠR’] the people of Harmekh to clear away [during the festival week growths obstructing]the canal.
>
> (b. M.Q. 4b)

> Rava allowed [ŠR’] bleeding of cattle during the festival week... Rava allowed fulled clothes to be rubbed. Rava said, “With regard to one who clears his field [of chips of wood] if it is for gathering fire wood, it is allowed, but if for clearing the ground, it is forbidden. How can we tell? If he picks up the larger pieces and leaves the smaller, it is to gather fire wood... Rava said also, “With regard to one who opens sluices to let water run off into his fields, if to get the fish, it is permitted; to water the soil, forbidden. How can we tell?...” Rava further said, “With regard to one who trims his palm tree, if it is for [food for] the beasts, it is allowed, but for the palm’s sake, it is forbidden. How can we tell?...”
>
> (b. M.Q. 10b)[2]

---

[1] = b. Shab. 148b. Italics supplied.

[2] Note also Rava’s lecture, b. Beẓ. 33a.

According to the interpretation of R. Ḥananel, the following took place on the festival:

> Some rams once came to [were brought for sale] Mabrakta [near Maḥoza] and Rava permitted the people of Maḥoza to buy them [and take the purchases back to town...] (After some discussion, Rava changed his ruling and said), "Let them be sold to the people of Mabrakta...."
>
> (b. ʿEruv. 47b)

The ruling of Abaye seems unequivocal. At his say-so, the people cleared out the water-channel serving their village. The several rulings of Rava cited in the second source are in varying forms; the first two state that Rava allowed (ŠR') certain actions, in the latter ones, he merely *said* ('MR) they might be done. Whether the difference in language implies a difference between a case and a merely theoretical ruling I cannot say. The third case clearly refers to Rava's administration of the markets. By contrast, in the several examples given earlier, the activities of private persons were at issue, and the rabbis may not have had equivalent control of what people did at home and on their farms. The question, "How do we know what a person's intent is," is important. It leads to the inference that rabbis, who might observe a man's work in the fields, wanted to know whether they should intervene or not. If so, one may suppose that had they observed illegal action, they might declare a ban, as happened in earlier times.[1] Upon that basis, I suppose that the Rabbi's several rulings were actually enforced.

The rabbis' hosts, that is to say, inn-keepers, brought them a number of questions concerning the rules about work on the intermediate festival days, including the following:

> The host of Rav b. R. Ḥanan had bundles of mustard stalks and asked him, "Is it permissible to crush it on the festival and eat of it." He could not answer, so he turned to Rava, who ruled...
>
> (b. Beẓ. 12b)

> The host of R. Papa—some say it was another who came before R. Papa—had some eggs from a Sabbath [which he wished to prepare] on the following day [Sunday, a festival]. He came and asked him, "Is it permitted to eat them tomorrow?"...
>
> (b. Beẓ. 4a)

The inquiry to a rabbi would have been natural. The innkeeper certainly did not want to serve foods or act in a manner prohibited

[1] Vol. II, p. 253 and vol. III, pp. 220-229.

by the law, and with rabbis at hand, it was normal to inquire about doubtful matters. Such inquiries would suggest that the rabbis had influence over the people among whom they lived, indeed whose patrons they were, as is to be expected, but they lead to no further inference. We have stories, moreover, about how the rabbis themselves acted on the festival-week, including the following:

> R. Joseph had beams of timber brought in in daylight...
> (b. M.Q. 12b)
>
> Rain trickled into Abaye's mill-room, and he asked Rabbah...
> (b. Beẓ. 36b)
>
> The wife of R. Joseph sifted flour...
> (b. Beẓ. 29b)
>
> R. Ḥama had a folding bed which was put up on festivals. Rava was asked whether it was permitted....
> (b. Shab. 47b)
>
> [R. Joseph said] "...it once happened that at Dura deRe'uta an alley ended in a backyard, and when I came to ask Rav Judah [or, when the case came to...] he ruled..."
> (b. 'Eruv. 7b)

Academic discussions touched upon many practical matters, such as sharpening a knife on the festival-week,[1] putting out a fire,[2] burial,[3] and the like.[4]

Purim and Ḥanukkah: The rules about reading the *Megillah* (Scroll of Esther) were extensively discussed. Rava held that reading it was more important than the service in the Jerusalem Temple,[5] that one was duty-bound to get drunk on Purim,[6] and that one must not recite the *Megillah* from memory but from a proper scroll. Rava[7] and R. Papa discussed the blessing to be recited before reading the *Megillah* and the division of the lections.[8] Rabbah and R. Joseph explained why the

---

[1] b. Beẓ. 28a-b, R. Nehemiah b. R. Joseph before Rava, etc.

[2] b. Beẓ. 22a, Abaye asked Rabbah.

[3] b. M.Q. 19b, Abaye asked Rabbah; b. Beẓ. 6a, Rava says gentiles take charge of the corpse on the first day of a festival.

[4] b. Beẓ. 8b, Rava on preparing dirt before the Sabbath or festival to cover excrement; b. Beẓ. 8b-9a, Rabbah on covering blood on the festival; b. Beẓ. 18b, R. Naḥman b. Isaac on bathing on the festival; b. Beẓ. 23a, Rabbah and R. Joseph on using perfume on the festival; b. A.Z. 6b, the general principles of laws of work on the festival, explicated by R. Naḥman b. Isaac.

[5] b. Meg. 3b.

[6] b. Meg. 7b.

[7] b. Meg. 18a.

[8] b. Meg. 21b.

Megillah was not to be read on the Sabbath.[1] Rava said that the *Hallel* was not recited on Purim.[2] Among numerous sayings and stories, none pertains to what ordinary people did or did not do. Since the *Megillah* was read in the synagogues, the rabbis' rulings were theoretically relevant, but I have found no evidence that they were actually carried out.

Two stories, both involving sages, were told about the observance of Ḥanukkah, first, Rabbah's practice in regard to the oil used in the Ḥanukkah light,[3] second, R. Huna b. Judah's confusion about when to say the Ḥanukkah prayer in the Grace after Meals, during his visit to Rava's school.[4] Other sayings relate to the blessing over the Ḥanukkah lights,[5] where they should be placed for public display at home,[6] the reason for the (earlier) prohibition of counting money by the Ḥanukkah lights,[7] prohibited and permitted uses of the Ḥanukkah lights[8] and other matters.[9] While the Ḥanukkah lights involved legal issues, no other aspect of the festival celebration was discussed. The issues pertained therefore to the Grace after Meals, of importance in the academy, and to the preparation and placement of the Ḥanukkah lights, done at home. Nothing tells us what ordinary people did.

XII. Court and Rite (v): The Sabbath

Certain aspects of Sabbath observance were well within the power of the courts, and others quite beyond it. Two kinds of laws were publicly enforced by the rabbis, concerning, first, "working" on the Sabbath, and second, the establishment of Sabbath limits.[10] In the former case, the rabbis' police power, combined with the weight of public opinion, gave them considerable ability to discourage outright Sabbath-breaking. In the latter, because they themselves could control the establishment of the Sabbath boundary, they had no difficulty whatever in doing as they thought proper. Where others established it, they increasingly did so under rabbinical supervision. Numerous other

[1] b. Meg. 4b.
[2] b. Meg. 14a.
[3] b. Shab. 23a, Abaye reports Rabbah's action.
[4] b. Shab. 24a.
[5] b. Suk. 46a, R. Naḥman b. Isaac.
[6] b. Shab. 22a, Rabbah.
[7] b. Shab. 22a, R. Joseph gives the reason for a ruling by R. Assi.
[8] b. Shab. 21b, Rava.
[9] b. R.H. 18b, Abaye and R. Joseph; b. Shab. 23b, Rava; b. Shab. 23a, R. Huna and Rava; b. Shab. 22b, Rava.
[10] See vol. I, pp. 148-149, vol. II, pp. 277-278, vol. III, pp. 243-252.

Sabbath laws, however, were by no means enforced among common people, so far as we know.

The Sabbath boundary: We have many instances in which rabbis supervised the preparation and placement of the Sabbath boundary:

> Rava b. R. Ḥanan said to Abaye, "What is the law [about the thickness of the sideposts]?" He replied, "Go and see what the people do [DBR]."
>
> (b. ʿEruv. 14b)[1]

> There was at Pum Nahara an open area. One side opened into an alley in the town, and the other into a path between vineyards that terminated at the river bank. Abaye said, "How are we to proceed? Should we put up for it a fence..." Rava said to him, "Would not people infer [from Abaye's ruling] that a sidepost is effective..."
>
> (b. ʿEruv. 24b)

> R. Safra said to Rava, "Behold the people of Ctesiphon for whom we measure the Sabbath limits from the further side of Ardashir, and the people of Ardashir for whom we measure the Sabbath limits from the further side of Ctesiphon..."
>
> (b. ʿEruv. 57b)

> Once the warm water [for a child's circumcision, prepared the day before the Sabbath]was spilled. "Let some warm water be brought for him from my house," Rabbah said...
>
> (b. ʿEruv. 67b)

> Once the warm water of a certain child was spilled out. Rava said, "Let us ask his mother. If she needs any, a gentile may warm some for him indirectly...
>
> [A similar incident.] Rava said, "Remove my things from the men's quarters to the women's and I will go and sit there, so that I may renounce in favour of the tenants of the child's courtyard the rights I have in this one..."
>
> (b. ʿEruv. 68a)

> Some men from Qorqonai [Circesium]once came to R. Joseph, and said to him, "Send us a man to prepare an *ʿeruv* for our town'" He said to Abaye, "Go and prepare the *ʿeruv* for them, but see there is no outcry against it at the school house." He went, and observed that certain houses opened on the river...
>
> (b. ʿEruv. 60a)

> Mar Judah saw the people of Mabrakta depositing their *ʿeruv* in the synagogue of Be'Agobar, and said to them, "Go deeper into the interior so that you may be allowed to walk a greater distance..."
>
> (b. ʿEruv. 61b)

[1] Compare the saying of R. Ashi, above, p. 161.

There was a certain alley in which Laḥman b. Ristak [a gentile] lived. The other residents [who were Jews]asked him, "Will you let us your domain" [for the Sabbath, so they may prepare an *'eruv*]? He refused. They went to Abaye and reported it to him. [Abaye told them how legally to get around the difficulty.]

(b. 'Eruv. 63b)

R. Tavla, visiting Maḥoza, saw a bolt suspended from the side of a doorway, and made no remark whatsoever about it...

(b. 'Eruv. 102a)

On the rabbis' own practices, we have the following stories:

A number of skin bottles were once lying in the manor of Maḥoza. While Rava was coming from his discourse, his attendant carried them in...

(b. 'Eruv. 44b)[1]

Rabbah and R. Joseph were once under way [on the eve of Sabbath before dusk], when Rabbah said to R. Joseph, "Let our Sabbath base be under the palm-tree that is supporting another tree...."

(b. 'Eruv. 51a)

The above stories are not of the same probative significance. The first indicates only that R. Joseph asked about the law in a certain situation, but does not say whether R. Joseph thereupon went and enforced it or not. As to Abaye's advice to see what the popular practice is, it may indicate that he thought the people were bound to be doing the right thing, or he may have felt that the question was of no importance, and so the peoples' practice should be relied upon and not disturbed. In either case, however, it does indicate that Abaye thought the ordinary people *were* keeping the laws on *'eruvin* so that they would exhibit *some* practice in a particular detail. It seems to me probative evidence that some laws of *'eruvin* were, in fact, widely observed. Since these laws represented a Pharisaic-rabbinic tradition, it is important to note that by the middle of the fourth century, they were probably observed among the masses.[2] The same inference is to be drawn from Rava's comment to Abaye in the case in Pum Nahara. There Rava was afraid that the ordinary people might draw the wrong conclusions from Abaye's teaching and practice. What is clear, therefore, is that the people were interested in these laws and apparently were prepared to observe them. The measurement for the people of

---

[1] Trans. and interpretation of W. Slotki (London, 1948), p. 306.

[2] For discussion of the evidence pointing to the expansion of rabbinic Judaism *by* this time, see below, pp. 256ff.

Ctesiphon and Ardashir again leads to the supposition that some Jews in these major cities were concerned about the laws of *'eruvin* and expected that the rabbis would explain how they were to be fulfilled.

The three cases on the spilled water are less decisive, for they indicate only the behavior of people who dwelt in close proximity to a rabbi.

The request to R. Joseph, by contrast, is striking. The later commentaries try to explain why at just this time the people of Circesium asked for a rabbi to prepare an *'eruv* for the town. The obvious implication was that formerly, no *'eruv*, or no rabbinical *'eruv*, was available. Upon this basis alone we can hardly conclude that some mass conversion to keeping the *'eruv*-laws had taken place. It seems likely, however, that the request indicated greater rabbinical supervision than formerly existed. The advice contributed by Mar Judah and requested from Abaye strikingly reveals once again the concern of ordinary people to keep these particular rules.

The case reported to Abaye is of special interest, for one may suppose that the Jews and gentile had lived for a long time without such arrangements. In that case, the question was a new one, and the need for Abaye's advice leads to the inference that these Jews too now wanted to keep laws they had formerly ignored. If we knew when Laḥman b. Ristak moved into the alley, we would have a clearer idea when Jews began to keep these laws. The story about R. Tavla, like those cited from the preceding generation,[1] suggests that had R. Tavla said anything about the matter, he would probably have been able to correct the situation.

The stories about the rabbis' own practices, on the other hand, simply illustrate that they continued strictly to observe the laws. Rava's instructions to his attendant not to repeat the action reported above were intended to prevent the people who accompanied him from gaining a false impression about the law. By contrast to the limited evidence of popular obedience to, and rabbinic enforcement of, other laws, we can only regard the above stories as an impressive indication of widespread conformity to the laws of *'eruvin*.

Academic discussions such as the following would therefore have reflected practical problems:

> There was a certain piazza at the house of Bar Ḥabu [one of whose supporting poles was situated at the entrance to an alley] and Abaye and Rava were forever disputing about it...
>
> (b. 'Eruv. 15a)

---

[1] Vol. III, p. 245.

Rabbah was asked, "What is the ruling where a man [beyond the Sabbath limit] had to attend to his needs?" He replied, "Human dignity supersedes a negative commandment..."

(b. 'Eruv. 41b)

Abaye asked Rabbah, "What is the ruling according to R. Meir, where one extended the corner piece..." He replied, "You have learned [in the Mishnah]..."

Abaye asked Rabbah, "What is the ruling according to R. Judah..." He replied, "You have learned [in Tannaitic tradition]...."

Abaye asked Rabbah, "Is a mound that rises to a height of ten [handbreadths] within an area of four cubits treated as a corner-piece or not?" He replied, "You have learned, 'R. Simeon b. Eleazar ruled...'"

(b. 'Eruv. 19b)[1]

The academic study of the law is illustrated in the above citations. The rabbis would argue about practical cases, respond to what must have been theoretical inquiries (for in the case brought to Rabbah, one can hardly suppose a man was then awaiting his comment or authorization), and inquire of the masters about various issues of legal theory. None of these cases, however, would have been remote from daily life, and doubtless rabbinical studies would eventually have resulted in practical application of the law in specific circumstances. Other issues under discussion included the following: How much food is required for the *'eruv*?[2] What is the law for an alley in the shape of a centipede?[3] Under what circumstances does the presence of the property of a gentile result in restrictions upon Jews?[4] How does one measure distances?[5] and the like.[6]

Other Sabbath Laws: The observance of the Sabbath formed a central theme in the rabbis' theology. Abaye taught that Jerusalem was destroyed only because of profanation of the Sabbath[7] and R. Naḥman b. Isaac said, conversely, that one who delights in the Sabbath is saved

[1] Further such inquiries by Abaye of Rabbah follow in the same place.

[2] b. 'Eruv. 29a, R. Joseph, Rabbah, and Rava.

[3] b. 'Eruv. 8b, Rava and Abaye.

[4] b. 'Eruv. 67b, Rabbah and R. Joseph.

[5] b. 'Eruv, 57a, Rava re Num. 35:4; Rava and Abaye; 58a, R. Joseph on rope used for measuring; b. 'Eruv. 56b, the surveyor bar Adda explained to Rava and Abaye about surveying; b. 'Eruv. 48a, R. Papa on rabbinical measurements.

[6] E.g. b. 'Eruv. 5a, Abaye and R. Joseph; 12a, R. Joseph and Abaye on a decision by Rav Judah; 16a, Abaye; 21b. R. Papa; 22b, Abaye on Babylonia as surrounded by rivers and therefore theoretically a single domain; 24a, Mar Judah visited R. Huna b. Judah; 31a = 82a, R. Joseph on the *'eruv* as a religious duty only; 45b, Abaye; 52b, Rabbah b. R. Ḥanan corrected by Abaye.

[7] b. Shab. 119b.

from the subjugation of exile.[1] The rabbinic discussions of Sabbath law were extensive, detailed, and searching. It is quite striking, therefore, that among all the traditions, we find only the following stories about enforcement of Sabbath laws or popular Sabbath observance:

> A certain person once came before Rava and asked whether it was permissible to perform a circumcision on the Sabbath. He replied that it was. After the person left, Rava thought, "Is it likely that he did not know it was permissible to perform a circumcision on the Sabbath?" He followed him and asked, "Tell me the circumstances of the case." The man replied, "I heard the child cry late on the Sabbath eve but it was not born until the Sabbath...."
>
> (b. Nid. 42b)

> A corpse was lying in Derokeret. R. Naḥman b. Isaac permitted it [over the objections of R. Naḥman brother of Mar son of Rabbana...] to be carried out into an area which was neither public nor private domain.
>
> (b. Shab. 94b)

> A person came before Rava, and he gave a ruling in accordance with his view [on bathing a new-born infant on the Sabbath in the usual way]. Rava fell ill. [He ascribed the illness to his erroneous ruling.]
>
> (b. Shab. 134b)

One also recalls that Rava told the Maḥozans how to carry soldiers' garments on the Sabbath.[2] These stories hardly constitute a rich body of case-reports. In the first, Rava assumed it was commonly known that circumcision may be performed on the Sabbath, and that ordinary people kept that law. In the third, he was asked about a parallel situation. The second involved what to do with a corpse on the Sabbath, a problem which must have arisen many times before R. Naḥman b. Isaac finally gave his ruling. On the basis of these three cases, one can hardly reach any firm conclusions about the extent of rabbinical influence over popular Sabbath observance. The only significant evidence is that ordinary folk were thought by the rabbis to know a simple, basic law regarding circumcision on the Sabbath. When one considers the enormous range of rabbinical laws pertaining to the Sabbath, the above evidence seems impoverished and limited. No one asked, so far as we know, about the numerous laws of work, carrying, clothing, cooking on the Sabbath, or of the various rites and rituals connected with the holy day.[3] The extensive reports of rabbinic enforcement of

---

[1] b. Shab. 118b.
[2] b. Shab. 147b, see above, p. 46.
[3] See below, pp. 324-330, on liturgy.

the laws in connection with the Sabbath boundary hence present a noteworthy contrast.

It should not be supposed that no one kept stories or traditions on how the Sabbath laws were actually carried out. We have a considerable number of such accounts, and *all* of them deal with what one or another rabbi did, refrained from doing, or inquired about. So there is no doubt that when stories about fulfilling the Sabbath laws were available, they were preserved and discussed in the schools. Among such stories about rabbis and their families are the following:

> [Regarding killing vermin on the Sabbath]: Rabbah killed them. R. Sheshet killed them. Rava threw them into a basin of water...
>
> (b. Shab. 12a)

> R. Joseph's wife used to kindle [the Sabbath lamp] late. R. Joseph [corrected her].
>
> (b. Shab. 23b)

> R. Joseph said, "I saw the calves of R. Huna's house go forth with their cords round about them on the Sabbath..."
>
> (b. Shab. 52a)

> R. Huna b. R. Joshua said, "I saw that my sisters were not particular about [openwork bands on the Sabbath...]"
>
> (b. Shab. 57a)

> R. Judah brother of R. Salla the Pious had a pair of sandals...He went to Abaye and asked him [about tying them on the Sabbath]
>
> (b. Shab. 112a)

> R. Mari b. Raḥel had some pillows lying in the sun. He went to Rava and asked whether they may be moved... Rava was walking in the manor of Maḥoza, when his shoes became soiled with clay. His attendant took a shard and wiped it off. The rabbinical disciples rebuked him...
>
> (b. Shab. 124b)

> Abaye's [foster-] mother prepared [a certain food on the Sabbath] for him and he would not eat it....
>
> (b. Shab. 140a)

> R. Aḥa b. Joseph was walking along, leaning on the shoulder of R. Naḥman b. Isaac, his sister's son.... He asked him, "How about rubbing linen..."
>
> (b. Shab. 140a)

[In preparing for the Sabbath] Rabbah and R. Joseph chopped wood.

(b. Shab. 119a)

Abaye placed a ladle on a pile of sheaves. Rava placed a knife on a young dove and handled it [R. Joseph ridiculed their actions...]

(b. Shab. 142b)

Abaye was standing before R. Joseph. He (R. Joseph) said to him, "Give me my hat." Abaye saw some dew on it, and hesitated to give it to him. "Shake it and throw it off," R. Joseph ordered, "we are not concerned at all about it."

(b. Shab. 147a)

R. 'Avia was sitting before R. Joseph, when his hand became dislocated. He asked him [whether it was permitted to reset it. Meanwhile] the hand slipped back...

(b. Shab. 148a)

Abaye found Rabbah letting his son slide down the back of an ass [on the Sabbath]. He said, "You are making use of animals?"...

(b. Shab. 154b)

The stories cited above should indicate that the rabbis recorded how various authorities behaved, criticized one another, consulted one another, instructed disciples properly to keep the Sabbath, and in all, carried out the law according to their own traditions or opinions. There can be no doubt that such stories were preserved to illustrate the way the law was to be kept. In no instance have we seen a non-academician's turning to a rabbi for advice. Numerous questions on Sabbath laws came to the rabbis, but few, if any, from ordinary people. I should therefore suppose that the rabbis' behavior on the Sabbath was one of the distinctive marks of their estate, and like their manner of saying Grace after Meals and other ritual actions, it indicated that a man was a rabbi or disciple. On the other hand, one cannot conclude that ordinary people did not keep the Sabbath. It is simply inconceivable to suppose that the masses of Jews did other than refrain from work on that day. I doubt that they refrained from work in just the manner the rabbis said they should or paid close attention to rabbinical laws about other details of Sabbath observance.[1]

---

[1] Among the numerous teachings about Sabbath laws and observances were the following: b. Shab. 12a, R. Joseph, an important law on Sabbath observance is that one must examine his garments before darkness on the eve of the Sabbath; b. Shab. 7b, Abaye vs. Rava on whether cavities of a private domain are regarded

XIII. Summary and Conclusions

The rabbinical courts administered laws pertaining to the market-place, including the abattoir, and supervised the collection and division of funds for the poor.[1] Clearly the courts had no difficulty in overseeing commercial life, ascertaining that butchers slaughtered and sold meat which conformed to Jewish ritual requirements, and exercising other functions relevant to public welfare. The courts manifestly took full responsibility for the establishment of the Sabbath limits, entirely within their control as communal administrative agencies. Certain other kinds of law which ordinary people intended to keep were probably carried out according to rabbinical rules, because rabbis were presumed to know what Scriptures required. These pertained to a few agricultural offerings and gifts to priests, taboos against sexual relations with a menstruating woman, and the like. I assume that the rabbis' reputation as men of great learning, rather than their position in the courts, accounts for success in guiding popular observance of those particular laws. Yet that same reputation seems to have had little or no affect upon other rites. The rabbinical rules about mourning, the ob-

as private or public; b. Shab. 3b, Abaye on whether a man's hand is like public or private domain; b. Shab. 8a, Abaye vs. Rava on the law about throwing a large round vessel into the street; b. Shab. 20b, R. Joseph on fires kept burning on the Sabbath; b. Shab. 49b, R. Joseph and Abaye on forms of labor which are prohibited and permitted; b. Shab. 60a, Rava, R. Joseph, and Abaye on what a woman may wear in the streets; b. Shab. 69b, Rava on how a man in the wilderness will observe the Sabbath; b. Shab. 70b, Rava and Abaye on reaping and grinding corn the size of a fig on the Sabbath; b. Shab. 73b, Rava on the punishment for filling up a hole on the Sabbath, see also b. Shab. 81b, Rabbah on the same subject; b. Shab. 74b, Rava and Abaye on the number of different counts for which a person would incur guilt by making an earthenware barrel on the Sabbath, or a wickerwork barrel; b. Shab. 74b, Rava vs. Abaye on untying on the Sabbath; b. Shab. 72b, Abaye vs. Rava on whether one is guilty who intended to lift up something detached from, but instead cut off something attached, to the ground; b. Shab. 91a, Rava asked, What if one carries out as much as a dried fig for food and then decides to use it for sowing; b. Shab. 92a, Rava and Abaye on carrying; b. Shab. 99b-100a, Rava and Abaye on throwing, and on covering a pit in the road with a mat; b. Shab. 102a, Rava and Rabbah on throwing; b. Shab. 107b-108a, Rava and Abaye on picking fungus; b. Shab. 117b, Rava on saving objects from a fire on the Sabbath; b. Shab. 123a, Rabbah and Abaye on forbidden labors; b. Men. 64a-b, Rabbah and Rava on desecrating the Sabbath in order to save lives; b. Ber. 31b, R. Naḥman b. Isaac on fasting on the Sabbath; b. Ḥag. 5a, Rava on sending on the evening of the Sabbath to one's wife meat which has not been porged; b. Shab. 50b, R. Joseph and Rava on what may be used to clean one's face on the Sabbath; b. Shab. 35a, Abaye asked Rabbah the law about removing honey from a honeycomb on the Sabbath; b. Shab. 141a, Abaye and Rava on cleaning clay from one's foot.

[1] See vol. III, pp. 266-271.

servance of holy days, festivals, and the Sabbath (except for the laws of *ʿeruvin*), the preparation and use of amulets, charms, and holy objects —these seem to have produced little or no impact upon popular behavior. People buried their dead, kept the Jewish festivals, resorted to amulets to guard their houses from demons, prepared and read sacred Scrolls, and the like. Yet the role rabbis played in these matters, if any, is simply not revealed by the evidence in our hands. Had we no stories about what *anyone*, rabbi or common folk, actually did, and no case reports or records of inquiries to the rabbis from ordinary people, then we could offer no hypothesis whatever. We do, however, have a considerable body of evidence about how some laws were enforced, and none at all about others. I can see no reason why, if cases on the others had arisen, stories about them should not have been preserved. Therefore since none is preserved, I suppose the reason was that people outside of the schools hardly could have kept, or cared about, these particular rabbinical laws.

The rabbinical courts, therefore, served mainly to administer public affairs and had slight direct impact upon the homes and synagogues of common people. Since the rabbis carefully defined laws pertaining to ordinary life, and not merely to the specific matters under their control, the reason for their failure to effect common practice was not that they did not aspire to direct it, but rather that they were unable to do so. Presumably either the exilarch or the Persian government did not let them. The original agreement between the exilarch, through Samuel, and the Sasanians in the time of Shapur I had specified that the Jewish courts would not transgress Persian law.[1] The cases cited in connection with Samuel's saying that government-law is law involved the payment of taxes, the adjudication of property rights, including the status of heathen property, and the means by which property is acquired. In ritual matters, the Jewish courts were probably left free to decide as they liked—if they could. It is hard to see how the Persian government would have cared whether or not rabbis told ordinary Jews what to do on the Sabbath. So if the rabbis' power over ritual life seems to have been narrowly restricted to public, administrative roles, the exilarch, and not the Persians, would have set that restriction. For him, the rabbis served as useful court officials. Their knowledge of law purported to have been given by Moses was considerable. They formed a disciplined, dependable party, or estate.

[1] Vol. II, pp. 64-72.

People must have looked up to them on account of their theurgical abilities.[1] The exilarch, however, was probably opposed to their making unrestricted use of the courts to control people's behavior. It was one thing to care for the poor, collect taxes, preserve an orderly, and ritually acceptable market. It was quite another to intervene in the lives of private people.

The contrast in Sabbath laws is suggestive. If ordinary folk liked, they could ask the rabbis about keeping the Sabbath, and occasionally, some people did so. But if not, the rabbis apparently had little power to punish people who from their viewpoint had sinned. Sabbath limits meant nothing to people who did not want to be guided by them. The rabbis, however, could do as they liked, for their public position as community administrators left them free to set up the boundaries. Had ordinary people simply ignored the Sabbath, and gone about their daily business, the rabbis would surely have punished them—and would have been expected to. But I feel certain very few people actually did so. Where rabbinical power was *both* necessary *and* lacking was in the middle ground between uncommon public violation of the biblical rules against work, and unopposed public administration of rabbinical rules about the Sabbath limit. What people wore or carried on the Sabbath or how they prepared food at home—these kinds of matters were essentially private, so far as the exilarch was concerned, and beyond rabbinical regulation.

Yet I do not mean to suggest that an individual's religious observance would greatly have varied from that of the community in which he lived. Such a supposition would be an anachronism. What was from the court's perspective "private," that is, beyond court authority, was, from the exilarch's and the peoples' viewpoint alike, most probably the accustomed way of doing things. As I have said, the prerabbinic patterns of Babylonian Judaism must have been deeply rooted. These were doubtless shaped by biblical laws and local customs, *ad hoc* decisions, and ancient, accepted exegeses of Scripture. For many centuries Babylonian Jews had kept the Sabbath and festivals, offered synagogue prayers and read the Torah, buried the dead, and observed other rites, laws, and taboos. The exilarch was hardly prepared to allow the disruption of popular and accepted practices or to provoke a revolution. So if, as seems clear, the rabbis' control over many rites was slight, except in such ways as the people invited their rulings, the reason was

[1] On which more below, Chapter Five.

that the exilarch did not find it in the public interest to allow rabbinical intervention.[1]

The people seem not to have asked the rabbis about Sabbath observance, festivals, holy objects, and the like, but they wanted their advice about some of the purity laws and food taboos. In either circumstance, the rabbis' powers were circumscribed. The rabbis did control other, equally ancient practices, such as the manner of slaughtering animals. Here, however, the rabbis' administrative duties produced considerably greater power. The courts' administrative functions were, on the whole, minor and tangential. The chief power of the courts, revealed above only with reference to the marketplace and abattoir, derived from the power to decide issues or cases of personal status and to litigate conflicting property claims. People did not have to come to court for advice about synagogue prayers or burial rites, although many may have respected the views of the holy men of the schools on these matters as well. Ordinary folk assuredly did have to bring property adjudications to rabbinical courts or to obtain their authorization, confirmation, or recognition for changes in personal status, as we shall now see.

[1] Perhaps the exilarch's failure to support the rabbis' effort to control Sabbath observance accounts for their harping on how he himself did not properly keep the Sabbath and on how his house-servants were thoroughly unreliable.

CHAPTER FOUR

BABYLONIAN JEWISH GOVERNMENT (II): THE RABBI AS JUDGE

I. Introduction

We turn to study the judicial functions of the Babylonian Jewish government. As earlier, we shall review the case reports indicating that in a specific litigation, a court decision was issued in accordance with a given law. I have already argued at length[1] that case reports constitute probative evidence, while academic discussions on legal issues at best provide equivocal testimony about practical law enforcement. One cannot readily rely upon "common sense" to distinguish between theoretical and practical law, for, as I have demonstrated,[2] statutes pertaining to dedications of property and personal value to the Temple of Jerusalem, in ruins for two centuries and more, most certainly were obeyed at the end of the third century A.D. in Babylonia. Without case reports, no one guided by "common sense" could have supposed that people would devote valuable property to a sanctuary which was no longer in existence. Nor can we rely upon legal theory to indicate that laws which were not supposed to apply in the diaspora, including Babylonia, were not obeyed. The evidence of rabbinical and popular practice has already suggested a confused state.[3] Some believed agricultural offerings and taboos did not pertain, at all or in part, to Babylonia. Others, by contrast, gave some of the offerings and observed the taboos.

It is important, however, to delimit the probative value even of case reports. I have argued that laws on civil litigations and personal status[4] were probably enforced by the Jewish judiciary. The *extent* of enforcement of these laws, however, cannot be easily estimated. The case reports derive mostly from courts associated with the schools and the exilarchate. On the other hand, we do not know much, if anything, about

[1] Vol. II, pp. 251-260, vol. III, pp. 202-213.
[2] Vol. III, pp. 207ff.
[3] Vol. II, pp. 260-261, vol. III, pp. 295-302, and above, pp. 143-149.
[4] Vol. III, pp. 317-338.

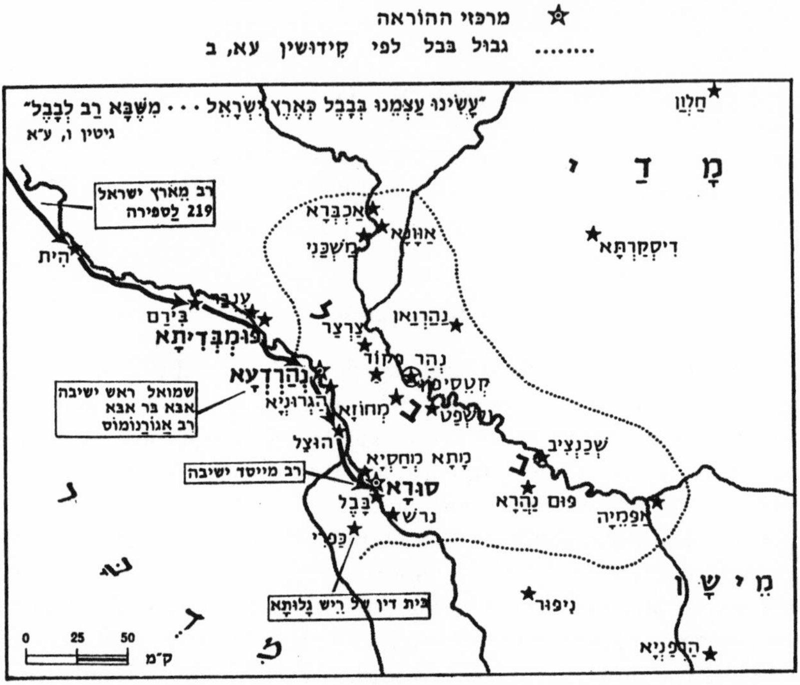

V. Centers of Rabbinical Schools and the Boundary of Babylonia according to b. Qid. 71b.
Source: Michael Avi-Yonah, *Carta's Atlas of the Period of the Second Temple, the Mishnah, and the Talmud.* (Jerusalem, 1966: Carta, Jerusalem), p. 98, Map #153.

towns outside of exilarchic, and therefore, academic, jurisdiction. M. Beer persuasively argued[1] that the exilarch about whom we have information in the Babylonian Talmud governed the Jews in Babylonia only. In second-century Nisibis, an exilarch or *archisynagogus* is mentioned.[2] An exilarch ruled in Apamea in this period, and Abaye and Rava supposed that his name would not be commonly known in Babylonia, as in the following:

> *Resh Galuta* Isaac, son of R. Bebai's sister, once went from Kurdafad [near Ctesiphon] to A[s]pamea and died there. A message was sent from there, "*Resh Galuta* Isaac, son of R. Bebai's sister, went from Kurdafad to Apamea and died there." The question arose whether [the possibility of] two [men by the name of] Isaac is taken into account or not. Abaye said that it was, Rava said that it was not. (b. Yev. 115b)[3]

[1] *Ẓiyyon*, 28, 1963, 1-33, see vol. III, pp. 87-95.
[2] Vol. I, p. 124, n. 2.
[3] On the place names, see Obermeyer, *op. cit.*, p. 183, n. 1.

So an exilarch lived at Apamea at the southern limit of Babylonia on the Tigris, and was apparently not well known in Babylonia. We have very little evidence about the situation in Mesene, Elam, Persia Proper (Fars), Hycrania, Khorrasan, or Khuzistan, not to mention more distant satrapies. We have an apparent reference to Seistan, and a number of stories about Jews from nearby Khuzistan in Babylonia. The Babylonian schools preserved no data whatever about Armenian Jewry, though we know full well that Jews lived there, and that thousands of families were deported from Armenia to Fars during Shapur's campaigns of ca. 365-375.[1] No reason whatever exists to suppose that the Babylonian exilarch controlled courts or schools outside of Babylonia itself, or that the Babylonian schools issued decrees concerning, or even discussed the affairs of, Jews outside of that satrapy. The situation within Babylonia itself is somewhat clearer. There, rabbinical courts did exert substantial authority in the towns where they were located. We may be reasonably certain that in Maḥoza, Nehardea, Sura, Pumbedita, Nersh, and the other larger towns, the courts proved effective instruments of administration and justice. Nearby villages, along the same canal or in the hinterland, could not have been quite so easily controlled. On the other hand, when the villagers brought their produce to market they would have come into contact with rabbinical administrators. These authorities certainly did whatever they could to guide, and where possible, to control life in the outlying villages.[2]

Even though numerous case reports were attached to discussions of specific Mishnaic laws, on that account we cannot conclude that all of the laws in a specific tractate were everywhere enforced in Babylonia. As we have seen,[3] case reports generally are grouped in discussions about a few specific laws. Those of Rava's decisions about wine taboos, for example, suggest that he had considerable power.[4] Yet that power pertained to the marketing of wine alone. Upon the basis of these case-reports, one can hardly conclude that he could effect all laws pertaining to relationships between Judaism and idolatry. Only where we can offer an explanation of why courts were able to issue effective decisions are we able finally to conclude that a specific body of laws was normally carried out. I have tried to offer such an explanation, based upon a

---

[1] See above, p. 16.

[2] But see b. B.B. 133b, a reference to uninformed judges by Rava, below, pp. 218, 222. Note by contrast the instructions to villagers who came to the towns on the Day of Atonement, above, p. 163.

[3] Above, p. 59, and vol. III, pp. 317ff.

[4] See above, p. 59.

comprehensive view of the evidence. I do not propose to utilize the individual case reports as proof-texts.[1] We must attempt as comprehensive and cogent an account as seems possible. My purpose here is only to describe the workings of Babylonian Jewish government, not to exposit specific laws, and hence the citations of case reports will be accompanied by as brief an explanation of their content as seems absolutely necessary.[2]

II. Capital Jurisdiction

When a miscreant died while being flogged at the order of Rava's court, the Iranian government made immediate inquiries into the matter.[3] From the advent of Sasanian rule, it was clear that the Jewish

[1] Therefore the narrow issue of "historicity" seems irrelevant here. It is of course interesting to know that a given rabbi at a given time and place "really" made such-and-such a decision. What is beyond doubt, however, is that in the schools, such a decision was believed to have been made. The report of various decisions is given *en passent* and in no way suggests that the tradent hoped to prove such-and-such a law was "really" enforced by the rabbi. It was self-evident to him that the case came to judgment and provided illustration of some principle of law. Even though theoretical statements about the law may not have been made by one or another authority to whom they were attributed, as in vol. II, p. 267, and below, pp. 193 and 196, case reports were generally tested, and all kinds of evidence were preserved about them, from whatever eyewitnesses or traditions of the event were available. So whether Rava "really" decided about wine-taboos in the marketplace I cannot say. Perhaps his school, or an agent of the school made such decisions, and not Rava himself. But there seems no valid reason to doubt such decisions were actually made and enforced as described in the traditions. I distinguish, therefore, between the historicity of an attribution to a given authority in a specific place or time, on the one hand, and of the narration of a given court action on the other. The former may be tendentious, the latter probably was not. At the very least, we have a perfectly factual account of the scholastic traditions about the enforcement of various laws through the courts. I can think of no reason to doubt the accuracy of the schools' information on the subject. I find no evidence to suggest academic traditions were intended to establish the claim of a wider range of court power than actually existed.

[2] Below, pp. 253-254, I shall discuss the issue of when does a case-report or story report an actual court case, and when is it merely a fictional narration of a point of law in the guise of a case. Clearly the language "If so-and-so does such-and-such, Rabbah says the law is so-and-so" does not preserve an actual case-report. On the other hand, in many instances of civil law, such language may well be the form in which actual court actions were preserved. We have a few such instances, as in vol. II, p. 267, and below, pp. 193, 196 and 217, in which we can show that the casuistic form did conceal an actual event. On the other hand, the language "A certain man did so-and-so. Abaye said... Rava said..." may just as well have constituted the way theoretical law was preserved, and sometimes may not report an actual court action.

[3] See above, p. 36, b. Ta'anit 24b.

courts could not impose capital punishment,[1] so the case in the time of Shapur II indicates that Sasanian policy had not changed. Jewish courts were not deprived of the right to try cases of theft, murder, and other serious offenses. The following indicates the punishment they might inflict:

> Bar Ḥama killed a man. The exilarch said to R. Abba b. Jacob, "Go, examine the matter. If he certainly killed, put out his eyes." Two witnesses came and testified against him that he had certainly killed [a man]. The accused came and brought two witnesses. They testified against one of the hostile witnesses. One said, "Before me he stole a *kav* of barley," and one said, "Before me he stole the handle of a *burtya* [spear, javelin]." [R. Abba] said to him, "What is your view? [To disqualify this man in accordance] with the view of R. Meir? But wherever there is disagreement between R. Yosi and R. Meir, the law follows R. Yosi, and R. Yosi said, 'A witness who is refuted in matters of money is acceptable to testify in capital cases.'" R. Papi said to him, "But that ruling [concerning legal disputes between R. Meir and R. Yosi] applies only where the Tanna has not stated R. Meir's view anonymously. Here however he has... [R. Papi proved his point.]" Thereupon Bar Ḥama arose and kissed his knees, and took upon himself his [R. Papi's] poll-tax for the rest of his life.
>
> (b. Sanh. 27a-b)

Bar Ḥama was certainly tried for murder, and had he been convicted, he would have received corporal, but *not* capital punishment. Blinding one's eyes was an exceptional punishment, not provided for in rabbinical law.[2] The traditional commentaries were troubled by that fact, and interpreted "blinding" to mean that the murderer's property would be confiscated, and hence the indemnity would have entered the category of a fine. (Of course, fines were supposedly not imposed in Babylonian courts.) The language seems satisfactorily clear, however, and quite unambiguous. The exilarch, not following rabbinical rules in such a matter as this, was prepared to blind a convicted murderer. He obviously could not put him to death.

Whether the accused enjoyed the services of a defense attorney or not is not specified. R. Papi's defense manifestly could not have been offered by an ordinary person, for it required detailed knowledge of Tannaitic traditions and Amoraic principles on how to resolve moot points. He gave it, by all accounts, because he "happened" to be present at the examination of the case. Bar Ḥama's joy was quite well justified. Whether Bar Ḥama himself otherwise would have had to know the

---

[1] Vol. II, pp. 30-35. But compare below, p. 188.

[2] Nor is it referred to in the Pahlavi law code, so far as I can see.

laws of refuting hostile testimony we cannot say. The account simply said that he brought two witnesses to discredit the accusing parties, so I suppose he knew enough law to be prepared on that account.

What is most important here is the fact that the exilarch took responsibility for murder trials. We have no earlier capital case. Whether the exilarch succeeded at this time—I should estimate about 350 A.D.—in regaining jurisdiction of murder cases in the Jewish community after the long lapse of nearly two centuries, or whether he had had it all along, I cannot guess. In any event, it is clear from the aftermath of Rava's case, and from the above, that capital penalties could not be imposed by the Jewish government. It is striking that the exilarch, and not a rabbinical court, judged the only murder case known to us to have been tried in the fourth-century. It may be that the exilarch was supposed to judge such cases, and did not leave them for the normal, town-courts to decide. On so slight evidence as a single case, however, we cannot come to a firm conclusion.

Other evidence relating to the death penalty includes the following sayings and stories:

> He who is born under Mars will be a shedder of blood. [R. Ashi observed, "Either a surgeon, a thief, a slaughterer, or a circumciser."] Rabbah said, "I was under Mars." Abaye replied, "You too punish and kill."
>
> (b. Shab. 156a)

> R. Joseph said, "Once...a Jewish court condemns to death, the condemned man is executed." Abaye replied, "Even in a Jewish court it is possible that something may be found to mitigate the sentence..."
>
> (b. Git. 28b-29a)

> Rava said, "If a man bound his neighbor and he died of starvation, he is not subject to execution... If he tied him up in the sun, or in a cold place, and he died, he is liable... If he tied him before a lion, he is not liable; before mosquitoes, he is."
>
> (b. Sanh. 77a)[1]

> A man came before Rava. He said to him, "The master of my village said to me, 'Kill so-and-so, and if not, I shall kill you.'" Rava replied, "Be killed, but do not kill. How do you know that your blood is redder? Perhaps that man's blood is redder."
>
> (b. Yoma 82b)[2]

---

[1] Further such examples of culpable negligence are cited, b. Sanh. 77a-78a.

[2] See also b. Sanh. 15a, Abaye and Rava on the death penalty applied to an ox.

Birth under the sign of Mars had not, Rabbah claimed, made him into a shedder of blood. Abaye's reply was that he did kill. We have no examples whatever of Rabbah's decreeing the death penalty, and I do not believe he did inflict it. The story is part of the tradition about Abaye's pointing out to Rabbah how unpopular he was in his town and cannot be interpreted to show that Rabbah actually put people to death. R. Joseph's and Abaye's comments on a decree of execution in a Jewish court, and Rava's about possible situations of manslaughter, culpable negligence, and the like, are quite theoretical. None of the numerous examples discussed by Rava is accompanied by the slightest hint that such events ever took place or came before Rava's court. We cannot suppose that they were too far-fetched. But we do not know that they ever actually happened, and I doubt that they did.

The inquiry to Rava was a strange one; if the master of a man's village was powerful enough to order a man to kill another, then he might well have had the power to force him to do so immediately. Consulting the rabbi does not, in any case, permit the inference that Rava would have been able to punish the man had he not followed rabbinical advice.[1] We do not know whether the master of the village was a Jew or not; he certainly was not a rabbi.

The Jewish court was quite able, on the other hand, to punish petty crimes such as theft, and to adjudicate the disposition of property which had been stolen. The following cases exemplified that power:

> A man of Nersh stole a book and sold it to a man of Papunia for eighty *zuz*. The latter went and sold it to a Maḥozan for hundred and twenty *zuz*. The thief was caught. Abaye said the owner of the book could come and pay the man of Maḥoza eighty *zuz*, and get his book back, and the Maḥozan could get the other forty *zuz* from the man of Papunia. Rava disagreed... Rava said... (b. B.Q. 115a)

> Rava was robbed of some rams when a thief broke in. The thieves subsequently returned them, but he refused to accept them... (b. Sanh. 72a)

One can only suppose that the thieves returned the rams because they were caught, as in the earlier case, and so it seems likely that there *was* someone who was supposed to catch and punish them, and also to return stolen property to the original master. That person must have restored Rava's rams, and Rava's refusal to accept them, based upon

[1] See also b. Sanh. 74a, and David Daube, *Collaboration with Tyranny in Rabbinic Law* (London, 1965), p. 27.

rabbinical theories about changes in the ownership of property, could not have been anticipated by the Jewish policeman. Had he known and accepted the rabbinical viewpoint, he would not have returned the rams to begin with. So the courts controlled by rabbis would have refrained, in certain circumstances, from making restitution of property recovered by police or agents of the exilarch, who would have naturally assumed it right and proper to recover and restore stolen goods. This is the only instance where a victim refused restitution. I should imagine ordinary folk would not have followed the rabbinical law, but would have expected that whatever could be recovered would return to their possession. What the courts controlled by rabbis would have been willing to do in such a circumstance is not clear. If the law prohibited the restoration of stolen property in specific circumstances, then the rabbinical courts would hardly have mandated restitution. On the other hand, if the people expected to get their property back, they would have demanded that the police who had caught the thief give them back what was theirs. In such a case, the police (or, the persons who recovered the property) would not have had to repair to the court for a decision, unless some contrary claim existed. In the absence of a contrary claim, the police would have given the property back to the original owner, thus bypassing the court. In any case, there can be no doubt that the Jewish courts did adjudicate cases of theft, and we may assume that thieves were punished when apprehended, though it is difficult to say just what that punishment was in this period. We have already noted earlier cases in which the courts tried and punished thieves.[1] It is clear, therefore, that the judiciary was responsible for crimes against persons and property, but that the penalties which might be imposed were limited. The court could inflict bodily punishment, not only in the rabbinically approved form of flogging, but also in the quite irregular form of corporal punishment through blinding, cutting off hands, and the like. The Sasanian government relied upon the Jewish administration to maintain peace and order within the Jewish community, but set limits to the means that might be employed to achieve it.[2] The courts nonetheless possessed very substantial power over the property of ordinary Jews.[3]

---

[1] See vol. III, pp. 302-305.

[2] I cannot, however, explain why courts which could inflict extreme corporal punishment could not also impose the death penalty. It is perfectly evident that the Sasanians never allowed the latter, and I suppose that their policy was based upon clearcut reasons. But I do not know what they were.

[3] For enslavement as a judicial penalty, see vol. III pp. 26-29.

III. Betrothals and Marriage Contracts

Two factors led to court supervision of the institution of marriage, first, the need for court action, either immediately or in case of later litigation over the marriage contract, and second, the occasional resort to the courts for a decision upon whether a betrothal had been properly carried out.[1] Court powers to certify that a betrothal was valid, or to require, through appropriate legal procedures, clarification or dissolution of a doubtful or improper betrothal, were considerable. It was not necessary for the court officials to cajole or persuade, for their power over the property cases which easily might emerge and over determinations of personal status was not limited. In some cases it was necessary for the rabbi as court official to make and effect an uninvited decision, but in most, conflicting parties came before him for decision. We shall here review cases of betrothal, dowry and marriage-contract, and below (section iv), contrast these with the good advice and counsel offered by rabbis upon marriage and family life. Wise counsel was rarely, if ever, accompanied by court action, but by promises or threats; property litigations and investigations of the validity of betrothals and marriages by contrast were rarely accompanied by moral maxims. The two sorts of sayings reflect entirely different circumstances and were based upon differing bases of public influence and leadership.

Betrothals: In the following cases, the courts' power over marriage derived from their right to determine whether or not the gift of betrothal was worth the stipulated amount, a few *zuz*, or not:

> A certain man betrothed with silk. Rabbah ruled, "No valuation is necessary [to ascertain whether it is worth the minimal sum for a betrothal]. R. Joseph held, "It must be valued [= evaluated]."
>
> (b. Qid. 7b)[2]

> A certain man betrothed with a mat of myrtle twigs. It was said to him, "But it is not worth a *perutah*." "Then let her be betrothed for the four *zuz* it contains," he replied. Having taken it, she remained silent. Rava said, "It is silence after receipt of the money, and such silence has no significance." [She knew the matting was not worth a *perutah*, and it was unnecessary for her to reject the proposal. Subsequent silence meant nothing.]
>
> (b. Qid. 12b)[3]

---

[1] Vol. II, pp. 268-274, and vol. III, pp. 274-283.
[2] Trans. H. Freedman (London, 1948), p. 27. Further discussion follows.
[3] *ibid.* p. 50.

A certain man betrothed with a myrtle branch in the marketplace. R. Aḥa b. Huna sent to R. Joseph, "What is the rule in such a case?" He replied, "Have him flogged ... and demand a divorce..."

(b. Qid. 12b)

A woman was washing her feet in a bowl of water. A man came, grabbed a *zuz* from his neighbor, threw it to her, and said, "You are betrothed to me." Then he went before Rava [to confirm the betrothal]...

(b. Qid. 52b)

A certain sharecropper betrothed with a handful of onions. When he came before Rava, Rava said to him, "Who renounced it in your favor [for the onions belong in part to the landlord]?" [Hence it was not wholly his property to begin with.]

(b. Qid. 52b)

A certain brewer [who brewed beer from dates provided by farmers, and received a fixed proportion of the returns] betrothed with a measure of beer. The owner of the beer came and found him. He said to him, "Why did you not give this beer, which is stronger?" When the matter came before Rava, Rava said...

(b. Qid. 52b)

In the above instances, the issue was clear, namely, did the gift of betrothal constitute a sufficiently valuable item, and was it the property of the giver? On the other hand, what is *not* clear to me is how the courts came to rule on the issue in the first place. If both parties were satisfied with the betrothal, then no court decision would have been solicited, and consequently, none given. In this instance, the groom claimed the woman was married to him, and she claimed she was still a free-agent. Her status was thus called into question. Both parties would therefore want to come to the rabbinical court, the one to protect his alleged marriage, the other to establish her alleged unmarried status.

In such a case, the rabbis' power would have come to bear. By contrast, in the following instance, no litigation came to court, and the rabbis could do little except "remain aloof." What that means is simple: the rabbis would do everything in their power to discourage their followers from marrying into that particular family.

Some of the family [which had descended from a marriage disapproved by Abaye and Rava on account of a legal principle] remained in Sura, and the rabbis held aloof from them (not because they agreed with Samuel but because they agreed with Abaye and Rava).

(b. Qid. 12b)

The courts had to decide other issues of betrothal concerning, specifically, the intent of one who gives his word to betrothe his daughter to a certain person, the rules of when one might effect betrothal, and finally, the conditions of a donation in connection with betrothal. In these instances, the courts' role was clear. In the first case, the conflicting claims for the daughter had to be settled. In the second, information was requested from a rabbi. In the third, property had to be equitably divided according to law. The cases were as follows:

> [A couple disputed on whom their daughter should marry.] She nagged him until he told her that the daughter could be married to her relative. While they were eating and drinking [at the betrothal festivities], the father's relative went up to a loft and betrothed her. Abaye said, "It is written, 'The remnant of Israel shall not do iniquity, nor speak lies' (Zeph. 3:13)." [The father gave his word, and could not therefore have consented to the betrothal which actually took place.] Rava said, "It is assumed that one does not trouble to prepare a banquet (for betrothal) and then destroy it." (b. Qid. 45b)

> Abaye's sharecropper once came to him and asked, "Is it permitted to betrothe [a nursing woman] fifteen months after [her child's birth]?" He replied... (b. Ket. 60b)

> Rava said, "Such a deed (of gift) can serve as a *moda'ah* (notification of gift) in respect of another." R. Papa said, "*This statement attributed to Rava was not explicitly made by him, but was inferred* [incorrectly] from the following case: A certain man wanted to betroth a woman. She said, 'If you assign to me all your property, I shall become engaged to you, but otherwise I shall not.' He did so. Meanwhile, his oldest son came and said, 'What is to become of me?' He took witnesses and said, 'Go hide yourselves in the Southside ['Ever Yemina, a suburb of Maḥoza] and write out [an assignment of my property] to him.' The case came before Rava who ruled..." (b. B.B. 40b)[1]

Actions on the validity of betrothals thus could have come to court if one of the parties sought an annulment and return of all property, or, less likely, if both parties sought court confirmation of what they had already done. In the cases of betrothal with silk and with a mat of myrtle twigs, the difficulty was whether sufficient property had changed hands. The betrothal with silk ought not to have produced a court case. Perhaps it did not, for the issue may have been a *post facto* rabbinical discussion of what *might* have been required in a litigation, had a case

[1] Trans. M. Simon (London, 1948), p. 175. Italics supplied.

arisen. Rabbah's and R. Joseph's rulings do not hint that the case had actually come before them, and the matter may just as well have been phrased in theoretical, casuistic language. The betrothal with a *zuz* hidden in a mat of myrtle twigs, by contrast, does seem to have involved a litigation, for the woman's silence is at issue. I suppose that she had subsequently become disaffected with the original arrangement. The cases of betrothal with a myrtle branch in a marketplace, the latter setting certainly contrary to the rabbis' rules, and of the family in Sura, indicate two means of rabbinical, or court, enforcement of the law. In the instance of the family at Sura, the rabbis could do little but discourage their followers from marrying into a family whose ancestry was of dubious legal standing. In the matter of an open, flagrant, and one-time violation of rabbinical laws, the court could also order a flogging. It would be meaningless to do so to descendants of the family of Sura.

The rabbis' presuppositions on the intentions of ordinary people were revealed in the suit of the secret betrothal that ended in Abaye's court. Abaye and Rava both assumed that people were of upright character, did not give their word and intend to break it,[1] and did not arrange a festive banquet only to hoodwink the other party. The reference to how the "remnant of Israel" will conduct itself is important. For the rabbis, honest behavior must always characterize that remnant. Those who did not act uprightly thereby testified they were not part of the "remnant of Israel" which would be saved.

The three cases of betrothal by means of disputed property, or of property not wholly belonging to the man, reveal little about why courts had to intervene. In the first, it is clear that the man sought confirmation of a contested betrothal, but we may only suppose it was the woman who was contesting it. The second and third cases seem even less clear. What is important in the final case is R. Papa's report of an actual court action before Rava. It is evident that the action involved a clearcut property dispute. We know in this instance who initiated action and why. R. Papa's criticism and correction of the saying attributed to Rava, like similar, false attributions to Rav and Samuel, upon the basis of a misinterpretation of court action, occurred

---

[1] But contrast Abaye's vow, cited above, p. 138, in a similar case. I suppose the difference is that in the case involving Abaye himself, he took a vow and meant to keep it, and hence had to come to court to annul it, but intended no dishonest or surreptitious action. Here on the other hand, the intention of the father in agreeing to a betrothal was at issue, and the presupposition of the rabbis seems clear.

specifically in matters of property litigation.[1] What happened is obvious. Rava made a ruling in a case. That ruling was preserved in the form of an abstract opinion, "Rava said, 'Such a deed of gift can serve...'" Had R. Papa not criticized the tradition, we should not know that Rava had actually so ruled in a practical case. But R. Papa did criticize the abstract tradition upon the basis of his own observation and interpretation of an event. This case, standing by itself, indicates only that some rabbinical sayings were carefully evaluated by the succeeding generation. One cannot conclude that all such sayings were critically studied. It is, however, significant that all the abstract sayings which were corrected by the subsequent generation upon the basis of the recollection of court action pertain to matters of property or cases of personal status also involving property transactions. Where court action was not taken, as in the teachings of Rava about culpable negligence in homicide,[2] no such criticism was possible. I should suppose that a great many other sayings about betrothals would have been effectuated through the courts, though it is difficult to know which ones actually came to trial.[3]

Marriage-Contracts: Court rulings on dowries and marriage-contracts obviously effected property exchanges or judgments between conflicting claims. Generally the marriage-contract would produce litigation after the death of the husband, when the widow sought payment of the sums of money and property specified in her marriage-contract. The rabbis held that a woman could not remain with her husband without the protection of such a contract. The wife of a rabbi inquired about whether that rule applied in practice. A third kind of litigation involved the disposition of property covered by the marriage contract during the life of the marriage, as in instances of the husband's misappropriation or misuse of such property. Cases of court adjudication of issues pertaining to dowries and marriage contracts included the following:

> The sister of Rami b. Ḥama was married to R. 'Ivya' and her marriage-contract was lost. When they came before R. Joseph [to

[1] See below, p. 196, for a second such case involving property litigation. See vol. II, p. 267 for R. Ḥisda's criticism of sayings attributed to Rav and Samuel, based in fact upon court actions and not scholastic lectures.

[2] Cited above, p. 188.

[3] See for example b. Qid. 7a-b, Rava said that partial betrothal was permitted; b. Qid. 6b, Abaye said one cannot betroth with a debt; Rava added, or with a gift which is to be returned. Rava held that the rabbinical rules were supported by Scriptures, b. Qid. 9a; R. Naḥman b. Isaac on Ex. 22:15, b. Qid. 46a. Note also b. Ket. 8a, Rava on saying a certain prayer included in the Grace in a home where a marriage takes place.

ask whether she may continue to live with her husband without it], he ruled... (b. Ket. 56b-57a)

Rava said, "At first I thought, a woman is entitled to seize money-bags of Maḥoza for her marriage-contract [payable from the deceased husband's estate]...When I observed, however, that they took them and went out with them [to the market], and as soon as a plot of land came their way they purchased it with this money, I decided that they only rely upon land [and hence should not be allowed to seize money]." (b. Ket. 67a)

The question was raised, "What is the ruling where a husband sold property for usufruct?"...Judah Mar b. Meremar replied in Rava's name, "Whatever he has done is done." R. Papa in the name of Rava said, "His act has no validity." R. Papa said, "*The ruling reported by Judah Mar b. Meremar was not explicitly stated, but arrived at by inference.* A woman once brought her husband two bondwomen [in her dowry.] The man went and married another wife and assigned one of them to her. She [the first wife] came to Rava and cried, but he disregarded her. One who observed it formed the opinion that Rava's view was, whatever the husband did is valid, but in fact it is not so..." (b. Ket. 80a-80b)[1]

A certain widow once seized a silver cup on account of her marriage-contract, and then claimed maintenance. She appeared before Rava, who told the orphans, "Provide maintenance for her...." (b. Ket. 98a)

A woman once brought into her marriage a robe of fine wool as part of her marriage-contract. When the man died, the orphans took it and spread it over the corpse. Rava ruled the corpse had acquired it [as a shroud]. (b. Yev. 66b)[2]

The first case does not indicate that ordinary people would have made such an inquiry, and we do not know whether others beside rabbis were so scrupulous about the required document. The saying of Rava is probative, for it indicates that women ordinarily did have

[1] Italics supplied.

[2] See also b. Ket. 104b, cited below. If so, the sumptuary laws concerning modest burial rites could not have been observed by the family or enforced by the court. No criticism of the use of such an expensive cloth for a shroud was recorded by the rabbinical judge. He did not enforce the recommendation against it, and I should therefore assume he could not do so. The court (perhaps after the fact) could not tell the people how to bury their dead, but it could determine to whom property used in connection with burial actually belonged. Compare above, p. 157.

marriage-contracts and usually collected them. So the law was both enforced and obeyed. The suits that came for trial must have represented only a small and hardly significant proportion of the instances in which the law was properly carried out without court action. R. Papa criticized Judah Mar b. Meremar's saying in Rava's name. He based his view upon actual observation of a court litigation over property covered by a marriage-contract. This suggests that other sayings would have been based upon inference from observed actions, rather than upon teachings handed on in school. The fourth and fifth cases record court actions of Rava in litigations over property involved in a marriage-contract. We have no reason to wonder how such cases came to court, for it is clear that the conflicting parties brought them, specifically because they wanted the court to rule on who should receive disputed property, or who must pay a contested claim. It seems reasonable to suppose that numerous other relevant sayings would have guided court decisions.[1]

To summarize: The courts therefore exerted considerable influence over certain aspects of the marriage-relationship, in particular, the disposition of property exchanged in effecting betrothals, the supervision of documents drawn up for dowries and marriage-contracts, and the adjudication of property claims resulting from conflicts over such documents. The cases mostly devolve upon narrow property claims and generally inconsequential sums. The rabbis' views of proper conduct in effecting betrothal, right motivation in choosing a spouse, the importance of finding a wife who would bring up one's children according to the Torah as the rabbis exposited it, and similar religious matters—these played no role whatever in court actions. When an ordinary person such as Abaye's sharecropper came for advice, the rabbi gave it, but not in his capacity as judge of a local court. By contrast, the case before Rava concerning a suitable legacy to one's eldest son involved fair division of an estate. On the whole, one gains the impression that the courts could not have significantly affected most normal marriages. Where the betrothal was beyond legal doubt, the marriage perfectly regular, the necessary documents in order, and the marriage-contract legally paid out, the courts had no role whatever. If, however, when these things were not correctly done, the court could act, then the possibility of court action must have encouraged normal people to obey the law to begin with.

[1] E.g., b. Ket. 52b, Abaye and Rava on how great a dowry may be given to a daughter; b. Ket. 53a, Rava on the sale of a marriage-contract.

IV. Family Life in Practice and Theory

While scholastic discussions on family affairs included attention to matters which could not have posed much practical difficulty, for instance the laws pertaining to the Temple rite of trial for a woman accused of adultery[1] and to the suitable candidates for marriage to the High Priest in the Temple of Jerusalem,[2] one can not so easily distinguish among more practical sayings. We shall first review the case reports, and then examine some rabbinic sayings about marriage and family life.

Adultery and Illegitimacy: The following relate to instances of adultery and other forms of illicit sexual relations:

> Rabbah said, "If [a woman's] husband is in town, we do not suspect [the results of] privacy [of a woman and another man]." R. Joseph said, "If the door opens to the street, we have no fear on that account." R. Bibi visited R. Joseph. After [eating] he [R. Joseph, who was going to a lower room with his wife, leaving R. Bibi above, and then planned to leave the house] said to the servants, "Remove the ladder from under Bibi."
>
> (b. Qid. 81a)

> A certain man was alone in a house with a [married] woman. Hearing her husband come in, the [supposed] adulterer broke through a hedge and fled. Rava ruled, "The wife is permitted [to remain with her husband]. If he had committed wrong, he would have hidden himself [in the house]."
>
> (b. Ned. 91b)

> A certain adulterer visited a woman. Her husband came, and the adulterer went and hid behind a curtain before the door. Some cress was lying there, and a snake (ate of it). The husband was about to eat the cress without his wife's knowledge. The [supposed] adulterer warned, "Do not eat it, for a snake has tasted it." Rava ruled. "The wife is permitted. Had he committed wrong, he would have wanted the husband to eat and die..."
>
> (b. Ned. 91b)

The first story reported that R. Joseph was extreme in his observance of the laws prohibiting a married woman from remaining by herself

---

[1] E.g., b. Sotah 6a, R. Joseph, on whether the "water of cursing" actually affects the accused woman or not; b. Sotah 17a, Rava on why dust is put into the water, with reference to Gen. 18:27; and 17a-b, on writing the scroll; b. Sotah 26b, Abaye and Rava on Num. 5:13, what did the husband actually warn against; b. Sotah 5b, R. Joseph says a suspected adulteress performs *ḥaliẓah*.

[2] E.g., b. Qid. 78a, Rava and Abaye on the marriage of a high priest; b. Sotah 44a, Rabbah on Lev. 21:15; b. Yev. 22b, Rava on Lev. 18:10 and 18:17.

with a man other than her husband. It was characteristic of the rabbis, like other holy men, to observe very strictly such laws of separation.[1] But no legal action could have come of it. The cases that came to Rava devolved upon the principle of whether a woman who had seemingly been compromised may remain with her husband. A property issue emerging in such cases was, Would the woman retain a right to her marriage-contract? If convicted, she would lose it. Upon that issue, litigation would have to take place. Nonetheless, the rabbis' administrative authority may have been sufficient so that had Rava only ruled upon the narrower issue of adultery, as the case reports indicate, he may have been able to decree that the woman must leave her husband in disgrace. He followed R. Naḥman's principles in deciding these cases.[2] (A story was also told of how 'Imarta daughter of Tali, a priest, committed adultery, and R. Ḥama b. Tobiah ordered her to be burned at the stake.[3] R. Joseph criticized his decree. However, Funk holds that this particular R. Joseph was the first Saboraic authority, in the time of the Jewish independent state under Mazdak. He points out that only in a situation of independence could a Jewish court have issued a death sentence. In vol. V, we shall return to the situation of the Jews in the time of Mazdak.)

Two cases in which rabbis decided questions of legitimacy were as follows:

> A betrothed couple once came before R. Joseph. She said [concerning her premarital pregnancy], "He is from him," and he admitted it. R. Joseph ruled...
>
> (b. Ket. 13b-14a)

> A woman came to R. Joseph and said to him, "Sir, I was unmarried after my husband [died] for ten years, and now I gave birth to a child." He said to her, "My daughter, do not discredit the word of the sages!" She confessed, "I had intercourse with a non-Jew."
>
> (b. Yev. 34b)

In these cases no property claim was at issue. They indicate that the courts were able to judge cases of personal status, in particular the

[1] See vol. III, pp. 195-202, 142-145. See Rava's action in enforcing such a strict separation in his court, b. Ket. 28a.

[2] Vol. III, pp. 275-276. Rava's opinion in b. Ket. 51b, on the right of a woman who has been raped to remain with her husband, is consistent.

[3] b. Sanh. 52b. A. Hyman, *Toledot Tanna'im ve'Amora'im* (London, 1910), II, p. 461, reports of R. Ḥama b. Tuviah only this pericope, and says, "From here we see that he was the head in his town." However, no firmer date on when he lived is given. S. Funk, *Juden in Babylonien*, II, 123 comments on the peculiarity of the case and its punishment.

legitimacy of the child, and to punish presumptive adultery or illicit sexual relations. The punishment would have been flogging or excommunication. Rava also ruled that R. Mari b. Raḥel, Samuel's grandson born of the relationship between Samuel's daughter and a non-Jew, was legitimate and even allowed him to hold office.[1] So the future status of a child born of a questionable relationship could also be determined. The courts could also see to it that fathers supported their families,[2] and order that maintenance be paid from estates for daughters as well as sons.[3]

Pure Lineage and Other Non-Litigable Matters: The rabbinical discussions about the boundaries of Babylonia[4] were intended to specify the towns or districts from which rabbinical Jews might take wives. Babylonia was believed to be the only "pure" country. That is to say, only in parts of Babylonia were the rabbis certain that Jews had observed the rabbinical laws about proper selection of mates. Hence the inherited "merit" of Babylonian Jews was undiminished by illegal or improper ancestral relationships. R. Joseph said that a person who spoke with a Babylonian accent might take a wife of superior birth.[5] So when Abaye asked him about the limits of Babylonia on the west side of the Euphrates, R. Joseph replied.

> "What is your motive? On account of Biram? The most distinguished [people] of Pumbedita took [wives] from Biram."
>
> (b. Qid. 72a)

Naturally, people who were stigmatized by the rabbis became outraged. They would, after all, have difficulty in finding suitable wives for their sons, and husbands for their daughters, if the word of the rabbi about their unsuitability was widely accepted. The following story suggests what might happen:

> R. Zera lectured in Maḥoza, "A proselyte may marry a bastard." [Since there were many proselytes in Maḥoza], everyone threw *etrogs* at him. Rava commented, "Is there anyone who lectures thus in a place where proselytes abound?" Rava lectured in Maḥoza, "A proselyte may marry the daughter of a priest," so they loaded him with silks. Then he lectured, "A proselyte may marry a bastard." They said to him,

---

[1] b. Yev. 45b.
[2] b. Ket. 49b, Rava compelled fathers to support their children, see above, p. 140.
[3] Below, pp. 213f.
[4] See vol. II, pp. 240-250. For this generation, note also R. Joseph, b. Git. 6a, and b. Ber. 59b.
[5] b. Qid. 71b.

> "You have destroyed your first. [That is, you took away what you gave.]" He replied, "I have done the best for you. If one wishes, he can may here [priests], if he wishes, he can marry there [bastards]."
>
> (b. Qid. 73a)

It is clear that the people of Maḥoza took quite seriously the rabbis' traditions about genealogy.[1] The Maḥozans were concerned about R. Zera's and Rava's rulings. On the other hand, while the rabbis could keep their distance from a family of whose marriage they disapproved, as we noted above,[2] they could not impose a divorce upon a happily married couple. Hence their teachings were important, but hardly litigable, and so the rabbis buttressed the law with fanciful warnings about the poor quality of the off-spring of such a marriage or about the bad luck destined to afflict one who married unwisely, as in the case of Abaye:

> Rava said, "...a man should not take a wife either from a family of epileptics or from a family of lepers...This applies, however, only when it has happened in three cases..." Abaye...married Ḥoma daughter of 'Isi b. R. Isaac son of Rav Judah, although Reḥava of Pumbedita and R. Isaac b. Rabbah b. Bar Ḥana had both married her and died. After he married her, he also died..."
>
> (b. Yev. 64b)

Rava taught that before one marries, he should find out about the woman's brothers.[3] He also recommended that a woman be similarly concerned. Commenting on R. 'Aqiva's saying, that when a husband and wife are unworthy, fire consumes them, Rava said that the fire of the wife was worse.[4] There were many rules about prohibited relationships, and such sayings would have encouraged some people to learn what the rabbis had to say about them.[5] One inquiry was recorded, from the "men of Be Miqse" to Rabbah about the status of the child of a man who was half-slave and half-free and a Jewish woman.[6] Rava taught that a foundling was fit for Jewish marriage.[7] R. Naḥman asked him whether a person who has "lifted up his hands" in priestly blessing of the congregation was thereupon elevated to full status as a priest.[8]

---

[1] See vol. III, p. 66, for Rav Judah's similar lecture.

[2] Above, p. 192.

[3] b. B.B. 110a, with reference to Ex. 8:23.

[4] b. Sotah 17a.

[5] E.g. b. Yev. 21a, Rava on the biblical origins of the prohibition of relations in the second degree; b. Yev. 21b, Abaye gives examples of prohibited connections.

[6] b. Yev. 45a. But such inquiries generally came from the local school-house.

[7] b. Qid. 73b.

[8] b. Ket. 24b. I assume it was R. Naḥman b. Isaac.

Such questions would quite naturally come to the rabbis as teachers, but whether court action resulted is not clear. If the courts could certify that a man was truly a priest, he hence might receive and consume priestly gifts. They could allow a foundling to benefit from community philanthropy, enter into a Jewish marriage, and declare his children to be Jewish. They could certify the child of a mixed marriage whose mother was Jewish to be similarly acceptable. We have no examples of such court action.

Sayings about normal married life were of another order entirely, for they constituted merely a corpus of good advice and wise counsel. The rabbis hardly expected to enforce these teachings through court action, which was either irrelevant to begin with or unthinkable. Such sayings convey the values of the schools. How much or how little they shaped the values of the streets we can hardly estimate. It was not through the courts that the rabbis could act in the following:

> Rava said..."Until the age of twenty, the Holy One blessed be He sits and waits [wondering], 'When will (a man) take a wife?' As soon as he reaches twenty, and has not married, he exclaims, 'Blasted be his bones!'" (b. Qid. 29b)

> Abaye said, "With a husband (the size of an) ant, her seat is placed among the great." (b. Yev. 118b)[1]

> Rava said, "Whoever has intercourse with a whore in the end will go begging a loaf of bread." (b. Sotah 4b)[2]

> Rava said to the people of Maḥoza, "Honor your wives, that you may be enriched." (b. B.M. 59a)

> Rava said, "It is meritorious to divorce a bad wife[3]... A bad wife who owns a large marriage-contract should be given a rival at her side[4] ...A bad wife is as troublesome as a very rainy day[5]... Come and see how precious is a good wife and how baneful is a bad wife[6]...." (b. Yev. 63b)

[1] See *Oẓar HaGeonim*, ed. B. M. Lewin, VII, p. 233.
[2] With reference to Prov. 6:26.
[3] With reference to Prov. 22:10.
[4] See also b. Yev. 12b, Rava on permission to marry the "rival" of a woman incapable of bearing children.
[5] See also Prov. 27:15.
[6] See also Prov. 18:22 and Qoh. 7:22.

Rava said, "A man may marry wives in addition to his first wife, if he can support them." (b. Yev. 65a)

R. Joseph taught that Gen. 35:11 indicates that a woman may use contraceptives, though a man may not.[1] Rava explained why in some situations, one had to wait as long as ten years between one marriage and the next.[2] R. Naḥman b. Isaac said that a barren woman ('YLW-NYT) was a "ram-like man."[3] Rabbah and R. Joseph discussed compensation for rape.[4] Rabbah held that if the wife of a priest was raped, her husband might be flogged if he had sexual relations with her thereafter.[5] Most of these sayings could hardly lead to court action. If a man did not marry before twenty, God might curse him, but the rabbis could do little to force him to marry. A woman might be proud to have any sort of a man, rather than none at all, but the rabbis could hardly find a husband for everyone. Whatever the disastrous results of intercourse with prostitutes, the rabbis could only admonish. People had better honor their wives; riches would result. If they did not honor wives, however, rabbinical intervention would hardly follow in most circumstances. Rabbis could not punish men's use of contraceptives; indeed it would be difficult to see how evidence could come to court on such a matter.

To summarize: The authority of the courts extended to abnormal situations, such as cases of adultery, pre- and extra-marital pregnancies, and the like. The rabbinical court could determine that adultery had been committed or that a child was not the true heir of his supposed father. While the rabbis would merely instruct the people about whether proselytes might marry illegitimate women or the daughters of priests, proselytes certainly cared what they said. Whether they would then do what the rabbis taught is not revealed in the sources. For all we know, they were angry at the insult to their honor, but would continue to marry as they pleased. Finally, the rabbis could impress upon ordinary people their ideas about entering into early marriage, refraining from intercourse with prostitutes, divorcing bad wives, honoring spouses, and the like. One cannot suppose that the courts could ever make judgments about violations of such good

[1] b. Yev. 65b.

[2] b. Yev. 42a. He himself waited ten years before marrying his wife, R. Ḥisda's daughter, b. Yev. 34b. See also b. Yoma 18b, If one has proposed marriage, the couple wait seven "clean" days, that is, days without a sign of menstrual blood.

[3] b. Ket. 11a.

[4] b. Ket. 42b, re. Deut. 22:29.

[5] b. Yev. 56b.

counsel. No litigation would conceivably result. Yet it was the good counsel of the rabbis that pertained most widely and directly to the everyday lives of common people, who did not normally commit adultery, dishonor their wives, father or bear extra-marital progeny. The rabbis' ideals for the normal marriage were accompanied by promises of heavenly favor or threats of heavenly disfavor precisely because no earthly power could effect such ideals. The reputation and influence of the rabbis rather than their court powers affected the normal and regular circumstances of life, while decisions made by rabbinical judges usually came to bear upon abnormal and irregular events alone.

v. Dissolution of Marriages

While the rabbis had no role in the ritual of marriage, they had considerable power over the formalities of its dissolution. Marriages were dissolved through either death or divorce.[1] If through death, the biblical provisions, where applicable, concerning levirate marriage were carried out in the courts. Divorce documents had to conform to court rules, or they would not be confirmed. Lack of judicial recognition meant that the parties could not remarry. Lack of confirmation meant that the woman could not collect her marriage settlement.[2] So under practically no circumstance, except the normal one of the death of a man whose wife had borne children, could a marriage come to an end without provoking some sort of rabbinical involvement.

Levirate Ceremonies: When a man died childless, his widow was supposed either to contract a levirate connection or to carry out a ceremony of *ḥaliẓah*, as the Bible prescribed, with the surviving brother. Since biblical rules were quite explicit, the people expected the courts to oversee, and where necessary to enforce, the law. The courts assuredly did so. The following cases were reported of fourth-century masters:

> Abaye once stood before R. Joseph, when a sister-in-law came to him to perform *ḥaliẓah*. He said to Abaye, "Give him your sandal," and Abaye gave his left sandal...
>
> (b. Yev. 103b)

> A daughter of R. Papa's father-in-law fell to the lot of a levir who was unworthy of her [but insisted upon contracting the levirate marriage]. When he came before Abaye, Abaye said, "Submit to her *ḥaliẓah*

[1] See vol. III, pp. 274-283.

[2] We shall consider the administration of estates below, pp. 212-220.

and you will thereby marry her." [R. Papa suggested to Abaye a better way out, that Abaye order him to submit to *ḥaliẓah* in exchange for a large sum of money. Abaye so ordered.][1] After the levir had submitted to *ḥaliẓah*, Abaye said to her, "Go and give him." R. Papa replied, "She was merely fooling him."..."Where is your father," Abaye asked [the levir].[2] "In town," he replied. "And your mother?" "In town." He (Abaye) set his eyes upon them and they died.

(b. Yev. 106a)

A couple both of whom admitted [after the levir had declared that consummation of marriage had taken place] that they had lied [and no levirate marriage had taken place]: Rava ordered the disciples to arrange for *ḥaliẓah* and to dismiss the case......

(b. Yev. 112a)

A certain man was known to have no brothers [or sons], and at the time of his death he so declared. R. Joseph said, "What is there to apprehend [in permitting the widow to remarry]?"...

(b. B.B. 135a)

The above accounts make it quite clear that *ḥaliẓah* ceremonies were conducted by rabbinical courts. The story of Abaye's decision about the levirate claim of an "unworthy" man who chose to marry into a rabbinical family presents a strange contrast. On the one hand, the court could not legally forbid the man from entering a levirate marriage. On the other, it was quite determined to prevent it. So the court tricked the man into a *ḥaliẓah* ceremony. The imprecision of the distinction between what the rabbi could do as judge and what he could only do as holy man here is most clearly revealed. He could not legally prevent the levirate marriage—but he could try to stop it in any other possible fashion, including casting an evil eye on the man's parents.

Other sayings on the laws of levirate marriage included the following: R. Naḥman b. Isaac held that it was better to arrange a ceremony of *ḥaliẓah* than to permit levirate marriage;[3] Abaye asked Rabbah about the divorce of a levirate wife;[4] Rabbah and Rava discussed accidental intercourse between a levir and his sister-in-law;[5] Rava taught a tradition on the place of a *ḥaliẓah* ceremony, how it should be read, the certificate of *ḥaliẓah* and its wording.[6] The certificate was as follows:

---

[1] I shall discuss the tendency of rabbis to favor one another in court, below, pp. 309f.

[2] Rashi: He asked R. Papa, for they must have sharpened his mind to think of such deceit.

[3] b. Yev. 39b.

[4] b. Yev. 52a.

[5] b. Yev. 54a.

[6] b. Yev. 101b.

"We have read for her from 'My husband's brother refuses' (Deut. 25:7) to 'will perform the duty of a husband's brother unto me,' and we have read for him from 'not' to 'take her,' and we have read for her from 'So' to 'him that had his shoe drawn off' (Deut. 25:9)."

(b. Yev. 106b)

The laws regarding levirate marriages and *ḥaliẓah* ceremonies were wholly in the hands of the courts. I have no doubt whatever that in practically all relevant details, whatever legal discussions and theories were transmitted in the schools represented law which was actually enforced. The laws of levirate marriage and *ḥaliẓah* did not entail an exchange of property. In the latter instance they were quite simply ritualistic. Nonetheless the people kept these laws and supported all rabbinical court rules necessary to do so properly. The reason was, as I said, that the Scriptures clearly imposed the requirement, and the people fully intended to live by the revelation of Moses.

Divorces: The rabbis determined the exact language and form of divorce-documents, the means by which they were to be delivered from the husband into the possession of the wife, and the consequences of such a divorce-action. Few, if any, laws pertaining to divorce can be thought to have been of mere theoretical consequence. Most of them were actually enforced through the courts, and the rest through the influence or intimidation represented by the potentiality of court action. The following divorce-cases pertained to this period:

A man went to the synagogue, took a scroll of the Torah, and gave it to his wife, saying, "Here is your divorce." R. Joseph ruled, "Why should we take any notice of it...."

(b. Git. 19b)

In the case of a bill of divorce which was found among the flax in Pumbedita, Rabbah acted according to the rule just laid down [that the divorce is to be delivered as written unless two factors mitigate against it].

(b. Git. 27a=b. B.M. 18b)

A certain man sent a divorce to his wife, telling the agent not to give it to her until thirty days had passed. Before then, the man found he could not carry out the commission, and therefore consulted Rava.... He said to the man, "Transmit your commission to us, so after thirty days we can appoint a bearer who will give the divorce to the wife..."

(b. Git. 29b)

A certain man said to the court, "If I do not make up with her in thirty days, it will be a [bill of] divorce." He went and tried, but she was not reconciled. R. Joseph said, "Has he offered her a bag of gold coins and still been unable to appease her?" According to another version, he said, "Must he offer her a bag of gold coins? He has done his best to make it up with her, but she would not be reconciled..."

(b. Git. 30a)

Giddal b. Reʿilʾai sent a divorce to his wife. The bearer went and found her weaving. He said to her, "Here is your divorce." She said to him, "Go away now and come back tomorrow." The agent returned [to Giddal] and told him, and he [Giddal] exclaimed, "Blessed be he who is good and does good." Abaye said, "Blessed is he who is good and does good, and the divorce is not cancelled," and Rava ruled, "Blessed...but the divorce is cancelled."

(b. Git. 34a)[1]

A certain man who was dying wrote a divorce for his wife[2] on the eve of the Sabbath, but had no time to give it to her [before the Sabbath]. The next day he was critically ill. Rava was consulted, and ruled, "Go and tell him to make over to her the place where the divorce is, and [let her acquire that place] and take [the formal] possession...."

(b. Git. 77b)

A certain man threw a divorce to his wife as she was standing in a courtyard, and it fell on a block of wood. R. Joseph said, "We have to see..."

(b. Git. 77b)

A certain divorce was dated by the term of office of the *astandara*[3] of the town of Bashkar. R. Naḥman b. R. Ḥisda sent to Rabbah to ask how to deal with it. He replied....

(b. Git. 80b)

Abaye once found R. Joseph at court, compelling [certain men[4]] to give a bill of divorce....

(b. Git. 88b)

A certain priest married a proselyte who was under the age of three years and one day. R. Naḥman b. Isaac said to him, "What is this?"

---

[1] Two further such cases are cited, in which the disagreement of Rava and Abaye is noted, but we have no evidence of court action on account of their respective comments.

[2] So that she would be free of the obligation of levirate marriage.

[3] *Astandara*=istandara, Levy, *Wörterbuch*, s.v., I, p. 120, der Depeschenüberbringer.

[4] Following Rashi's interpretation.

[That is, on whose authority do you contract such a marriage?] The other replied [quoting a rabbi's view of the law]. "Go and arrange for her release, or else I will pull R. Jacob b. 'Idi out of your ear," R. Naḥman b. Isaac replied.

(b. Yev. 61a)

A divorce was once found in Sura, and in it appeared the following, "In the town of Sura, I, 'Anan son of Ḥiyya of Nehardea, released and divorced my wife so-and-so." When the rabbis searched from Sura to Nehardea, there was no other 'Anan b. Ḥiyya except one, of Hagra, who was then in Nehardea, and witnesses came and declared that on the day on which the bill of divorce was written, 'Anan b. Ḥiyya of Hagra was with them. Abaye said.... Rava said....

(b. Yev. 116a)

Once a certain man was dying. He was asked to whom his wife might be married, and replied, "She is suitable for a high priest." Rava said, "What is there to apprehend [for if a man says he divorced his wife, he is believed]...."

(b. B.B. 135a)

Moses b. ' Azri was guarantor for his daughter-in-law's [marriage contract]. His son, R. Huna, was a rabbinical disciple and in need of money. Abaye said, "Is there no one to advise R. Huna to divorce his wife so she may claim her marriage-contract from her father-in-law and he may then take her back." Rava said to him, "But we have learned, 'He must vow that he will not derive further benefit from her'?" Abaye's reply was, "Does every one who divorces his wife do so before a court?" [Only in a court would such a vow be enforced, but a divorce can be given outside of court.]....

(b. 'Arakh. 23a)

A man once bought a boat-load of wine, but had nowhere to store it. He asked a woman, "Do you have a place for rent?" She said no. He married her, and she gave him a place for storage. He went home, wrote a divorce, and sent it to her. She went out and hired carriers (to pay them of that wine) and had it put out in the road. R. Huna b. R. Joshua ruled....

(b. B.M. 101b)

In general the cases cited above all pertained to court recognition of the validity of a bill of divorce. Special cases were before the courts, for ordinary ones would not require court action. In the first two instances, the issue was whether a valid bill of divorce had actually been handed over. In the third, fourth, and fifth, the question was whether the interposition of an agent had resulted in complications either on account of delivery or on account of postponement of delivery. In the sixth and seventh, the question was whether a woman was legally able to acquire the divorce under special circumstances. In the eighth, the dating of the divorce document was in doubt. The ninth and tenth cases show that as earlier, the courts were able to force a man to prepare, or approve the preparation of, a bill of divorce for his wife. The eleventh case indicates how carefully the rabbis investigated the status of divorce documents which had been discovered in unusual circumstances, and the twelfth, similarly, shows that the courts meticulously investigated the intent of the husband. The thirteenth and fourteenth cases indicate that in extraneous matters, in which a divorce was used for some ulterior purpose, the rabbis were still able to rule on the validity of the document.

Divorces were not prepared by the courts. But all who hoped to have court backing for their documents had to conform to court rules. Only a few cases seem to have come for direct litigation. In most, as I said, the rabbis were asked to comment upon exceptional problems. R. Joseph's ruling in the first case represented such a court decree, for by saying that he would take no notice of the man's action, he ruled that the couple was still married and required a proper bill of divorce to be written. The consultation of Rava in the third case was probably more representative of what generally took place. The conflicting traditions attributed to R. Joseph pose a problem, for if the divorce were regarded as invalid, there is no reason why another could not have been issued. The only practical consequence of the divorce of the dying man and of R. Joseph's comment could have come because of some extenuating circumstance. Had the man in the meantime died without issue, his wife would have been subject to the law of levirate marriage. Hence the length of time in R. Joseph's case might have created a practical issue where none, in fact, would ordinarily have existed. The divorce of Giddal b. Reʿilʾai reveals no such practical outcome, and I suppose there was none. In such an instance, the report of a "case" does not prove there was actual court action but may represent mere scholastic discussion. On the other hand, the inquiry of R. Naḥman b. R. Ḥisda was important, for it involved how a divorce should be properly dated.

The enforcement of divorce-documents found in the street raised a number of practical problems. Had the woman denied receiving the document, the validity of the divorce would depend upon the testimony of those who had witnessed and delivered it. The final two cases show that divorces were relatively common and lightly given. The opinion attributed to (though not necessarily said by) Abaye was that most people did not in fact divorce their wives before a court. What is especially interesting is that R. Naḥman b. Isaac and R. Joseph were able to force men to divorce their wives, on grounds specified in the law, and so had the power to disrupt a marriage. This was a most irregular procedure, and Abaye specifically commented on R. Joseph's exceptional act. Nonetheless, R. Joseph defended himself, and since we have earlier evidence of similar powers, we need not doubt that the courts could do what R. Joseph was said to have done. So the rabbis' extended discussion of points of divorce law reflected the exact procedures and practical requirements of their courts.[1]

Three further cases illustrate other powers of the courts:

> A man once drowned in the Tigris and after five days was hauled up at the Shebistana bridge, and on the evidence of the groomsmen, Rava permitted the wife to marry again.
>
> (b. Yev. 121a)

> A man once went around saying, "Alas for the valiant rider who was at Pumbedita, for he is dead." R. Joseph [or Rava] allowed his wife to remarry.
>
> (b. Yev, 121b)

> A certain pagan once said to a Jew, "Cut some grass and throw it to my cattle on the Sabbath or I will kill you as I killed so-and-so, that Jew, to whom I said, 'Cook me a dish on the Sabbath' and whom I killed when he refused." The wife [of the man who had refused to cook on the Sabbath] heard, and she came to Abaye. He kept her waiting for three festivals. R. 'Adda' b. 'Ahavah said to her, "Apply to R. Joseph whose knife is sharp." She turned to him, and he ruled...
>
> (b. Yev. 121b-122a)

It is clear from these instances that the courts could rule upon the validity of a claim that a man had died, and so in still a third way could control the dissolution of a marriage. Such a ruling was particularly important. If a woman did not obtain it, she could be prevented from

[1] Note for example the long opening discussion, b. Git. 2aff., on how the bearers of a bill of divorce must testify concerning the preparation of the document; b. Git. 21a, Rava, if a man writes a divorce for his wife and gives it to the slave for delivery; b. Git. 67b, Rava on the orders of the bearers of a bill of divorce; b. Git. 72b, 83b-84a, Rava on a conditional bill of divorce; b. Git. 75b, Rava on the language of a conditional bill of divorce; b. Ket. 2b, on a plea in regard to divorce; b. A.Z. 37a, Abaye on a bill of divorce after death; b. Qid. 5a, Rava on a divorce through a written document and not through a money-payment, etc.

remarrying. If she did remarry, her future children could be stigmatized as illegitimate, of impure or tainted genealogy, being the children of adultery.

To summarize: A combination of circumstances therefore endowed the rabbinical courts with substantial power over dissolution of marriages. First, the people believed that the Scriptural requirements about levirate marriages and *ḥaliẓah* ceremonies must be fulfilled. They came to the courts for execution of the latter and for rulings about the former, as the occasion required. Second, the Scriptural requirement that a bill of divorce be issued made it necessary to provide such a document. Because of the ramifications of an improper document, it was necessary to draw it up according to rabbinical rules so the courts would enforce it. The bill of divorce had, moreover, to be conveyed, or handed over, to the wife according to rabbinical law. Whatever conditions the husband set had to be carried out, or the document was invalidated. While ordinary divorces obviously would not provoke intervention, extraordinary circumstances would lead directly to court. Common people therefore tried to do things to begin with to conform to rabbinical regulations. Third, in both levirate connections and bills of divorce, the most practical issue concerned the status of future progeny of the respective parties. If a woman was not satisfactorily freed of her obligations to her levir or to her former husband, then her children out of a later marriage would be illegitimate. Nothing mattered more to Babylonian Jewry than purity of lineage. The people would do everything to make certain their descendants would not be stigmatized. Besides the requirements of Scripture and the possibility of court action, the most important impulse to keep the law therefore lay in the fear of tainting one's descendants. Fourth, since the courts could compel the payment of sums pledged in marriage contracts, and now due on account of divorce or death, it was necessary not only to consult rabbinical judges, but also to apply to them for court orders when payment was not satisfactorily forthcoming. Fifth, the right of the courts to declare that a man was legally dead gave them further power over women who claimed they had lost their husbands, and hence required no bill of divorce before remarrying. So the courts' power over the dissolution of marriages was practically unlimited. I doubt that in enforcing any other part of the law they possessed practical power to a greater degree than here.

VI. Wills and Estates

The predominant issues in the above cases concerned the personal status of individuals, for example whether a woman was betrothed or not, married or properly divorced, indisputably widowed, free of levirate obligations, and the like. In actions of personal status, the exchange of property, while important, was secondary to, and dependent upon, the determination of an individual's legal circumstance. We turn now to the wide variety of cases in which the disposition of property was the primary and central issue. In all commercial, business, real estate, and other property matters, the courts could transfer possession from one man to another, confirm rights of ownership, and settle every sort of conflict. From the viewpoint of the exilarch, the adjudication of property disputes represented the courts' chief task, and the rabbis' laws about such issues therefore were easily effected.

The point at which the courts entered into a case now is no longer in doubt. Earlier we found occasion to wonder why the rabbis offered an opinion in matters which seemed to be phrased as cases, "A certain man did so-and-so." In property litigations we need no longer speculate on how a given issue came before the courts, for in most instances it is clear that either the possessor of a property requested court confirmation of his rights, or a plaintiff challenged them, or property in the hands of neither had to be properly adjudicated, or an alleged malefactor damaged the rights or property of another.

Most closely associated with family life, the settlement of wills and division of estates constituted an important source of litigation.[1] Nonetheless it was only when such matters were disputed that the courts' power came to bear. A person could ordinarily give instructions about the disposition of his property to three men, who might thereupon draw up and witness a will or actually execute it on the spot. The desired division did not require the supervision or intervention of the courts. Earlier the largest single group of cases dealt with the issues of gifts in contemplation of death, mainly because of R. Naḥman's innovations in the law covering that circumstance.[2] In this period, no single principle similarly predominated in litigations.

Wills and estates produced three kinds of court cases, first, the final disposition of contested wills, second, applications for maintenance

[1] Vol. II, pp. 263-264, and vol. III, pp. 286-295.

[2] Vol. III, pp. 288-290. See also b. B.B. 149a, and Rabbah, b. B.B. 175a.

from legacies for widows and orphans, and third, the sale of estates under various conditions. The third kind of case was by far the most frequent. Our brief review of the case-reports will indicate that the rabbinical courts had no difficulty in making and executing judgments, because in all instances, property was at issue. Litigations of wills yielded the following case reports:

> A certain man declared (in his will), "Give four hundred *zuz* to so-and-so and let him marry my daughter." R. Papa said, "He receives the four hundred *zuz*, but as for the daughter, if he wishes, he may marry, but he need not..."
>
> (b. Beẓ. 20a)

> A man once declared (in his will), "Give four hundred *zuz* [of the value] of this wine to [my] daughter." The price of wine rose. R. Joseph ruled that the profit goes to the orphans [that is, to the residuary estate].
>
> (b. Ket. 54a-54b)

In both of the above cases, the task of the court was to interpret the language and intent of the will. Both involved substantial sums of money. Hence we may suppose that the cases were actually brought to court for litigation, in the first instance by the daughter, whom the man refused to marry, or by the man, whom the daughter refused to pay; in the second, by either party seeking to gain the excess value of the original quantity of wine.[1]

The rights of the widow to be supported by her deceased husband's estate conflicted with the interest of the orphans, in many cases born of a different, perhaps earlier marriage. The rights of both parties were carefully protected by the courts. In general litigations devolved upon two issues, first, by what procedures and from what possessions the widow receives her marriage settlement, and second, what are the obligations of the estate to support her and other female legatees. The following cases were recorded:

> A similar case [of a daughter claiming maintenance out of her deceased father's estate] came before R. Joseph, "Give her of the dates that are spread on the reed-mat" [that is, movable property]. Abaye said to him....
>
> (b. Ket. 50b)

> A male and a female orphan came before Rava, who said, "Raise [a larger maintenance] for the male, for the sake of the girl [that is, an allowance sufficient for both]." The rabbis said to Rava....
>
> (b. Ket. 51a)

[1] On inheritances, see also Abaye and Rava, b. B.B. 111b.

Ḥoma, Abaye's widow, came to Rava and asked him to grant her an allowance of board, and he did so. She asked for an allowance for wine, but he said, "I know that Naḥmani did not drink wine." [She swore that he gave her wine]. "By the life of the Master, he gave me to drink from horns [ŠWPRZY] like this." As she was showing to him, her arm was uncovered and light shone upon the court. Rava rose, went home, and solicited [his wife] R. Ḥisda's daughter. "Who has been today at the court?" she asked. "Ḥoma, the widow of Abaye," he replied. Thereupon she followed her, striking her with the straps of a chest until she chased her out of Maḥoza. "You have already killed three men, and now you come to kill another?"

(b. Ket. 65a)

The wife of R. Joseph b. Rava came before R. Neḥemiah the son of Joseph and said to him, "Grant me an allowance of board," which he did. "And of wine!" He granted it to her, saying, "I know the people of Maḥoza drink wine."

(b. Ket. 65a)

The wife of R. Joseph son of R. Menashia of Devil came before R. Joseph and asked for an allowance of board and wine, which he granted. "Grant me an allowance of silk." "Why of silks?" he asked. "For your sake and for the sake of your friend and for the sake of your colleagues."[1]

(b. Ket. 65a)

The mother-in-law of R. Ḥiyya 'Arika was wife of his brother, and when widowed, she lived in her father's house. R. Ḥiyya maintained her for twenty-five years at her maternal home. At the end, she said, "Supply me with maintenance." He denied she had a further claim. "Pay me my marriage-contract," and he denied her right to it. She summoned him to court before Rabbah b. Shila [who ruled in her favor]. R. Ḥiyya disregarded the ruling, so the judge wrote out for her an *'adrakhta'* (a document). He came and appealed to Rava....

(b. Ket. 104b)[2]

In these cases, the issue was whether and how a wife was to be supported from her late husband's estate. The first case was cited to show what an orphaned daughter was given, namely, movables, but not real property. In the second, the son's portion was increased so he might support his sister. Three of the four cases of widows, apparently all of rabbis, claiming that the court should provide for them out of their deceased husbands' estates, involved the appropriate extent of

[1] To keep up her social standing.

[2] See below, p. 243, for further discussion of this case.

that support. The claim to wine was thought to be excessive unless the woman and her husband usually made use of it. The same issue pertained to the provision of silk garments. In the final case, the issue was whether a woman, having been maintained for many years outside of her late husband's household, still would be able to demand the settlement of her marriage contract. Having sustained her claim, the court then issued an appropriate document so that she might collect her dues. Among other sayings about maintenance of a widow and orphans were those of R. Joseph, that daughters must be maintained until they are married, and that if the widow painted her eyes or dyed her hair, she lost her claim to maintenance, and the like.[1]

The courts exercised guardianship over the estates of widows, orphans, the deaf, and others who were not wholly able to manage their own affairs. An example of control of the property of a deaf man is as follows:

> A deaf man once lived in the neighborhood of R. Malkio, who arranged for him to take a wife to whom he [R. Malkio] assigned in writing the sum of four hundred *zuz* out of his estate. Rava remarked, "Who is so wise as R. Malkio...."
>
> (b. Yev. 113a)

The rabbinical court sought the ablest guardians:

> Abaye said [after deciding a case involving orphans' land], "Anyone who appoints a guardian should appoint one like this man, who understands how to turn the scales in favor of orphans."
>
> (b. Ket. 109b)

A more difficult case in which the courts ruled on the settlement of estates follows:

> A certain old woman had three daughters. She and one of them were taken captive. Of the remaining two daughters, one died, leaving a child. Abaye said, "What shall we do? Shall we (temporarily) assign the estates to the (third) sister? But perhaps the old woman is dead, and a relative is not permitted to enter upon a minor's estate. Shall we assign the estates to the child? But perhaps the woman is not dead, and a minor cannot enter a captive's estate." Abaye ruled, "Therefore half is given to the (last) sister, and a guardian is appointed over the other half in the child's behalf." Rava commented...
>
> (b. B.M. 39b)

---

[1] b. Ket. 53b-54a; see also b. Qid. 17b, Rava said that by biblical law, a pagan is entitled to receive an inheritance from his father, based upon Lev. 25:50.

The case would have come to court when the settlement of the deceased daughter's estate was demanded. The court appointed a guardian to administer the child's property. The power of the court over the disposition of orphans' property, illustrated in the several claims for widows' maintenance from estates and in the above cases, extended also to marketing or sale of land and other holdings, as in the following:

> Reḥavah was in charge of an orphan's capital. He went before R. Joseph to ask permission to use it. He replied...
>
> (b. B.M. 29b)

> A certain man once made a field a boundary mark for another person. When one of the witnesses who contested the ownership died, a guardian was appointed over the estate, who came before Abaye...
>
> (b. Ket. 109b)

In these two cases, the court's approval had to be obtained for the disposition of the funds and property of an orphan. The guardians appointed by the court came under supervision later on, and could be removed or even fined for misappropriation of funds. In the following, more direct court action was involved, because of conflicting claims:

> It was rumored that Rava b. Sharshom [a guardian of orphans' property] was using for his own benefit land that belonged to orphans. Abaye summoned him and said, "Tell me the facts." He said, "I took over this land from the father of the orphans as a mortgage and he owed me other funds in addition...." [Abaye ruled against him].
>
> (b. B.B. 32b-33a)

> Did not Rava order some orphans to return a pair of shears for clipping wool and a book of *'Aggadah* which were claimed from them, though the claimants adduced no proof [that they had loaned them to the father]....
>
> (b. B.B. 52a)

The two cases reflect the difficulties of settling an estate. It was not always clear what the deceased had done. The courts had therefore both to protect orphans' rights and to see that debts were paid and loans returned, so that legitimate property relationships would be not disrupted by the possibility of sudden death. Hence in the first instance, the court had to protect the orphans' rights, and in the second, Rava ordered the return of property the deceased had borrowed and the heirs retained as their own. The sale of property by minor-orphans was carefully regulated, as in the following instances:

Rava in R. Naḥman's name said that the intervening period [the eighteenth year] was regarded as being under age.... *That view of Rava was not stated explicitly but through inference.*[1] [Italics supplied] A certain youth during his intervening period sold the estate [of his deceased father]. He came before Rava who decided the sale was illegal...

(b. B.B. 155b)

A certain youth under twenty sold his inherited estate. When he was to appear before Rava [desiring to withdraw from the sale, on the plea of being a minor] the relatives told him, "Go, eat dates and throw the pits at Rava" [to show the boy was irresponsible]. He did so, and Rava said, "The sale is no sale." When the deed was written out the buyers said, "Go tell Rava, the scroll of Esther may be obtained at a *zuz*, and the court deed may be obtained at a *zuz*!" He went and delivered the message. Rava then changed his mind and ruled that the sale was legal [as the boy was knowledgeable.] When the relatives said that the purchasers had so instructed the lad, he replied, "But he understands what is explained to him, and if so, he possesses intelligence, so his earlier act was due to exceptional gall."

(b. B.B. 155b)

In the above instances, the right of under-age orphans to dispose of their inheritances was at issue, and the principle was that if the minor knew what he was doing, he could not retract his action. The second case is of great interest, for it shows that the relatives and the aggrieved

[1] It is particularly curious that what was incorrectly attributed to Rava was not a simple saying, but an alleged attribution *by* Rava *to* R. Naḥman. The passage begins with a legal question, followed by "Rava said in the name of R. Naḥman..." and then, "Rava b. R. Shila said in the name of R. Naḥman...", each supplying a tradition of R. Naḥman's supposed opinion. The account proceeds as given here. Hence it was "originally" supposed that Rava merely transmitted an opinion of the earlier master. If so, the person who witnessed Rava's court-decision thereupon presumed that he had acted in accordance with R. Naḥman's teaching. Why the supposition was not simply concerning Rava's *own* opinion I cannot say.

Perhaps the apparent existence of a tradition on the subject in R. Naḥman's name led the tradent to assume as follows: "Rava could not have acted contrary to R. Naḥman's tradition, as cited by Rava b. R. Shila, unless he actually held a contrary teaching from the master, for Rava would otherwise hardly act contrary to the acknowledged and known dictum of R. Naḥman." So four separate thought-processes had to intervene between event and the false tradition. The witness to Rava's court decision had first to take note of it, and, second, to compare it with an existing tradition of R. Naḥman. He, thirdly, had to reflect that since Rava could not "possibly" contradict R. Naḥman, he therefore must have followed another tradition in R. Naḥman's name. Finally, the tradent(s) would have rendered the tradition as we have it, "Rava in the name of R. Naḥman said ... Rava b. R. Shila in the name of R. Naḥman said...." Later on, it was added, "Rava did not really *say* anything of the sort, but in court he *ruled* as follows. By false inference his principle was supposed to be such-and-so; yet that was not the principle by which he acted at all."

purchasers both knew full well upon what basis the court would make its decision, and tried to conform to the conditions necessary to achieve, in the one case, confirmation, in the other, retraction, of the sale. The following instance shows that the courts could oversee how the orphans carried out the instructions of a will:

> A dying man gave orders to give a palm tree to his daughter. The orphans divided the estate and did not do so. R. Joseph intended to rule ... But Abaye said to him...
>
> (b. Ket. 109b)

Other rulings about the disposition of estates[1] included the following:

> A certain man bought a field adjacent to his father-in-law's estate. When they came to divide the latter's estate, the man said, "Give me my share next to my own field." Rabbah said, "This is a case where a man can be compelled [to act generously, and] not to act after the manner of Sodom." R. Joseph objected, "The brothers can claim the field to be especially valuable..."
>
> (b. B.B. 12b)

> Rava b. Ḥinnena and R. Dimi b. Ḥinnena were willed by their father two female-slaves, one of whom knew how to cook and bake, the other to spin and weave. They came before Rava [to decide whether one could force the other to divide them, the one who received the more valuable to compensate the other]. He said to them...
>
> (b. B.B. 13b)

> A certain man once said to his fellow, "My estate will be yours, and after you, it will go to so-and-so." The first was entitled to be his heir. When [both the testator and] the first man died, the second came to claim the estate. R. ʿIlish proposed in Rava's presence to decide that the second was also entitled to receive the bequest. Rava said, "Such decisions are given by arbitration judges..."[2]
>
> (b. B.B. 133b)

> A certain man said to his wife, "My estate will belong to you and your children." R. Joseph said, "She acquires the ownership of half of it."
>
> (b. B.B. 143a)

---

[1] See also b. Ket. 98a, Rabbah b. Rava asked R. Joseph whether a woman is required to take a court-oath who sells an estate without court supervision or authorization; b. Ket. 100b, R. Joseph on the sale of an estate without public bidding; b. Shev. 46b, Rava on orphans' property.

[2] Rashi: Arbitration judges are not experts in the law, and divided property in half, as in the case of money whose ownership was disputed.

A certain person once said, "My estate is to go to my sons." He had a son and a daughter. Do people call a son "sons" or perhaps he meant to include his daughter in the gift. Abaye said ... and Rava said ... and R. Joseph said....

(b. B.B. 143b)[1]

A certain man died and left a brother. [The case involved a loan. The lender died childless and left a brother as heir. The borrower had died and left children. The lender's brother now claims the debt from the borrower's children.] Rami b. Ḥama thought of ruling ... Rava corrected him...

(b. Shev. 48b)

The above cases involved several different issues. The first and second centered upon the fair assessment of one's share in an estate. If a man signified that he desired his share of land in a particular place, in this case near his own property, that land would have therefore become more valuable to him than otherwise, and that added value had to be taken into account in settling the estate. In the second case the issue was whether the special skills of slaves had to be compensated for. In the third, fourth, and fifth cases, the language and intent of the testator were at issue. In the final case, settlement of the deceased's loan was arranged by the court.

The wide range of cases concerning the disposition of estates and the interpretation of wills leaves no doubt that the court had full power to decide such matters. Litigations involved rather specialized questions, for instance, the fulfillment of a condition set by the testator, as "Give him money and let him marry my daughter," or the unusual situation in which the interpretation of the testator's language would affect considerable property (as in the case of the rise in the price of wine). Several widows' claims were reported. In general the courts had to rule on the fairness of those claims, for the rights of others, particularly orphans, had to be protected. Excessive claims would be denied. Further, the courts were supposed to see that minor-orphans' property, as well as that of incompetents, was protected. They therefore appointed and supervised guardians, who had to apply to the court for permission to use the orphans' funds, and who had also to explain their actions to the court when called upon. When orphans acted in their own account, the courts could also examine their competence, and decide whether their action was legal or not. In the final group of cases, other aspects of the settlement of estates by the courts were illustrated.

---

[1] Quoting biblical language, Gen. 46:23, Num. 26:8, and I Chron. 2:8.

The courts exercised no monopoly on the settlement of estates, for arbitrators[1] might give decisions, and the relatives of orphans might also take a hand in protecting their rights and property. Nonetheless the fact that the courts were ready to intervene and preserve the rights of all concerned would have set high standards for the whole community. In the end, one could always appeal for justice to the rabbinical authority, so the law might as well be kept to begin with. The Iranian government clearly expected that orderly community life would be maintained by all sub-groups in its empire. One of the characteristics of an orderly community was that the rights of widows and orphans were carefully protected. From prophetic times onward, Jews also believed that, being weak and without protection, widows and orphans were the objects of special heavenly concern. So both social and religious policy required the courts to take an active interest in the fair settlement of estates and related issues. With sufficient political power and religious warrant, the courts were well able to do so.

vii. Mortgages, Debts, and Bonds

Normal commercial relationships did not provoke the courts to intervene.[2] People usually paid their debts, did not cheat or defraud one another, did not enter disputes about ownership of goods or property, and did not, therefore, have to resort to the courts for judgment. The fact that the courts were prepared to act and had the power to do so, however, provided ordinary folk with security. If the law could be enforced, then most people would keep it even when no political authority was actually present to make them do so. The few cases cited below merely adumbrate the many instances in which life went on uneventfully and correctly. Three sorts of cases involving mortgages, bonds, and debts, now came before the courts, first, collection of debts, second, disposition of pledges and security given for loans, and third, the prohibition of interest. In all three, court action proved quite sufficient to settle litigations.

Debt collections came to court generally because of a claim of fraud. The debtor claimed that he had paid the debt, and the creditor denied it. Rava held[3] that if one lends money in the presence of witnesses, he must

---

1 On the significance of Rava's reference to arbitrators, see above, p. 185.
2 See Vol. III, pp. 295-302.
3 b. Shev. 41b.

also collect it before witnesses to prevent cases of fraud, such as the following:

> There was a certain person who said to his neighbor, "When you repay me, repay me before Reuben and Simeon."[1] He went and repaid before two others. Abaye said, "He told him to repay before two witnesses, and he repaid before two." Rava said to him, "For this reason he said, 'before Reuben and Simeon,' so he should not be able to put him off [by saying he had repaid before two others who were not available. It is no excuse, and he must pay.]"
>
> (b. Shev. 41b)

> A certain man said to his neighbor, "Give me the hundred *zuz* I lent you." [The other denied the loan.] The lender went and brought witnesses that he had lent, [but they also said] that the debtor had already paid the money. Abaye said, "What shall we do? They say he lent, but they themselves say he was also repaid." Rava said, "If the borrower said, 'I did not borrow,' it is as if he said, 'I did not repay.'"
>
> (b. Shev. 41b)

> There was a certain man who said to his neighbor, "Give me the hundred *zuz* I claim from you." The man replied, "Did I not repay before so-and-so and so-and-so?" The two alleged witnesses came and denied the event ever happened. R. Sheshet thought of ruling that the man was proved a liar. Rava said to him, "Anything which does not rest upon a man [= for which he is not obligated] he will do unconsciously [lit.: is not in his mind.]"
>
> (b. Shev. 41b)

> A certain man claimed, "Give me the six hundred *zuz* that I claim from you." The other replied, "Did I not repay you a hundred *kavs* of gallnuts which were worth six per *kav*?" He replied, "No, they were worth four per *kav*." Two witnesses came and said they were indeed worth four. Rava said, "He is proved a liar" [and must pay the difference.] Rami b. Ḥama said, "But you said that anything which does not rest upon a man he will do unconsciously?" Rava replied, "But people remember the market price."
>
> (b. Shev. 41b-42a)

> A certain man said, "You are believed by me whenever you say to me that I have not paid you." He went and paid before witnesses. Abaye and Rava both said, "Behold he believes him."
>
> (b. Shev. 42a)

---

[1] These would be conventional names, like Smith and Jones, but an actual case could well be reported according to such fixed conventions, and this is not necessarily a theoretical account. Another such convention must be "four hundred"-*zuz*, barrels of wine, etc., which would mean, "a great quantity."

Twelve thousand *zuz* were owed to R. Papa by people in Khuzistan. He transferred ownership of them to Samuel b. 'Abba' [or, 'Aḥa'] by means of the threshold of his house....

(b. B.Q. 104b)[1]

A certain judge once allowed a creditor to take possession of the property of the debtor before he had sued the debtor. R. Ḥanin b. R. Yeva' removed him [= gave the property back to the debtor]. Rava said, "Who would have been so wise as to do such a thing if not R. Ḥanin...."

(b. B.B. 174a)

The central issue in the above cases was whether and how a debt had actually been paid. In the first, the lender had set a condition that certain witnesses must attest to the repayment of the debt. When the man alledgedly repaid before others, the court had to rule on whether the borrower had fully conformed to the conditions originally agreed upon. In the second suit, witnesses attested to the loan, but went on to say that the borrower had already repaid it. The court had to evaluate their testimony. In the third, the witnesses simply denied that they had seen the transaction to begin with. In the fourth, the issue was whether a loan had been repaid in kind and devolved upon the value of what had been handed over in payment. In the fifth case the original stipulation was tested in court. In the sixth, the conditions of repayment of a loan of a considerable sum were described, in particular the means by which ownership of property in settlement of the debt was transferred. In the seventh case, the right of the lender to seize property of a delinquent debtor without appropriate court action was at issue, and Rava set aside the judgment of what was apparently a lower court. Two further debt cases, both involving rabbis, were those of Abba b. Martha's debt to Rabbah, in which the law of the Seventh Year remission of debts was observed,[2] and the action of R. Papa and R. Huna b. R. Joshua in seizing a ship from the estate of Yemar b. Ḥashu, as cited above.[3] R. Joseph said that the law of *'anparut* (a debt payable by installments with forfeiture if a payment is missed) does not apply in Babylonia.[4] Rava held that creditors might repossess lands sold by a debtor to others and resold by them, while Abaye held that the creditor could not repossess land already resold.[5] Rava held that it was permitted to repay a large

[1] Also b. B.B. 77b, 150b.
[2] b. Git. 37b, See *Ozar HaGeonim*, X, p. 73.
[3] b. Ket. 84b-85a, see above, p. 135.
[4] b. Git. 58b. See also *Ozar HaGeonim*, ed. B. Lewin, X, p. 124.
[5] b. B.Q. 8b.

debt in very small parts. Though the lender might bear resentment against the borrower for dissipating his capital, he could not repair to the court for any reason.[1] Abaye and Rava judged a case involving commercial paper:

> A certain deed of [debt] acknowledgement did not contain the phrase, "He said to us, Write it, attest and give it to him [to the creditor]." Abaye and Rava both said...
>
> (b. Sanh. 29b)

The clerks of their courts knew the law, and hence they usually drafted such documents correctly. It is likely that the courts prevented the need to litigate a larger number of cases by seeing to it that loans were properly documented.

Biblical laws about holding and returning security for a debt were naturally enforced in the courts, as in the following cases:

> A certain heathen gave a house in pledge to R. Mari b. Raḥel and then sold it to Rava. R. Mari waited a full year and collected the rent, and then offered it to Rava [for the coming year]. He explained to Rava, "The reason I did not offer you rent before this is that an unspecified pledge is a year. Had the heathen wished to make me quit [within the year], he would have been unable, but now you may take rent for the house." He replied, "Had I known it was pledged to you, I should not have bought it. Now I will treat you according to their law. Until they redeem the pledge they receive no rent. So I will take no rent from you until you are paid out."
>
> (b. B.M. 73b)

> A man once pledged an orchard to his neighbor for ten years. After the creditor had taken the usufruct for three years, he proposed to the debtor, "If you will sell it to me it is well. If not, I will hide the mortgage deed, and claim I have bought it." Thereupon the debtor transferred the property to his son (a minor), and sold it to him. The sale is certainly no sale, but the purchase money—is it accounted as a written debt and collectable from mortgaged property, or perhaps it is only a verbal debt, which cannot be collected from mortgaged property? Abaye said ... Rava said...
>
> (b. B.M. 72a)

> A certain man pledged an orchard for ten years, but it aged after five. Abaye said, "The [aged trunks] rank as produce." Rava said, "As principal. Therefore land must be bought therewith, and the mortgagee enjoys the usufruct."
>
> (b. B.M. 109b)

---

[1] b. B.M. 77b.

> A certain man took a butcher's knife in pledge. On coming before Abaye, Abaye ordered, "Go return it, because it is a utensil for preparing food, and then come to stand at judgment for the debt." Rava said, "He need not stand at judgment for it, but can [now] claim the debt up to the value of the pledge"....
>
> (b. B.M. 116a)

In the first case, Rava purchased a property from a non-Jew after it had been pledged as security for a loan. R. Mari b. Raḥel held the land and enjoyed the usufruct, as was his right, and then transferred ownership to Rava. Rava responded by saying that the land held as security should be retained by the original lender until the debt was paid out, and then he would accept ownership. This was, he said, according to "their" law. In the second instance, the creditor attempted to force the debtor to sell him the land which he had held for three years. Since in Jewish law, three years of usufruct unimpeded by protest constituted the *prima facie* establishment of ownership through squatter's rights, the lender would, he supposed, have a strong case in court. The debtor protected himself against fraud as best he could. The issue before the court did not devolve upon the fraud, but rather upon the disposition of money transferred by the debtor in the act of self-protection. The fourth case involved a change in the condition of the security. The fifth was closest to the original biblical requirement about returning the pledge if it was used for the maintenance of life. R. Joseph held that a court officer must recover the pledge, but that the creditor ought not to do so, should he have a claim on it according to the biblical law (Deut. 24:6).[1] Rava said with reference to Deut. 24:13 that a man may take as a pledge an item of clothing worn by day and hold it through the night, but he must return it in the morning.[2] He also said that if one declares his slave to be security for a debt and then sells the slave, the creditor can seize the slave, but if he so declares of an ox or an ass and sells them, the creditor cannot seize them.[3]

Whether bonds had been paid was at issue in the following case:

> Once R. Papa and R. Adda b. Mattena sat in [Rava's] presence when a bond was brought to him. R. Papa said to him, "I know that this bond has been paid." Rava asked, "Is there anyone with the Master to confirm the statement"....
>
> (b. Ket. 85a)

[1] b. B.M. 113a.
[2] b. B.M. 114b.
[3] b. B.B. 44b. For another opinion of Rabbah, see b. B.Q. 49b.

We shall see (below, p. 227) the discussion of the case of a bond issued against the children of R. 'Ilish, in which the possibility of usury was discussed. Rava held that a man possessing a bond of one hundred *zuz* cannot have it converted into two bonds each worth fifty *zuz*, nor can two bonds of fifty be converted into one for one hundred.[1] Such bonds of indebtedness would have to be drawn up, if not by court-appointed scribes, then according to the rules which would render them negotiable in the courts; contested bonds would have to come to courts. Hence there was no practical limit upon the enforcement of the rabbinical laws covering bonds.

Biblical prohibitions against taking interest on loans were clear and unequivocal. Legal fictions intended to circumvent the prohibitions were strongly disapproved, and documents to effect such fictions would not be enforced by the courts. Usury was regarded by Rava as equivalent to robbery whether the victim willingly paid it or not.[2] He also said that the exodus from Egypt was mentioned along with laws of interest, fringes, and weights (Lev. 25:36-38; Num. 15:38, 41, Lev. 19:38) because God thereby wished to say, "It is I who distinguished in Egypt between the firstborn and others. Even so, it is I who will exact vengeance from him who ascribes his money to a gentile and [directly] lends it to a Jew on interest, or who steeps his weights in salt, or who uses fringes dyed with vegetable blue and maintains that it is real blue."[3] Such a saying would suggest that the courts were unable to act against a man who surreptitiously made use of a gentile as a front for usurious practices within the Jewish community. Hence the divine curse was invoked, there probably being no satisfactory, this-worldly alternative means to prevent the practice. On the other hand, Rabbah and R. Joseph ruled that dealings in futures were legitimate. A man may therefore contract to supply provisions at the current market price, even though the price may change later on.[4] One who lends money at the early market price must personally appear at the granary.[5] Abaye and Rava both held that the courts would reclaim funds paid in usury, and in compelling repayment of a debt, would check on the possibility of usury.[6] A mortgage, on the other hand, was understood as a temporary sale, so that the lender's right of usufruct did not constitute usury.

[1] b. B.B. 172a.
[2] b. B.M. 61a.
[3] b. B.M. 61b.
[4] b. B.M. 63b.
[5] b. B.M. 63b.
[6] b. B.M. 65a.

Nonetheless, Rava strictly required the creditor to allow a fixed deduction of the debt annually, even though the usufruct was less than that amount.[1] Rava said,

> "The law permits neither the credit interests of R. Papa, nor the bonds of the Maḥozans, nor the tenancies of the people of Nersh."
>
> (b. B.M. 68a)

The first reference was to R. Papa's view that beer sold for credit might be priced higher than when paid for in cash. R. Papa held that the beer would not deteriorate. Since the brewer did not need the money, he merely conferred a benefit on the purchaser by giving it to him earlier than otherwise.[2] The purchaser paid a higher price. The Maḥozan bonds would add the (estimated) profit to the principal and record the whole in a bond, so that the lender's share of the profits of a commercial loan was guaranteed at the outset. Since there was no certainty that profit would accrue and also no sharing of risk, it was in fact a usurious clause. In the tenancies of Nersh, they wrote the following clause, "*A* mortgaged his field to *B*, and then the debtor rented it from him." The rental was fixed and paid in produce. Since the creditor had not in fact acquired the land which he has allegedly rented to the debtor, and therefore the land has not been formally transferred to the debtor, it is a thinly disguised form of direct interest. Rava provided for a "proper" kind of interest:

> Rava said, "One may say to his neighbor, 'Take these four *zuz* and lend money to so-and-so' [on interest] for the Torah prohibited only usury which comes directly from the borrower to the lender ... One may say to his neighbor, 'Here are four *zuz*, and persuade so-and-so to lend me money.' The neighbor merely receives a fee as advocate [and is not guilty of usury]."
>
> (b. B.M. 69b)

With so simple an alternative at hand, it is easy to see why the rabbis' rules could otherwise be strict. Both the laws of Moses and the needs of a highly developed commercial life could be easily satisfied. Three practical cases were recorded:

> A woman once told a man, "Go and buy me land from my relatives," and he went and did so. The seller said to the agent, "If I have money, will she return it to me?" "You and Navla," he replied, "are relatives [so she will certainly permit you to repurchase the land when you are

[1] b. B.M. 67b.
[2] b. B.M. 65a.

able to do so]." Rabbah b. R. Huna said, "Whenever one says 'You ... are relatives,' the seller relies upon it, and does not completely transfer [the object of sale]. The land is returnable, but what of the crops? Is it direct usury, which can be legally reclaimed, or indirect usury, and not reclaimable? Rabbah b. R. Huna said it must be considered indirect usury and cannot be reclaimed in court. Rava similarly ruled, "It is considered indirect usury and cannot be reclaimed in court."

(b. B.M. 67a)

A bond was issued against the children ot R. ʿIlish, stipulating half profits and half loss [that is to say, a bond whereby R. ʿIlish undertook to trade on these terms, and this is regarded as usury]. Rava said, "R. ʿIlish was a great man[1] and would not have fed another person with forbidden food [resulting from profits such as these]. It must be taken to mean, either half profit and two-thirds loss, or half loss and two-thirds profit. [That is, the borrower must have agreed to receive half the profits but to bear two-thirds of the loss, or if R. ʿIlish were to stand half the potential loss, he must receive two-thirds of the profit]."

(b. B.M. 68b-69a)

Rava advised those who watch over the fields, "Go and find some work in the barn so that your wages may not be payable until [that work is done], since wages are not payable until the end, it is only then that they remit in your favor" [what they pay over and above the stipulated wage].

(b. B.M. 73a)

The watchers were not paid until the wheat was winnowed, though wages were due immediately after the harvest. In consideration, they were given something above their due, which appeared to be usurious interest. Rava advised them to keep busy, so their wages would not actually be payable until they received their pay, in which case the additional payment would not come on account of their having waited, hence as interest on their salary, but rather as a gift.

In the first case, therefore, the issue was whether land was intended to be given over for acquisition by the lender, and what was the status of the usufruct in reference to the prohibition of usury. In the second, the issue was whether a contract had actually stipulated an arrangement of profits and loss which the rabbis regarded as usurious. Rava said that it was unthinkable for so great an authority as R. ʿIlish to have stipulated a usurious agreement, and he therefore interpreted the language of the bond to conform to the law. In the third instance, Rava advised workers how to avoid violating the law against usury.

---

[1] See vol. III, p. 134.

The courts' supervision of collections of mortgages and debts generally came in consequence of violation of the law. Otherwise there was no need to intervene. The cases of alleged fraud in repayment of debts would have been brought to court by the borrower, from whom excessive payment was demanded, or by the lender, who found himself unable to recover his funds, or by both, when the two issued conflicting claims. By contrast, cases of alleged usury would not necessarily have come before the courts at all if both parties had mutually agreed to the arrangement, unless some extraneous factor led to court action and thus revealed an illegal agreement. Rava could only advise the workers how to avoid breaking the law of usury, but no actual case could arise. In other cases, the basic agreement was regarded as sound and enforceable, but the issue of what to do about subsidiary or tangential returns had to be settled. It is striking to note the limited range of cases. We have no instance where the court simply had to force a recalcitrant debtor to pay his debt or to issue a decree against him. Doubtless such cases did arise, and we can only assume that they were not of sufficient legal or scholarly interest to warrant inclusion in a legal commentary upon the Mishnah. The only cases actually set down involved unusual circumstances or exemplified exceptionally interesting principles of law. We must therefore suppose that many more cases involving the collection of mortgages and debts, the transfer of ownership of pledges or securities for debts which had been defaulted, and the like, came to the courts. And, as I said, still more transactions would have been legally carried through without eliciting court action of any sort.

VIII. Contracts

Contracts of various kinds, involving the exchange of property or services, would naturally come to the courts if not properly carried out, or if the original conditions required the judges' interpretation. Cases included these:

> R. Papa and R. Huna b. R. Joshua bought some sesame on the bank of the Royal Canal and hired some boatmen to bring it across, with a guarantee against any accident that might happen to it. After a time the canal was stopped up. The rabbis said to the boatmen, "Hire asses and deliver the material to us, since you guaranteed against any accident that might happen." The rabbis then appealed to Rava, who said to them, "White ducks who want to strip men of their cloaks![1] It is an

[1] Compare above, p. 135.

exceptional kind of accident [for which no one is responsible]."

(b. Git. 73a)

A certain man said to his sharecropper, "The general rule is that one irrigates the land three times annually, and takes a fourth of the produce. You irrigate four times, and take a third of the crop." Before he finished, the rain came. R. Joseph said, "He has not actually irrigated [the fourth time]." Rabbah said, "There was no need [for the fourth]...."

(b. Git. 74b)

A certain person sold a field to his neighbor, with a guarantee against any accident that might happen to it. They turned a canal through the land. The seller consulted Rabina, who said that he must go and clear the land, since he had guaranteed it against accidents. R. Aḥa b. Taḥalifa remarked to Rabina that it was an unusual accident ... The matter at last came before Rava, who ruled that it was an exceptional accident [and not covered by the agreement of sale].

(b. Git. 73a)

A certain man once leased a field from his neighbor and said, "If I do not cultivate it, I shall give you a thousand *zuz* [as a percentage of the lease]." He left a third of the field uncultivated. The Nehardeans said, "It is just that he should pay him 333 1/3rd *zuz*." Rava ruled, "It is an *'asmakhta* [an assurance that one will pay in case of non-fulfilment of a condition which a man is confident he will fulfill] which is not enforceable...."

(b. B.M. 104b)

A person once hired out an ass, and said to the hirer, "Do not go by way of Nehar Peqod, where there is water, but by way of Nersh, where there is none." He went by way of Nehar Peqod, and the ass died. He came before Rava, and made the plea, "I went by way of Nehar Peqod, but there was no water." Rava ruled....

(b. Bekh. 36a)

A certain man gave money for poppy seed. The price went up, and the vendor retracted, and said, "I have no poppy seed, take back your money." He would not take his money, and it was stolen. When they came before Rava, he ruled, "Since he told you to take back your money and you refused, he is not accounted as a paid bailee, and is not even an unpaid one...."

(b. B.M. 49a)

A certain man leased a field by the bank of the Old Royal Canal [near Maḥoza] on a money rental for sowing garlic. The Old Royal Canal was dammed up. When the man came to Rava, he said to him, "It is unusual for the Old Royal Canal to be dammed. It is a widespread blow. Go and deduct..."

(b. B.M. 106b)

Rava also commented on the *'isqa*, or business-partnership contract, whereby a man invested money with a trader who traded on their joint behalf. The investor took a greater share of the risk than of the profit (as in the case of R. 'Ilish above), receiving either half the profit and two-thirds of the loss, or a third of the profit and half the loss. The arrangement prevented the possibility of usury. The Nehardeans held that such an agreement was part-loan, part-bailment. If the partner dies, the funds cannot be held to be movable property in the heirs' hands, Rava held. He said also that if a man accepted an *'isqa* and suffered a loss, but then made it good, and had not yet informed the investor, he cannot then say to him, "Deduct the loss." The latter can reply, "You took the trouble of making it good to avoid being called a poor trader." Similarly, Rava said, "If two men accept an *'isqa* and profit, and one wants to divide before the agreed schedule to wind up the agreement, and the other objects and wishes to earn more profits, he can legally restrain him from closing the transaction."[1]

In the first three cases as well as the last cited above, the issue was whether a catastrophe constituted a foreseeable event which the contract would have covered, or so extraordinary a happening that no contract could have conceivably taken it into account. The decision of the courts rested upon their assessment of the possible intent of the contract, and this depended upon the nature of a disaster. The courts were therefore able to decide what private parties had intended by their original accord in ordinary times. In the fourth instance, similarly, the intent of the lessor had to be determined by the court. If he had merely promised something in full certainty that he would be able to carry it out, then it was not his intention to give over to the owner such a substantial claim. Rava's view was that it was a mere encouragement to complete the contract, but no enforceable stipulation. In the fifth case, the issue was whether the condition set forth in a contract was to be narrowly or broadly interpreted. If the owner said not to take a certain route because of the water, and no water in fact impeded the road, then the hirer could not be held responsible, the original clause having been irrelevant to the facts of the case. In the sixth story default on a contract caused an impasse, at which the injured party tried to force the vendor to keep his agreement. Rava ruled in favor of the vendor, and the injured party's error in failing to resort to court action, rather than attempting to force the issue on his own, became evident. (One recalls that the canals were dammed up, and then cleared out, in the course of

[1] b. B.M. 104b-105a.

the Romans' campaign in central Babylonia. It took place, however, after the death of Rava, and the normal management of the canals, not the exceptional situation brought on by the tactics of war, produced the cases cited here.) Rava's comments on the *'isqa* contract seem quite practical. There was no reason why the courts could not easily enforce rabbinical rules, and in fact the case of R. 'Ilish, cited earlier, must be interpreted in the light of Rava's comments on the business-partnership agreements permitted by the courts.

We once again note that the chief issues in fourth-century cases were exceptional. Normally the occurrence of an unusual event preventing fulfillment of a guaranteed contract would not have forced litigation over that contract. The language of contracts was usually sufficiently clear so that court interpretation was unnecessary. We have no cases in which the sole issue was, What do you do if one party simply fails to keep his part of a contractual agreement? The reason was surely *not* that no such cases came to court, but rather that they were not of sufficient interest for preservation.

We may reasonably assume that the courts enforced the provisions of a great many unremarkable agreements of all kinds, but that the bulk of their decisions therefore were not preserved, being of no special legal interest.

IX. Other Commercial Transactions

One cannot readily distinguish between commercial transactions and the various issues of debts, contracts, mortgages, bonds, and other loans, already considered above.[1] Here we shall review cases which do not readily fall into the earlier categories, but indicate more general supervision of market litigations. Such cases included the following rulings on transactions in wine, an expensive and perishable commodity:

> Rava once brought wine from a shop. After diluting it, he tasted it, found it was sour, and returned it to the shop. Abaye protested....
> (b. B.M. 60a)

> R. Joseph decided a case [in which wine went sour]....
> (b. B.B. 96b)

> A man was once moving a barrel of wine in the market [RYSTQ'][2]

[1] See pp. 220ff. Note also the decisions on the suitability of wine for sale, cited above, pp. 59-60, and see also b. B.B. 24b, 98a-b, for a similar case.

[2] Ristaqa = market-place outside of town, cf. Jastrow, s.v., II, 1475b.

of Maḥoza, and broke it on a projection, so he came before Rava, who ruled...

(b. B.M. 83a)

A man told his neighbor to buy four hundred barrels of wine. He did so. [He then claimed they had soured.] ... The case came before Rava, who said, "When four hundred barrels of wine turn sour, the facts should be widely known. Go and bring proof that the wine was originally sound..."

(b. B.M. 83a)

Rava said that if a man sold wine to a shopkeeper intending to retail it, with the shopkeeper keeping a percentage of the proceeds, and when about half had been sold, the wine soured, then the vendor must take the wine back from him. If a man accepted wine intending to sell it in the market of Vologasia, and the price fell by the time he got there, the original owner must bear the loss in value.[1]

Other kinds of commercial judgments involved renunciation of sale, when the seller wanted to cancel an agreed and completed transaction, or sale of movables or land on some contingency, as follows:

A man had silk beads [WRŠKY] for sale. He demanded six [*zuz*] while they were worth five. If five and a half were offered, he would have accepted it. A man came and said, "If I pay him five and a half, it is renunciation [since the overcharge was less than a sixth, it was not actionable]. Therefore I will pay six and sue him." When he went to Rava, he ruled [that he had no claim of fraud].

(b. B.M. 51a)

A certain man sold property intending to emigrate to Palestine, but when in the act of selling, he said nothing. Rava ruled, "It is a mental stipulation and not recognized."

(b. Qid. 49b)

A certain man sold his property with the intention of emigrating. He migrated but could not settle down. Rava ruled, "When one goes there, it is with the intention of settling, but this man has not done so. [The sale is cancelled]." Others state that he ruled, "He sold it intending to emigrate, and has done so. [The sale is valid.]"

(b. Qid. 50a)

On the laws of overcharge, Rava held that one may legally withdraw from a sale on account of any fraud in measure, weight or number, even if less than the standard of overreaching.

Still another kind of case centered upon what was included in an agreement of sale, as follows:

[1] b. B.M. 56b.

> A certain man said to another, "I sell you this olive press and all its accessories." There were shops abutting on to it on [the roofs of] which they used to spread out sesame seeds. R. Joseph was asked [whether they were included in the sale]. He said....
>
> (b. B.B. 68a)

The law long ago had provided numerous rules for such a situation as this, and the court had no difficulty in settling the case according to rabbinic traditions.

These cases all arose in normal market transactions. In the first two, the tendency of wine to sour or to fluctuate in price raised a number of issues, mainly to do with who must bear the loss. In the third, the willingness of the courts to set aside transactions in which fraud or overcharge had taken place was tested by a shrewd buyer. In the next two cases, the intent of a stipulation was at issue. It was made clear that a stipulation had to be stated expressly, but the more difficult matter of whether it had been met or not resulted in an ambiguous tradition in Rava's name. In the final case the issue was simply what had been comprehended in a sale-agreement.

Commercial transactions, contracts, various kinds of documents and deeds, debts, bonds, and mortgages—all of these matters could easily be settled by the Jewish courts. The Iranian government would certainly not trouble itself with such petty matters. Appeal of court rulings in such inconsequential cases, small sums or minor issues was hardly practical. One might, therefore, suppose that the Jewish courts were effective mainly in matters of commerce and disputes over movables, contracts, and the like, but not in far more important suits, such as real estate cases or litigations over immovables, for such cases could never have been finally decided without Persian confirmation.

x. Litigation over Immovable Property and Real Estate

The right of Jewish courts to decide cases about property rights obviously depended upon Iranian approval. In cases of immovables, there was always time to appeal to Iranian courts, which might have produced a different decision if appeal were possible. In such a situation, the Jewish courts could have done little to support their decisions. Commercial or contract cases, by contrast, produced a very quick result. Whether or not appeal was theoretically possible, the Jewish courts could so rapidly have effected their decisions as to present a *fait accompli*. In immovable property cases, on the other hand,

Iranian courts could always intervene. They probably never did, for an appeal, successful or otherwise, was never recorded or referred to. Litigations over immovables by Jewish courts therefore prove beyond any doubt that the Iranian government supported the Jewish court-system, validated its decisions when necessary, and refused to consider appeals from its courts, even in real estate cases, so long as decisions were congruent to Persian law.[1]

Reports of actual real estate cases include the following:

> A man against whom was a claim of a thousand *zuz* had two houses ['PDNY], each of which he sold (to a single person) for five hundred. The creditor thereupon came and seized one of them, and was going to seize the other. The purchaser took one thousand *zuz*, and went to the creditor and said, "If the one is worth one thousand *zuz*, well and good, but if not, take your thousand *zuz* and go [give up both houses]." Rami b. Ḥama proposed ... but Rava said to him...
>
> (b. Ket. 91b)

> A certain man against whom was a claim for a hundred *zuz* had two [small] plots of land each of which he sold for fifty [to the same purchaser]. The creditor came and seized one of them, and them came to seize the other. The purchaser took a hundred *zuz* and went to him and said, "If one is worth a hundred *zuz*, well and good, but if not, take the hundred *zuz* and go." R. Joseph proposed to say ... But Abaye said to him...
>
> (b. Ket. 91b)

Two further cases, one to Abaye, the other to Rami b. Ḥama, involved the same principle. In both, the borrower had not guaranteed the sale against further claims, so the purchaser had to make good on legitimate claims against his property. The courts commented upon, but do not seem to have intervened in, the matter. The discussions presupposed the possibility of intervention if necessary. Further land disputes coming before the courts included the following:

> R. Papa bought a field from a certain person who claimed it contained an area of twenty *griva*, but it contained only fifteen. He came before Abaye, who said to him, "You surely realized the size and accepted..."
>
> (b. B.B. 106a-b)

> A man once said to a neighbor, "If I sell this land, I will sell it to you," but he went and sold it to another person. R. Joseph said that the first one had acquired it. Abaye said to him, "But he had not settled the price..."
>
> (b. A.Z. 72a)

[1] See vol. III, pp. 334-335. Note the contrast in criminal matters, in which excessive punishment provoked state inquiries.

In the above cases, the courts were able to decide whether fraud had been committed in the sale of land, and whether a man had acquired an option to buy land, thus preventing others from purchasing it. More commonplace issues pertained to the settlement of disputed boundaries, as in the following:

> A certain man once made a boundary mark for another, [and one of the witnesses to whom he sold a nearby field] contested its ownership. The man died, and a guardian was appointed over his estate. The guardian came to Abaye...
>
> (b. Ket. 109b)

Many other sayings were handed on concerning the sale of houses and land, and what was included in such sales.[1] Rabbah said that if a man who owns half a field sells it and says, "I sell you the half which I have in the land," he sells half of the whole. If he says, "I sell half of the land that I have," he sells a quarter of the whole. If a man writes in the deed, "The boundary of the land is the land from which half has been cut off," he sells half.[2] Rava said, "If the seller says, 'I sell you a residence,' it means that he refers to apartments."[3] He also ruled about riparian sales, and held that if a man sells the shore of a river and its bed, the purchaser takes possession of the shore and the bed separately.[4] Other riparian cases included the following:

> Certain [farmers]in Be Ḥarmakh [near Pumbedita] went and dug a trench from the upper [waters of the] Shanvata [SNWWT'] canal and brought it around via their fields to the lower waters. Those higher up came and complained to Abaye, saying, "They are spoiling our canal [by slowing the current]." He said to them, "Deepen the bed a little." They said to him, "If we do so, the trenches will be dry." He replied [to the first group], "Then leave the canal alone."
>
> (b. Git. 60b)

The state made a continuing investment in the management and repair of the canals, which fructified Babylonia. Without the canals, nothing would grow. The right of the rabbinical court to decide a case in which water rights were at issue testifies to state authorization to do so, for without it, Abaye could have issued no such decree, nor, indeed, could he have heard the case at all. By contrast, the rabbinical courts had no authority whatever over non-Jewish property rights, including

---

[1] For comments of R. Joseph and Rava, b. B.B. 61a-62b.
[2] b. B.B. 62b.
[3] b. B.B. 67a.
[4] b. B.B. 67a.

rights to use of the canal-water, and could not order outsiders to obey Jewish law, as the following indicates:

> Rabbah b. R. Huna had a forest by the canal bank. He was asked to make a clearing [by the water's edge] and replied, "Let the owners above and below me first clear theirs, then I will clear mine." ... The neighboring forests belonged to the Chief Gendarme.[1] Therefore Rabbah b. R. Huna said, "If they cut down theirs, I will do so also, but if not, why should I? For if the ropes can be still hauled, they have room for walking. If not, they cannot walk there no matter what I do." Rabbah b. R. Naḥman was traveling in a boat and saw a forest on the canal bank. He said, "To whom does it belong?" "To Rabbah b. R. Huna," he was told. He cited the Scripture (Ezra 9:2), "Yea, the hand of the princes and rulers has been chief in this trespass." He ordered, "Cut it down, cut it down." Rabbah b. R. Huna came and found it cut down. "Whoever cut it down, may his branches be cut down." They say that during Rabbah b. R. Huna's lifetime, none of the children of Rabbah b. R. Naḥman remained alive.
>
> (b. B.M. 107b-108a)

First, Rabbah b. R. Huna clearly had no recourse, nor could he sue the rabbi who ordered his trees cut down. Hence he resorted only to a curse. On the other hand, the Jewish court manifestly had no power to order the Iranian official to cut down his trees and clear the passage. Rabbah b. R. Huna originally relied upon that fact. So the Jewish court *could* make rulings over Jewish property, but not over that of others, certainly not over state lands, in matters of riparian rights. No case more clearly illustrates the nature of Jewish courts' authority. Where they had power, it was complete, and appeal for restitution was not possible. Where they had no power, it was possible to do absolutely nothing.

Many cases arose from disputes about squatters' rights. Such disputes, in which the right of possession was disputed by owners unable to evict squatters, depended upon the rule that three years' actual possession conferred presumptive right [*ḥazaqah*]. R. Joseph found biblical evidence for the rule in Jer. 32:44. Rava held that the reason was that a man may forgo his rights of usufruct for a year or two, but not for three years.[2] The following litigations were recorded:

> A certain man said to another, "What right have you [lit: What do you want] in this house?" The other replied, "I bought it from you, and have used it for the period of [three years of] *ḥazaqah*." The other said, "I was in foreign markets [and could not protest]." "But I have

[1] *Bozorg Rufila*, see vol. III, p. 20, n. 1.

[2] b. B.B. 29a, Abaye and Rava discuss the matter further.

witnesses to prove you used to come here for thirty days every year." "Those thirty days," he replied, "I was occupied with my business." Rava ruled, "It is quite possible for a man to be fully occupied with his business for thirty days."

(b. B.B. 30a)

A certain man said to another, "What right have you on this land?" He replied, "I bought it from so-and-so, who told me he had bought it from you." The first said, "You admit that this land was once mine and that you did not buy it from me. Clear out then, you have no case with me." Rava ruled, "He was quite within his rights in what he said" [for the squatter had no proof that the man from whom he bought it had bought it from the original owner].

(b. B.B. 30a-30b)

A certain man said to his neighbor, "What right have you on this land?" He replied, "I bought it from so-and-so and have used it for [three years]." The other said, "So-and-so is a robber." The first replied, "I have witnesses to prove that I came and consulted you and you advised me to buy the property." The plaintiff replied, "The reason is that I preferred to go to law with you than with him." Rava ruled, "He replied quite legally...."

(b. B.B. 30b)

A certain man said to another, "What right have you on this land?" "I bought it from so-and-so, and I have had the use of it for [three years]." The first one said, "So-and-so is a robber." The other said, "But I have witnesses to prove that you came the evening [before] and said to me, 'Sell it to me.'" "My idea was to buy [what I was already] legally entitled to," the plaintiff answered. Rava ruled, "It is not unusual for a man to buy what he is already legally entitled to."

(b. B.B. 30b)

A certain man said to his neighbor, "What right have you on this land?" He replied, "I bought it from so-and-so and have had use of it for the period of the *ḥazaqah*." The other said, "But I have a title deed to prove I bought it from him four years ago." The other replied, "Do you think when I say the period of *ḥazaqah*, I mean only three years? I mean a lot of years." Rava said, "It is not unusual to refer to a long period of years as 'the period of *ḥazaqah*'...."

(b. B.B. 30b)

This man claims, "This land belonged to my father" and the other, "To my father." One brought witnesses to prove it belonged to his father, and the other did so to prove he had used it for the period of *ḥazaqah*. Rabbah said, "What motive did [the occupier] have to lie? He could [merely] have pleaded that he had purchased it and used it for the period of *ḥazaqah*...."

(b. B.B. 31a)

None of these cases contested the principle that *ḥazaqah*, or squatters' rights, might be attained through sufficient use of property. The issues were narrower and concerned various claims which came, or might have come (as in the final instance), before the court. Rava ruled that a man might claim he had no occasion or opportunity to inspect his property, and consequently to enter a protest against illegal occupation of his land; that a weak claim could be thrown out of court; that the owner might arrange by subterfuge for the recovery of his property, either by permitting a weaker party to purchase the land from a stronger one, or by promising to repurchase what was legally his own land. The conflicting claims before Rava, in which one party attempted to weaken the plea of another to have completed the period of the *ḥazaqah*, required the court to interpret the language of the first litigant. In the final suit, the court of Rabbah confirmed [or, was willing to confirm, in case litigation should arise] possession in the hands of the party who already possessed the land. Rava's rulings seem generally to have favored the plaintiff against the alleged squatter, but only a thorough survey of all such traditions could show whether in fact he consistantly *intended* to do so on principle. Other real estate cases involved the plea before Rabbah that a deed to land was forged,[1] a plea before Abaye in which the litigant brought only one witness in support of his claim,[2] and the decision of R. Naḥman b. R. Ḥisda about the inquiry of the people of Pum Nahara on whether ploughing a fallow helps to confer *ḥazaqah* or not.[3] In the case of the seizure by Tai tribesmen of land around Pumbedita, one recalls, Abaye was asked to register duplicate deeds, in case one was forcibly seized from them, and Abaye said it would be illegal to do so.[4] We have two further cases of eviction,[5] and one concerning the assignment of the cost of building a fence between land.[6] Other rulings concerned the following issues: making parapets for the roof of a house;[7] digging a pit near one's neighbor's boundary;[8] and setting up the bounds of a property.[9]

To summarize: The Jewish courts clearly had full control of cases involving real estate litigations among Jews. Normal issues of contested

[1] b. B.B. 32a-b.
[2] b. B.B. 33b-34a.
[3] b. B.B. 36b.
[4] b. B.B. 168b.
[5] See below, pp. 244-245.
[6] b. B.B. 5a, to Rava.
[7] Abaye, b. B.B. 6b.
[8] Abaye vs. Rava, b. B.B. 17b.
[9] R. Joseph, b. B.M. 103b.

ownership as well as boundary questions came to trial, along with cases on rights to the use of irrigation water, and on the duties of riparian owners to clear their banks. The courts could transfer ownership from one party to another, and settle other cases in whatever manner they thought legal. Actions in such matters testify, as I said, to the perfectly regular status of Jewish court decisions. If Jews did not voluntarily acquiesce in such decisions, they could have had no recourse to other authorities. I can think of no more striking evidence of the normality of Jewish community life, for were a serious persecution intended by the Sasanian administration, the first act would have been to strip the Jewish courts of all powers and subject the Jews to Sasanian court jurisdiction.[1]

xi. Bailments

Disputes arising from bailments were well within the courts' jurisdiction in earlier times.[2] In this period, the following litigations were reported:

> There was a shepherd to whom people daily entrusted cattle in the presence of witnesses. One day they did so without witnesses. Subsequently he completely denied [receipt of the cattle]. Witnesses testified he had eaten two of them. R. Zera ruled ... Abaye answered him...
>
> (b. B.M. 5a)

The discussion had to do with court procedures, specifically whether or not the bailee had to take an oath in connection with his claim. In the following cases, the dispute was over restitution for loss of the bailment:

> A certain man deposited money with his neighbor, who placed it in a cot of bulrushes. It was stolen. R. Joseph said, "Though it was proper care in respect to thieves, it was negligence in respect to fire. Hence the beginning [of the incident] was with negligence though its end was through an accident, and he is liable..."
>
> (b. B.M. 42a)

A certain man deposited money with his neighbor. When he demanded the return of the money, the bailee claimed, "I do not know

[1] Just as the Catholicus was the first target of persecution, so the exilarch would have been. The Iranian State could simply have removed the legal foundations for the exercise of exilarchic functions and thereby suspended the operations of the Jewish courts. I think it is obvious that the State did no such thing, and had not the slightest intention of upsetting the old arrangements with the Jewish community.

[2] Vol. III, pp. 316-317.

where I put it." Rava ruled, "Every plea of 'I do not know' constitutes negligence, so go and pay."

(b. B.M. 42a)

A certain man deposited money with his neighbor, who gave it over to his mother. She put it in her workbasket and it was stolen. Rava said, "What ruling shall judges give in this case? Shall we say to him, 'Go and repay?' He can reply, 'All who deposit do so with the understanding that the wife and children [may be entrusted with the bailment].' Shall we say to the mother, 'Go and pay?' She can plead, 'He did not tell me the money was not his own, that I should bury it.' Shall we say to him 'Why did you not tell her?' He can argue, 'I told her it was mine, so she was more likely to guard it well.' But he must swear that he entrusted that money to his mother and she must swear she had placed that money in her workbasket and it was stolen. Then the bailee goes free."

(b. B.M. 42a-b)

A certain steward for orphans bought an ox on their behalf and entrusted it to a herdsman. Having no [proper] teeth to eat with, it died. Rami b. Ḥama said, "What verdict shall judges give in this case? Shall we say to the steward, 'Go and pay?' He can reply, 'I entrusted it to the herdsman.' Shall we say to the herdsman, 'Go and pay?' He can plead, 'I put it together with other oxen and gave it food. I could not know it was not eating'...."

(b. B.M. 42b)

A shepherd was once pasturing his sheep by the Papa canal, and one slipped, fell into the water, [and drowned] ... Rabbah exempted him, with the remark, "What could he have done? He guarded them in the usual way." Abaye protested...

(b. B.M. 93a-b)

When a man did not accept responsibility for a bailment, Rava held that he is completely free from responsibility, and so ruled in an actual claim.[1] In the case of bailee's negligence, if the bailee afterward died a natural death, Abaye in Rabbah's name held that his estate was liable, and Rava in Rabbah's name held that the estate was not liable.[2] Rava ruled that a paid bailee who hands over his charge to another retains liability for all consequences.[3] Rabbah said that a person who took charge of a lost article which he has found and has to return to the owner is in the position of an unpaid bailee, and R. Joseph thought he

[1] b. B.M. 49b, see above, the case of the sesame sale, pp. 228-229.
[2] b. B.M. 36b.
[3] b. B.Q. 11b.

was a paid bailee.[1] In the following, Abaye as finder became such an unpaid bailee:

> Abaye was sitting before Rabbah when he saw some lost goats standing, and he took a clod and threw it at them. Rabbah said to him, "You are now liable for them, so get up and return them [to their owner]."
>
> (b. B.M. 30b)

Other possible cases were discussed, and there is no doubt that practical situations would have arisen in which the conclusions would have been put into effect.[2]

XII. Documents and Deeds

Proper documents could produce court action, and those improperly drawn up resulted in considerable loss, not only in relationships of marriage and divorce, but in all business, commercial, and property transactions. The court scribes drew up such documents, and others who did so had to conform to the court rules. In consequence, the courts exercised substantial authority over all kinds of legal documents and deeds, as illustrated by the following cases of deeds of gift:

> A certain woman came before Rava [to ask for a ruling on a deed of gift in which she wrote, 'From life'. She now wished to withdraw the gift.] Rava decided in accordance with his tradition [that she was not entitled to withdraw]. She nagged him. He said to R. Papa b. R. Ḥanan, his scribe, "Go, write for her..."
>
> (b. B.B. 153a)

> A certain deed of gift was witnessed by two robbers. R. Papa b. Samuel wished to validate it on the grounds that their ineligibility as witnesses had not been made public. Rava said to him...
>
> (b. Sanh. 26b)

> A certain deed of gift was attested by two brothers-in-law. R. Joseph thought to validate it...
>
> (b. Sanh. 28b)

Forgery of a deed was discovered in court, as in the following:

> In a certain [deed] it was entered, "a third of an orchard", and subsequently the buyer [forged the document to read] "and an or-

---

[1] b. B.Q. 56b.
[2] b. B.Q. 108b.

chard". He appeared before Abaye, who said to him, "Why has the *vav* so much space around it?" Having been bound, the man confessed.
(b. B.B. 167a)

In a certain deed was entered, "The portion of Reuben and Simeon, brothers". They had a brother whose name was "Brother", ['ḥy] and the buyer added to it a *vav*, and converted [the word into] 'and Brother'. [w'ḥ'y] When the case came before Abaye [the purchaser claimed the third share], Abaye said to him, "Why is there so little space around the *vav*." The man was bound and confessed.
(b. B.B. 167a)

A certain deed bore the signatures of Rava and R. Aḥa b. Adda. The holder of the deed came before Rava, who said, "This signature is mine. However I never signed before R. Aḥa b. Adda." The man was bound and confessed. Rava asked him, "I can understand how you forged mine, but how could you manage R. Aḥa b. Adda's, whose hand trembles." The man replied, "I put my hand on a rope bridge..."
(b. B.B. 167a)

The courts therefore were quite able to detect, and punish forgeries of commercial documents. In the following cases, we see that they were empowered to determine the disposition of other issues involving forged legal documents:

A certain man said to another, "What are you doing on this land?" He replied, "I bought it from you, and here is the deed of sale." "It is forged," said the first. The other party whispered to Rabbah, "It is true that it is a forged document. I had a proper deed but I lost it, so I thought it best to come to court with some sort of document." Rabbah ruled [in his favor].
(b. B.B. 32a-b)

A certain man said to another, "Pay me the hundred *zuz* that I claim from you, and here is the bond." The other claimed it was forged. Leaning over to Rabbah, the first admitted it, but claimed he had lost the genuine document. Rabbah ruled [in his favor].
(b. B.B. 32b)

Abaye ruled in a case in which a man paid a lender in behalf of another man and reclaimed his bond, which he presented to the court.[1] R. Joseph adjudicated a case in which two deeds of sale relating to the same field came before R. Joseph. One was dated "On the fifth of Nisan" and the other "In Nisan." R. Joseph confirmed the property in the hands of the person whose document read "Fifth of Nisan." The

[1] b. B.B. 32b.

other then requested that the court write a *tirpa*, a document authorizing seizure of property sold to a third party, so that he might seize and recover his money.[1] Rava similarly examined a court document, found it improperly drawn up, and refused to enforce it.[2] Abaye interpreted the language of a deed:

> In a certain deed it was written, "Six hundred and a *zuz*". R. Sheravya' asked Abaye, "['Does it mean] six hundred *'istira* and a *zuz*, or six hundred *perutot* and a *zuz*?" He replied, "Dismiss the question of *perutot*, which could not have been written in the deed, since they would have been added up and converted into *zuzim*...."
>
> (b. B.B. 166b-167a)

Abaye also held that one who had to present his signature at court (for example, to help the court determine that his signature is the same as one appearing to attest a court document) must not present it at the end of a scroll, for a stranger might find it and write in that he had a claim of money upon him.[3] Rava held that a document in Persian which has been handed over in the presence of Jewish witnesses was sufficient warrant for recovering property on which there was no previous lien.[4] When R. Papa had to deal with a Persian document drawn up in a Persian archive, he would have two Persians read it separately, without telling them his purpose. If their readings agreed, he would permit recovery, on the strength of such a document, even of mortgaged property.[5] Rava would give his scribes careful instructions on how to draw up a bill of divorce[6] as did Abaye.[7] Rava laid down the formula as follows,

> "We are witnesses how so-and-so son of so-and-so dismissed and divorced his wife from this day and for all time...."
>
> (b. Git. 85b)

These cases and stories of court actions show that the Jewish judges were fully able to require proper preparation of such papers, knew how to detect forgeries, displayed great care in the choice of language for deeds and documents, and were able to interpret that language in court-actions. In the first instance, Rava decided on the basis of the legal

---

[1] b. Ket. 94b. See *Ozar HaGeonim*, vol. VIII, p. 329.
[2] b. Ket. 104b.
[3] b. B.B. 167a.
[4] b. Git. 11a.
[5] b. Git. 19b.
[6] b. Git. 84b.
[7] b. Git. 85b.

formula whether a deed of gift was revocable; in the second, R. Papa b. Samuel evaluated attestation of a document by people whose testimony would normally not be accepted in court, and in the third, a similar issue, for other reasons, came before R. Joseph. Abaye's and Rava's rulings on forged documents suggest that the courts would not hesitate to force a suspect to testify against himself. Claims of forgery were not however always decisive, for a man could admit a forgery and by so doing, establish the truthfulness of a more important claim. In the two cases above, Rabbah thought that the man could simply have denied the forgery and so establish his claim upon the basis of the document he actually held in his hand. Admitting the forgery when he did not have to, the man was able to secure greater credibility than otherwise. Bonds and two deeds of sale for the same field were likewise adjudicated. The language of deeds was not always clear, and Abaye's ruling was based upon common sense. The rabbis could understand spoken Pahlavi, but could not read it (which is not surprising, given its defective alphabet). They nonetheless managed with the help of Persians to judge cases based on Pahlavi documents. They could scarcely hope to reject out of hand all documents written in Persian, especially if they expected the Persian government to respect bills issued in their courts. A court system had to have the power to issue legal documents, to control their enforcement, and to judge cases upon their basis. It is clear that the Jewish courts had all the necessary power to do so.

XIII. Workers and Slaves

The courts judged cases involving payment of workers' salaries and the rights of sharecroppers. Slaves were regarded as property pure and simple, and so numerous decisions concerning their disposition came to court. The fourth-century rabbis never condemned the institution of slavery. It was an accepted part of economic life. Because of their jurisdiction over property, the rabbis had considerable authority over slaves, never used to mitigate the conditions in which slaves lived out their lives.

Two cases of eviction of sharecroppers were recorded in this period:

> R. Joseph had a gardener, who worked for one-half the profits. He died and left five sons-in-law. R. Joseph said, "Beforehand, there was one, now there are five. Beforehand they did not rely on each other [to do the work] and so caused no loss, while now they will." He said to

them, "If you accept the improvements due to you and quit, it is well. If not, I will evict you without [even] giving you the improvements..."

(b. B.M. 109a)

Ronia was Rabina's gardener. He spoiled the garden, and was dismissed. He then went to Rava and [complained about how he was treated]. Rava ruled, "He has acted within his rights." "But he gave me no warning," the gardener claimed. "No warning was necessary," Rava answered. Rava held that elementary teachers, gardeners, cuppers, butchers' and the town scribe were all regarded as on permanent notice...

(b. B.M. 109a-b)

These cases both involved rabbis who knew their rights and exercised them. Rabbah b. R. Huna held that the market traders of Sura are not guilty of transgressing the commandment not to hold back wages when they do not pay them promptly, because they pay on the market-day. All tacitly understand that under that stipulation the workers are employed.[1] There can be little doubt that the contrary view would have led to action on the part of Rabbah b. R. Huna to see to it that the workers were paid day by day. As a result, the workers must have had to wait for their wages, perhaps to borrow to obtain immediate necessities until that time.

Rava held that if one engaged laborers to cut dikes, and rain fell so that the work was impossible, if the employer inspected the situation in the previous evening, the loss is the workers'; otherwise the loss is the employer's. He said that if one hired workers for irrigation and it rained, the workers lose; if the river overflowed, the employer must bear the loss, but he pays them at the reduced rate of unemployed laborers.[2] Rava ruled that if one engaged workers for work, and they finished it in the middle of the day, he can give them easier work, or work of the same difficulty, but not of more difficulty; he must pay them for the full day of work.[3] These rulings reveal an effort to come to a just appraisal of the rights of both parties.

Slaves had few, if any rights. The rabbis did not favor the emancipation of non-Jewish slaves, and did little to secure the emancipation of Jewish ones, beyond the biblical requirements. The following reveals the contemporary view:

[1] b. B.M. 111a.
[2] b. B.M. 76b-77a.
[3] b. B.M. 77a.

> There was a certain female slave in Pumbedita who was immorally used by men. Abaye said, "Were it not for the opinion of Rav Judah in Samuel's name, that whoever emancipates his heathen slave breaks a positive commandment, I would compel her master to make out a deed of emancipation for her ...."
>
> (b. Git. 38a)

Rabbah similarly said that men become impoverished for emancipating slaves, inspecting property on the Sabbath, and taking their main Sabbath meal when the sermon was given in the school.[1] *Refraining* from freeing slaves was thus equated with observance of the Sabbath and hearing the Sabbath lesson, as an act of very great religious consequence. We do not know whether ordinary people frequently emancipated their slaves, so necessitating a rabbinic pronouncement against it. In any case, we know full well that Rabbah thought it a sin equivalent to violating the Sabbath. These views were quite consistent with those of the earlier generation.[2]

Contested title to a slave was litigated in the following case:

> Rami b. Ḥama and R. ʿUqba b. Ḥama bought a female slave in partnership. The arrangement was that one should have her services during the first, third, and fifth years, the other during the second, fourth, and sixth. The title was contested, and the case came before Rava. He said to the brothers, "Why did you make this arrangement? So that neither of you should obtain the presumptive right [*ḥazaqah*] against the other? Just as you have no presumptive right against each other, so you have no presumptive right against outsiders ...."
>
> (b. B.B. 29b)

In general, Jews were enslaved because they had to sell themselves to obtain funds, either to feed their families, or to pay debts or taxes, as in the following cases:

> Some of the servants of R. Joseph b. Ḥama used to seize slaves of people who owed them money, and made them perform work. Rava (his son) said to him, "Why do you allow this to be done?"...
>
> (b. B.Q. 97a)

> R. Papa said to Rava, "The master must have observed the men of Papa b. Abba's house, who advance sums of money on people's accounts to pay their head taxes, and then force them into their service. Do they, when set free, required a deed of emancipation or not?" He replied, "... thus said R. Sheshet, The surety of these people is deposited

---

[1] b. Git. 38b.

[2] Vol. III, pp. 24-29.

in the king's archives, and the government has ordained that whosoever does not pay his tax must become the slave of him who pays it for him...."

(b. Yev. 46a=b. B.M. 73b)

In the former instance, the slave was treated as property, to be seized in payment of debts just like land or movable goods. In the latter, the rabbis found themselves in the position of having to approve the practices of the Iranian government. In no instance did they collect funds to pay such a tax and so prevent people from being enslaved. They apparently did not use charity funds for that purpose.[1] Hence poor people must have found that the Jewish government did little, if anything, to prevent their enslavement.

Other opinions on slavery include that of R. Naḥman b. Isaac, If a man bought a slave on condition that he would set him free, he would give him a written declaration, "Your person shall become yours as from now as soon as I have bought you."[2] He held with reference to Ex. 21:3, that if a slave has a wife and children when entering service, his master may give him a heathen slave to beget further slaves; but if not, his master may not do so.[3] Abaye tended to interpret Scriptures applying to slaves in a lenient manner, and held that God had favored slaves.[4] Rava held that the Jewish slave belongs bodily to his master.[5] Rava also said that if a master emancipated his slave, a creditor could not reenslave him.[6]

XIV. Damages

In the exceptional situations created by damages and torts, the rabbis' task was to maintain public order. Their main concern was to assure that people did not have to take the law into their own hands but

[1] Yet such funds *were* collected to ransom captives.
[2] b. Yev. 93b.
[3] b. Git. 8b, 45a, b. B.Q. 20a.
[4] b. 'Arakh. 30b, b. B.Q. 20a.
[5] b. Qid. 28a.
[6] b. B.Q. 90a, Ket. 59b, Git. 40b, etc. See also *Oẓar HaGeonim*, ed. B. M. Lewin, X, p. 81. For a brief account of Christian attitudes toward slavery, see Marvin R. Vincent, *A Critical and Exegetical Commentary on the Epistles to the Philippians and to Philemon* (N.Y. 1897) pp. 162-169. Note also the remarks of Vladimir G. Lukonin, *Persia II*, trans. from Russian by James Hogarth (N.Y.-Cleveland, 1967), *passim*. I regret I do not now have access to the scholarship of Soviet Iranists, in particular on the question of slavery and other social-economic relationships, except for the relevant passages of N. Pigulevskaja, *Les Villes de l'État Iranien* (Paris, 1963), pp. 79-92, 141-150, etc.

could resort to the courts for quick and effective justice. R. Naḥman b. Isaac and Rava both were firm in holding that one may not execute his own justice.[1]

Evidence that the fourth-century masters judged cases of damages in the law courts derives from the following cases:

> In a case where a goat noticed turnips on top of a cask and climbed up and consumed them and broke the jar, Rava ordered full payment....
> (b. B.Q. 20a)

> The goats of Be Tarbu used to damage R. Joseph's [fields]. He said to Abaye, "Go tell their owners to keep them indoors." Abaye said, "What is the use? Even if I go, they will say to me, 'Let the master build a fence....'" It was announced by R. Joseph, or, some say, by Rabbah, "[that...] in the case of goats kept for the market but meanwhile guilty of causing damage, a warning is given to their owners. If they comply, well and good, but if not, we tell them, 'Slaughter the animals immediately, and sit at the butcher's stall to get whatever money you can.'"
> (b. B.Q. 23b)[2]

> Such a case occurred [in which a utensil was broken] in Pumbedita and Rava ordered compensation to be paid.
> (b. B.Q. 27b)

> A certain woman once entered the house of another to bake bread, and the goat of the owner came, ate up the dough, became sick and died. Rava ordered the woman to pay damages...
> (b. B.Q. 48a)

> An ass once bit off the hand of a child. R. Papa b. Samuel ruled in the case, "Go forth and assess the value...." Rava said to him, "Have we not learned..." Abaye replied... The father of the child said, "I do not want [this method of valuation] as it is degrading." They said, "What right have you to deprive the child of his payment?" He replied, "When he comes of age, I shall reimburse him..."
> (b. B.Q. 84a)

> An ox once chewed the hand of a child. The case came before Rava, who said, "Go and assess the child as if it were a slave..."
> (b. B.Q. 84a)

What is most important in these cases is the fact that the courts decided them. In the first and third, the court determined that the owner was liable, and ordered payment for damages. In the second, Abaye

---

[1] b. B.Q. 28a. But rabbis could do so, see below, p. 314.

[2] See B. M. Lewin, ed., *Ozar HaGeonim* XII, p. 26.

was unable to protect R. Joseph's property, because the neighbors had a perfectly legitimate response. R. Joseph, or Rabbah, was able to announce a public ruling which would protect the entire community from similar inconvenience. On the other hand, we do not know whether the ruling was carried out, or whether it constituted a mere threat. In the fourth case, the task of the court was to determine whether the woman was liable for the death of the goat. In the fifth and sixth, the issue was how to determine the exact amount of compensation. There was no doubt however that compensation would be ordered, assessed by court procedures, and duly paid. In the following, the issue was the extent of secondary liability for damages:

> R. Huna b. Judah happened to be at Be 'Evyone and visited Rava, who asked him, "Have any cases recently been decided by you?" He replied, "I had to decide the case of a Jew whom pagans forced to show them another's property, and I ordered him to pay." Rava said, "Go and reverse the judgment in favor of the defendant...."
>
> (b. B.Q. 117a)

> Two men were quarreling about a net. Both claimed it. One went and surrendered it to the royal *frahanga*[1] [who confiscated it, for by Sasanian law, all ownerless objects belong to the state]. Abaye ruled... Rava said... Rava therefore said, "We would have to impose an excommunication upon him until he brings back [the net] and appears before the court."
>
> (b. B.Q. 117a)

> A certain man had a silver cup which had been deposited with him, and when attacked by thieves, he took and handed it over to them. He was summoned before Rava [current printed text: Rabbah], who declared he was exempt. Abaye said, "Was he not rescuing himself by means of another man's property?"...
>
> (b. B.Q. 177b)

> A certain man had a purse of money for redemption of captives deposited with him. When attacked by thieves, he handed it over. Rava ruled he was exempt...
>
> (b. B.Q. 117b)

> A certain man managed to get his ass on a ferry boat before the people in the boat had disembarked. The boat was in danger of sinking, so a man came along and pushed the ass into the river, where it drowned. When the case came to Rava, he declared him exempt...
>
> (b. B.Q. 117b)

---

[1] On *parangaria*. See '*Arukh* VI, 415A, and I, s.v. 'PRHNG. The meaning here is *judge*.

In the above cases, the courts had to determine whether a man could be held liable for causing loss to another through no ultimate act of his own. In the first, the man was forced to reveal property for tax purposes; the property was confiscated, and the court had to decide whether the informer was liable. In the second, a man had in anger destroyed property which might actually belong to another, by giving it over to the state. In the third, fourth, and fifth cases, a man saved himself by giving up another's property to thieves or other misfortune. In all cases, the liabilities were determined by the court, which enjoyed full authority.

Other litigations of damages included the following:

> Two men were traveling together, one tall, the other short. The tall one was riding on an ass, and had a [linen] sheet, while the short one was wearing a cloak, and walked on foot. On coming to a river, he took his cloak and placed it on the ass, and took the linen and covered himself with it [since linen could stand the water better than wool]. Then the water swept the sheet away. They came before Rava, who ruled...
>
> (b. B.M. 81b)

> Some porters broke a barrel of wine belonging to Rabbah b. R. Huna. He seized their garments, and they complained to Rava, who ordered their return....
>
> (b. B.M. 83a)

> A man borrowed an axe from his neighbor, and it broke. Rava said to him, "Go and bring witnesses that you did not put it to unusual use, and you are free from liability..."
>
> (b. B.M. 96b)

> Meremar b. Ḥanina hired a mule to the people of Khuzistan, and went out and helped them to load it. Through their negligence, it died. Rava held them liable...
>
> (b. B.M. 97a)

> Rava b. R. Ḥanan had some date trees adjoining a vineyard of R. Joseph, and birds used to roost in the trees and fly down and damage the vines. Rava b. R. Ḥanan told R. Joseph to cut down his trees. The latter said, "But I have kept them [the proper distance] away..."
>
> (b. B.B. 26a)

These cases pertained to negligence, and the rabbinical courts had no problem in determining liabilities and inflicting penalties. The claim of Rabbah b. R. Huna against the workers was not evaluated; he simply could not seize their garments to compensate the damage he had suffered. In the case of the borrowed axe, the issue was whether the man had done anything out of the ordinary; if not, he incurred no special liability. The same rule pertained to the case of the hired mule. In the final case, the issue was whether the owner had done all he was required to do to prevent damages. Other sayings included many which must have guided court decisions in practical cases.[1] Court rulings in cases of torts and damages generally resulted in exchanges of property, either as a penalty or in compensation for damages. Control of the courts over the possessions of the Jewish community made it easy to enforce all such rulings. In consequence, people could normally look to the courts for quick and fair actions and did not have to undertake vigilante justice.

XV. Summary and Conclusions

Babylonian Jewish government consisted of more than what rabbis said and did, but the bulk of our information tells us little more than that. I have stressed the circumstances which produced cases, as earlier,[2] since my interest is not in the history of Jewish law, but in the substance of Jewish politics and of religious-historical sociology. It is perfectly clear that the political structure, constituted by a Jewish millet-regime headed by the exilarchate, supported and legitimized by the Sasanian authorities, actually was made up of local courts and related authorities responsible for maintaining an orderly and peaceful community life. These courts were staffed by the graduates of rabbinical law-schools. By the fourth century, the schools had produced a considerable number of well-trained lawyers, and these graduates served as the chief, though probably not the only,[3] means by which the exilarchate carried out its political responsibilities.

What, exactly, did the Sasanians expect the Jewish courts to adjudicate? I think it clear that determinations of personal status and litigations over property of all kinds were the sole state-recognized functions. When, moreover, we review the kinds of examples, we cannot suppose the Jewish courts were particularly important. On the whole, the size of litigations corresponded to those likely to come before a small-claims

[1] E.g., b. Git. 50a, Rava on land payments for damages, also b. B.Q. 7a, Abaye and Rava, b. B.Q. 85b, Rava, etc.

[2] See Vol. II, pp. 251-260, and Vol. III, pp. 319-334.

[3] Note above the reference to uninformed "arbitrators," who not knowing the law simply divided disputed property among the several claimants, rather than coming to a decision based upon a true assessment of what Jewish law required.

court in modern society. Thefts involved a book, or a few rams. Betrothal cases concerned a few *zuz*, a willow-branch, some onions, or a piece of silk. Settlements of marriage-contracts required litigation of a robe of fine wool, a silver cup. A few cases of alleged adultery were recorded, all of sufficient innocence for the court to rule that no adultery had taken place. Ceremonies of *ḥalizah* and the preparation and delivery of proper divorce documents hardly amounted to weighty matters of state. The exilarchate itself could not have paid much attention to the technicalities of the dissolution of a marriage. Divorce litigations in any event were provoked by peculiar and exceptional circumstances; normally a man could divorce his wife without court intervention. The settlement of estates entailed somewhat larger sums of money. "Four hundred *zuz*," a round number, represented approximately enough capital for two years' maintenance of a woman, it is generally supposed. The provision by the court for widows—of food, wine, clothing—represented humble and more typical matters. Even most estate-cases pertained to rather small claims, such as a few trees, a slave, the choice plot of ground. Settlement of debts, collections of mortgages and bonds, and the like required rulings on somewhat more substantial sums, but the real issues were still relatively inconsequential, a hundred *zuz*, or whether a pledged spoon or knife had to be returned. Broken contracts likewise were entered into by a few ferrymen and sharecroppers, or devolved upon a hired ass, the purchase of some wine or poppy-seed, a flooded field. Other commercial litigations demanded that the courts decide about a few *zuz* worth of silk beads, some sour wine, the sale of a wine press or of a field. Property cases similarly involved alleged fraud in a relatively small plot, the supposed existence of an option to purchase a field, the use of some canal water, and very frequently, squatter's rights over a house or a field the owner had not seen for some time and the eviction of tenant farmers. Damages were done to a jar or utensil, a dead goat, a silver cup, a purse of money stolen in part through negligence, a broken ax and a broken wine-barrel. I have continually stressed the circumstances and facts of cases because it seems to me these clearly reveal the real substance of issues left in the rabbis' hands. With a few exceptions, strikingly petty sums of money or barely consequential amounts of property were all that the courts actually adjudicated. So in general the affairs of mainly the lower classes of society were subject to rulings by the rabbinical courts. Large commercial transactions, for many thousands of *zuz* worth of silk or pearls, wine, or beer, enormous property transactions involving a whole village or town, claims of a considerable number of workers against a single employer, or vice versa, the affairs of large estates, rich landowners, big businessmen, important officials—none of these occur with any frequency, if at all, in the reports available to us. The reason only in part was that not many Jews seem to have been located in the higher strata of society. In part, it must have been that the rabbinical courts' jurisdiction was limited. The absence of significant criminal actions, apart from the single murder case before the exilarch, moreover is suggestive. It would indicate that some other authority than the rabbinical courts was responsible for criminal prosecutions. I therefore suppose that the exilarch must have held the chief responsibility—if the Sasanian courts did not retain it for themselves—for anything that really mattered.

The rabbis could not have agreed, however, that the humble and petty issues before them were of no consequence. It was their view, a very old one in Judaism, that the least and humblest affairs, as much as the largest and most weighty ones, testified to Heaven about the moral state of society. If Amos had condemned Israel of old because a poor man was cheated of his shoes, then one can hardly be surprised that a later rabbi insisted upon the return of a cooking utensil given in pledge. What was important to the rabbis was that justice should prevail. They knew that if justice did not characterize the streets, petty trading market, small farms and shops, then great affairs of commerce and the state would not likely prove to be morally superior. We have already stressed that the ethics of daily life—and that meant the life of exchanges of onions and the use of water in a small canal—determined the destiny of Israel according to rabbinic theology.[1] So the petty cases settled by courts controlled by the rabbis mattered very much to them.

As I said, it may be that some of the instances we have cited above do not always necessarily report actual court cases. The fixed language of so many reports, beginning "A certain man...," the conventional sums of money, such as a hundred or four hundred *zuz*, and the fairly fixed and limited forms in which the cases were written down—these characteristics raise some doubt in my mind that every report actually recorded a real case. Moreover, we have already wondered about the circumstances which led to some court decisions, for occasionally, the reason a case came to court is not at all obvious. We can readily assume that in litigations of property, one or both parties brought the case to court. In other matters, however, one can only assume that if a rabbi gave a decision or an opinion, and if that decision or opinion is recorded

[1] Vol. II, pp. 52-57, 180-187, 236-240.

in the context of a specific circumstance, then some actual event underlay it. Even in such "cases" as did not really come to court, however, the story of a theoretical event does provide helpful information about what the schools and the tradents thought was taking place in court—and what was not coming to rabbinical courts at all. Hence at the very least, we have an accurate picture of the mind of the schools about the raw material of the courts. On the other hand, some theoretical dicta may in fact conceal actual court action, as in the false ascription of an opinion to Rava.

We need not dwell too long on the curious contrast between reports about observance of the laws on ritual matters and those dealing with personal status and property transactions. The former clearly revealed that the rabbis could do little if anything through their political position to enforce, or even to guide, the observance of many laws related to the Sabbath and festivals, holy objects and taboos about sex, food, and clothing, and the like. The exceptions to the rule were mostly explicable in terms of the rabbis' public position. They supervised the marketplaces, and so could determine what kind of meat and wine was suitable for sale and what was not. They could thus instruct the butchers and supervise the abattoirs. As communal officials, they could also see to it that the Sabbath-limits were properly established. They did not have to wait to be consulted, but simply went and carried out the law as they saw fit. On the other hand, having no special place in the synagogue, they had more influence over the disposition of synagogue property than over the rites and prayers normally carried on there. They could preach, as we shall see, and so acquired some further influence over the ordinary people through public instruction in the synagogue. But that influence cannot be confused with power exerted by public officials and judges. On the other hand, the extensive legal discussions about Grace after Meals, prayers to be said on various special occasions, Sabbath and festival rites and taboos, the preparation of the home for Passover, the conduct of the Passover *Seder*, building the *Sukkah*, observance of the New Year and the Day of Atonement, special fast days, reading the Scroll of Esther on Purim, conduct on the intermediate days of festivals, not to mention the whole range of laws dealing with other aspects of ritual life—few if any of these discussions produced such significant exemplifications of popular obedience in this or any earlier period as to persuade us that ordinary people were much affected. It is similarly curious, as I said, that while the courts could easily determine proper judicial procedure, decide on how documents were to be drawn up, determine the rules of evidence and oath-taking, by contrast the Talmudic discussions on the laws of the Sanhedrin and the structure of Jewish judiciary do not indicate that Babylonian courts were even set up according to rabbinic tradition. I should suppose that the exilarch organized the courts and administration without reference to rabbinical traditions on the subject. Once set up, however, they were run as the rabbis wanted.

It is therefore clear that for the rabbis, the limited control they now enjoyed could not have been wholly satisfactory. They did not regard the Mishnaic laws about civil damages and torts as holier than those about prayers or the Sabbath. It was simply that their circumstances permitted them to enforce the former in court, but only to teach about the latter in school. The reason they acquiesced in an only partially acceptable situation was that they hoped in time to improve it. They could not have aspired to less than complete, public, communal conformity to the "whole Torah," both the written part all the people seemed to know about, and the oral traditions only the rabbis now possessed. They chose to cooperate with the exilarchate to enforce as much of the law as they could—and dared. But in time, they intended to reconstruct Jewish community life so that the whole Torah would pertain, so far as relevant. And, as I said, when they succeeded, they fully expected that all of it *would* be relevant, for on that day, the Messiah would come, the Temple would be rebuilt, and the Jewish people would be restored to its own land and to its own government. In Meanwhile, they wanted to construct as full a replica of that ideal situation as was possible before redemption, so as to effect that redemption. The school, like the monastery of the Christian community nearby,[1] would provide the opportunity. There the Torah was studied and carried out in all possible detail by the masters and disciples. In the school, man in the image of God and society in the paradigm of the heavenly academy were to be embodied. And from the school students and masters would go forth to exemplify the will of God, eventually to reshape the life of the streets, homes, farms, and marketplace to conform to it.

The remarkable fact is that the rabbis were able to see themselves as lawyers and politicians at all. They exercised no sovereignty. The state was alien. Outside pressure laid stress upon keeping a peaceful and orderly community, but certainly not upon keeping to the laws of Moses just exactly as the rabbis in particular exposited them. Thus the

---

[1] Vol. III, pp. 195-202.

cohesion of the Jewish community produced by that external pressure did not in any way depend upon, or result in faith in, the supremacy of *rabbinic* law.[1] The state lent a measure of sovereignty to an exilarch from whom the rabbis were increasingly alienated. To the rabbis, the State gave no sovereignty whatever, nor in effect did the exilarch. The schools were their nation and constituted their real sovereignty. If their laws were academic laws, for their part, rabbis made no distinction between theoretical and practical law nor recognized as final or acceptable a disjuncture between sacred law and the reality of actual practice. When Pharisaic-Tannaitic-Rabbinic Judaism determined to conquer a nation through the steady extension of its concept of the school to all of national life, I cannot say. But it was when the last Jewish state before the present one lost all semblance of sovereignty, with the fall of Jerusalem in 70 A.D., that R. Yoḥanan ben Zakkai actually made the schoolhouse into the sole legitimate instrumentality of Jewish sovereignty. From that time onward, sovereignty as others knew it began to pass out of the hands of other powers in Jewry and into the houses of study, so far as the rabbis were concerned. In time, they proved in practice to be quite correct.

One must ask, To what degree did the rabbis now approach the realization of this ideal? The following tables survey the reports of cases and other evidence suggesting that the rabbis were able either to enforce the law or to influence people to keep it. The tables are not meant to provide more than suggestive evidence. Some items which have been excluded would lead to the supposition of rather widespread law enforcement or obedience. For example, while I have not counted as a "case" Abaye's saying that one should see how "the people" say a blessing over water, that dictum may be significant. It may mean that he was willing to rely upon popular practice and therefore approved it. Or it may mean that he meant by "people" *the common practice of the schools*. Similarly, though more conclusively, the saying that one posts public notices to inform people of the dates of holidays has not been counted. Nonetheless, that saying presupposed that people did keep Passover and the Day of Atonement, and provides important evidence that the rabbis decided when these festivals took place. Other bracketed examples are included to indicate the range and quality of evidence testifying to rabbinical authority and influence.

---

[1] Compare Joseph Schacht, *An Introduction to Islamic Law* (Oxford, 1964), pp. 2-3.

I. *b. Berakhot*

	Ca. 310-330 [*Rabbah, R. Joseph*]	*Ca. 330-350* [*Rava, Abaye*]
Court Cases		
Questions from Outside of the Academy		1. b. Ber., 54a. Man saved by miracle told by Rava what blessing to say.
Stories and Sayings about Enforcement of, or Obedience to, Law Outside of the Academy	**1. [b. Ber. 31a (= b. Nid. 66a), R. Zera, Israelite women are strict about menstrual taboos.] 2. b. Ber. 33b, Rabbah comments on error in disciple's prayer, in synagogue.	*[1. b. Ber. 45a, *Re* blessing for water, Abaye (or R. Joseph), "Go see what the people do."] 2. b. Ber. 50a, Rava comments on disciple's error in synagogue prayer at Abi Gobar.

* General statement, not counted as a case.
** Duplicate. Duplicates are signified by [—] and are counted only once.

II. *b. Shabbat*

	Ca. 310-330 [*Rabbah, R. Joseph*]	*Ca. 330-350* [*Rava, Abaye*]
Court Cases		
Questions from Outside of the Academy		
Stories and Sayings about Enforcement of, or Obedience to, Law Outside of the Academy		1. b. Shab. 94b, R. Naḥman b. Isaac permitted carrying a corpse out of the house on the Sabbath. 2. b. Shab. 134b, Rava ruled a man might bathe an infant on the Sabbath in the usual way. 3. b. Shab. 147b, Rava told Maḥozans how to carry soldiers' cloaks on Sabbath.

III. *b. 'Eruvin*

	Ca. 310-330 [*Rabbah, R. Joseph*]	*Ca. 330-350* [*Rava, Abaye*]
Court Cases		
Questions from Outside of the Academy		
Stories and Sayings about Enforcement of, or Obedience to, Law Outside of the Academy	1. b. 'Eruv. 60a, Men of Qa gonai asked R. Joseph to send a man to prepare *'eruv* for their town. 2. b. 'Eruv. 67b, Rabbah advised on getting hot water for circumcision on Sabbath	*[1. b. 'Eruv. 14b = b. Ber. 45a Abaye said to see what blessing people said for water]. 2. b. 'Eruv. 15a, Abaye and Rava disagreed about sidepost of house of Bar Ḥabu. 3. b. 'Eruv. 24b, Abaye ruled on *'eruv* for open area at Pum Nahara. 4. b. 'Eruv. 40a, Rava permitted people to buy turnips which came to Maḥoza on festival. 5. b. 'Eruv. 47b, Rava permitted Maḥozans to purchase rams though Gentiles had brought them from beyond Sabbath limit. 6. b. 'Eruv. 57b, R. Safra told Rava how one measures Sabbath limits for people of Ctesiphon and Ardashir. 7. b. 'Eruv. 61b, Mar Judah told people of Mabrakta where to place their *'eruv*. 8. b. 'Eruv. 63b, Abaye advised neighbors of Gentile on preparing *'eruv*. 9. b. 'Eruv. 68a, Rava advised on getting hot water for circumcision on Sabbath. 10. b. 'Eruv. 68a, Rava.

* Duplicate.

III. *b. ʿEruwin*

	Ca. 310-330 [*Rabbah, R. Joseph*]	*Ca. 330-350* [*Rava, Abaye*]
		*[11. b. ʿEruv. 102a, R. Tavla did not object to Maḥozan practice.] *[12. ʿEruv. 102a, R. ʾIvya did not object to Nehardean practice.]

* — Inconclusive. Not counted.

IV. *b. Pesaḥim*

	Ca. 310-330 [*Rabbah, R. Joseph*]	*Ca. 330-350* [*Rava, Abaye*]
Court Cases		
Questions from Outside of the Academy		
Stories and Sayings about Enforcement of, or Obedience to, Law Outside of the Academy	1. b. Pes. 50b, R. Joseph told Jews of Khuzistan they do not have to separate *ḥallah* on rice.	1. b. Pes. 5b, Rava told Maḥozans to remove the leaven left by troops in their houses before Passover. **[2. b. Pes. 25b, Rava told man not to kill, even if it meant being killed.] 3. b. Pes. 40b, Rava permitted wet grain to be sold to Gentiles before Passover. *[4. b. Pes. 76a=b. Ḥul. 112a, R. Ḥinena b. Rava of Pashronia permitted a pigeon which fell in dairy-relish].

* Duplicate. Not counted.
** Not counted. Inconclusive.

V. *b. Yoma, Sukkah, Bezah* [= Y., S., B.]

	Ca. 310-330 [*Rabbah, R. Joseph*]	*Ca. 330-350* [*Rava, Abaye*]
Court Cases		
Questions from Outside of the Academy		1. b. B. 12b, Host of Rav b. R. Ḥanan asked about crushing mustard stalks on Festival.
Stories and Sayings about Enforcement of, or Obedience to, Law Outside of the Academy	1. b. Y. 77b, R. Joseph permitted people of Be Tarbu to walk through water to hear the lecture on the Day of Atonement.	1. b. Y. 56b, Rava corrected prayer of synagogue prayer-leader on Day of Atonement. 2. b. Y. 77b, Rava permitted people of ʿEver Yemina to walk through water to guard crop on Day of Atonement. *[3. b. Y. 82b (= b. Pes. 25b) Rava tells man not to kill.] 4. b. B. 27b, Rava ruled on firstling. **[5. b. B. 30a, Rava enacted in Maḥoza *re* carrying on festival.]

* Duplicate.
** General rule, not a case. Not counted in summary table.

VI. *b. Rosh HaShanah, Taʿanit* [= R.H., T.]

	Ca. 310-330 [*Rabbah, R. Joseph*]	*Ca. 330-350* [*Rava, Abaye*]
Court Cases		
Questions from Outside of the Academy		
Stories and Sayings about Enforcement of, or Obedience to, Law Outside of the Academy	1. b. T. 24a, Rabbah decreed a fast.	1. b. T. 24b, Rava decreed a fast. 2. b. T. 24b, Rava ordered corporal punishment for intercourse with Gentile woman.

VII. *b. Megillah, Mo'ed Qatan, Ḥagigah*

	Ca. 310-330 [*Rabbah, R. Joseph*]	*Ca. 330-350* [*Rava, Abaye*]
Court Cases		
Questions from Outside of the Academy		
Stories and Sayings about Enforcement of, or Obedience to, Law Outside of the Academy	1. b.Meg. 25a, Rabbah corrected synagogue prayer of prayer-leader.	1. b. Meg. 26b, Rava told priests what to do about corpse in synagogue. 2. b. M.Q. 4b, Abaye allowed people of Ḥarmekh to clean canal during festival week. 3. b. M.Q. 10b, Rava allowed bleeding. 4. b. M.Q. 16a, Abaye and Rava excommunicated butcher who was insolent to rabbis. 5. b.M.Q. 22a, Rava told Maḥozans *re* mourning.

VIII. *b. Yevamot*

	Ca. 310-330 [*Rabbah, R. Joseph*]	*Ca. 330-350* [*Rava, Abaye*]
Court Cases	1. b. Yev. 34b, Paternity case to R. Joseph. 2. b. Yev. 103b, R. Joseph officiated at *ḥalizah*. 3. b. Yev. 121b, R. Joseph permitted woman to remarry. 4. b. Yev. 122a, R. Joseph permitted woman to remarry.	1. b. Yev. 45b, Rava declared man legitimate and gave him public office. 2. b. Yev. 66b, Rava ruled corpse acquired cloak [*re Ketuvah.*] 3. b. Yev. 97a, Rava instructed how to ascertain impotency. *[4. b. Yev. 100a, Rava *re* court procedure] 5. b. Yev. 106a, Abaye officiated at *ḥalizah*. *[6. b. Yev. 106b, Abaye

* Not counted. Example of court procedure.

VIII *b. Yevamot*

	Ca 310-330 [*Rabbah, R. Joseph*]	*Ca 330-350* [*Rava, Abaye*]
		on text of *ḥalizah* certificate.] 7. b. Yev. 112a, Rava officiated at *ḥalizah*. 8. b. Yev. 114b, Rava permitted woman to remarry. 9. b. Yev. 115b, Abaye permitted woman to remarry. 10. b. Yev. 116a, Abaye on bill of divorce. 11. b. Yev. 121a, Rava permitted woman to remarry.
Questions from Outside of the Academy	1. b. Yev. 45a, Men of Be Mikse to Rabbah.	
Stories and Sayings about Enforcement of, or Obedience to, Law Outside of the Academy		

IX. *b. Ketuvot*

	Ca. *310-330* [*Rabbah, R. Joseph*]	*Ca. 330-350* [*Rava, Abaye*]
Court Cases	1. b. Ket. 13b-14a, R. Joseph ruled on legitimacy of child. 2. b. Ket. 50b, R. Joseph ruled on maintenance for daughter from estate. 3. b. Ket. 54b, R. Joseph ruled on legacy to daughter. 4. b. Ket. 57a, R. Joseph ruled on lost *ketuvah*. 5. b. Ket. 65a, R. Joseph ruled on maintenance for widow.	*[1. b. Ket. 27b (=b. Bekh. 36a), Rava ruled on case of hired ass.] 2. b. Ket. 28a, Rava ruled in case of betrothed and former fiancé. 3. b. Ket. 49b, Rava ruled *re* non-support. 4. b. Ket. 49b, Rava in case of R. Nathan b. Ammi, forced gift for charity. 5. b. Ket. 51a, Rava ruled on maintenance of orphans from estate.

* Duplicate.

IX. *b. Ketuvot*

	Ca. 310-330 [*Rabbah, R. Joseph*]	*Ca. 330-350* [*Rava, Abaye*]
	6. b. Ket. 61b, R. Joseph ruled *re* settlement of estate. 7. b. Ket. 91b, R. Joseph ruled *re* collection of debt. 8. b. Ket. 94b, R. Joseph ruled *re* dispute of sale of land. 9. b. Ket. 109b, R. Joseph ruled *re* legacy to daughter. 10. b. Ket. 111a, R. Joseph banned man for moving from Pumbedita.	6. b. Ket. 65a, Rava ruled on maintenance for widow. **[7. b. Ket. 76a, Rava observed women's preference for land.] 8. b. Ket. 67b, Rava provided charity for applicant. 9. b. Ket. 80b, Rava ruled *re ketuvah*. 10. b. Ket. 84b-85a, Rava ruled *re* collection of debt. 11. b. Ket. 85a, Rava ruled *re* collection of debt. 12. b. Ket. 85a, Rava ruled *re* bond of indebtedness. 13. b. Ket. 86a, R. Papa and R. Hama discussed case decided by Rava *re* debt. 14. b. Ket. 91b, Abaye ruled *re* debt. 15. b. Ket. 91b, Rava ruled *re* sale of *ketuvah*. 16. b. Ket. 98a, Rava ruled *re* collection of *ketuvah*. 17. b. Ket. 104b, Rava ruled in appeal *re* collection of *ketuvah*. 18. b. Ket. 109b, Abaye ruled *re* contested land.
Questions from Outside of the Academy		
Stories and Sayings about Enforcement of, or Obedience to, Law Outside of the Academy		

** Not counted as a case.

X. *b. Nedarim, Nazir, Sotah* [= *Ned., Naz., S.*]

	Ca. 310-330 [*Rabbah, R. Joseph*]	*Ca. 330-350* [*Rava, Abaye*]
Court Cases	*[1. b. Ned. 23a, R. Joseph absolved Abaye of oath.]	1. b. Ned. 21b, Rabbah b. R. Huna absolved oath. 2. b. Ned. 25a, Rava judged case of debt collection. 3. b. Ned. 91b, Rava ruled in case of suspected adultery. 4. b. Ned. 91b, Rava ruled in case of suspected adultery.
Questions from Outside of the Academy		
Stories and Sayings about Enforcement of, or Obedience to, Law Outside of the Academy		

* Not counted. Pertinent to law-enforcement in schools only.

XI. *b. Gittin*

	Ca. 310-330 [*Rabbah, R. Joseph*]	*Ca. 330-350* [*Rava, Abaye*]
Court Cases	1. b. Git. 19b, R. Joseph ruled on *get*. 2. b. Git. 30a, R. Joseph ruled on conditional *get*. 3. b. Git. 74b, R. Joseph ruled in contract dispute. 4. b. Git. 77b, R. Joseph ruled on acquiring *get*. 5. b. Git. 88b, R. Joseph forced men to to give divorce.	*[1. b. Git. 6a, Rava generally required declaration of witnesses *re get* in Maḥoza.] 2. b. Git. 29b, Rava ruled on delivery of *get*. 3. b. Git. 34a, Abaye and Rava ruled on validity of *get*. 4. b. Git. 60b, Abaye ruled in case of riparian rights. *[5. b. Git. 67b, Rava instructed how to prepare *get*.] 6. b. Git. 73a, Rava ruled in contract dispute.

* Not counted. Description of court procedure, not a case.

XI. *b. Gittin*

	Ca. 310-330 [*Rabbah, R. Joseph*]	*Ca. 330-350* [*Rava, Abaye*]
		7. b. Git. 77b, Rava advised on how to acquire *get* on Sabbath. *[8. b. Git. 84b, Rava instructed scribes who wrote *get*.] *[9. b. Git. 85b, Rava laid down text of *get*.] 10. b. Git. 89b, Rava suppressed a rumor.
Questions from Outside of the Academy		
Stories and Sayings about Enforcement of, or Obedience to, Law Outside of the Academy		

* Not counted. Description of court procedure, not a case.

XII. *b. Qiddushin*

	Ca. 310-330 [*Rabbah, R. Joseph*]	*Ca. 330-350* [*Rava, Abaye*]
Court Cases	1. b. Qid. 7b, Rabbah ruled on validity of betrothal with silk. 2. b. Qid. 12b, R. Aḥa b. Huna ruled on betrothal with myrtle branch in market.	1. b. Qid. 12b, Rava ruled on validity of betrothal with myrtle twigs. 2. b. Qid. 45b, Abaye and Rava commented on disputed betrothal. 3. b. Qid. 49b, Rava ruled on retraction of sale of property. 4. b. Qid. 50a, Rava ruled on sale of property. 5. b. Qid. 52b, Rava ruled on disputed betrothal. 6. b. Qid. 52b, Rava ruled on disputed betrothal. 7. b. Qid. 52b, Rava ruled on disputed betrothal.

XII. *b. Qiddushin*

	Ca. 310-330 [*Rabbah, R. Joseph*]	*Ca. 330-350* [*Rava, Abaye*]
Questions from Outside of the Academy		
Stories and Sayings about Enforcement of, or Obedience to, Law Outside of the Academy		1. b. Qid. 73a, Rava lectured about whom proselytes may marry, and was alternately honored and threatened.

XIII. *b. Bava' Qamma'*

	Ca. 310-330 [*Rabbah, R. Joseph*]	*Ca. 330-350* [*Rava, Abaye*]
Court Cases	1. b. B.Q. 93a, R. Joseph ruled on liability for charity purse. 2. b. B.Q. 117b, Rabbah ruled on misappropriation of bailment. 3. b. B.Q. 117b, Rabbah ruled on drowning of ass to save boat.	1. b. B.Q. 20a, Rava judged case of damages by goat. 2. b. B.Q. 48a, Rava judged case of damages by dough to goat. 3. b. B.Q. 84a, R. Papa b. Samuel assessed damages done by ass to child. 4. b. B.Q. 84a, Rava assessed damages done by ox to child. 5. b. B.Q. 115a, Abaye ruled on sale of stolen book. 6. b. B.Q. 117a, R. Huna b. Judah ruled about liability of Jew who was forced by Gentiles to show another's property [for confiscation]. 7. b. B.Q. 117b, Abaye ruled on misappropriation of bailment.
Questions from Outside of the Academy		

XIII. *b. Bava' Qamma'*

	Ca. 310-330 [*Rabbah, R. Joseph*]	*Ca. 330-350* [*Rava, Abaye*]
Stories and Sayings about Enforcement of, or Obedience to, Law Outside of the Academy	*[1. b. B.Q. 23b, R. Joseph and Abaye despaired of ending damage from goats.]	

* Not counted. Inconclusive.

XIV. *b. Bava' Meẓi'a'*

	Ca. 310-330 [*Rabbah, R. Joseph*]	*Ca. 330-350* [*Rava, Abaye*]
Court Cases	1. b. B.M. 18b, Rabbah decided on validity of *get* discovered among flax. 2. b. B.M. 42a, R. Joseph ruled on bailment. *[3. b. B.M. 81b (=b. Ket. 27b, etc.), Rabbah (N.B.) ruled on case of hired ass.] 4. b. B.M. 93a, Rabbah ruled on liability for drowned sheep. 5. b. B.M. 101b, R. Huna b. R. Joshua ruled on dispute over rental of warehouse.	1. b. B.M. 5a, R. Zera ruled in case of bailment. 2. b. B.M. 23b, Abaye ruled on possession of wine. 3. b. B.M. 24b, Abaye ruled on ownership of meat dropped by vulture. 4. b. B.M. 28b, Rabbah b. R. Huna ruled on restoration of lost ass. 5. b. B.M. 31b, Rabbah b. R. Huna ruled on business litigation. 6. b. B.M. 39b, Abaye ruled on estate of captives. 7. b. B.M. 42a, Rava ruled on bailment. 8. b. B.M. 42a-b, Rava ruled on bailment. 9. b. B.M. 49a, Rava ruled in case of futures. 10. b. B.M. 49b, Rava ruled in case of bailment. 11. b. B.M. 51a, Rava ruled on fraud through renunciation of sale. 12. b. B.M. 67a, Rabbah b. R. Huna ruled on land purchase.

* Duplicate. Not counted.

XIV. *b. Bava' Meẓi'a'*

	Ca. 310-330 [*Rabbah, R. Joseph*]	*Ca. 330-350* [*Rava, Abaye*]
		13. b. B.M. 68a, Rava ruled on bond in which interest seemed stipulated. 14. b B.M. 69a, Abaye ruled on division of herd. 15. b. B.M. 72a, Abaye ruled on disposition of pledged field. 16. b. B.M. 81b, Rava ruled on liability for lost cloak. 17. b. B.M. 83a, Rava ruled on liability for broken wine barrel. 18. b. B.M. 83a, Rava ruled on liability for sour wine. 19. b. B.M. 96b, Rava ruled on liability for broken ax. 20. b. B.M. 97a, Rava ruled on liability for ass. 21. b. B.M. 104b, Rava ruled on contract dispute. 22. b. B.M. 106b, Rava ruled on dispute over lease. 23. b. B.M. 109b, R. Papa b. Samuel ruled on whether tenant farmer may receive value of improvements. 24. b. B.M. 109b, Rava ruled on litigation over pledge. 25. b. B.M. 116a, Abaye ruled on disposition of pledge. 26. b. B.M. 116a, Rava ordered orphans to return borrowed implements.
Questions from Outside of the Academy		

XIV. *b. Bava' Meẓi'a'*

	Ca. 310-330 [*Rabbah, R. Joseph*]	*Ca. 330-350* [*Rava, Abaye*]
Stories and Sayings about Enforcement of, or Obedience to, Law Outside of the Academy		

XV. *b. Bava' Batra'*

	Ca. 310-330 [*Rabbah, R. Joseph*]	*Ca. 330-350* [*Rava, Abaye*]
Court Cases	1. b. B.B. 8a, Rabbah levied charity tax on orphans. 2. b. B.B. 12b, Rabbah ruled on division of estate. 3. b. B.B. 31a, Rabbah ruled *re ḥazaqah*. 4. b. B.B. 32a-b, Rabbah ruled on forged deed of sale. 5. b. B.B. 32b, Rabbah ruled on forged deed of sale. 6. b. B.B. 68a, R. Joseph ruled on disputed sale. 7. b. B.B. 96b, R. Joseph decided case *re* sour beer. 8. b. B.B. 135a, R. Joseph ruled on need of *ḥaliẓah*. 9. b. B.B. 143a, R. Joseph ruled on disposition of estate.	1. b. B.B. 9a, Rava ruled on contract of butchers. 2. b. B.B. 13b, Rava ruled on division of estate. 3. b. B.B. 24a, Rava permitted use of wine discovered between tree trunks. 4. b. B.B. 29b, Rava ruled on title to female slave. 5. b. B.B. 30a, Rava ruled *re ḥazaqah*. 6. b. B.B. 30a-b, Rava ruled *re ḥazaqah*. 7. b. B.B. 30b, Rava ruled *re ḥazaqah*. 8. b. B.B. 30b, Rava ruled *re ḥazaqah*. 9. b. B.B. 30b, Rava ruled *re ḥazaqah*. 10. b. B.B. 32b, R. Idi b. Abin ruled *re* bond of indebtedness. 11. b. B.B. 33a, Abaye ruled *re* trusteeship of orphans' estate. 12. b B.B. 33b, Abaye's disciples ruled *re ḥazaqah*. 13. b. B.B. 40b, Rava ruled *re ḥazaqah*. 14. b. B.B. 106b, Abaye judged case of misrepresentation of real estate for sale.

XV. *b. Bava' Batra'*

	Ca. 310-330 [*Rabbah, R. Joseph*]	*Ca. 330-350* [*Rava, Abaye*]
		15. b. B.B. 126a-b, Rava ruled on disposition of estate. *[16. b. B.B. 130b, Rava instructed R. Papa and R. Huna b. R. Joshua not to tear up his decisions, nor to infer after death laws from them.] 17. b. B.B. 133b, R. 'Ilish before Rava ruled on division of estate. 18. b. B.B. 135a, Rava ruled on alleged divorce of wife of dying man (*re ḥaliẓah.*) 19. b. B.B. 143b, Abaye ruled on language of will. 20. b. B.B. 153a, Rava ruled on deed of gift. 21. b. B.B. 155b, Rava ruled on disposition by minor of estate. 22. b. B.B. 155b, Rava ruled on disposition by minor of estate. 23. b. B.B. 167a, Abaye ruled on forged deed. 24. b. B.B. 167a, Abaye ruled on forged deed. 25. b. B.B. 167a, Rava ruled on forged deed. 26. b. B.B. 167b, Abaye ruled on forged receipt. 27. b. B.B. 168a, Abaye ruled on forged receipt. 28. b. B.B. 168b, Abaye ruled on making duplicate deeds. 29. b. B.B. 174a, R. Ḥanin removed creditor from property of debtor.

* Court procedure.

XV. *b. Bava' Batra'*

	Ca. 310-330 [*Rabbah, R. Joseph*]	*Ca. 330-350* [*Rava, Abaye*]
Questions from Outside of the Academy		
Stories and Sayings about Enforcement of, or Obedience to, Law Outside of the Academy		

XVI. *b. Sanhedrin*

	Ca. 310-330 [*Rabbah, R. Joseph*]	*Ca. 330-350* [*Rava, Abaye*]
Court Cases	*[1. b. Sanh. 5a, R. Joseph told Mar Zutra b. R. Naḥman what to do when he erred in a case.] 2. b. Sanh. 28b, R. Joseph ruled on deed of gift.	*[1. b. Sanh. 25a, Rava ruled on eligibility to give testimony.] 2. b. Sanh. 26b, R. Papa b. Samuel ruled on deed of gift witnessed by robbers. 3. b. Sanh. 27a, R. Aḥa b. Jacob tried murder case. 4. b. Sanh. 29b, Abaye and Rava ruled on deed of debt acknowledgement. **[5. b. Sanh. 74a, Rava told man not to kill.] 6. b. Sanh. 100a, Rava judged suspected *trefa*.
Questions from Outside of the Academy		
Stories and Sayings about Enforcement of, or Obedience to, Law Outside of the Academy		

* Not counted. Court procedure.

** Not counted. Inconclusive.

XVII. *b. ʿAvodah Zarah*

	Ca. 310-330 [*Rabbah, R. Joseph*]	*Ca. 330-350* [*Rava, Abaye*]
Court Cases	1. b. A.Z. 39a, R. Joseph was asked to rule on possible fraud. 2. b. A.Z. 49a, R. Joseph ruled on use of manure from. idolatrous source. 3. b. A.Z. 72a, R. Joseph ruled on disputed land sale.	1. b. A.Z. 22a, Rava ruled on partnership of Jewish and Gentile farmer. 2. b. A.Z. 22a, Rava permitted partnership of Jewish and Gentile farmer. 3. b. A.Z. 40a, Rava prohibited purchase of fish. 4. b. A.Z. 57b, Rava ruled on ritual fitness of wine. 5. b. A.Z. 61b, Rava ruled on ritual fitness of wine. 6. b. A.Z. 61b, Rava ruled on ritual fitness of wine. 7. b. A.Z. 65b, Rava permitted wheat into which unfit wine had fallen to be sold to Gentiles. 8. b. A.Z. 70a, Rava ruled on fitness of wine. 9. b. A.Z. 70a, Rava ruled on fitness of wine. 10. b. A.Z. 70a, Rava ruled on fitness of wine. 11. b. A.Z. 70a, Rava ruled on fitness of wine. 12. b. A.Z. 70a, Rava ruled on fitness of wine. 13. b. A.Z. 70a, Rava ruled on fitness of wine. 14. b. A.Z. 70a, Rava ruled on fitness of wine. 15. b. A.Z. 70a, Rava ruled on fitness of wine. 16. b. A.Z. 70b, Rava ruled on fitness of wine. 17. b. A.Z. 72b, Rava ruled on fitness of wine.
Questions from Outside of the Academy		

XVII. *b. ʿAvodah Zarah*

	Ca. 310-330 [*Rabbah, R. Joseph*]	*Ca. 330-350* [*Rava, Abaye*]
Stories and Sayings about Enforcement of, or Obedience to, Law Outside of the Academy		

XVIII. *b. Horayot, Shevuʿot, Makkot* [= H., Sh., M.]

	Ca. 310-330 [*Rabbah, R. Joseph*]	*Ca. 330-350* [*Rava, Abaye*]
Court Cases		1. b. Sh. 41b, Abaye ruled in case of debt repayment. 2. b. Sh. 42a, Rava ruled in case of debt repayment. 3. b. Sh. 42a, Abaye and Rava ruled in case of debt repayment. [4. b. Sh. 46b, Rava ruled orphans must return objects borrowed by father.] 5. b. Sh. 48b, Rami b. Ḥama ruled in debt collection.
Questions from Outside of the Academy		
Stories and Sayings about Enforcement of, or Obedience to, Law Outside of the Academy		

XIX. *b. Zevaḥim, Menaḥot, Ḥullin*

	Ca. 310-330 [*Rabbah, R. Joseph*]	*Ca. 330-350* [*Rava, Aabaye*]
Court Cases		
Questions from Outside of the Academy		
Stories and Sayings about Enforcement of, or Obedience to, Law Outside of the Academy	1. b. Ḥul. 39b, Inquiry to R. Joseph on deal with Arabs to share animal. 2. b. Ḥul. 43b, Case to Rabbah about bird that may have been clawed.	*[1. b. Zev. 116b, Rava ordered offering of sacrifice of Ifra Hormiz.] **[2. b. Men. 40a-b, Rava said we rely on public notices to inform people of the dates of Passover and the Day of Atonement.] 3. b. Ḥul. 31a, Rava examined arrow for R. Jonah b. Taḥalifa. 4. b. Ḥul. 43b, Rava ruled on improperly slaughtered ox. 5. b. Ḥul. 44b, Rava declared animal permitted and bought the meat. 6. b. Ḥul. 49b, Rava ruled on case of perforation. 7. b. Ḥul. 49b, Rava ruled on uncovered pot of honey. 8. b. Ḥul. 50a, Rava ruled on perforated intestines. 9. b. Ḥul. 57a, Rava ruled on birds with broken legs. 10. b. Ḥul. 77a, Abaye ruled on animal with broken leg. 11. b. Ḥul. 112a, R. Ḥinena b. Rava of Pashrunia permitted pigeon which fell into milk. 12. b. Ḥul. 133a, Abaye used to receive priestly dues.

XIX. *b. Zevaḥim, Menaḥot, Ḥullin*

	Ca. 310-330 [*Rabbah, R. Joseph*]	*Ca. 330-350* [*Rava, Abaye*]
		13. b. Ḥul. 133a, Rava used to receive priestly dues. 14. b. Ḥul. 141b, Rava was asked about trapping a certain bird.

* Inconclusive and irrelevant. ** Not counted. General rule, not a case.

XX. *b. Bekhorot, ʿArakhin, Temurah, Keritot, Meʿilah, Tamid*

	Ca. 310-330 [*Rabbah, R. Joseph*]	*Ca. 330-350* [*Rava, Abaye*]
Court Cases		1. b. Bekh. 36a, Rava ruled in case of hired ass.
Questions from Outside of the Academy		
Stories and Sayings about Enforcement of, or Obedience to, Law Outside of the Academy	1. b. Bekh. 27a, Rabbah ate heave-offering.	1. b. Bekh. 3b, Rava told woman proselyte about partnership in animal with heathen.

XXI. *b. Niddah*

	Ca. 310-330 [*Rabbah, R. Joseph*]	*Ca. 330-350* [*Rava, Abaye*]
Court Cases		
Questions from Outside of the Academy		*[1. b. Nid. 20b, Ifra Hormiz to Rava *re* meaning of blood.]
Stories and Sayings about Enforcement of, or Obedience to, Law Outside of the Academy	**[1. b. Nid. 66a, R. Zera said Israelite women were strict about menstrual taboos.] 2. b. Nid. 32a, R. Joseph said infant was to be immersed to protect heave-offering from uncleanness. 3. b. Nid. 67b, Rabbah permitted immersion on eighth day.	

* Inconclusive and irrelevant. Not counted. ** General rule, not a case.

XXII. *Summary*

	Ca. 310-330	*Ca. 330-350*	*Total*	*Approximate Percentage of Total*
Civil Law (including commercial and real estate, settlement of estates, gifts to charity, maintenance of widows and orphans, collection of debts, marriage contracts, damages and liabilities).	26	90	116	51.1%
Personal Status (including marriage, divorce, *ḥaliẓah*, etc., excommunication for moving from place to place, adultery).	13	22	35	15.0%
Food and Sex Taboos (including slaughter and ritual fitness of wine).	3	28	31	13.7%
Fasts, Holidays, Sabbath.	3	13	16	7.1%
Sabbath Limits.	1	5	6	2.6%
Synagogue Liturgy (including blessings).	2	4	6	2.6%
Punishment of Common People for Disrespect to Scholars; Suppression of Rumors.	2	2	4	1.7%
Mourning.	—	1	1	0.4%
Vows.	1	1	2	0.8%
Agricultural Rules.	3	3	6	2.6%
Capital Crimes.	—	2	2	0.8%
Total	54	171	225	98.4%

XXIII. *Comparisons*

	Ca. 220-265		*Ca. 265-310*		*Ca. 310-350*	
	Number	*Per Centage*	*Number*	*Per Centage*	*Number*	*Per Centage*
Civil Law (including commercial and real estate, settlement of estates, gifts to charity, maintenance of widows and orphans, collection of debts, marriage contracts, damages and liabilities).	23	33.8%	85	52.1%	116	51.1%
Personal Status (including marriage, divorce, *ḥaliẓah*, etc., excommunication for moving from place to place, adultery).	16	23.5%	24	14.1%	35	15.0%
Food and Sex Taboos (including slaughter and ritual fitness of wine).	15	22.0%	21	12.9%	31	13.7%
Fasts, Holidays, Sabbath.	10	14.7%	19	11.6%	16	7.1%
[Sabbath Limits.	7	—	7]	—	6	2.6%
Synagogue Liturgy and Blessings	3	4%	2	1.2%	6	2.6%
Punishment for Disrespect to Scholars.	—	—	2	1.2%	4	1.7%
Vows and Dedications.	—	—	7	4.2%	2	0.8%
Agricultural Rules.	1	1%	3	1.8%	6	2.6%
Capital Crimes.	—	—	—	—	2	0.8%
Total by periods	68	99.0%	163	99.1%	224	98.0%

The table of comparisons (XXIII) shows general consistencies between the periods ca. 220-310 and 310-350 both in the absolute number of case reports, and in the proportions of cases pertaining to various categories of law. Approximately 60% of all instances pertained to matters of civil law and personal status; approximately 15% to food and sex taboos; approximately 20% to Sabbath and festival observances, of which approximately half involved the *'eruv*. The scattering of cases and other exemplifications of law-enforcement among other categories of law proved consistently inconsequential. It is difficult to see any striking increase in the number of stories. The preservation of these accounts was certainly the result of literary and academic, not historical or sociological factors. (Almost all cases in third and fourth-century strata derive from, or were attributed to, the courts conducted by heads of schools, Samuel, Rav, Rav Judah, R. Naḥman, R. Huna, R. Ḥisda, Rabbah, R. Joseph, Abaye, and Rava.) Had there been noteworthy increases in the number of cases from one period to the next—as indeed there seems to be from 220-265 to 265-310, and from 310-330 to 330-350—one still could not persuasively argue that such an increase by itself proves there was an increment in the rabbis' influence or power over Jewry. The phenomenon remains at best suggestive, but hardly probative.

It is nonetheless clear that almost all instances of law enforcement derived from the rabbis' narrow judicial and administrative role in the Jewish community or from their supervisory functions in the marketplace. In addition to court adjudication of civil law and determinations of personal status, most, though not all, decisions on religious taboos (food, Sabbath law, menstrual separation) were made possible by the rabbis' communal position. Of the thirty-one instances of the enforcement of food-taboos listed on Table XXII, approximately twenty-six related to ritually-contaminated wine or the slaughter of animals, both being aspects of market-supervision. Of the twenty-two exempla of enforcement of Sabbath and festival law, six in this period, and a much greater proportion earlier, pertained to the Sabbath limits. On the other hand, a number of cases, sayings, and stories, either not counted here at all, or counted as merely a single exemplification of law enforcement, permit the inference of fairly widespread popular observance of certain laws, all of biblical, not rabbinic, origin. It is hardly necessary to recapitulate our earlier conclusions.[1] As I said, whatever rabbinical law-enforcement actually took place generally depended upon the rabbis' position in the Jewish government headed by the exilarch and recognized and legitimated by the Iranian government.

[1] Vol. III, pp. 334-336.

BROWN JUDAIC STUDIES SERIES

140001	*Approaches to Ancient Judaism I*	William S. Green
140002	*The Traditions of Eleazar Ben Azariah*	Tzvee Zahavy
140003	*Persons and Institutions in Early Rabbinic Judaism*	William S. Green
140004	*Claude Goldsmid Montefiore on the Ancient Rabbis*	Joshua B. Stein
140005	*The Ecumenical Perspective and the Modernization of Jewish Religion*	S. Daniel Breslauer
140006	*The Sabbath-Law of Rabbi Meir*	Robert Goldenberg
140007	*Rabbi Tarfon*	Joel Gereboff
140008	*Rabban Gamaliel II*	Shamai Kanter
140009	*Approaches to Ancient Judaism II*	William S. Green
140010	*Method and Meaning in Ancient Judaism*	Jacob Neusner
140011	*Approaches to Ancient Judaism III*	William S. Green
140012	*Turning Point: Zionism and Reform Judaism*	Howard R. Greenstein
140013	*Buber on God and the Perfect Man*	Pamela Vermes
140014	*Scholastic Rabbinism*	Anthony J. Saldarini
140015	*Method and Meaning in Ancient Judaism II*	Jacob Neusner
140016	*Method and Meaning in Ancient Judaism III*	Jacob Neusner
140017	*Post Mishnaic Judaism in Transition*	Baruch M. Bokser
140018	*A History of the Mishnaic Law of Agriculture: Tractate Maaser Sheni*	Peter J. Haas
140019	*Mishnah's Theology of Tithing*	Martin S. Jaffee
140020	*The Priestly Gift in Mishnah: A Study of Tractate Terumot*	Alan J. Peck
140021	*History of Judaism: The Next Ten Years*	Baruch M. Bokser
140022	*Ancient Synagogues*	Joseph Gutmann
140023	*Warrant for Genocide*	Norman Cohn
140024	*The Creation of the World According to Gersonides*	Jacob J. Staub
140025	*Two Treatises of Philo of Alexandria: A Commentary on De Gigantibus and Quod Deus Sit Immutabilis*	David Winston/John Dillon
140026	*A History of the Mishnaic Law of Agriculture: Kilayim*	Irving Mandelbaum
140027	*Approaches to Ancient Judaism IV*	William S. Green
140028	*Judaism in the American Humanities*	Jacob Neusner
140029	*Handbook of Synagogue Architecture*	Marilyn Chiat
140030	*The Book of Mirrors*	Daniel C. Matt
140031	*Ideas in Fiction: The Works of Hayim Hazaz*	Warren Bargad
140032	*Approaches to Ancient Judaism V*	William S. Green
140033	*Sectarian Law in the Dead Sea Scrolls: Courts, Testimony and the Penal Code*	Lawrence H. Schiffman
140034	*A History of the United Jewish Appeal: 1939-1982*	Marc L. Raphael
140035	*The Academic Study of Judaism*	Jacob Neusner
140036	*Women Leaders in the Ancient Synagogue*	Bernadette Brooten
140037	*Formative Judaism: Religious, Historical, and Literary Studies*	Jacob Neusner
140038	*Ben Sira's View of Women: A Literary Analysis*	Warren C. Trenchard
140039	*Barukh Kurzweil and Modern Hebrew Literature*	James S. Diamond
140040	*Israeli Childhood Stories of the Sixties: Yizhar, Aloni, Shahar, Kahana-Carmon*	Gideon Telpaz
140041	*Formative Judaism II: Religious, Historical, and Literary Studies*	Jacob Neusner

BROWN JUDAIC STUDIES SERIES

140042	*Judaism in the American Humanities II: Jewish Learning and the New Humanities*	Jacob Neusner
140043	*Support for the Poor in the Mishnaic Law of Agriculture: Tractate Peah*	Roger Brooks
140044	*The Sanctity of the Seventh Year: A Study of Mishnah Tractate Shebiit*	Louis E. Newman
140045	*Character and Context: Studies in the Fiction of Abramovitsh, Brenner, and Agnon*	Jeffrey Fleck
140046	*Formative Judaism III: Religious, Historical, and Literary Studies*	Jacob Neusner
140047	*Pharaoh's Counsellors: Job, Jethro, and Balaam in Rabbinic and Patristic Tradition*	Judith Baskin
140048	*The Scrolls and Christian Origins: Studies in the Jewish Background of the New Testament*	Matthew Black
140049	*Approaches to Modern Judaism I*	Marc Lee Raphael
140050	*Mysterious Encounters at Mamre and Jabbok*	William T. Miller
140051	*The Mishnah Before 70*	Jacob Neusner
140052	*Sparada by the Bitter Sea: Imperial Interaction in Western Anatolia*	Jack Martin Balcer
140053	*Hermann Cohen: The Challenge of a Religion of Reason*	William Kluback
140054	*Approaches to Judaism in Medieval Times I*	David R. Blumenthal
140055	*In the Margins of the Yerushalmi: Glosses on the English Translation*	Jacob Neusner
140056	*Approaches to Modern Judaism II*	Marc Lee Raphael
140057	*Approaches to Judaism in Medieval Times II*	David R. Blumenthal
140058	*Midrash as Literature: The Primacy of Documentary Discourse*	Jacob Neusner
140059	*The Commerce of the Sacred: Mediation of the Divine Among Jews in the Graeco-Roman Diaspora*	Jack N. Lightstone
140060	*Major Trends in Formative Judaism I: Society and Symbol in Political Crisis*	Jacob Neusner
140061	*Major Trends in Formative Judaism II: Texts, Contents, and Contexts*	Jacob Neusner
140062	*A History of the Jews in Babylonia. I: The Parthian Period*	Jacob Neusner
140063	*The Talmud of Babylonia: An American Translation. XXXII: Tractate Arakhin*	Jacob Neusner
140064	*Ancient Judaism: Debates and Disputes*	Jacob Neusner
140065	*Prayers Alleged to Be Jewish: An Examination of the Constitutiones Apostolorum*	David Fiensy
140066	*The Legal Methodology of Hai Gaon*	Tsvi Groner
140067	*From Mishnah to Scripture: The Problem of the Unattributed Saying*	Jacob Neusner
140068	*Halakhah in a Theological Dimension*	David Novak
140069	*From Philo to Origen: Middle Platonism in Transition*	Robert M. Berchman
140070	*In Search of Talmudic Biography: The Problem of the Attributed Saying*	Jacob Neusner
140071	*The Death of the Old and the Birth of the New: The Framework of the Book of Numbers and the Pentateuch*	Dennis T. Olson

BROWN JUDAIC STUDIES SERIES

140072	*The Talmud of Babylonia: An American Translation. XVII: Tractate Sotah*	Jacob Neusner
140073	*Understanding Seeking Faith: Essays on the Case of Judaism. Volume Two: Literature, Religion and the Social Study of Judaism*	Jacob Neusner
140074	*The Talmud of Babylonia: An American Translation. VI: Tractate Sukkah*	Jacob Neusner
140075	*Fear Not Warrior: A Study of 'al tira' Pericopes in the Hebrew Scriptures*	Edgar W. Conrad
140076	*Formative Judaism IV: Religious, Historical, and Literary Studies*	Jacob Neusner
140077	*Biblical Patterns in Modern Literature*	David H. Hirsch/ Nehama Aschkenasy
140078	*The Talmud of Babylonia: An American Translation. I: Tractate Berakhot*	Jacob Neusner
140079	*Mishnah's Division of Agriculture: A History and Theology of Seder Zeraim*	Alan J. Avery-Peck
140080	*From Tradition to Imitation: The Plan and Program of Pesiqta Rabbati and Pesiqta deRab Kahana*	Jacob Neusner
140081	*The Talmud of Babylonia: An American Translation. XXIIIA: Tractate Sanhedrin, Chapters 1-3*	Jacob Neusner
140082	*Jewish Presence in T. S. Eliot and Franz Kafka*	Melvin Wilk
140083	*School, Court, Public Administration: Judaism and its Institutions in Talmudic Babylonia*	Jacob Neusner
140084	*The Talmud of Babylonia: An American Translation. XXIIIB: Tractate Sanhedrin, Chapters 4-8*	Jacob Neusner
140085	*The Bavli and Its Sources: The Question of Tradition in the Case of Tractate Sukkah*	Jacob Neusner
140087	*The Talmud of Babylonia: An American Translation. XXIIIC: Tractate Sanhedrin, Chapters 9-11*	Jacob Neusner
140089	*The Peripatetic Saying: The Problem of the Thrice-Told Tale in Talmudic Literature*	Jacob Neusner
140090	*The Talmud of Babylonia: An American Translation. XXVI: Tractate Horayot*	Martin S. Jaffee
140091	*Formative Judaism V: Religious, Historical, and Literary Studies*	Jacob Neusner
140093	*The Integrity of Leviticus Rabbah*	Jacob Neusner
140096	*The Memorized Torah: The Mnemonic System of the Mishnah*	Jacob Neusner
140099	*Major Trends in Formative Judaism III: The Three Stages in the Formation of Judaism*	Jacob Neusner
140102	*Sifra: The Rabbinic Commentary on Leviticus*	Jacob Neusner/ Roger Brooks
140103	*The Human Will in Judaism*	Howard Eilberg-Schwartz
140104	*Genesis Rabbah: Vol 1. Genesis 1:1 to 8:14*	Jacob Neusner
140105	*Genesis Rabbah: Vol 2. Genesis 8:15 to 28:9*	Jacob Neusner
140106	*Genesis Rabbah: Vol 3. Genesis 28:10 to 50:26*	Jacob Neusner
140108	*Genesis and Judaism*	Jacob Neusner
140109	*The Talmud of Babylonia. An American Translation. XXXV: Tractates Meilah and Tamid*	Peter J. Haas
140110	*Studies in Islamic and Judaic Traditions*	William Brinner/Stephen Ricks

BROWN JUDAIC STUDIES SERIES

140111	*Comparative Midrash: The Plan and Program of Genesis Rabbah and Leviticus Rabbah*	Jacob Neusner
140112	*The Tosefta: Its Structure and its Sources*	Jacob Neusner
140113	*Reading and Believing*	Jacob Neusner
140114	*The Fathers According to Rabbi Nathan*	Jacob Neusner
140115	*Etymology in Early Jewish Interpretation: The Hebrew Names in Philo*	Lester L. Grabbe
140116	*Understanding Seeking Faith: Essays on the Case of Judaism. Volume One: Debates on Method, Reports of Results*	Jacob Neusner
140117	*The Talmud of Babylonia: An American Translation. VII: Tractate Besah*	Alan J. Avery-Peck
140118	*Sifre to Numbers: An American Translation and Explanation, Vol 1: Sifre to Numbers 1-58*	Jacob Neusner
140119	*Sifre to Numbers: An American Translation and Explanation, Vol 2: Sifre to Numbers 59-115*	Jacob Neusner
140120	*Cohen and Troeltsch: Ethical Monotheistic Religion and Theory of Culture*	Wendell S. Dietrich
140121	*Goodenough on the History of Religion and on Judaism*	Jacob Neusner/ Ernest Frerichs
140122	*Pesiqta DeRab Kahana I: Pisqaot One through Fourteen*	Jacob Neusner
140123	*Pesiqta DeRab Kahana II: Pisqaot Fifteen through Twenty-Eight*	Jacob Neusner
140125	*Comparative Midrash II*	Jacob Neusner